THREE YEARS IN CALIFORNIA

William
Perkins'
Journal

OF LIFE AT SONORA, 1849–1852

William Perkins. *Miniature painted by Alfred Waugh, 1845.*

THREE YEARS IN CALIFORNIA

William Perkins' Journal

OF LIFE AT SONORA, 1849–1852

With an Introduction and Annotations by

DALE L. MORGAN & JAMES R. SCOBIE

1964

University of California Press

Berkeley and Los Angeles

University of California Press
Berkeley and Los Angeles, California

Cambridge University Press
London, England

© 1964 by the Regents of the University of California

Library of Congress Catalog Card Number: 64-21141

Designed by Theo Jung

Printed in the United States of America

TO JORGE WALTER PERKINS

What is here?

Gold? Yellow, glittering, precious gold!
Thus much of this will make black, white;
foul, fair; wrong, right; base, noble;
old, young; coward, valiant.

—TIMON OF ATHENS

CONTENTS

Introduction

The journal of William Perkins is a personal record unlike any other in the literature of the California Gold Rush. Most Forty-niners have much to say about their trials and tribulations in getting to California, little about their experiences after arriving. Perkins gives a cursory account of his travels in 1849 by land and sea, but he opens up like a flower in the sun on reaching the diggings, and the area about which he wrote was extraordinarily interesting.

It is our good fortune that Perkins made for the Southern Mines at a time when most Forty-niners were swarming into the Northern diggings; doubly so that he went to the "Sonoranian Camp." Circumstances made Sonora, in what soon would become Tuolumne County, unique among the California mining towns, for from the beginning, as its name indicates, it was a center for the foreign-born and afterward a champion of their interests. Moreover, while Perkins was establishing himself, and almost until his final departure in 1852, Sonora was unique among the mining towns in being blessed with a fairly numerous female population. Sonoran and Chilean Forty-eighters and Forty-niners brought their women with them; and as time went on Sonora attracted French and other women. On many counts Sonora had a remarkably varied society, which interested William Perkins beyond the mechanics of making a fortune. His journal—or the book he fashioned from his journal—glows with the color this society gave his world, and we have a richer appreciation of California for the record Perkins bequeathed to us.

William Perkins has been little more than a name in the annals of Tuolumne County. That he was an early Sonora merchant and town official is almost all that was known of him. With the publication of his Sonora journal, he becomes one of the notable figures of Gold Rush history. Perkins was born, we understand, on April 17, 1827, in

Toronto, Canada.[1] Little is known about his early life. The opening
pages of his narrative do not even reveal where he was living when he
joined the Gold Rush, though eventually he tells us that he had set out
from Cincinnati, and we infer from his portrait that he had made his
way to the Queen City as early as 1845. In chapter xxx Christmas
memories recall to him "the wild grounds of Argentieul . . . the old
Farm and Homestead; my Father, my brothers, and sisters around me,
and dim memories of a Mother!" On leaving California, he harks back
to "my bachelor quarters in C[incinnati]" and "the quiet but jolly
nights at the '*Den*' where George Woodward, John Groesbeck, George
Febuger and Tom Gallagher used to stroll in to play cribbage at a
cent a point." "I shall ever remain famous," he maintains, "as having
introduced cribbage into C———." We must take William Perkins'
earlier life for granted and accompany him to California by one of the
less-traveled routes.

We have a parallel account of his journey across Mexico in the
narrative published in 1850 at Columbus, Ohio, by Samuel McNeil,
Perkins' fellow traveler. A self-revelation by a crusty individualist, not
less than a personal record of the Gold Rush, *McNeil's Travels in
1849, to, through and from the Gold Regions, in California* must have
given Perkins mixed feelings if the pamphlet ever fell under his eye.
McNeil did not think much of his companion, but because he writes
long where Perkins writes short, he is not to be relegated to a note, and
we have thought best to quote much of his account of the journey.
McNeil's dates may not be uniformly correct, but they are indicative,
and place his travels in solid perspective:

Being a shoemaker, and ambitious to rise somewhat over the bench, it
is no wonder that the discovery of gold in California excited my fancy and
hopes; believing that the celebrated *Golden Age* had arrived at last . . . I

---

[1] We follow the birth date given for Perkins in the brief biography by a local
historian of Santa Fe, Argentina, Juan J. Gschwind, *Guillermo Perkins, su
contribución al progreso económico argentino* (Rosario, 1936). The portrait
painted in 1845 does not suggest an 18-year-old; there is some doubt whether a
22-year-old would have been named captain of the company in crossing Mexico;
and when the "1850" census enumeration was made in Tuolumne County in
May, 1851, Perkins' age was recorded as 33, the same as that of his partner
Theall, which would date his birth 1818. Such census records were often
erroneous, but the question remains.

joined a respectable company [from Lancaster, Ohio] going to the promised land. The company consisted of [Hugh] Boyle Ewing, a son of the Hon. Thomas Ewing, Secretary of the Interior; James Myers, a capable and honest constable; [W. R.] Rankin, State Attorney; Jesse B. Hart, a shrewd lawyer; Benjamin Fennifrock, a farmer; Samuel Stambaugh, a merchant; Joseph Stambaugh, a druggist; Edward Strode, a potter, from Perry county; John McLaughlin, from the same county; [H. B.] Denman, nephew of the Hon. Thomas Ewing; William F. Legg, from Columbus, and [George] Liverett, from the same.

February 7, 1849, we started by coach, from Lancaster, Ohio, passing through Columbus, to Cincinnati, remaining a week at the latter place, where we obtained the necessary outfit, consisting of two years' provisions and the appropriate weapons of defence. The articles were sea biscuit, side pork, packed in kegs; six tents, knives, forks, and plates; each man a good rifle, a pair of revolvers, a bowie knife, two blankets, and crucibles, supposing that we would be obliged to melt the ore, not knowing that nature had already melted it to our hands.

A little later McNeil mentions others who joined at Cincinnati, "Ferguson, Chaney, Miller, Effinger, Emmet [Enyart], and Perkins." His list of the company may be compared with one given by C. W. Haskins in *The Argonauts of California* (New York, 1890), p. 398: "S. G. Stambaugh, W. R. Rankin, Jos. Stambaugh, R. P. Effinger, J. M. Myers, H. B. Ewing, P. Kraner, L. Baker, H. B. Denman, S. McNeal, B. F. Finefrock, J. B. Hart, O. Chaney, Thos. Wilson, E. Strode, Jas. Miller, W. F. Legg, Geo. Leverett, Jno. McLaughlin, L. McLaughlin, Capt. W. Ferguson, Wm. Perkins, Lieut. Wm. P. Rice." This second list is obviously defective in not including David Alexander Enyart, then about twenty-four years old, who set out from Cincinnati with Perkins and became his partner. According to Haskins, these men "left Cincinnati, for California, Feb. 20th." McNeil presents a different picture:

February 15, started in steamer "South America," commanded by Capt. Logan, for New Orleans, 1600 miles, costing each $10 in the cabin. I cannot omit saying that we found Capt. Logan a perfect gentleman, fit for a higher station, and his boat one of the best in the western waters. The trip was made in six days. . . . As usual, we found a crowd of gamblers on the steamer, who, like the Devil, are going to and fro on the earth seeking whom they may devour. . . . We observed one of them fleece a lieutenant in the army out of $50; the latter rising calmly from the table observing that he had paid a big sum for a little amusement, when he ought to have had sense enough to know that he had been cheated, and courage enough to have chastised the gambling robber. Those gamblers have certainly forgotten how their comrades were hung at Vicksburg, or they now would not be increasing their numbers, and acting as boldly as their predecessors did. At Paducah, in Kentucky, a gentleman came on board to see the adventurers who were going to California, and observed, with a very long face—much longer than a flour barrel—that we had experienced our last of comfort and civilization, as our difficulties and privations were commencing, and that we had better return and be satisfied with the little which Providence had placed in our hands, which would be a great treasure if enjoyed with a contented mind. I admired him for his philanthropic feeling, but considered his philosophy unsound, for I believed that that same Providence was influencing us to seek the gold regions. . . .

About one hundred and sixty miles above New Orleans our California expedition appeared to be brought almost to a close. About 10 o'clock at night a tremendous storm from the south assailed our steamer, forcing the waves over the hurricane deck, exposing us to two fatal dangers, explosion of the boilers and wreck of the vessel in a spot where escape was impossible. When the Captain became alarmed we thought it time for us to be somewhat uneasy. If the storm had been fatal, the loss would have been great in life and property, as the passengers in the cabin and on deck, and the crew, amounted to about one hundred and seventy-five, and we had a very valuable freight on board. But few had the courage to swear, and many had the wisdom to pray, who afterwards were the foremost in drinking and gambling. . . . To preserve our vessel from being broken asunder by the mountain billows, or whelmed beneath the raging waves, the captain caused the steamer to be anchored near a high shore, so that we might be somewhat shielded from the raging storm, where we remained until morning.

As our steamer was detained five hours at Baton Rouge . . . we visited the residence of Gen. Zachary Taylor, or rather President Taylor. Of course, he was absent, but he had left his glorious mark on the place, everything being good and in its place according to regimental rule. The new State House, in the course of erection, commanded our admiration. . . .

On the 20th of February we arrived at New Orleans, and sojourned at the Planter's Hotel, conducted by Chandler, who is the most accommodating and most reasonable host I have met in all my travels. . . . He not only gives the best that the New Orleans market affords, but he gives his delicacies at the cheapest rates, and by his friendly face and manners makes one feel perfectly at home.

Perkins dismisses the voyage thus far in a sentence or two, though telling us that in New Orleans three gentlemen from Maryland joined the party. Charles Hyde was one, Corse or Course another, but the third is identified only as B——.[2] (McNeil says that the first two came from Alexandria, Virginia, and this more specific statement may be correct.) Perkins relates that he took passage from New Orleans on the *Sarah Sands* (a simple mistake for the *Maria Burt,* as will be seen later), but McNeil indicates that he was to have sailed to Chagres in the *Alabama.* McNeil never quite explains his remark; yet Perkins is not actually included in the passenger list of the *Maria Burt.* As McNeil recounts the rest of the journey:

Understanding that the steamship "Maria Burt" was about starting for Chagres, we employed one of our comrades, named Stambaugh, to engage passage for us. Finding that he desired to place some of us in the steerage, while himself and a few select friends wished to occupy the cabin, we altered the plan by bringing all together into the cabin, wishing to bring all on a level both as to comforts and privations. Perhaps he thought some of us could not bear the cabin expenses—if so, he is excusable; but if any other motive impelled his movements, he is willing to have a burden on his heart which we would not have on ours for a considerable sum. The steamship "Alabama," belonging to government, was also ready to start for the same point, with Col. Weller and suite, appointed to assist in fixing or running the boundary line between the *extended* United States and Mexico. Some comrades, who joined us at Cincinnati, Ferguson, Chaney, Miller, Effinger, Emmet [Enyart], and Perkins, by some stroke of shrewd policy, got excellent berths on the "Alabama,"[3] which we also would have obtained had not another Stambaugh, with the different name of Ferguson, been rather smarter with the tongue on the occasion.

Feb. 28th, we started from New Orleans in the "Maria Burt," intending to go to Chagres, but as the reader will shortly see, we were obliged to take

---

[2] The passenger list for the *Maria Burt* printed in the New York *Herald,* March 13, 1849, lists in sequence "Hyde, Brent, Corse," and so on. However, a Dr. William T. Brent, apparently from New Orleans, is mentioned in the correspondence of John E. Durivage when the latter crossed Mexico soon after. "B——" may have been L. Baker; see page 88.

[3] At least one of the party went on to the Isthmus, whether or not in the *Alabama,* for when McNeil was returning to the States in September, at San Diego he met Thomas Wilson, who had started with him from Lancaster, gone via Chagres, and sailed north in an unlucky vessel, the *Two Friends.* Wilson was then still trying to reach San Francisco.

a different route. Shortly after passing the Balize in the Gulf, the vessel sprang a leak, and leaked so much that we returned with difficulty to New Orleans. As the "Alabama" had departed, we took passage in the steamship "Globe" going to Brazos in Texas. On that vessel we found Col. Webb's company, consisting of one hundred men, bound for California. They were fine looking intelligent gentlemen, well calculated to be successful in such an expedition. Also, Simons' New Orleans company, comprising forty stalwart adventurers bound for the same promising land, our own company at that time consisting of twenty persons, all inspired by hope and joviality. But, in the course of ocean events, this hilarity was doomed to come to an end, when the mountainous billows of the Gulf commenced operating on the susceptible frames of the landsmen, all suffering from sea-sickness except myself and another person, which afflicted them until our vessel arrived at the Brazos. . . .

We arrived March 4th [actually March 7, March 4 having been the date of departure from New Orleans], at Brazos, a small town consisting of about fifty houses at the mouth of the Rio Grande river, from Fort Brown twenty-five miles by land, and sixty by water. Col. Webb's company proceeded by steamer two hundred miles up the Rio Grande to Davis' ranche, consisting of a store, grocery, and farm. Thinking that it would be dangerous to take about $11,000 extra, with them, Col. Webb placed it in the hands of a bar-keeper at the ranche, who said that not long afterwards it had been stolen from him. With the loss of their money came the desolating Cholera, which swept off about forty [*i.e.,* eight] of their number, and [some of] the rest returned to New Orleans, the very picture of despair, without money and without health. I had before frequently advised my companions not to take so much provision and baggage with us, but was constantly opposed; but they found at last that the shoemaker prophet was inspired for the occasion. At the Brazos we purchased a wagon and six mules for the conveyance of our goods, and a horse for each, the horses costing from ten to fifty dollars. At Fort Brown we were obliged to purchase an additional wagon and four mules. I tried there to pursuade them to sell the wagons and mules, and proceed on horses, but without effect. The others concluded to elect a captain, which I opposed, stating that if we could not rule ourselves for the good of the whole, and each take care of his own money, we were not fit for the journey to California, but I was not successful in my argument. We then elected for our captain, a Mr. Perkins of Cincinnati, an overbearing ignorant Englishman, who did not suit my strict republican principles. I feel convinced that the spending bump was so prominent on his head, that he would have foolishly expended more than the $11,000 Col. Webb lost, if he had possessed entire sway. Six of the mules he was permitted to purchase soon dropped dead, and the company were displeased with me, because I would not permit him to purchase one for myself. I selected and bought one which I rode safely and happily one thousand miles. On 8th of March, we started from Fort Brown for Reynosa, 60 miles, on the Rio Grande, experiencing much difficulty in keeping the road, and finding water for ourselves and mules. At Charcoal Lake, about half way, we hired a guide and interpreter, for $300, to take us through to Mazatlan, on the Pacific ocean, one thousand miles from the Brazos. We remained at this lake three days. Although the water of it was so stagnant that the fish were lying dead upon its shores, we were obliged to cook with and drink it. We then proceeded to Reynosa, at which place we arrived on the 20th. Finding there that our complement of wagons would not conveniently carry our goods, obliging us to drag along at the rate of ten miles per day, we purchased another wagon and four mules, which I also opposed, but with the same want of success. I was actually enraged at the increase of our expenses. We had then about $1000 worth of wagons and mules, and were now obliged to pay a duty of $60 on each wagon on passing from Texas into Mexico, our personal baggage having already cost more than its value. Firmly believing that Perkins would wastefully spend all our money, if permitted to have his own way, we ejected him from his office, electing in his stead, to act as governors, a committee of three persons, viz.: Stambaugh, Hart, and Perkins. At this place the cholera appeared in our band, attacking Brown, of Alabama, who joined our company at Brazos, and Stambaugh, from Lancaster, but fortunately both recovered. It, and apprehended difficulties, so frightened Brown, that he left our company and returned. We remained ten days encamped on the bank of the river opposite Reynosa. From our encampment every morning and every evening we heard about three hundred bells ringing in Reynosa, so terrifically that we thought at first the town was on fire, or about to be attacked by some enemy, and felt inclined to cross the river to render our assistance; but found afterwards they were ringing for religious purposes. The Mexicans called them *Joy Bells*, but it was an obstreperous joy to which we were not accustomed. . . .

On the 30th we crossed to Reynosa, in canoes, taking our wagons to pieces and crossing them in the same way, swimming over our mules, which occupied us three days. Of course we were soon saluted by the custom house officers, for their dues. While our committee waited on them to settle that matter, the rest of our company rushed into the Rio Grande to bathe, which proved a delicious treat. . . . Some señoritas, married and unmarried, I presume, had been watching us, and came down to bathe and show off their celestial charms, stripping to the skin while talking like so many parrots, and then mingled with us in the nautical amusement. As we had too much modesty to do in Mexico what they do there, we left the watery angels to their sweet selves, and going ashore, dressed, and watched them a considerable time while they scrutinized us critically. There must be much vice where such freedoms are permitted. . . .

Reynosa contains about 3000 inhabitants, who were terribly frightened and scathed by cholera, during our stay of three days in the place. The day we left, sixty persons died in the place from its effects. In fact, every house we passed in our progress from Fort Brown to Saltillo, had one or more persons in it dead from cholera. . . .

Proceeding we reached, after two days travel, a town called Chenee [China], on a river pronounced San Whan [San Juan], one of the tributaries of the Rio Grande, 50 miles from Reynosa. We arrived at 11 o'clock at night, finding the frolicking part of the inhabitants—which means the whole, as the Irishman says—in an awful predicament. They had been enjoying a fandango that Sunday night, which was suddenly interrupted at 9 o'clock by the priest, who would not give them license to dance until twelve o'clock, as they desired, he believing that there is a time to dance as well as a time to sleep. We sympathized with the inhabitants with all our hearts and with all our legs, as we greatly wished to exercise the latter in that innocent and exhilarating amusement. . . . We only stopped long enough to get some hay for our mules, being determined to encamp at a country ranche not far beyond, where we might have our wants supplied more readily. We found the hay stacked in the trees so that the cattle could not reach it; a necessary precaution as they have no fences, and the cattle are herded in droves. Progressing, we lost our way, in attempting to find the ford across the San Whan, so that we were obliged to encamp on this side of it. A singular occurrence happened that night. Baker and myself were on guard. Suddenly we were startled by the screaming of Strode, who, in his fright, declared that he saw a Camanche Indian or Mexican crawling towards the encampment. Leverett, who had slept in the same tent, took the alarm in a worse form, and, wrapping a blanket around him, rushed into the chapparel, shrieking that the Indians were about massacreing the whole band. Of course, we wakened the others, and all who remained prepared in military order for the expected combat . . . [but] found the enemy to be—not a Camanche Indian, not a renegade Mexican, or a wild beast—but an expanded umbrella rolling on the ground towards us, moved by a gentle breeze. Before retiring that night, one of our comrades had occasion to use that umbrella, and left it expanded on the ground, which made some of us run away and some of us laugh excessively.

The next morning we forded the San Whan. In doing so, one of our comrades named Course, from Alexandria, in Virginia, came near being drowned. Being on a very small weak mule, the force of the current swept both away into deep water. As he could not swim, his situation was a critical one. Stripping as fast as possible, I leaped in to his rescue, and succeeded, after much difficulty, in bringing him to shore. The mule, after losing the saddle, swam out.

On the 10th of April, we arrived at Monter[r]ey. As the cholera was raging badly in the town, we disputed whether we should remain or proceed to a mill five miles farther, where there were many conveniences both for health and comfort. The committee determined that we should remain there, which highly displeased the rest of the company. That night, about 6 o'clock, Course and myself were attacked by cholera. At 6 o'clock the next morning Course died, but fortunately I recovered to tell the readers my adventures. We buried Course at the Walnut Springs, about eight miles from the city, as we could not be permitted to bury him in a Catholic burial ground in Monter[r]ey, the deceased having been an Episcopalian. . . . A Mr. Hyde, from the same place in Virginia, and belonging to the same Episcopal Church, after helping to drink or finish three kegs of the best 4th proof French brandy, preached an appropriate funeral discourse over our deceased comrade before starting to the grave, reading in the appropriate places the suitable prayers; Perkins, McLaughlin, and the Lancaster lawyer [Hart] acted as mourners on the occasion, and for the life of me I could not tell which made their eyes the reddest, the tears or the brandy.

Passing from Monter[r]ey to Saltillo, we saw nothing extraordinary except many inviting palmetto and prickly pear trees. Saltillo contains 8000 inhabitants, and has in its place, a magnificent fountain pouring out water towards every point of the compass. We did not linger long at Saltillo, and passed on to the Buena Vista battleground, 8 miles, where we encamped, employing as much time as we could spare, in viewing its celebrated localities, remembering that there one of the greatest victories was gained by Gen. Zachary Taylor, who with 5000 troops, principally volunteers, conquered Santa Anna, commanding 25,000 lancers and infantry. Buena Vista means in English a *Fine View* or *Grand Sight,* and it was, indeed, a *Grand Sight* for our troops to see the Mexicans scampering away as if fifty-thousand devils were at their heels. . . . We visited the graves in which our heroes, who fell on that glorious occasion, had been interred. They were buried, layer upon layer, in two large pits—of course, covered with uncommon glory as well as with common dirt. . . .

We proceeded to Paras [Parras], finding the road skirted luxuriantly with the palmetto, prickly pear, and a plant called the King's Crown. We stayed three days at Paras, where we got our wagons repaired and the mules shod, and disposed of some of our loading in order to facilitate us on our journey. Thence to Quinquema [Cuencamé]. At this point the Camanche Indians became numerous. Eight miles from that town before reaching it, nine of those Indians attacked a Mexican train, consisting of mules packed with silver, which thirty Mexicans were taking to Durango. We saw the transaction. The Indians left the silver on the ground and drove off the mules, as the Mexicans ran to us for protection. We tried to save a wounded Mexican, but seeing us hastily approaching, the Indians killed him and rapidly fled. The inhabitants of Quinquema hailed us as if we were delivering angels, and the alcalde offered us $50 each, if we would lead the citizens against those Camanches, who are the noblest of the Indians in Mexico, but we concluded not to interfere as it might afterwards hinder our journey and endanger our lives, should those Indians hear of our interference. That afternoon, before we started, the Mexicans had a battle with them, in which the former had five killed and twelve wounded. But one Camanche was killed, and he was dragged into town at the end of a lasso, the other end being affixed to the horn of a saddle occupied by a vaunting Mexican. Thence to Durango, where we arrived April 19th. It is one of the largest and oldest cities in Mexico, containing, as I thought, about 125,000 inhabitants. The houses look like prisons, the doors and windows being plentifully supplied with iron bars, as if to prevent the beaux from carrying off the ladies or the Indians from capturing the whole family. The roofs are flat, and may appropriately be used for forts in time of war. The churches are among the most splendid in the Roman Catholic world. . . .

At this place I determined to use my best efforts to have our wagons and mules sold in order to go the rest of the land journey on pack mules, and also to stop the joint-stock eating business, as I had frequently bought chickens and eggs, which I never saw, much less eat of afterwards. Aided by others, who saw the existing evils we succeeded, and the wagons, mules, and some other articles were sold; $1000 worth of property brought but $450. We then hired a train of thirty mules, accompanied by six muleteers, to convey our decreased baggage and goods to Mazatlan, 160 miles distant, on nothing but a mule path. . . . At Durango, finding that my own mule had so sore a back that I could not ride it, I hired one at $1 per day.

Started from Durango, April 22d. The first night after leaving that city, Strode and Denman lost their mules, either strayed or stolen, so they were obliged to foot it. . . . Stambaugh showed how curiously jealousy can operate on the human heart. In passing over the mountains he exhibited a great deal of timidity, driving his mule before him instead of riding it where there was not the least danger. My courage and skill in riding up and down the precipices, showed his fearfulness in a rediculous light, so much so that he advised me to do as he did, only riding on the levels on the summits of the mountains. I told him that if he was willing to give $1 per day for the privilege of driving a mule up hill and down, he might do it, but that for myself I had given $1 per day for my mule for the privilege of riding whenever it suited my convenience, and that was all the time. I also observed that he had better return to Durango and persuade Gen. [José] Urrea to believe that he was a male angel, unfit for travel over Mexican mountains, as I had heard through our interpreter, that the Lancaster lawyer [Hart], Perkins, Hyde (the man who preached the sermon) and himself, had while in Durango palmed themselves off to Gen. Urrea as very wealthy gentlemen, travelling only to see the country, implying that myself and a few others were their escort or servants. While the fact was, I shone the most prominent in that city. All the rest shaved except myself, so that my beard reached almost to my knees, and, consequently, with my long silver mounted rifle and other accoutrements, I presented a truly formidable appearance, and attracted general attention and admiration wherever I went. This, of course, excited the jealousy of Stambaugh and a few others. As Gen. Urrea had been the greatest cut-throat in murdering our straggling soldiers during the war with Mexico, it showed rather a traitorous disposition to visit him, which should cast some discredit on those who honored, or, perhaps, dishonored him by a visit. . . .

On the fifth day from Durango, we reached the summit of the highest mountain, where I thought I was nearer to the good world than I would ever be again, from which we enjoyed a glorious prospect of mountains and plains, and, towards the east [west] a glimpse of the Pacific Ocean, which seemed pacifically inviting us to its borders.

As we progressed, we had ice and snow on the mountains, where we encamped at night; and by day in threading the valleys we enjoyed a delicious climate, water-melons, peaches, grapes, cocoa nuts, oranges, lemons, bananas and plantains. This truly romantic and solemn scenery affected us considerably. Previously, we had almost constantly passed through scrubby chapparel, and frequently could not find enough of wood to cook our meals; but here, almost for the first time since leaving the Brazos, we were traversing primeval forests, some of the trees of which had witnessed (if trees have eyes) the exploits of the soldiers of Cortez and Pizarro. . . .

In those mountains we passed silver mines every day, some of which were worked by English companies. At the bottom of the highest mountain I mentioned, was a very singular rock, about two thousand feet high, while its base was only about one hundred feet square. On its summit towered a beautiful pine tree, 60 feet in height. Nothing more of note happened until we arrived at Mazatlan on the Pacific ocean. Here we found a French brig

and a Danish schooner, both bound for San Francisco. I was informed that
the Lancaster lawyer observed to the French captain that he would induce
our company, and two or three other companies which had arrived by way
of Mexico City, to prefer his vessel, if he would give him his passage free.
As the Lancaster lawyer acted in this way, and as I also knew that while in
Durango he borrowed fifty dollars in silver of a negro, on the credit of the
company, and which still remained unpaid, telling the negro (in order to
get that sum) that our gold pieces would not pass for their full value in
Durango, but would in Mazatlan, I determined to quit so mean a person,
and forsake the company who would countenance him. I at once took
passage on the Danish schooner, named "Joanna Analuffa," commanded by
a gentlemanly German, paying $75, the distance from Mazatlan to San
Francisco being 1500 miles. Started from Mazatlan May 10th, with 200
passengers on board. I left $100 worth of articles with the company which
went in the French vessel, for which I never received a cent. Mazatlan contains about 10,000 inhabitants. Before leaving, Stambaugh observed to me
that I could do nothing without the company, and that I would certainly
be murdered in California without its protection, when I observed that I
would rather die than travel any further with such a swindling company.
This greatly enraged him, and the Lancaster lawyer picked up a gun to
shoot me. I then coolly told them that I did not wish wilfully to kill any
body or to be killed in an ordinary brawl, but that I was stout and stout-
hearted, and either with rifle, pistol, or bowie knife, I was honorably willing
to fight either of them on the spot. This latter offer neither of them thought
proper to accept. But now to the voyage.

After getting far out into the ocean, we ran a north-east course, towards
the destined port. When a week from land, we were supplied with wormy
bread, putrid jerked beef, musty rice, and miserable tea, there not being
enough of tea to color the water, the water was colored previously, to
deceive us, but we were too wide awake for the captain, and, being 200
in number, we determined to have the worth of our money, as the Yankee
boys are number one on sea as well as on land. We threw those articles of
food overboard, telling the captain we must have better. This infuriated
him, and he swore that if we did not become satisfied with the food he gave
us, he would take us back to Mazatlan, and have us tried and imprisoned
for mutiny. We as furiously told him that hunger knew no law, and that as
soon as he turned the vessel towards Mazatlan we would shoot him, and
moreover, that he must not only keep on his proper course, but give us
proper food, or we would take all the ship matters into our own hands. He
became as cool as a cowed rooster, kept on his course, and afterwards gave
us the best he had. We caught and ate a few sharks on the passage; and I

saw for the first time in my life whales every day, and porpoises darting about in every direction, like artful politicans, turning summersets occasionally to suit their respective views, and show the other fish their superiority.

In this fashion, says McNeil, on May 30 he arrived at San Francisco. His date is incorrect, for the *Alta California* of June 14, 1849, reports the arrival on Saturday, June 9, of the Danish schooner *Johanna & Oluffa,* Capt. Engers, 23 days from Mazatlán, cargo to Huttmann, Miller & Co., with 100 passengers. McNeil's tale has strange aspects, for Perkins says the whole company, himself included, came up from Mazatlán on the *Johanna and Oluffa.*[4] From San Francisco, McNeil made for Sacramento and the Northern Mines. Late in the summer, before starting homeward with his modest "stake," he visited the Southern Mines, encountering Perkins while the latter was suffering from poison oak. McNeil got back to Cincinnati October 12, 1849, and soon after was embracing his wife in his Lancaster home. Nearly three years passed before Perkins followed him back up the Mississippi, and thereby hangs our tale.

Perkins does not say what led him to find his star of fortune rising over the Southern Mines. He may have been contrary enough, independent enough, or merely sensible enough to conclude that if so many were going north, he might make out better in less crowded parts. He traveled first to Stockton, thence to Sullivan's Diggings, going to Sonora in the beginning only because he was stricken by poison oak. This region was comparatively unknown as yet, and we must develop something of its history down to the time Perkins arrived.

James W. Marshall's initial gold discovery, at Coloma on the South Fork of the American River, was made January 24, 1848. The

---

[4] The "French brig" which McNeil mentions is not identifiable. The *Alta California* of June 14 mentions the arrival at San Francisco on June 12 of the "Fr bark Olympa Capt Dansos, 40 days from Mazatlan, cargo to M. Dufford— 97 passengers." But the same issue records the arrival of the *Johanna & Oluffa* on June 9, a mere 23 days from Mazatlán. On June 21 the *Alta* notes the arrival on the 15th of "Mex brig Two Brothers, Udin, 31 days from Mazatlan, cargo to order—53 passengers." Finally, on June 28 the *Alta* records the arrival on June 22 of "Am schr Mazatleca, Faughton Master, 40 days from Mazatlan—17 passengers." No other arriving vessels seem to fit into McNeil's context.

significance of his find dawned slowly upon the people of California, and not until spring was it reflected in a rush to the diggings, that rush being to the American River. In late March or early April Charles M. Weber got together a small party at his establishment Tuleburg, the future Stockton, and set out to examine the Stanislaus River. Finding nothing, he and his men, who included a few Mexicans, turned north toward the Mokelumne, where they found their first color. Encouraged, they pursued their investigations and halted finally on Weber's Creek, at what became known as the Dry Diggings, near the site of Placerville. By summer many were mining in this area. Weber and a few associates formed a "Stockton Mining Company" and induced some Tuolumne Indians to learn the rudiments of mining. These Indians were then dispatched to the Stanislaus and Tuolumne rivers to dig gold. The plan was successful enough that in August, 1848, the "Stockton Mining Company" removed to the Stanislaus, and, though the company as such broke up the following month, the Southern Mines now existed.

That is the tale related in George H. Tinkham, *History of Stockton* (San Francisco, 1880), pp. 71–74, and proof has slowly come forth to establish its correctness. James H. Carson, who contributed a series of "Early Recollections of the Mines" to the Stockton *San Joaquin Republican*, commencing in January, 1852,[5] wrote as a participant and much closer to the actual events. He himself made his way to the mines from Monterey in May, 1848; he says that in June, July, and August the "old dry diggings . . . situated at the future Placerville, otherwise called Hangtown, in El Dorado county," were "the centre of attraction for gold diggers," with a heterogeneous population of some three hundred, exclusive of Indians.

In August, the old diggings were pronounced as being 'dug out,' and many prospecting parties had gone out. Part of Weber's trading establishments had secretly disappeared, and rumors were afloat that the place where all the gold "came from" had been discovered South, and a general rush of the miners set that way. . . . I would remark, that the South and North fork of the American river, Feather and Yuba rivers, Kelsey's and the old Dry Diggings, were all that had been worked at this date. The Middle, and North fork were discovered by a few deserters, in September, where in the

    ⁵ These *Early Recollections* were reprinted at Stockton in pamphlet form later in the year; they are cited in their newspaper occurrence to establish how early they were written.

space of a few days they realised from five to twenty thousand dollars each, and they left California by the first conveyance. . . .

The discovery of Sutter's Creek and Rio Seco was made in July, and the Moquelumne river diggings, at which there was but little done, that season. Mr. Wood, with a prospecting party discovered, at the same time, Wood's Creek on the Stanislaus [Tuolumne], out of which the few who were there then were realising two and three hundred dollars per day, with a pick and knife alone.[6]

Carson [*i.e.*, himself], who had been directed by an Indian, discovered what has since been known as Carson's Creek; in which himself and a small party took out, in ten days, an average of 180 ounces each. [George] Angel also discovered Angel's Creek, at which he wintered in 1848. Ever first with the discoveries were Capt. Weber's trading stores; John and Daniel Murphy, and Dr. Isabell [James C. Isbell] being with them. . . .

The gold discoveries reached no farther south during 1848—with the exception of the Tuolumne, on which gold was known to exist, only. The rains commenced on the last of October, which drove full two thirds of the diggers out to the towns on the coast. . . . Those who remained in the mines, during the winter of '48, made but little at mining, as the supplies for their subsistence were so high as to absorb all they made—but the traders amassed fortunes. . . .

Although written so soon after the events, Carson's account is nevertheless in retrospect; contemporary documentation for the opening of the Southern Mines is our pressing want. When Colonel R. B. Mason visited the mines in July, 1848, preliminary to writing his famous official report of August 17, he examined the diggings at Weber's Creek and obtained from Charles M. Weber a large lump of

---

[6] The Mr. Wood who gave name to Woods Creek would seem to have been the Benjamin Wood who was murdered by Indians on the Middle Fork of the American River, as recorded in the San Francisco *Alta California*, April 12, 1849 (thus also giving name to Murderers Bar). He came to California from Oregon in 1848. In preparing his *Annals of Tuolumne County* in 1861, Thomas Robertson Stoddart identified the man for whom Woods Creek was named as "the Rev. Jas. Woods, of Philadelphia," and later writers have elaborated a virtual mythology from this reference. Apparently Stoddart had in mind the Presbyterian minister, James Woods, who, as related in his *Recollections of Pioneer Work in California* (San Francisco, 1878), left New York in the *Alice Tarlton* with his family on May 17, 1849, and by a voyage of nearly eight months reached San Francisco, shortly afterward opening his ministerial labors in Stockton.

gold to be sent to Washington.[7] Nothing was then being said about gold farther south. But on August 15, a correspondent who signed himself "J. B." wrote a letter from " 'Dry Diggings,' Gold Placero," published in the San Francisco *Californian* of September 2, 1848, which said in part, "News has just arrived that new 'diggins' have been discovered on the Stanislaus river, and about 200 persons leave this morning for the new prospect, myself among the number. . . ." Chester S. Lyman, afterward a professor at Yale, who spent some time in the mines between June and August, all the while detailing his activities in a diary, set out for San Jose toward the end of the summer. On August 25, soon after leaving William Daly's ranch on the Cosumnes, he recorded meeting

Mr. Montgomery returning from an exploration of the various new diggings. He had been as far as the Stanislaus & reports gold in greater or less abundance on that & all the intermediate streams from 30 to 50 miles in from their mouths or midway in the Mts. as on the Am[erican] Fork. But as yet the gold tho beautiful does not seem to be so abundant as at the dry digging. It is more water worn & consequently smoother & more rounded. He showed some specimens which he had obtained; himself & his companions dug 6°ˣ in 2 or 3 hours. This was in a ravine 4 or 5 miles from the river Stanislaus. There are not many digging yet besides Indians.[8]

Apparently it was word of these new diggings that impelled Walter Colton to try his hand at gold washing. In his *Three Years in California* (Philadelphia, 1850), Colton tells of setting out from Monterey on September 21 to reach the diggings on the last day of the month. He is rather vague as to just where he traveled (place names were just being established), but eventually makes it clear that he had come to the Stanislaus. Since he mentions meeting Colonel Mason and the young Lieutenant William Tecumseh Sherman on September 30, the first diggings he reached can be located with some precision, for a letter written by Sherman to E. O. C. Ord from the vicinity of Sutter's, November 14, 1848, tells of this same tour of investigation. According

---

[7] See 30th Congress, 2d Session, *House Executive Document* 1 (Serial 537), pp. 56–64.

[8] For this and other quotations from Chester S. Lyman's diary, see Frederick J. Teggart, ed., *Around the Horn to the Sandwich Islands and California 1845–1850* (New Haven, 1924), pp. 275–286. Lyman had noted on August 23 that "Webber has moved his camp to the new diggings further south," an evident reference to the Stanislaus.

to Sherman, a long ride south from the Calaveras had brought the Army officers to the Stanislaus about twenty miles from its mouth, "at the Old Rancheria of José Jesus"—the future Knights Ferry. The diggings were a few miles above that point, near a place the miners were calling "the Crater." [9]

On October 18 Colton mentions being camped "in the centre of the gold mines, in the heart of the richest deposits which have been found, and where there are many hundred at work." Next day he tells of a rumor "that a solid pocket of gold has been discovered in a bend of the Stanislaus," so that the miners stampeded in that direction, only to return sheepishly later in the day. On the 20th Colton set out "for a cañada, about ten miles distant," clearly Woods Creek, and by a mountain trail reached what he calls "the great camp of the Sonoranians," where "hundreds were crowding around" a monte table. ("It was in this ravine," Colton says, "that a few weeks since the largest lump of gold found in California was discovered. It weighs twenty-three pounds, is nearly pure, and cubic in its form. Its discovery shook the whole mines.") Colton has something to say about "Sonoranians" in the mines this fall, but that is a topic to which we shall return. He set out for home by way of Stockton in mid-November, saying rather preposterously that fifty thousand miners left the diggings at the onset of the rainy season.

While Colton was on the Stanislaus, Chester Lyman made his appearance there on a mercantile speculation, bringing goods furnished by Josiah Belden. Starting from San Jose on October 5, Lyman crossed the San Joaquin four days later, traversed a plain to the Stanislaus, and, via a mountainous road, on the 15th reached "an Indian Rancheria, where Dan Murphy has a camp selling goods for Webber." He went on to William Gulnac's camp a few miles above and there commenced his trading operations. "Did not sell very much however," Lyman says in his diary. "Many camps in this valley, little gold dug at present. Most people trading, market over-stock." More illuminatingly he writes under date of October 19–20:

Thurs & Frid. Very little trade, people leaving, diggings poor, few getting more than 1 or 2 oz per day.

---

[9] This unpublished letter, with another dated October 28, 1848, is in the Beinecke Collection, Yale University Library.

Examined the rich ravine where a piece said to weigh 15 or 20 lbs of pure gold was taken out. The rock on which the gold lies appears to be a species of gneiss, very hard & resembling basalt. The strata running about N N W & dipping 75° or 80° easterly. In passing down the creek to the lower camps 5 or 6 miles various successive strata of slates present themselves with about the same direction & inclination. The gold is found here as elsewhere only in the drift or diluvium. In this region most of the gold is taken from dry ravines setting into the main creek [undoubtedly Woods Creek] which runs into the river Tuallomy, in south westerly direction. 5 to 6 miles below where the deposit has been found very rich the gold occurs in the main stream resting on the same kind of rock mentioned above. Quartz is abundant in the region, & I noticed some dykes or beds of it several yards in thickness, between beds or strata of the slatey rocks.

On Sunday, October 22, Lyman adds: "Much noise & drinking in neighboring camps. A great deal of gambling done here. Gold sells for $5 to $8. per ounce."

Three days later, having sold out the remainder of his merchandise at cost, Lyman prepared to go home, he and his associates having cleared $450 apiece. "While we have done this others have done 10 to 20 times as much, especially those who sell grog, which I would not be engaged in for all the gold of the Placero. One man tells me that since he opened his grog shop 7 days ago he had made $7000 or over $1000 a day. Last Sunday he took in $2000 half of it in cash; the first day he cleared more than the whole cost of his stock. A dram costs on an average $2. or more." Lyman lists prices that had prevailed during the past month, then says, "From the Indians all sorts of prices are taken & much deception is practiced. [James] Savage used an ounce weight which counterpoised 11 silver dollars. A common practice is to use a two oz weight for an oz &c. Gold sells for 6 to 8 dollars an oz in cash. It has been down to 3 & 4 among the gamblers, who have been very numerous here. For the last two days several hundred people have left this valley, & it now looks quite desolate." Lyman left the diggings on October 26 and reached San Jose on November 1. Thus he had been gone nearly three weeks when Walter Colton departed. James H. Carson remembered three years later that the rains commenced at about the end of October, but the *Californian* observed on November 4, 1848: "Great numbers of the miners come down on every launch that arrives from the Sacramento, and the general opinion appears to be that the season for digging is pretty near over for this year. Though the rainy season has not yet set in, it was daily expected. . . ." The rains seem not to have come before late November.

We get the impression that at the close of 1848 no great excitement prevailed about the Southern Mines. A chronicle has yet to appear, written by one who wintered in the diggings; perhaps we will never have such a record. A change came over the region by spring. On March 28, 1849, E. C. Kemble wrote the *Alta California* from Sacramento:

. . . It is *Stanislaus* that has allured the uninitiated gold hunter to the early conquest—*Stanislaus* that has gathered the floating population of the mines during the past month—"*Stanislaus*" that has gone forth a rallying cry throughout the valley, and whose waters, it is said, have washed out the shining, beautiful gold as it was never washed out before. We yesterday was shown a piece of remarkable beauty and purity, weighing eleven ounces and three fourths, for the gold from that stream is generally in large pieces, more generally termed *slugs* or *coarse,* but very *fine* gold, if you please. The borders of this Stanislaus stream form an inexhaustable rich portion of the Placer, though because it is at this time "o'erflowing full," the heavier deposits cannot be reached, and labor generally is suspended in consequence.

A country that had seemed barren of place names when winter set in flowered with names in the spring, used as though they had always existed. Characteristically, a letter in the *Alta California* of May 31, written by a correspondent who signed himself "S. W.," dated Stanislaus diggings, Jamestown, five miles from the river, May 13, 1849, tells of reaching that vicinity May 7 (a mistake for April 7). Jamestown, said he, was "named in honor of Mr. James, who is an Alcalde, 'as is an Alcalde,' and who dispenses grub and justice to the satisfaction of all." (James & Co., he further related, had a large tent, kept as a combined store and hotel.) [10] On April 13 large stories were

---

[10] George F. James, later well-known as a San Francisco lawyer, apparently did not reach California until 1849. Stoddart, who was under the impression that he came to the Tuolumne country in 1848, says that he entered largely into mining speculations which finally obliged him to leave Jamestown bankrupt. "By his departure, many men lost their earnings . . . and in revenge they called the place by the name of American Camp. It only held this name, however, a short time, when the old one of Jamestown was again taken up, and never since dropped or altered."

being told "of the Mormon and Sullivan's diggings above, but on investigation I find although some have got out a pound and more, that the proportion of the fortunes is about the same throughout the mines." In passing he mentions a recent murder "at Carson's creek, ten miles from here." A later Jamestown letter of May 29, printed in the *Alta* of June 21, by the same correspondent, refers casually to "Wood's camp—1½ miles below." The Sonoranian Camp, or Sonora, came into existence in April, 1849, as Perkins himself tells us in the last of his letters printed in the Appendix. But we must go back to 1848 to approach this history from another vantage point.

A well-developed legend has it that large numbers of Sonorans were in the diggings as early as the summer of 1848. Undoubtedly there were a few, but they must have been Sonorans visiting in California when news of the gold discovery first began to spread; most American miners were incapable of distinguishing between Sonorans, New Mexicans, and their Spanish kinsmen, the native Californians. José Francisco Velasco, *Noticias Estadísticas del Estado de Sonora* (Mexico, 1850), pp. 289–290, records that the first caravan from Hermosillo, Sonora, did not set out until October, 1848. Cave Johnson Couts, a second lieutenant in the First Dragoons, marched from Monterrey, Mexico, to Los Angeles in the fall of 1848. On reaching the Colorado River at the present city of Yuma during the last week of November, he remarked in his diary: "A small party of Mexicans passed on 25th from California, 'Los Angeles' going after their families in Sonora. News of California favorable. Got from these a paper published in San Francisco dated Sept. 16th, 1848, and which was greatly sought by all, as the *circulating medium* was very interesting, if not equally amusing. Gold dust $16 to oz. announced the arrival of Ingall's age." It may be that these were returning miners, but Couts is not specific.

After crossing the Colorado, Couts noted during the second week of December that Mexicans from Sonora were daily passing "on their way to the *abundancia*, the gold mines!" And on December 17:

The whole state of Sonora is on the move, are passing us in gangs daily, and say they have not yet started. Naked and shirttailed Indians and Mexicans or Californians, go and return in 15 or 20 days with *over a pound* of pure gold each, per day, and say "they had bad luck and left." In Los

Angeles and San Diego a man in fitting out a party of 5 or 10 men for the mines has only to go to a merchant and borrow from one to two thousand dollars and give him an "order on the gold mines." Nothing apparently sells for less than ounce of gold.[11]

It may be doubted that Sonorans in any numbers reached the Southern Mines before February, 1849. We would exhibit a more sweeping skepticism except for Walter Colton's account of the Stanislaus diggings in the fall of 1848. On October 27 Colton wrote in his journal:

I have just returned from another ravine, five miles distant, where there are eighty or a hundred gold-diggers. They are mostly Sonoranians, and, like all their countrymen, passionately devoted to gambling. They were playing at monté; the keeper of the bank was a woman, and herself a Sonoranian. . . . A Sonoranian digs out gold simply and solely that he may have the wherewithal for gambling. This is the rallying thought which wakes with him in the morning, which accompanies him through the day, and which floats through his dreams at night. For this he labors, and cheerfully denies himself every comfort.

In the course of the next two weeks Colton made other allusions to the Sonoranians, including their mode of "dry washing" gold. Some of them may have been Sonorans once removed, migrants to southern California from the country east of the Colorado and south of the Gila; but Colton had been for two years a resident of California, and some powers of discrimination should be granted him.

It is nevertheless probable that many of these "Sonorans" actually were Californians. One such was Antonio Franco Coronel, who had come from Mexico in 1834 and was destined to become mayor of Los Angeles in 1853 and state treasurer in 1867–1871. Coronel dictated his reminiscences in 1877. In this illuminating manuscript, now preserved in the Bancroft Library,[12] Coronel recalls that after confirmation of the

---

[11] Henry F. Dobyns, ed., *Hepah, California! The Journal of Cave Johnson Couts* (Tucson, 1961), pp. 82–88.

[12] Antonio Franco Coronel, Cosas de California, dictated to Thomas Savage for the Bancroft Library, 1877 (C-D 61). A more extended excerpt from the Coronel manuscript is translated as an appendix to Richard Henry Morefield, "The Mexican Adaptation in American California: 1846–1875" (M.A. Thesis, University of California, Berkeley, 1955).

gold discovery, several parties left for the north from the Los Angeles area. The group that he accompanied consisted of about thirty men, including Ramón Carrillo, Narciso Bottello, Dolores Sepúlveda, Narciso José Antonio Machada, one of the Osunas, and "several Sonorans." They made their way to Pueblo de San José, and in August, 1848, set out for the Dry Diggings.

As translated from the Spanish, Coronel's dictation says:

Upon arrival at the San Joaquin River . . . we met Father José María Suarez del Real who was a true *vaquero* and who had a great deal of gold with him. He told us that he came from Stanislaus Camp—recently discovered—which was a placer rich in gold. We went there and found the camp of some New Mexicans who had come from Los Angeles and who had recently settled there, one or two Americans or foreigners, and several other parties of Spanish people who came from San José and other nearby points.

[With his companions Coronel settled in the center of the main ravine which served as an encampment.] A little before sunset, there arrived at our camp seven tame Indians, each one with little sacks of gold shaped like sausages, of an average length of ten to twelve inches. I was leaning on my saddle and on top of the saddle bags that I was carrying were several ordinary blankets which were used as saddle blankets. They were used and dirty and their value when new had been two pesos each. One of the Indians took one of them and pointed to the sack filled with gold; he pointed out on a certain spot as the amount he was offering for the blanket. There was then in that area no way to acquire anything to replace that blanket so I refused the offer of the Indian. He increased it in the same manner, lowering the place where he pressed on the sack with his thumb; I refused again. He increased again and then one of my servants asked me why I did not give it to him—that he would make some saddle blankets of grass.

I took a tin plate that we had and the Indian emptied the gold into it, and after giving him the blanket I weighed it; there were seven and one quarter ounces—the first gold from the gold mines of California that I obtained. Immediately another Indian made the same offer for the other blanket that I had left. I refused two or three offers before I accepted; after giving up the blanket I weighed the gold—a little over nine ounces.

I had a serape from Saltillo for my own use. The Indians began to examine it and to make me offers for it, gathering four of their small bags which altogether contained about *three and one half pounds* of gold. I refused all offers because that serape was my main covering. One of my servants—Benito Perez—sold them in the same manner a serape from New

Mexico that had cost him nine pesos and which was a year old—for two pounds three ounces of gold.

This Benito Perez was experienced in gold mining and suggested to me that it would be well to follow these Indians to find out from where they brought the gold—to give him a companion and he would follow them. The Indians continued buying several other objects by the same system and among the purchases they made was an old horse from a certain Valdes, giving him nearly two pounds of gold. After dark the Indians retired from our camp and Benito Perez followed them, accompanied by one of my servants (one of the mute Indians I had with me, named Agustin, whom I had raised as a member of the family.) . . . They followed them to their camp which was not far away; it belonged to Captain Estanislao whose name had been given to the area. Perez camped on a hill in front of the Indian camp and spent the night there waiting for the Indians to leave. The next morning the seven Indians who had visited us left the camp and crossing some hills headed east. Perez followed them without being seen. The Indians stopped at a ravine called Cañada del Barro and with some wood sticks began to dig for and gather gold. Perez went down to where the Indians were; they seemed unfriendly, but he insisted in digging in a place next to theirs and right away he found gold, and by digging with his knife he gathered three ounces of thick flakes. It already being late, he made sure of the location and that there was plenty of gold, and returned to my camp to report to me all that had happened.

Perez and I agreed to go immediately to take possession of the spot without being noticed; but as I had companions I felt that it would be wrong if I did not give them a share, especially as Perez had informed me that this was a large and rich area. Probably the news spread like magic and I knew that my movements were being watched. I then ordered Perez with my two mute Indians to leave without being seen to take possession of the land which he considered to be the richest. They did so; and when I was assured that he had gained his objective, I started out late at night, followed by some of the Spanish people who were in the camp.

All marked out their plot of ground, guarding it to begin work the next day. On October 7, 1848, everyone began to work at daybreak. After a little digging we came upon the gold deposits and everyone who was working was happy with the results. I, with my two mute Indians, recovered with that day's work about forty-five ounces of coarse gold, not counting the leavings which we saved for washing. Dolores Sepúlveda, who was next to my claim, dug up a *nugget* of a little more than twelve ounces, besides the rest of his gains. All the others, some one hundred-odd persons, had brilliant results.

The next day I continued on the same job and gathered, with my two mutes, thirty-eight ounces of coarse gold, not including the leavings I accumulated.

The third day I spent washing the dirt and it yielded fifty-one ounces.

The ravine, Cañada del Barro, was a thousand yards or more long; it was at its beginning that we obtained the results which I have described. From this point the ravine made a break and turned; here there was a sand bar about three hundred yards long. At the same time that I was working my claim, a certain Valdes, alias Chapanango, a native Californian from Santa Barbara, found on the sand bar that I mentioned a deposit of gold which was caused by a large rock located underground in such a manner that it obstructed the current, catching there quantities of gold. Valdes, having dug down some three feet, found another deposit and gathering it easily, he threw it into a sort of a towel until the towel picked up by the four corners would not hold any more. Fascinated by his great find, he went about boasting of it, and being satisfied, wished to leave the area.

Lorenzo Soto, of San Diego . . . was looking around for a claim and seeing that Valdés was not working his, offered to buy it. . . . Soto worked about eight days on his claim, and from the amount of gold I saw and from what he told me it weighed, he had taken out fifty-two pounds. The claim had reached water, and in this condition he sold it to some Machados from San Diego, who also took considerable gold from it.

I left my servants working my claim and went to examine the third sand bar in the Cañada del Barro. With me came one of the most famous *gambusinos* among the Sonorans, known by the nickname of "Chino Tirador." We stopped at a spot which we felt was favorable. . . . At a depth of four feet, he found a deposit of gold next to an underground rock that divided his claim from mine. This was about 9 a.m. He began to gather the gold with a horn spoon and with his hands, throwing it into a wooden bowl, and he would clean the dirt from it by shaking the bowl, or as the Sonorans say, "dry washing." He worked at this until 4 p.m., throwing the gold that was cleaned into his straw hat. I was observing the good fortune of this man, because I, with much more effort, had only been able to get six ounces of gold in the same period. The crown of his hat, which was of good size, being filled, he had left a good deal more in the bowl. I told him he should empty his hat into the bowl (which was large). This he did and he was hardly able to carry it. He said he was going to the camp and then I asked permission to work his claim. He cheerfully granted it, and the result was that I obtained seventeen ounces in some two hours of work.

"Chino" had gone to the camp with his gold, where it caused a great commotion. He went about offering to sell his gold for silver which was scarce. He had already sold some part of it to someone when I arrived. He proposed to sell me clean gold at *twenty reales* [two and one half pesos] *per ounce*. I bought seventy six ounces at this price; I did not have silver for any more. Other persons there bought the rest at about more or less the same price [but he gave a foreigner some two pounds for a partly-full bottle of aguardiente]. . . .

"Chino" used the silver which he had obtained by selling his gold to set up a monte bank on the ground on a sheet, because one must note that he did not have any clothes but a pair of cotton pants and a wool shirt, plus the wool sheet. By ten o'clock that night, or perhaps earlier, "Chino" was drunk from the aguardiente and without a cent. All his money had been won from him. On the next day he returned to the claim he had left, but during the night many people had worked it, even by candlelight, taking from it great quantities of gold; and when he examined it, it seemed to him that it would not yield enough to make his work worthwhile. This claim was taken over by Felipe García of Los Angeles and in three days he took out about twenty ounces from a pocket he found. . . .

I abandoned my claim in this area and returned to the one I was working previously. I continued there for about a month—perhaps a few days less.

By the beginning of winter all the people on the Stanislaus, with very few exceptions, had accumulated fairly large amounts of gold and wanted to return to the populated areas for the winter, because already the news had circulated that the snows on the Stanislaus were severe and could prevent the arrival of food supplies. But the people did not leave because of news of the operations of a band of thieves on the San Joaquin River.

Don Andres Pico had brought a party of Sonorans supplying them with all their needs from Los Angeles to this spot on the condition that they pay him for those supplies in gold at the going price as of that moment. In order to insure this payment, he had them working together under the supervision and care of a Spaniard named Juan Manso, one of the owners of the Administration of San Fernando. The departure of this party for San Jose had been announced, and when part of them left, the majority of the people on the Stanislaus departed for San Jose.

Coronel goes on to relate that he had concluded to winter on the Stanislaus, because his claim was very rich, and he had ground enough to work throughout the winter, weather permitting. He was preparing to build a house when he received a letter from Ramón Carrillo, inviting him to go to the Northern Mines. Coronel traveled north, only to learn on reaching the Feather River that Carrillo had left for Sonora. In consequence he went to Sonoma to winter, arriving there about the middle of December. Early in March, 1849, he set out for the diggings, again, intending to go to the Stanislaus, but in Sacramento "met people

who had returned from that area who gave me the news that the
Stanislaus was almost entirely overrun by all kinds of nationalities, but
especially by Sonorans."

Virtually unchronicled is this movement of Sonorans up from the
south and their overspreading of the basins of the Stanislaus and the
Tuolumne, but we get a glimpse of what had been going on through
the winter in the letter by the *Alta California's* Jamestown correspondent, "S. W.," which recounts events from May 14–29. As of May
14 he writes, "Twelve California carts, with four yoke of oxen each,
passed this valley last eve, and it was a scene of rural beauty, I have
seldom seen surpassed." On the 16th:

> The immigration for the past two days has been less than usual. Now
> and then, a party appears on its winding way, composed principally of
> Mexicans, with their lances and red flags. A party of them encamped near
> Jamestown and hoisted a small red flag over their tent, but a deputation of
> Americans waited upon the *gentlemen,* and soon gave them to understand,
> that such a proceeding would be looked upon as a natural insult, and
> challenge direct, and they instantly hauled the offensive banner down. This
> afternoon the line of march seems to be resumed, and the apparently in-
> terminable array is again in motion. One may well ask "where do they come
> from? and what country is likely to be depopulated?" for some parts of the
> world must be thinning their ranks very rapidly.

A correspondent of the New Orleans *Picayune* signing himself
"Freaner," who must have reached San Francisco about the same time
as Perkins, after a tour of the interior returned to the seaport to advise,
in a letter of June 30 printed by the *Picayune* on August 5, that about
twenty thousand people were at work in the Southern Mines, "including all ages, sexes, conditions and colors, taking out 1,000 pounds of
gold per day; whenever a miner gets less than an ounce a day, he thinks
he is not paid for his labor, and seeks some better place." Freaner
explained:

> The first of the mining region is on Woods's Creek, south of the
> Stanislaus. At present there are few working them, on account of the water
> flowing in on them from under ground. The people from the State of
> Sonora, Mexico, and those from South America, settled at this point; but
> owing to some difficulties likely to occur between them and the Americans,
> they moved out and established a camp about four miles distant [what he

terms "the Sonorian Camp."] The Mexicans and South Americans number about 8,000; they keep up all the customs and habits of their country— bull-fights, chicken-fights, dancing, gambling, etc. on Sundays and feast days. In all the other 'diggings' Sundays are respected, though I have not heard of any preaching in any of them.[13]

By the close of June, 1849, the differentiation of "the Placer" into Northern and Southern mines was established. In practical terms, the Northern Mines were dependencies of Sacramento, the Southern Mines of Stockton. The former were the diggings in the watershed of the Sacramento, the latter in the basin of the San Joaquin. But the Southern Mines were a continually growing area, by the summer of 1849 embracing diggings as far south as the Tulares. James H. Carson, in his recollections, tells in detail how this had come about.

The first expedition to explore the potential of the Tulares, Carson says, was led by William R. Gardner (Garnier) of San Jose, who set out early in 1849 for Kings River. He and some others were killed by Indians, and the expedition was driven out. A second party, consisting of "Messrs. Loveland, Curtis, Harris, Swain, and four others," reached the mountains March 20, approximately fifteen miles above the Merced and made the first gold discovery at what became known as "Burn's diggings." They in turn were put to flight by the Indians.

The next party of exploration were more formidable than the two first mentioned. This party consisted of ninety-two men, under the guidance of Carson, [i.e., himself], and Robinson, of Monterey; they were composed of dragoons and discharged teamsters from the command of Major Graham, which had arrived from Mexico, and a number of disbanded volunteers of Col. Stephenson's regiment, well armed and equipped. This party struck into the Sierra Nevada where the Mariposa enters the plains, and explored the adjacent country, finding gold in many places; they thence proceeded to the Merced and Tuolumne and found gold on these streams and tribu-

---

[13] One entertaining feature of "Freaner's" letter is an excerpt quoted from an "accont Buk of John McGuire and the people in thease diggins," *i.e.*, at Sonora, which identifies some of the "people" as "George Williams, the darkey white man," "Red that lives with Dancing Bill," "the man thats in his tent," "Inaca that has the woman with the big ring in her ear," "Chene" (i.e., Chino Tirador?), "John that speaks English," "Polenary flowris that cut of the china man's hair," "Manell Salyes, the Canaccer frenchman, that has the white wife." For the whole extraordinary account, see Carlo M. De Ferrari's note appended to Chapter IV of Stoddart's *Annals of Tuolumne County*, p. 79.

taries as far as they went. The reports of these expeditions soon peopled these regions. Col. Fremont and his party were about the first who dug for gold in the Mariposa region on what is known as Fremont's Creek in the spring of 1849.

Carson says he was not pleased with these new diggings and made his way north to Stockton at the beginning of May, finding that town already vastly changed. He then returned to the diggings of 1848, only to find Carsons and Angels creeks "filled with human beings," and Woods Creek worse:

On the long flat we found a vast canvass city, under the name of James-town, which, similar to a bed of mushrooms, had sprung up in a night. A hundred flags were flying from restaurants, taverns, rum-mills and gaming houses. The gambling tables had their crowds continually, and the whole presented a scene similar to that of San Francisco during the past winter. . . . Wood's creek was filled up with miners. . . . Mormon Gulch, Sol-diers' Gulch, Sullivan's Diggings, and the Rich Gulch of the Moquelumne, had been rich discoveries, made during the fall and winter, and were now centres of attraction. Curtis's creek and the rich diggings of the flats around Jamestown soon followed. In October, '48, a small party of us were en-camped on the flat near where Sonora now stands. Nightly a California lion greeted us with his long howl, on the hill now occupied by the town; he seemed to be conscious that the white man was approaching, and that his old playgrounds were soon to be occupied by a tented city.[14]

These were the scenes, this the country, that became the stuff of William Perkins' life. As he makes clear in the third of his letters printed over his nom-de-plume "Leo," reprinted in our Appendix, for him the Southern Mines were rather narrowly delimited, mostly that

[14] A bare beginning has been made in documenting the early development of the Southern Mines. Two doctoral dissertations concerned with various aspects of this history are Gregory F. Crampton, "The Opening of the Mariposa Mining Region, 1849–1859" (University of California, Berkeley, 1941); and, more germane to our present interest, William R. Kenny, "History of the Sonora Mining Region of California, 1848–1860" (University of California, Berkeley, 1955). The latter thesis elaborates Roberta Evelyn Holmes, "Early Development of the Sonora Mining Region" (M.A. thesis, University of California, 1925). A systematic search of American newspapers for letters written from the mines, especially in 1849–1852, will have to be carried out before the history of either the Southern or the Northern mines is placed on a sound footing.

part of the future Tuolumne County north of the Tuolumne River, and south of the Stanislaus which would separate Tuolumne from Calaveras County. Establishing himself at Sonora, that appropriately named center of the foreign miners, he became a prominent participant in its affairs and a warm and sympathetic chronicler of its life.

In 1848 there had seemed to be gold enough in California for all who had the will and the physical stamina to dig for it. Not until the spring of 1849 did James H. Carson hear of that innovation, the "miner's claim" (was the concept imported from Sonora by the experienced miners from that area?); anyone could dig where he chose. Nor was there any anti-foreign feeling in 1848. Except for the native Californians, everyone was spiritually a foreigner. The spoiling times came with the inrush of 1849.

Like most nations, the United States has a history of exploiting rather than of cherishing its minorities. Indians, Negroes, Irish, Mexicans, Chinese, and Japanese, to say nothing of Quakers, Mormons, Jews, and Catholics, at different times have been efficiently exploited; and in the 1840's a strong nativist political sentiment had begun to develop. General Persifor F. Smith, sent to California early in 1849 to assume military command, seems to have been infected by this sentiment, for in a proclamation issued at Panama in February, he declared that he would check the influx of foreigners into the gold region. No one paid much attention to this proclamation, not even the United States government, but an anti-foreign feeling manifested itself as the influx of Forty-niners into California continued.

The San Francisco *Alta California* on July 2, 1849, estimated that the California population at the beginning of the year approximated 15,000 (exclusive of Indians) of whom 1,000 were foreigners. Between January 1 and April 11 the number of land immigrants was estimated at perhaps 500 (who would have been mostly from Mexico), while arrivals by sea, the great majority of whom were foreigners, were known to have totaled 3,614. Between April 12 and June 30 the land immigration "from Sonora and other northern Departments of Mexico" was estimated at about 5,000, and 1,452 Mexican males were recorded to have arrived by sea. Of 5,677 males who from all points of the compass reached San Francisco by sea, 1,350 were from Chile, 1,251 from Panama, 370 from the Sandwich Islands, 227 from Peru, 120 from Tahiti, 43 from New South Wales, 34 from China, 28 from New Zealand, and 26 from Central America. Most of the 205 female arrivals came from Chile (70), Mexico (57), Panama (25), and Peru (21). With our special interest in Sonorans, let us note that on December 1, 1849, the *Alta* further estimated that 6,000 Mexicans in all might have reached California overland. These figures correspond with Velasco's estimate that from 5,000 to 6,000 Sonorans set out for the mines between October, 1848, and April, 1849.

By July, 1849, a general inclination developed to drive the Chileans and Peruvians from the American River. The movement spread, and soon even the naturalized Californians were being expelled from the mines on three hours' grace. Jealous greed easily masquerades as patriotism on such occasions. Foreigners were accused of having no interest in building up the country, of desiring only to strike it rich and go home, which was exactly the idea of the American miners. Only time, and the inability to raise a stake so as to return home, made permanent Californians out of many American goldseekers of 1849 and 1850. The same causes would have made naturalized citizens out of many foreigners, had events been left to take their own course.

Coronel, after wintering at Sonoma, set out for the southern diggings in March, 1849, only to learn that the region "was almost entirely overrun by all kinds of nationalities, but especially by Sonorans." He went to the Dry Diggings (Placerville) instead. He recalled later:

In this gold field, there was quite a population of Chileans, Peruvians, Californians, Mexicans, and many Americans, Germans, etc. The campsites were established separately, largely according to nationality. All—some more, some less—were profiting from the fruits of their labor. Then the news spread that the expulsion from the mines of all those who were not American citizens was being planned, because it was felt that foreigners had no right to exploit the mines.

One Sunday there appeared notices in The Pines and various other places that all those who were not American citizens had to leave the area within twenty-four hours, and that force would be used against those who failed to obey. This was supported by a meeting of armed men, ready to make good this announcement.

There were a considerable number of people of various nationalities to whom this order to leave applied. They decided to gather on a hill in order to be ready in case of an attack. The day on which the departure of the foreigners was supposed to take place, and during the next three or four days, both forces remained on the alert, but the situation did not go beyond shouts, gunshots and drunkenness, and finally everything calmed down and we returned to our work, although daily some of the weak were despoiled of their claims by the stronger.

A few days later, a Frenchman whom Coronel calls Don Augusto and a Spaniard named Luis were seized, having been accused by an old Irishman of having stolen four pounds of buried gold. Coronel and his fellows protested that the two were men of good standing and had sufficient money of their own, with no reason to steal. Moreover, Coronel proffered five pounds of gold gathered up in the camp for the benefit of the accused, one pound more than had assertedly been stolen. The man acting as chief of the Americans took the gold, saying he would talk with the committee, and told Coronel to return in a few hours. But before the appointed time the men were hanged and the same fate was promised to any who might defend them. "This act dismayed me," Coronel says, "and it had the same effect on many others. Two days later I packed up camp and went to the northern mines." But soon armed marauders were roaming the mines, jumping claims of the Spanish-speaking people. Coronel returned to his Los Angeles home. In his view, the reason for most of the antipathy against those of Spanish blood was that

the majority of them were Sonorans who were used to gold mining and consequently obtained quicker and richer results—as did the Californians who came first and acquired the same arts; those who came later were possessed of the terrible fever to secure gold, yet unable to satisfy it because they were not satisfied with what they got, hoping to enrich themselves in a moment. These, I saw, could not resign themselves patiently to the better fortune of the others. Add to this fever, that which comes from excessive use of liquor. Add also that, among so many people of so many nationalities, there were a great number of dissolute men, capable of every conceivable crime; and the circumstances of there being no laws or authorities to protect the rights and lives of men, gave these wicked men an advantage over peaceful and honorable men. Properly speaking, there was no law in those days but that of force; and in the end the decent people, in their own defense, had to establish law of retaliation.

Coronel is quoted at such length because he was himself of Spanish blood and Mexican descent, though a naturalized Californian; it is enlightening to hear from one of those William Perkins is presently defending. Through the summer of 1849 there was a considerable exodus of the foreign-born down into San Francisco, many being shipped home with the help of their governments. Less well reported at the time was an exodus from the Northern to the Southern mines, and a general buildup of the foreign population in the Sonora area where Perkins settled. But the animus of the Americans followed.

Charles Kirkpatrick, who had arrived by the overland route a few weeks before, was mining at Winters' Bar on the Mokelumne River when he wrote in his diary on Sunday, October 14: "As this is the day for doing up business here, and there being a great many foreigners at work all about us a meeting was called in the evening for the purpose of electing an Alcade or magistrate whose duty it should be to warn these foreigners that they are transgressing and that they must leave or as we say here 'Vamous.'"

Kirkpatrick was no desperado, like so many now in the mines, and one can discern a troubled moral sense in his diary entries of the next few days. He was finding mining very hard work—*"This gold digging I don't like atall."*—When he and two others labored until noon on the 17th, making only $7.50, they spent the afternoon vainly prospecting for a better locality. On the 18th:

This morning finding a hole deserted we tried our luck in it. Three of us in the day made $28.00, but part of this we stole—in this way—in Sunday's record I spoke of the foreigners having to leave and as the time in which they were to 'vamous' had elapsed, we thought there would be no harm in our laying claim to a fine pile of dirt brought down from the dry 'diggins' by an old Mexican, so at it we went; but in 15 or 20 minutes here came the old fellow 'mad as a hornet' and for some time we could not tell what he was going to do. All he could get out of *us* was for him to 'vamous.' This was indeed poor pay for the loss of his gold, but he took it, pocketed the insult and went to washing the pile himself while we went to work in another place. (The manuscript transcript of Kirkpatrick's diary made for H. H. Bancroft, is now in the Bancroft Library.)

Thomas Butler King's report on California, submitted to the Secretary of State in March, 1850,[15] held that the American emigration did not arrive by sea in force until July and August, and the overland emigration did not start to come in until the last of August and first of September. "The Chilinos and Mexicans were early in the country. In the month of July it was supposed that there were fifteen thousand foreigners in the mines." King's figures seem inflated, but he goes on:

At a place called Sonoranian camp, it was believed there were at least ten thousand Mexicans. They had quite a city of tents, booths, and log cabins; hotels, restaurants, stores, and shops of all descriptions, furnished with whatever money could procure. Ice was brought from the Sierra, and ice-creams added to numerous other luxuries. An inclosure made of the trunks and branches of trees, and lined with cotton cloth, served as a sort of amphitheatre for bull-fights; other amusements, characteristic of the Mexicans, were to be seen in all directions.

The foreigners resorted principally to the southern mines, which gave them a great superiority in numerical force over the Americans, and enabled them to take possession of some of the richest in that part of the country. In the early part of the season, the Americans were mostly employed on the forks of the American and on Bear, Yuba and Feather Rivers. As their numbers increased they spread themselves over the southern mines, and collisions were threatened between them and the foreigners. The latter, however, for some cause, either fear, or having satisfied their cupidity, or both, began to leave the mines late in August, and by the end of September many of them were out of the country.

Other comments of this kind could be quoted; King has been brought into these pages because he proposed a novel revenue measure, the exaction of

one ounce or $16 as the price of a permit or license to dig or collect gold for one year. This I regard as about the average value of one day's labor in the mines. This tax on fifty thousand miners, the probable number next summer, will give a revenue of $800,000. On one hundred thousand miners

---

[15] First printed as a government document, King's report was reprinted at New York in 1850 as *California: the Wonder of the Age*. It was also appended by Bayard Taylor to the second volume of his *El Dorado, or, Adventures in the Path of Empire* (New York, 1850), where it may be conveniently consulted.

—the probable number in 1851—it will give $1,600,000, besides the per centum on the vein-mines, and the sum received for town lots, timber, etc., which would probably swell the amount to at least $200,000.

King suggested that part of the money thus collected should be expended in constructing roads and bridges, to facilitate communication to and through the mining districts. "These facilities will so reduce the cost of living in the mines, that the miners will gain instead of lose by paying the tax." (One hears cheers by the taxpayers.) King went on to say:

I have proposed to exclude foreigners from the privilege of purchasing permits, and from working as discoverers of purchasers in the vein-mines. My reasons for recommending this policy are, that these mines belong to, and in my judgment should be preserved for, the use and benefit of the American people. I mean, of course, all citizens, native and adopted.

During the mining season of 1849, more than fifteen thousand foreigners, mostly Mexicans and Chilenos, came in *armed bands* into the mining district, bidding defiance to all opposition, and finally carrying out of the country some twenty millions of dollars' worth of gold dust, which belonged *by purchase* to the people of the United States. If not excluded by law, they will return and recommence the work of plunder. They may, with as much right, gather the harvest in the valley of the Connecticut, the Ohio, or the Mississippi. No other nation, having the power to protect it, would permit its treasure to be thus carried away. I would not allow them to purchase permits, or work vein-mines, because the contributions proposed to be required are so moderate that they will not cause the slightest inconvenience to the miners, and are not designed as an equivalent for these privileges. Foreigners, therefore, would willingly pay these small sums for permission to collect and carry away millions of dollars in value. The object is not only a suitable revenue, but to preserve for the use of our own fellow-citizens the wealth of that region.

The kind of thinking in which King indulged was also being done in the California legislature. On February 8, 1850, one of the Senators from Sacramento, T. J. Green, gave notice that at an early day he would introduce a bill entitled, "An Act for the better regulation of the mines and mining, until the action of the United States Congress shall be had thereon." On March 15 this bill was referred to the Committee on Finance, of which Green himself was chairman. Five days later he made a report in writing recommending passage, which was voted by seven yeas and four nays on March 30. After amendments in the Assembly and further amendments in the Senate, the bill became law on April 13, 1850.[16]

This measure attempted to deal with the problem of foreign miners from a revenue standpoint, decreeing that none but natives or naturalized citizens of the United States should be permitted to mine in California without a license. The Governor was required to appoint a Collector of Licenses for each mining county, and for the county of San Francisco, who should issue licenses to mine in a specified form, the cost of which would be $20 per month. Persons requiring to be licensed and not taking out licenses were to be stopped from mining, if necessary by sheriff's posse; and anyone continuing to mine after having been thus stopped would be guilty of a misdemeanor, the penalty for which was imprisonment for a term not exceeding three months and a fine of not more than $1,000. The law was to operate until the Governor should issue a proclamation announcing the passage of a law by Congress, regulating the mines of precious metals in California.

The report of the Senate finance committee held that the gold discovery threatened California "with an emigration overwhelming in number and dangerous in character," including "the worst population of the Mexican and South American States, New South Wales, and the Southern Islands, to say nothing of the vast numbers from Europe. Among others, the convicts of Mexico, Chili, and Botany Bay, are daily turned upon our shores, who seek and possess themselves of the best places for gold digging, whether upon their own or on account of foreign employers, and carry from our country immense treasure." Under the United States Constitution, immigration could not be prevented, but the bill would require the foreigner, "upon the plainest principles of justice, to pay a small bonus for the privilege of taking from our country the vast treasure to which they have no right." With something of King's optimism, Green's committee maintained: "This the foreigner will cheerfully do, because the permit which he carries upon his person will save him from the interruption of the stronger

---

[16] See *Statutes of California,* 1850, pp. 221–223; *Senate Journal,* 1850, pp. 142, 217, 221, 232, 250, 252, 257, 265, 298–299, 304, 309, 323–325, and the report of Green's committee, pp. 493–497; and *Assembly Journal,* 1850, pp. 1106, 1147, 1165, 1213.

power which is in our own people; at the same time our own citizen who delves side by side with these newcomers, will be content in knowing the fact that they are paying some tribute towards the heavy expenses of our new State." The anticipated revenue from this law was the considerable sum of $200,000 per month.

A booklength study could be made of the Foreign Miners' Tax, its roots in the California of 1850, its impact upon the State, and its tangled later history.[17] Here we are interested primarily in its effect upon William Perkins in Sonora. Himself a foreigner, he was exempt from the tax because he was a merchant rather than a miner. He would also have been exempt had he been a lawyer, cooper, or stonemason, which suggests something about the constitutionality of the statute. Even so, as a merchant he and many of his kind were immediately injured by efforts to collect the tax. As a matter of principle, but also as a matter of direct economic interest, he became a champion of the foreign element. His letter of May 19–22, 1850, to the Stockton Times, reprinted in our Appendix, was one of the earliest efforts to publicize the plight of the foreign miners and enlist the sympathy of the community in their behalf.

Since that letter and the parallel entries made in his journal may be read in the present work, it would serve no purpose to offer a summary in these introductory pages. But it may be enlightening to observe how the crisis precipitated in Tuolumne County by the advent of the Collector was reported by others.

The appointed Collector was Lorenzo A. Besançon, a lawyer of New York birth, more recently from Louisiana. The Stockton Times printed the text of the new law on April 27, 1850, alerting the Sonora community to what was in the wind, but it was not until two weeks later that Besançon prepared to license the miners.

On May 28 the Alta California reported:

There appears to be no little excitement among the foreign miners now in the Placer, who evince a determination to disregard the enactment taxing them for the privilege of obtaining the gold of California. A rumor was

---

[17] William R. Kenny, in the dissertation cited in note 14 discusses this tax; and information of value is presented by Carlo M. De Ferrari in annotating Stoddart's Annals of Tuolumne County. See also H. H. Bancroft, History of California (San Francisco, 1888), VI, 396–408.

prevalent on Sunday that General Besancon, one of the collectors was murdered in the endeavor to perform his duty. We are pleased to hear of his safety, however, by a recent arrival. The following is a letter addressed by him to Col. J. C. Hays, our Sheriff, accompanying which is a copy of an inflammatory placard, clearly exhibiting the way in which matters stand:—

COLUMBIA, May 16, 1850.

This is a copy of one among many inflammatory bills posted upon the trees in the diggings written in different languages.

My truest regards,
L. A. Besancon.

To Col. Hays.

NOTICE TO FOREIGNERS.

It is time to unite: Frenchmen, Chileans, Peruvians, Mexicans, there is the highest necessity for putting an end to the vexations of the Americans in California.

If you intend to allow yourselves to be fleeced by a band of miserable fellows who are repudiated by their country, then unite and go to the camp of Sonora, next Sunday: there will we try to guarranty security for us all, and put a bridle in the mouths of that horde who call themselves citizens of the United States, thereby profaning that country.

The *Alta California's* special correspondent, Robert Wilson, wrote from Stockton on May 22 about a recent visit to Sonora, concerning which he said, "Such a motley collection of Mexicans, Chilians, Frenchmen, Chinese, Jews, Jonathans, Paddies, and Sawnies, I had never seen together before in California . . . the centre of an extensive mining region—a winter depot for provisions—a place of recreation for the people of the surrounding settlements, and the head quarters of the Mexicans from the province of Sonora [where] the Mexicans and Chilians, who had been driven from other settlements, have always worked unmolested." At the moment of writing, Wilson reported, there was quite an excitement in Stockton, in consequence of reports received last evening from Sonora:

A number of foreigners at Sonora, having refused to comply with the requisitions of the "Act for the government of foreign miners," a time was fixed upon by the Collector of License to summon a posse of American citizens, to prevent them, forcibly if necessary, from continuing mining operations. The time fixed upon, I believe, was last Monday [May 13]. On Sunday there was quite an excitement among the foreigners. Guns and ammunition were purchased by them at one of the stores, and they paraded the streets armed and using threatening language. The sale of fire-arms was prohibited by the authorities, and couriers were dispatched to the surrounding settlements for reinforcements of Americans. In the evening the Sheriff, Mr. Work, was accosted by a Mexican who asked him if he was not an officer, or the officer who intended to enforce the payment of the license. On replying that he was, the Mexican made an attempt to stab him, when a person standing by, named Clark, with a single stroke of a bowie knife, nearly severed his head from his body. Thirty armed Americans soon arrived from Mormon Gulch, and the whole American population were on the alert all night.

At last accounts there were two or three hundred Americans at Sonora, under arms, and others were hourly arriving. On Monday the excitement had somewhat abated. Hundreds of the Mexicans and Chileans were packing up and leaving for Stockton. Many of them disclaimed having had any intention of resorting to arms, and all were evidently more or less frightened at the aspect of affairs. It appears that the Mexicans who took part in the disturbance, were led on by some hot-headed Frenchmen, lately arrived from France, of the Red Republican order. They found however, that the majority of the Spaniards were not disposed to join them, and it is supposed that the whole affair will blow over, without any very serious consequences. The affair will probably be a severe blow to business, for the present, in Sonora.

The Stockton Times of May 25 devoted an entire page to Perkins' letter respecting these events, and also printed excerpts of a letter signed "Hunt," written from the Mormon Diggings on May 20:

SIR,—We have had quite an exciting time for the last two or three days, and probably ere now a small "mess" in the shape of a civil war is going on at the Sonorian camp. I returned from there last night about 1 P.M. the "posse comitatus" having been called upon by the civil authorities to protect the town of Sonora. The American population rose en masse. I am glad to say that the officers appear firmly determined to carry the law into effect, and to perform their duty without flinching. Captain Besancon, the collector for this county, arrived at Sonora, on Friday last, and all the foreign population, composed principally of Mexicans, Chilians, and French, at once became excited on the subject of the license tax. They declared their intention, boldly and publicly, to oppose its payment, even threatening to meet force by force. Notices were posted up through Sonora and the new American camp [Columbia] calling a general rally of foreigners for the purpose of preventing the collector from proceeding in his duty. The excitement became great throughout the country, and although the American population in this country does not number one-fifth that of the foreigners, every man declared his intention to support the law. On Sunday afternoon the foreigners held their meeting, and at least 3,000 of them were prepared and armed for resistance. They proceeded tumultously into town, sweeping through the streets in crowds, boasting of their strength, and threatening in many instances to burn the town that night, etc. Many persons estimate the number of men then congregated at 5,000, and that force could easily be doubled in 12 hours. Inevitable bloodshed is feared by many. Judge Tuttle accordingly sent several expresses to the neighbouring diggings, and with such urgency was the message delivered that about 150 men were soon on a forced march. The main body, under Captain Allen, arrived before sundown, and were enthusiastically greeted by the Americans. Liberal provision was made for their comfort, as far as was possible—for each had seized his rifle and equipments, and nothing else, believing that his countrymen were in imminent danger.[18]

It was also reported that the Sonorians, Chileans, and French had each raised their national flags at the new diggings. Today the collector and sheriff will first proceed to Shaw's Diggings, and compel the foreigners to comply with the law; thence to the new diggings, etc. It is estimated that probably at least 1,000 armed Americans will rendezvous at Sonora before noon this day. I apprehend bloodshed.

Editorially the *Stockton Times* commented:

The news from the mines has spread an unwonted gloom over the markets of the river towns, and much anxiety is felt as to the ultimate effect of the tax on foreign miners in the district of San Joaquin. We again recommend a careful perusal of Leo's letter, and advise that the governor be memorialised to call an extra session of the legislature, which body may be

---

[18] Walter Murray published in the *Sonora Herald* in 1852 an entertaining account of this rescuing force which rode to Sonora from Mormon Gulch, an account afterward reprinted in Heckendorn & Wilson's *Miners and Business Men's Directory* for 1856, pp. 38–40, and in Lang, *A History of Tuolumne County*, pp. 29–33.

prayed to levy a tax of five, instead of twenty dollars, per month. We are echoing the sentiments of every merchant in Stockton.

On June 1 the *Stockton Times* printed a further communication from "Hunt," dated Mormon Diggings, May 25, 1850:

MR. EDITOR.—I wrote to you a couple of days ago the first chapter of the "Sonorian Campaign." And as all things seem to have settled down again into wonted quietude, I will wind up the yarn. On Monday morning our forces were augmented by the arrival of forces from Wood's Creek, the Pine Crossing, Sullivan's, Murphy's, Indian Gulch, Cuyota Creek, Carson's and all the diggings on the Stanislaus and Tualumne rivers.[19] As fast as the war cry rolled on from hill to dale, it was re-echoed from willing hearts and stalwart bearers of trusty rifles, who hastened to the rescue. The country was up, and as in the days of the revolution, homespun and corduroy covered patriotic hearts; check shirts were the predominant field uniform, and red flannels shone conspicuously.

The collector and sheriff proceeded to Shaw's diggings, and backed by an armed posse of some five hundred Americans, met with no resistance whatever. Some few paid the tax, others asked for time, as they had not the *oro*, whilst the greatest number had ceased operations. From there they proceeded to the new diggings, or American Camp, where, it was anticipated, there would be a general "muss." The evening before it had been rumored and positively asserted that the French, Mexicans, and Chilians had each raised their national flags, as rallying points for their forces, and

---

[19] A typed transcript of the diary of George E. Jewett in the Bancroft Library further documents these events. Jewett, who had been mining near Pine Crossing, writes:

"May 19th. Started for Jamestown found the people of Sonoria in a state of great excitement on account of the law imposing a tax of $20.00 per month on foreigners. They rose in a mass on being called on by the collectors declaring that they will not pay it & threaten to drive the Americans out of the country if they attempt to enforce it. The Americans are laying low to-day but they must look out tomorrow.

"May 20th. This morning before day there were about 500 or 600 Americans in Sonoria well arrived [armed]. The Greasers were all quiet but it was reported that some 2000 had been collected to make a stand at Columbia. 3 or 4 miles N. W. of Sonora. The Yankees were on the way in no time & when they arrived there they found a Mexican flag hoisted, and any quantity of Greasers. They marched into town, pulled down the flag, hoisting the stars & Stripes, fired a few rounds into the air which had a wonderful effect on the enemy for they made themselves scarce as soon as possible. The leaders were taken and put into jail. This I think is the last time they will attempt to oppose American laws."

the determination was fixed in all minds that if such was the case, those flags must come down. But when the posse arrived there, they found all things in order; they found all things presenting a sullen quietness, the foreigners generally collected in little knots, having ceased working. Here about the same state of things existed as at Shaw's Diggings. One Frenchman, who had been particularly conspicuous in heading the movements of yesterday, and who had expressed himself strongly in violent insurrectionary language was arrested and conveyed a prisoner to Sonora.

As the Americans could do nothing more, they elevated a tall pine, and flung from it the brilliant star spangled banner, saluting it with tremendous shouts of applause and vollies of small arms. The utmost enthusiasm prevailed, and the furor of the foreigners was most effectually quelled. Not a murmur was heard, although I expect, like the Irishman's owl, they "kept up a d—l of a thinking."

All hands then marched to the right about, leaving quiet and order behind them, and a perfect respect for the laws of our infant state. This prompt movement on the part of the Americans I am perfectly satisfied has exercised a most extraordinary influence upon the feelings, opinions, and movements of our foreign denizens. It is my opinion that but few of the foreigners will pay the tax of $20 per month; most will evade it by moving about from one place to another.

The *Stockton Times* expressed pleasure at learning that active opposition to the tax was quelled, law and order predominating. But editorially it had more to say, its views a restatement of Perkins' letter:

As we expected, the collection of the new tax is producing a ruinous effect upon the traders in the southern mines. Business, in many places, is at a complete stand still; confidence is shaken; there exists a universal feeling of distrust among the miners; man is set against man. None condemn more strongly than we do the violence that has been done to the law by the foreign population; but at the same time, few lament more sincerely the cause which awakened this opposition. We do not quarrel with the tax *per se*; we but deny the policy of the amount proposed to be collected from each miner. In the report on the bill, we remember that its authors stated the certificate would be a protection to the foreign miner, while at the same time it provided revenue for the state. Now we respectfully submit that as the tax stands, the legislature, in five cases out of ten, has placed it out of the power of the miner to obtain this protection, and we fear but a comparatively small sum will be collected for state purposes. Had the cost of the certificate been five instead of twenty dollars, every foreigner would have claimed that certificate as a boon. We sincerely believe that these sentiments are shared by nearly every American in this district.

Several storekeepers from the mines have called upon us, and described in graphic terms, the present state of trade. One gentleman said that in his store for some time past, previous to the advent of the collector, he has regularly taken across his counter the sum of six or seven hundred dollars per week; but during the past seven days he had not taken one hundred; another gentleman had broken up his establishment; a third had been compelled to curtail his purchases in Stockton, and countermand orders to a large amount. The universal feeling prevailing in this town is well embodied in the following memorial, which has been signed by nearly every merchant in Stockton, there being but one dissentient. We believe that the gentlemen who took the initiative in this matter are the members of the highly respectable firms of W. H. Robinson & Co., and Starbuck & Spencer, who have informed us that the universal sentiment was in favor of the petition.

To His Excel'y, PETER H. BURNETT, *Governor of California.*

The undersigned, resident citizens of the town of Stockton, county of San Joaquin, would respectfully represent to your excellency, that a law, passed and approved at the late session of the legislature of this state at San Jose, entitled "An Act for the better regulation of the Mines and the Government of Foreign Miners," is not affecting the objects for which it was passed, but is proving highly injurious and oppressive to a large majority of the people of this state. Your petitioners believe that the prominent object of the law was to collect a speedy revenue; but its operation has been to stop the labor of thousands of miners—to derange and almost to destroy business in all the inland towns—to create a feeling of disorder and discontent in the mines, where the most perfect order and harmony have existed for some time past, and which will greatly retard the prosperity of this country, if it does not ruin it.

Your petitioners represent that the price of a license, as fixed by the law referred [to], is oppressively high—that vast numbers of the foreign miners are unable to pay it, and even those who are able to do so, are tempted from the amount of the tax, to use every subterfuge to avoid its payment. And your petitioners are of the firm opinion, which is but an echo of the unanimous voice of the miners, that if the tax were placed at $5 instead of $20, it would be paid cheerfully, and an immense revenue would be collected.

Your petitioners would therefore respectfully pray your excellency to call an extra session of the legislature, to be held as soon as convenient, and to recommend the passage of a law amending the aforesaid law, in such manner that the price of a license shall be $5 per month instead of $20, believing as they do, that the expense of such session would be more than compensated by the amount of revenue collected under the law so amended, and fully justified by the urgent and absolute necessity of the case.

We trust that the governor will take into his serious consideration the claims of the vast interests embarked in the district of San Joaquin, where the burden of the tax is most severely felt.

As Perkins relates, the merchants at Sonora joined in this effort to effect a modification of the Foreign Miners' Tax. The effort is also described in the *Stockton Times* of June 8:

The merchants and other residents of Sonora met together on Friday last, May 31, to consider what measures it would be best to adopt in relation to the tax upon foreign mining. Dr. Dealey was appointed chairman, and the meeting was addressed very ably by several gentlemen. It was unanimously resolved that the tax was in direct contravention of the American treaties with foreign nations—in direct opposition to the treaty with Mexico made at the close of the late war—in direct opposition to the Americans in the San Joaquin district; and since the general belief was that the tax is so enormous that the foreigners cannot pay it, Mr. Heydenfeldt, be employed to take such legal measures as he may deem necessary to stop the proceedings of the collector. Several hundreds of dollars were subscribed on the spot; and we have been informed that some thousands can be raised, if necessary. We understand that Mr. Heydenfeldt is now in San Francisco, making an application to the supreme court in relation to the matter.

Three weeks later, on June 29, the *Stockton Times* reported that for the purpose of testing the constitutionality of the law, Judge Heydenfeldt had moved the Supreme Court for a writ of *quo warranto* against Col. L. A. Besançon, Collector for Tuolumne County, after unsuccessfully applying for such a writ from the District Judge having jurisdiction over Tuolumne County. The Supreme Court refused on grounds that the office of such a writ was to prevent the usurpation of any office, franchise, or liberty, as also to afford a remedy against corporations for a violation of their charters; that a jury trial was indicated, and that the Court had only appellate jurisdiction. The foreign element were not without legal recourse, but would have to present their grievances to the proper court.[20]

On what legal basis the modification was made is uncertain, but on August 3, 1850, Besançon issued a notice, distributed throughout Tuolumne County:

> The Collector of Taxes for foreign miners announces that he is now authorized by the government to receive $20 for the privilege of laboring in the mines until the last day of December next, and to issue a license for that period. He is instructed to protect all who comply with this requisition, and punish all others as violators of the law. The Collector's office is at the head of Washington Street, Sonora.[21]

Heydenfeldt's further recourse to the judiciary was unavailing, but on March 14, 1851, the legislature repealed the Foreign Miners' Tax.[22] The *Stockton Times,* which editorialized against the tax on March 5 ("a law for the killing of children to get their fat"), and printed proceedings of a Stockton meeting which declared that the tax was being collected in Tuolumne County without a shadow of right, exulted over the repeal in its issues of March 15 and 22, 1851. Perkins left California in the spring of 1852 gratified that he had had some part in the overthrow of this "odious measure," not knowing that the tax was being reënacted by the legislature then in session.[23]

How much damage was done the Southern Mines, and indeed all California, by the Foreign Miners' Tax and the effort to collect it? The violence that fills the pages of Perkins' journal after the events of mid-May, 1850, the murder and the rapine that appalled observers,

---

[20] For further comment, see chapter xi, note 2.

[21] Lang, *A History of Tuolumne County,* pp. 46–47.

[22] *Statutes of California,* 1851, chapter 108, p. 424.

[23] This act, approved May 4, 1852, had the somewhat specious title, "An Act to provide for the protection of Foreigners, and to define their liabilities and privileges" (*Statutes of California,* 1852, chapter 37, p. 84). The license was fixed at $3 per month. Next year, on March 30, 1853, the act was amended, raising the cost of a license to $4 per month (*Statutes of California,* 1853, chapter 44, pp. 62–65.) For later changes in the law, and general comment, see Bancroft, *History of California,* VI, 406–407. During the first year, the heavy tax brought in only $29,991; and the State found it difficult to collect from the Collectors, especially from Besançon.

clearly resulted from the violence done the fabric of society in the mines. The fact was well understood at the time. "We shall long remember," commented the *Stockton Times* on March 5, 1851,

how fatal were its universal results—how it ruined the trader, and was made a fearful instrument of oppression—how it robbed the poor—how it drove the desperado to the highway—how it turned one man against his neighbour—how it sharpened the assassin's knife and primed the barrel of his pistol—how it depopulated the hitherto flourishing settlements amidst the hills—how it made the air heavy with fear, as though a plague had swept over the land and had scattered destruction with its wings.[24]

Perkins is not the only chronicler of life in Sonora during these turbulent years 1849–1852. The diary and letters of Dr. Lewis C. Gunn and his wife, Elizabeth, have been edited by their daughter, Anna Lee Marston, as *Records of a California Family* (San Diego, 1928). Dr. Gunn came to California in 1849, mined at Jamestown, and carried on a general medical practice. He removed to Sonora in 1850, bought an interest in the *Sonora Herald,* and built an adobe house which still stands. He ceased to keep a diary before removing to Sonora, however; and the diary which his wife kept while voyaging around Cape Horn to join him in 1851 was laid aside after she reached San Francisco. She wrote many letters during the ten years the Gunns remained in Sonora, but without giving us such a sense of the place and its people as we derive from Perkins. The latter mentions her once in his journal, not favorably.

Enos Christman, who became an associate of Gunn in the publication of the *Sonora Herald,* kept a diary of his passage around Cape Horn in 1849–1850 and a journal of his experiences in the Southern Mines, at first in the Mariposa country, later on the Calaveras, and from August, 1850, at Sonora. He left Sonora for his Pennsylvania home shortly after Perkins' departure, taking passage on the next voyage of the *Winfield Scott,* in June, 1852. Christman's letters and journal have been edited by Florence Morrow Christman as *One Man's Gold* (New York, 1930), and this book may be enjoyably

---

[24] The *Alta California* shared generally in the view of the *Stockton Times,* approving the Foreign Miners' Tax in principle, but not the extortionately high rate, and noting the tendency of American miners to rob the foreigners by demanding license money which vanished into their own pockets.

compared with William Perkins' journal. A number of letters written
to his family by a deaf overland pioneer of 1849, dated "Jacksonville,"
Sonora, Chili Camp, Columbia, and Yankee Hill between August 11,
1850, and September 29, 1853, have been printed in *Edmund Booth
Forty-niner*, a 1953 publication of the San Joaquin Pioneer and
Historical Society. This bibliographical record could be greatly extended, but we must be content to mention, in addition, only Thomas
Robertson Stoddart's *Annals of Tuolumne County*, contributed as a
series of articles to the *Columbia Courier* in 1861, and reprinted in
book form by the Tuolumne County Historical Society in 1963 with
scholarly notes by Carlo M. De Ferrari. Although Stoddart did not
come to Sonora until about 1857 and could not write with personal
authority about the early history of the county, he interviewed a
number of the pioneers and drew liberally upon the files of the *Sonora
Herald* and Heckendorn & Wilson's *Miners & Business Men's Directory* of 1856. Much that has since been written about Tuolumne
County and Sonora, including [Herbert O. Lang's] *A History of
Tuolumne County*, published by B. F. Alley (San Francisco, 1882),
and Edna Bryan Buckbee's *The Saga of Old Tuolumne* (New York,
1935) owes much to Stoddart's labors.

After this has been said, the Perkins chronicle remains unique,
both as a record of life in Sonora and Tuolumne County and as an
account of experiences in California between 1849 and 1852. He
himself put this chronicle into book form; the present editors have used
his own contents page, followed his chapter structure, and incorporated
his notes, with due credit, into their own. Had the book been published
soon after it was written, a contemporary editor would probably have
changed Perkins' spelling and punctuation. We have preferred to treat
the manuscript as the primary document it is, reproducing it as
faithfully as circumstances permit. Various allusions in Perkins' text
indicate rather clearly that he wrote this book about 1862, some ten
years after his departure from California. He must have had contemporary memoranda to go upon, like the actual journal of which he
speaks in January, 1850, but these have disappeared; all that remains is
the manuscript preserved by his grandson, Jorge Walter Perkins of
Buenos Aires. Composed in English, this manuscript now consists of
274 leaves legibly written in brown ink, with the title, "El Campo de
los Sonoraenses or Three Years Residence in California by William

Perkins F.R.G.S. 1849, 1850 and 1851." A Spanish translation was printed in Buenos Aires in 1937, with a considerably reduced text. A few students have used the Argentine edition and a retranslation into English was serialized in ten issues of the *American Book Collector* in 1955–1956. Although the Spanish version is inferior, it has served history well by preserving the last part of Perkins' record of his homeward journey, some pages of the manuscript having been lost since 1937. Adding a retranslation of those pages from the Buenos Aires edition, the editors have now with great pleasure made the whole Perkins record available.

One other feature of the present book seems especially worthy of mention: its portrait of William Perkins as a young man. This portrait, a miniature preserved by his grandson, is signed "Waugh 1845." In 1951 John Francis McDermott edited, for publication by the Missouri Historical Society, a narrative entitled, *Travels in Search of the Elephant: The Wanderings of Alfred S. Waugh, Artist, in Louisiana, Missouri, and Santa Fe, in 1845–1846*. In his introduction McDermott concluded regretfully: "No busts or paintings of Waugh's have been identified; there is no way of judging his skill as painter or sculptor." Now a specimen of Waugh's work has been found, and we may conclude that his skill was considerable.

Perkins himself was artistically inclined, though not possessed of a professional talent, and one drawing which illustrates his book—a drawing probably done much earlier, for it is tipped into the manuscript—is reproduced herein. We have further enlarged the Perkins canon, as previously remarked, by reprinting three letters he wrote to the *Stockton Times* and the Stockton *San Joaquin Republican*, over his pen name, "Leo," while living at Sonora in 1850–1851.

Something remains to be said about Perkins' later life. At the time he left California he may have contemplated returning after a visit home, as his partners Theall and Enyart had done earlier. At various times he had hearkened to proposals that would have taken him from California to yet more distant parts; and he seems to have talked seriously with his Argentine friends, the Navarros, about the possibility of a new life in South America, but he gives us no intimation that such ideas had crystallized. We may wonder whether the great fire that occurred in Sonora shortly after his departure, on June 17, 1852, bankrupted Theall, Perkins & Co., for the losses of this firm were stated to total $30,000.[25] If, doubtfully, Perkins actually returned to California, he did not remain long. When next on record, we find him in South America.

During his California years Perkins had been attracted to Latin Americans. He found their way of life, their attitudes, and their culture to his liking. It is not strange that in the mid-fifties he sailed for Chile, there joining two of his Sonora friends, the Navarro brothers. Argentines from the northwestern province of Catamarca, the Navarro family had chosen exile during the arbitrary and de facto rule of Rosas. The two boys had been swept off to California by the gold fever which coursed through Chilean ports in those days. Rosas fell early in 1852; yet, like many Argentine expatriates, the Navarro family did not hurry home. In October, 1856, Perkins married a sister of his good friends, Parmenia Navarro Ocampo, at Concepción in southern Chile. He may have visited the western provinces of Argentina two years later with his wife and infant son, but it was not until 1860 that he settled at Rosario, in the eastern province of Santa Fe.[26] Although to the end of his life Perkins remained a Canadian and a British subject, he made his permanent home at Rosario, and there, with his three boys and four girls (two other children died in infancy), he became the progenitor of an important and extensive Argentine family.

Perkins not only liked Argentina; he also had unbounded faith in its future. Rosario in 1860 represented to him an opportunity to transform a pastoral frontier into a flourishing image of North America. During the political and economic struggles between the Argentine provinces and the city of Buenos Aires, Rosario had emerged as the chief port for the provinces. Trails and roads from the provinces and the projected railroad route from the major interior city of Córdoba ended in Rosario. Its location on the Paraná River was accessible

---

[25] Lang, A History of Tuolumne County, p. 87.

[26] The date of Perkins' arrival in Argentina has not been established. Gschwind, Guillermo Perkins, p. 9, selects 1858 as the date, but the introduction to the Spanish version of Perkins' book gives 1861 as the year. During 1860 Perkins sent articles to El Comercio of Valparaiso from the western Argentine province of San Juan, and his first article from Rosario was dated April 4, 1861. However, in a lecture he delivered in Simcoe, southwest of Toronto, published in the town's British Canadian, January 8, 1868, Perkins clearly stated: "When I first arrived in Rosario in 1860 . . ."

to ocean-going vessels, the high banks provided excellent loading facilities, and differential tariffs served to attract shipments directly from Europe. The foreign population, always in Argentina a barometer of commercial prosperity and opportunity, numbered one-quarter of the city's ten thousand inhabitants.

For more than a decade Perkins actively led efforts to bring railroads, immigrants, and prosperity to Argentine shores. During his first year in Rosario he demonstrated the range of his vision by attempting to manufacture windmills copied from a United States model, thus anticipating by two decades the importation of such equipment. As shown by the windmill, Perkins felt that he had extensive information and experience from his life in North America and from his continued contacts there that could prove invaluable to his new homeland. While in Chile he had published several articles on agriculture and commerce in *El Comercio* of Valparaiso. In 1862 he made his debut in the Argentine press with an extensive commentary on the agricultural potential, especially for cotton-raising, of the delta and islands of the Paraná River. Later that same year he became one of the editors of the Rosario newspaper, *La Patria*.

Rosario thought of little else in 1863 than the railroad which was to link it to Córdoba. William Wheelwright, a Rhode Islander by birth, a South American by adoption, and a builder of Peruvian and Chilean railroads, had undertaken, with British capital, to turn into reality a project which had been discussed since 1853. Perkins soon appeared as one of the local leaders in this enterprise. In February *La Patria* changed its name to *El Ferro Carril* (*The Railroad*) in accord with its editors' enthusiasm. Rarely a day passed that the principal concern of the editorial page was not an exhortation to commerce, investors, and the public in general to support the railroad venture. When in April the foreign business community gave a banquet to celebrate the start of construction, a ceremony attended by the Argentine president himself, Perkins was one of the principal speakers. The following year, in the face of general reluctance by Argentine investors to gamble on such a project, Perkins backed his words with money, putting his name down for twelve shares in the Central Argentine Railroad Company. At the same time he was made secretary of the provisional committee to raise local funds for railroad investment.

Railroads were only one of Perkins' many dreams for bringing prosperity and stability to Argentina. Hand in hand with improved communications went the need for immigrants, particularly farmers. After the fall of Rosas a few official attempts had been made to contract Europeans to settle on the Indian frontier, especially in the province of Santa Fe where pastoral industries had proved largely unsuccessful. Despite hardships, incompetence, and marginal location, in the 1860's some of these colonies began to prosper. But there was little practical recognition of their value either in Argentina or in Europe. At the invitation of Santa Fe's governor, Perkins in November, 1863, made a tour of three colonies near the provincial capital. His detailed report, the first extensive effort to publicize the colonization projects, was published in fifteen instalments in *El Ferro Carril* and reprinted the following year in amplified form in both English and Spanish as *The Colonies of Santa Fe. Their origin, progress and present condition with general observations on emigration to the Argentine Republic.*[27] Much of the "general observations" had formed part of his brief pamphlet of 1863, *Apuntes generales para los inmigrantes (Notes for the Immigrant.)* His work to educate public opinion continued in a series of articles on the provinces and on Paraguay, published in *El Ferro Carril* in 1864. Individual editorials show the scope of his interests: cotton cultivation in Argentina; tobacco cultivation in Santa Fe; the plow; immigration to Santa Fe; agricultural expositions; defense of the frontier; the trans-Andean railroad; public lands; street paving. Recognition of his journalistic and public leadership came in March, 1864, when he was elected to one of the six vacancies on the Municipal Council of Rosario. Three months later the president of Argentina named him a member and secretary of the local Commission for the Promotion of Immigration.

Journalism and public service hardly served to keep body and soul together in that era of Argentina's growth. Perkins consequently earned his livelihood as a merchant, hotel proprietor, real-estate agent, and exporter. As befitted one of Rosario's important businessmen, his offices were situated only a block from the main plaza and next to the port area. Typical of his widespread interests was the inauguration in July, 1864, of the Gran Hotel Central near the waterfront. Two

---

[27] A German translation of this pamphlet was also published.

months later, in partnership with Santiago J. Wild, he opened a general agency to handle real estate, exports, and imports.

Journalism, however, remained Perkins' great love and the instrument which he felt could best mold Rosario's, Santa Fe's, and the nation's development. Yet *El Ferro Carril,* almost since its inception, had demonstrated a split personality, a reflection of its editors' conflicting positions. Domingo F. Quijano was an interested and partisan observer of every political issue and personality that crossed the local and national stage. Perkins, meanwhile, never lost an opportunity to state his belief that Argentina's great handicap lay in too much passionate devotion to politics and too little dedication to the economic interests of the nation. In September, 1864, he withdrew from the editorship of *El Ferro Carril.*[28] Two months later he began his own daily, *El Cosmopólita,* of which he was the principal editor. In a statement of objectives, Perkins declared that this newspaper "will be essentially commercial in nature and will dedicate itself to questions of immigration, agriculture, arts and sciences, literature, transportation, and education."

In those years few newspapers in Argentina survived long. The audience was small, the cost of paper and printing high, and advertisements few. Subscriptions by governments, both national and provincial, frequently spelled the difference between survival and collapse, but such subsidies demanded that editors pay political homage to their benefactors, an obligation hardly compatible with Perkins' character and principles. The daily printing of *El Cosmopólita* ran from three to five hundred copies. For a while the paper received a subsidy from the national authorities. Perkins made continual adjustments in format, steadily reducing the size of the four pages, but problems continued. Meanwhile he carried on his battle: for street-paving, which he also fought for in the City Council; for immigrants from the southern United States now that the American Civil War was drawing to a close; for navigation of interior rivers such as the Bermejo; for a Foreigners' Social Club; for economic development of the Chaco frontier; for improved primary education; for a national postal service; for a national currency system and a National Bank; for greater exports

---

[28] Gschwind and all later commentators on Perkins' life mistakenly give September, 1864, as the date when he took over as editor of *El Ferro Carril.*

of Argentine salted beef; for new farm machinery; for a land mortgage bank. Besides, he carried on a running cross-fire with his former colleague, the editor of *El Ferro Carril*. For a moment in April, 1865, when a Paraguayan attack drew Argentina into the disastrous five-year Paraguayan War, he even had to stand off charges of treason and threats of physical violence which followed his declaration that commerce and economic development were as important as national honor. But his journalistic efforts attracted other forms of recognition as well. In May, 1865, the Royal Geographical Society in London made him a fellow. Subsequently Perkins proudly displayed the initials, F.R.G.S., on all his publications.

On October 17, 1865, *El Cosmopólita* appeared with a skull and crossbones, bordered in black, and a valedictory: "Our last word is a fervent plea to the public to realize that the salvation of this country lies in its material progress, that the peaceful labors of commerce, agriculture, and mining, the propaganda of immigration and expositions, will create a great and happy nation; while politics and personalized passions, the unworthy ambitions of its rulers, the arbitrary actions of its authorities, will condemn this land to the miserable and ignominious existence of the untutored and the ignorant." At the end of the year, *El Cosmopólita* began to appear again and for several months continued its campaign for colonization under the initials W. P., but it finally disappeared in March, 1866.

Perkins left a more enduring monument to his faith in a new Argentina than his courageous but ephemeral journalism. From the columns of *El Ferro Carril* and *El Cosmopólita* he had preached the need to develop the deserted Chaco region of northern Santa Fe and had suggested that the possible exodus of Southerners at the end of the Civil War could be tapped for Argentina's benefit. In 1865 he entered into correspondence with such a group, including acquaintances from his Californian days, and interested the Santa Fe government in an expedition to the Chaco to select land for North American immigrants. In February, 1866, the provincial authorities appointed him official agent to conclude arrangements with an advance party of these immigrants, and he accompanied the expedition to take notes on "the quality of lands, their physical aspect, the temperature, class of vegetation, courses of streams, etc." For two months, May and June, 1866, he and a party of North Americans and Argentines struggled across the morass of dense vegetation, swamps, and streams that make up much of the Chaco. From his experiences came a detailed scientific report and the first accurate map of this region, published in Rosario as *Relación de la espedición a El Rey en el Chaco*. More important for Argentine development, he helped the United States immigrants select and secure thirty-six square miles for their colony, to be known as New California, and consequently was listed as the "founder" of this frontier settlement. Early in 1867 several more families from California and some Welsh, who had moved from their colony on Argentina's southern coast, joined the advance party of twenty-three. The resourcefulness of these colonists and the good location near water-communication with the city of Santa Fe guaranteed the colony's stability despite the wildness of the surroundings and the presence of hostile Indian tribes.

During these same years Perkins, as secretary of the local Commission for the Promotion of Immigration, carried on an extensive correspondence with Europe, North America, Australia, and New Zealand. *The Standard*, the English newspaper of Buenos Aires, frequently reproduced portions of these letters which responded to endless queries on land values, agricultural opportunities, and local legislation affecting immigrants. One such letter directed to *The Standard* in early 1867 has a prophetic ring, although Perkins hardly set his sights high enough. After commenting on a recent auction of 1,683 square miles of Santa Fe lands, he emphasized the low prices: "A shilling an acre! And our great grandchildren will have to pay probably five pounds an acre for these same lands." Many of Perkins' letters were translated by Argentine immigration agents in Europe for the excellent and honest propaganda they contained, thus finding their way into German and French newspapers. An 1866 pamphlet published in Buenos Aires in both English and French, *The Agrarian Laws of Santa Fe . . . to which are added preliminary and explanatory observations on the nature and aim of the enactments translated from the Spanish,* further exemplifies his propaganda efforts.

Perkins maintained his close contact with the Central Argentine Railroad in those years while the tracks slowly advanced toward Córdoba, and from this came his greatest achievement in colonization. As part of the concession to the British company constructing the line, a strip three miles wide on each side of the track had been granted to a subsidiary, the Central Argentine Land Company, for colonization purposes. After some delay in expropriation and surrender of this land, the company was finally authorized in 1868 to proceed with its plans. Perkins was selected as the company's agent to recruit agricultural immigrants and departed for Europe late that same year. On his way, he visited his childhood home of Toronto and seized the opportunity to educate his fellow Canadians by speeches and newspaper articles on Argentina's agricultural promise. He went on to London, then passed to the Continent. There he opened a campaign for Swiss settlers, possibly because Switzerland had provided a large percentage of the early immigrants to the colonies of Santa Fe. He soon recognized that northern Italy was an even better source of agricultural colonists. But before he could move far in that direction, the company decided that Perkins' experience was urgently required in Argentina to establish the actual colonies.

The new director of colonies returned to Rosario in February, 1870, only two weeks before the first group of settlers was due. Yet he accomplished something never previously achieved, and repeated only infrequently in the annals of Argentine immigration. When the twenty-five families arrived, he had a train ready to take them directly to the surveyed lots at Roldán, twelve miles west of Rosario. Here wooden houses had been constructed, wells dug, food stocks laid in, horses, plows, and harrows obtained, and wire for fences made ready. Everything was prepared "so that the colonists could start work within an hour of their arrival." [29]

In May, 1870, the railroad was completed to Córdoba. For the next two and a half years Perkins, as director of the Land Company, worked hand in hand with his good friend, William Wheelwright, director of the Central Argentine Railroad, to string colonies along the Santa Fe portion of the track. Perkins' agents in Europe continued to collect groups of settlers and to dispatch them from Le Havre, Marseilles, and Genoa. During the first year of his directorship he tried to carry out a pet project and establish a wholly English colony at Cañada de Gómez, forty miles from Rosario. But the bad publicity Argentina had been receiving in the British press as a consequence of the murder

[29] Guillermo Wilcken, Las colonias: Informe sobre el estado actual de las colonias agrícolas de la República Argentina (Buenos Aires, 1873), p. 148.

of several English settlers cut immigration to a trickle and forced him to give up the idea of an English colony. More successful was his third colony, Carcarañá, twenty-six miles from Rosario, and, like Roldán (later renamed Bernstadt), primarily settled by Swiss and French families. In 1872 colonists from Lombardy and Piedmont in northern Italy arrived at Tortugas on the Santa Fe-Córdoba border to settle the fourth and last of the Company colonies established by Perkins.

Throughout his directorship Perkins maintained the same interest in and understanding of the colonists' welfare that he had demonstrated in the founding of Roldán. Both he and Wheelwright considered colonization a long-range investment—facilities and advantages given immigrants would attract settlement along the railroad's route, encourage development of towns and commerce, foment production of cereals, and eventually repay the railroad a hundred-fold in freight revenues. In this sense the four colonies with their three thousand inhabitants provided an important catalyst in the growth of Argentina. Agriculture, especially wheat-farming, ceased to be relegated, as it had been in the early Santa Fe colonies, to the fringes of a pastoral economy. The realization of Perkins' dream of a transformed nation, however, had to be left to private initiative and spontaneous immigration. Wheelwright died in 1873, and Perkins, without his friend and colleague to support him, faced a new directorate in London interested only in immediate profits. He resigned and so ended his valuable assistance to Argentina's development.

During the last two decades of his life Perkins disappeared from the public stage. Perhaps he was disillusioned, as he had been when *El Cosmopólita* folded in October, 1865: "We are tired. We have made many sacrifices; we have neglected our true interests; we have broken our health; and it is only natural that discouragement should have crept into our heart." At any rate, after his resignation as director of the Central Argentine Land Company, in 1873, he lived a semiretired life, occasionally serving as acting British vice-consul in Rosario. During the serious cholera epidemic of 1874 he appeared in three brief intervals as acting president of the Municipal Council of Rosario. For most of his remaining years he was the Rosario correspondent for *The Standard*. Sometimes monthly, occasionally every week, his articles, always with an agricultural or commercial slant, appeared over the initials W. P. Ill health finally forced him into complete retirement in 1890, and he died in 1893.

As several obituaries noted, it was fitting that he died on the Independence Day of a country whose imprint had been indelibly fixed on him in his youth. In California he found a blending of the Latin culture which so appealed to his spirit and which drew him southward to his permanent home in Argentina. Yet he never lost an opportunity to introduce that force he had known on the western frontier, the energy and ambition of the North American, into his dream for a new Argentina. The colony of New California, the colonies of the Central Argentine, his work as secretary to the Immigration Commission, his years of editorial advice in *El Ferro Carril, El Cosmopólita,* and *The Standard* were the fruition in Argentina of a character and a personality we come to appreciate in the pages of his book. On both frontiers he left an imprint and a record.

ACKNOWLEDGMENTS

This first publication of William Perkins' experiences in the California Gold Rush, presenting the text as he himself wrote it, has been made possible by the informed help of many people.

In May, 1960, the "poet of the Santa Fe colonies," José Pedroni of Esperanza, Argentina, pointed out to James Scobie a work by Guillermo Perkins, translated into Spanish as *El campo de los Sonoraenses: Tres años de residencia en California, 1849–1851* (Buenos Aires, 1937). Shortly thereafter the original English version of Perkins' manuscript was found in the possession of his grandson, Jorge Walter Perkins of Buenos Aires. He generously placed the manuscript in the hands of the editors, permitting it to be carried off to Berkeley, California, and also provided a photograph of the miniature portrait of his grandfather reproduced as the frontispiece of the present book.

Supplementing the personal information provided by Jorge Walter Perkins, useful counsel was given by Leopoldo Kanner and Augusto Fernández Díaz of Rosario, and valuable newspaper files were made available by the Biblioteca del Consejo Nacional de Mujeres, the Biblioteca Argentina, and *La Capital,* all of Rosario, and the Biblioteca Nacional of Buenos Aires. Particularly helpful was a scrapbook of newspaper clippings, possibly arranged by Perkins himself, in the Biblioteca Argentina of Rosario.

At the University of California the editors completed the work after close collaboration for an extended period. Patricia B. Scobie and Jordan R. Scobie transcribed Perkins' manuscript and helped in the labor of proofreading. At the Bancroft Library, George P. Hammond, Director, and Robert Becker, Assistant Director, took a lively interest from the beginning; and the enormous resources of that institution for the study of the Gold Rush did much to amplify the Perkins record. Lloyd G. Lyman and Maxwell E. Knight of the University of California Press contributed largely to the book now presented. Various scholars who for years have enthusiastically spaded the history of Sonora and Tuolumne County, especially Barbara Eastman of Oakland, and Donald Segerstrom, Edward M. Jasper, Carlo M. De Ferrari, Margaret H. Long, and Ruth A. Newport of Sonora, gave cordially of their time and knowledge but are not to be held accountable for shortcomings. Typing and research assistance was granted by the Institute of International Studies and the Institute of Social Sciences at the University of California; the California State Library provided the photograph of George Goddard's 1852 lithograph of Sonora; the Southwest Museum enabled us to reproduce J. W. Audubon's 1850 drawing of San Francisco; other illustrations were furnished by the Bancroft Library. We thank Alice Alden for the maps and Miriam Ash for the index.

Berkeley, California D. M. AND J. S.
April, 1964

THE JOURNAL OF

William
Perkins

CHAPTER I

CHAPTER II

CHAPTER III

CHAPTER IV

CHAPTER V

CHAPTER VI

Our house.—Amateur painting and carpentry.—The cost of a stovepipe.—
Christmas on the plains.—Prices of the necessaries of life in Sonora.—
Absence of crime.—Administration of Justice.—Sickness in the Mines.—
Man-traps.—Another Bear Story.—Golden operations.—A "chunk" or
"nugget."—Found drowned.—Washed out of bed.

CHAPTER VII

Depredations of the Indians.—Expedition to the mountains in pursuit.—
Following the trail.—Taking and burning of a Rancheria, and fight with
the Savages.—"Root-Diggers" and "Mission" Indians.—Mule flesh versus
Dog flesh.—Harrassed by the Indians.—Sufferings and dangers.—Safe re-
turn.—Gamblers.—Sunday in Sonora.—Immigration.—The soft sex in
California.

CHAPTER VIII

Which treats of a singular case of Somnambulism and other psychological
phenomena.

CHAPTER IX

A daring murder.—The Mexican "Greaser."—Valentine day.—Mission
Indians and Root-diggers.—Description.—Climate of California.—The
grand results of the discovery of gold in the Pacific.—Texans killed by
Indians.—Mules and Muleteers.—Progress of the Town.

CHAPTER X

The great Fire of the Second of May in San Francisco.—Energy of American character.—Horses, the breed in California.—A domestic tragedy.—
The town organized.—The famous tax on foreign miners.—Menacing attitude of the foreign population.—Observations on the illegality of this
tax.

CHAPTER XXXIII

CHAPTER XXXIV

CHAPTER XXXV

CHAPTER XXXVI

CHAPTER XXXVII

CHAPTER XLIV

PREFACE

The wonderful change that has operated in California and Australia within a dozen years; the civilization of savage wilds; the rise of important towns and wealthy mercantile Marts; the cultivation of wastes that had in all probability lain, untouched by the hand of man, from the commencement of the history of our globe; the immense territories reclaimed for the use of the over-crowded races of the Old World, have presented their miraculous phases with such astonishing rapidity, that the events of Today had the effect of oblitering those of Yesterday; and it is difficult even for the men, whose familiarity with these changes dates from the earlier epochs, to realize, in the progress and perfection of the Present, the labors, the sufferings, the crimes and the wonders of the Past.

To the many thousands whose residence in California was contemporaneous with my own, I address the present work; convinced that, while each one will readily acknowledge the faithfulness of the pictures delineated, their presentation will have the same pleasing effect on the mind as the viewing a painting in which is depicted some fearful scene in which one has been an actor, and the memory of which has become partly obliterated by others of equal magnitude.

Under this impression I have prepared, at this distant period, my book for the press.

To the English reader the contents of this volume may not be uninteresting, as from it, data may be obtained to form a comparison between the rival Gold regions, California and Australia; and although from the commencement, the vigilance of the British Government foresaw, and early took measures to guard against, the great accumulation of crime inevitable under such extraordinary circumstances, yet, from the fact of Australia being already cursed with many thousands of convicts at the time of the Gold discoveries, excesses of all kind have been as rife in one place as in the other, where no such precautionary measures were taken by the Authorities; and we may safely aver that a

71

picture of Life in California will bear many striking resemblances to one of Life in Australia.

In reference to the work presented to the reader, I shall only add that it pretends to nothing more than to depict the ordinary routine of life in one of the most popular and populous mining regions of California, Sonora, or the old Camp of the Sonoraenses, in an epoch when neither the laws of man nor God were respected. The scenes related were mostly written down at the time of their occurrence, in the unadorned language of every-day life; and with no effort to embellish or invent. During my residence in California, it might well be said that "Truth is stranger than Fiction." There was consequently little inducement to appeal to the latter.

THE AUTHOR

CHAPTER I

It was at the beginning of the year One thousand, eight hundred and forty-nine, and a short time after the receipt in the United States of the extraordinary tidings from California, and while the whole country, from Florida to Quebec, was in a state of wild excitement, that I was induced by my natural love of adventure, and perhaps influenced in part, like the followers of Cortes and Pizarro, by the more ignoble motive, the acquisition of that precious metal which has caused so many heroic as well as so many wicked deeds, to enrol myself in one of the many parties that daily were leaving the Atlantic for the distant Pacific coast.

The party which I joined was composed of a score of young men belonging mostly to the best class of society, one of them being the son of the then Minister of the Interior, Mr. Ewing.[1]

We proceeded to New Orleans, where we laid in the necessary supplies of clothing and arms, and where we were joined by three gentlemen from Maryland. We embarked on the Steamer *Sarah Sands*, bound for the Isthmus of Darien, with the intention of passing over to Panama, and there wait for an opportunity to transport ourselves to San Francisco. Our first start however, was unfortunate. Barely had we

---

[1] Thomas Ewing (December 28, 1789–October 26, 1871), first Secretary of the Interior, was not appointed to head the new department until March 7, after Perkins left for California. He had been Secretary of the Treasury during the Harrison and Tyler administrations, and for a short time in 1850–1851 represented Ohio in the Senate. His home was at Lancaster, from which his fourth child, Hugh Boyle Ewing (October 31, 1826–June 30, 1905), set out for California in company with Samuel McNeil, as related in the Introduction. Biographies of father and son are printed in the *Dictionary of American Biography*, with the information that Boyle in 1849 "was caught by the gold fever and made the journey to California by way of New Orleans and Texas, thence across Mexico to Mazatlán on the Pacific Coast and across the Cordilleras on muleback. . . . In 1852 he returned by way of Panama to Washington as the bearer of government dispatches." Later Boyle practiced law, served as a general officer during the Civil War, and from 1866 to 1870 was minister to Holland. One of his books is *The Black List; a Tale of Early California* (1893).

passed the Belize, and caught a glimpse of the Gulf of Mexico, when
the steamer sprung a leak, and the danger soon took such a magnitude,
that with difficulty we succeeded in putting back to New Orleans.[2]

Holding a council of war, we unanimously determined to change
our route, and, passing through Mexico, reach Mazatlán, where the
probabilities would be greater of finding a speedy conveyance to the
Golden Gate.

Fortunately for the success of our scheme, a steamer was to start
within a few hours for *Punta Isabel,* near the mouth of the *Rio Grande;*
so transferring our traps to this steamer, and furnishing ourselves with
passports at the Mexican Consul's office, we embarked a second time.[3]

A party of young men from New York, headed by Colonel Webb,
brother to the renowned Editor of that name, was on board the same
ship, also bound for *Punta Isabel,* but with the intention of taking the
upper route, by *Chihuahua,* and reaching California by land, through
what is called the Great Southern Pass.

I may as well here relate the fate of this party, which was composed
of gentlemen belonging to respectable families in New York. They
separated from us at Fort Brown, on the Texan side of the river,
opposite the Mexican town of *Metamoras,* and proceeded up the river
for Chihuahua; but they never got further than fifty or sixty miles up.
Here the cholera appeared amongst them; some died, and the rest,
disheartened and terrified, returned to the coast before my party had

---

[2] Perkins did not leave New Orleans in the auxiliary steamship *Sarah Sands,*
which was then on the Atlantic run (she sailed from New York for Liverpool on
March 1), though afterward she was sent around the Horn to run between San
Francisco and Panamá, first arriving in San Francisco June 5, 1850. Instead, as
seen by Samuel McNeil's narrative, quoted in the Introduction, Perkins originally left New Orleans in the *Maria Burt.* The New York *Herald* of March 13,
1849, records her departure on February 28, with a list of 82 passengers which
oddly includes neither Perkins nor his associate Enyart, though many familiar
names appear. On March 15 the *Herald* quotes the New Orleans *Delta* of
March 6: "The steamship Maria Burt, Captain Breath, hence for Chagres, in
going down the river on the night of the 1st instant, ran into the bank of the
river during a heavy fog, and received such damages as made it necessary for her
to return to this city for repairs."

[3] As related by Samuel McNeil, this second departure from New Orleans
was in the steamship *Globe.* The New York *Herald* of March 18, 1849, re-
publishes from the New Orleans *Picayune* an account of her sailing on March 4.
The *Picayune's* list of her 188 passengers does not name the "seventy-four on
deck" among whom were Perkins and his fellow refugees from the *Maria Burt.*

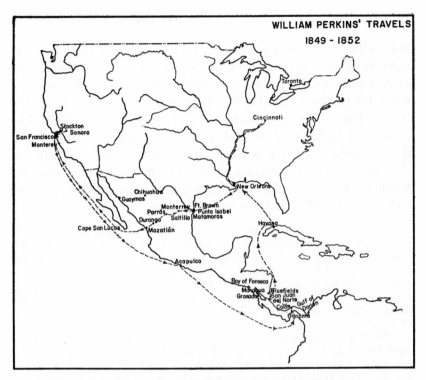

WILLIAM PERKINS' TRAVELS
1849 - 1852

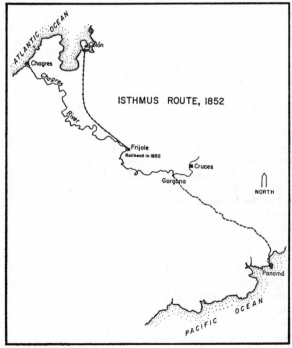

ISTHMUS ROUTE, 1852

crossed the river. I was told that Col. Webb, in order to inure his party to hardwork and suffering, made them chop wood for the steamer, and carry it on board. Such work in a broiling sun soon knocked up men whose life had been passed in Broadway, and whose toil had heretofore consisted in running up a column of figures or counting bankbills. The remnant embarked for New York, with the exception of Mr. Audibon, the son of the celebrated and lamented Naturalist, who, with two or three companions, courageously braved the dangers of the route, and finally reached California, long after my arrival there, and after having endured unheard of fatigues and sufferings.[4]

---

[4] Perkins recites in brief one of the more celebrated incidents of the Gold Rush. The company initially was headed by Henry Livingston Webb, elder brother of James Watson Webb, editor and proprietor of the New York Herald; he was born at Claverack, New York, February 6, 1795, settled in Illinois in 1817, served for many years in the Illinois legislature, became a major of volunteers in the Black Hawk War, colonel of the 18th U. S. Volunteers in the Mexican War, and a general of Illinois militia; he died at Makanda, Illinois, October 5, 1876.

Webb's second-in-command on the California venture was John Woodhouse Audubon, artist son of a distinguished father. As Perkins says, the ambitious enterprise broke up under the lash of cholera and other misfortunes, related in the New York Herald on April 2–3, and in fuller detail on April 6, where the Picayune of March 29 is quoted relative to nineteen who turned back and eight who died of cholera. Audubon and a few others reached San Diego early in November, 1849, and then made their way north via the San Joaquin Valley, reaching San Francisco December 21. Between January and May, 1850, Audubon spent considerable time in the Southern Mines, visiting Wood's Diggings, Jamestown, Yorktown, and Mormon Gulch in late March. All the while he occupied himself sketching the novel scenes. After returning to New York, he began publication of a work, Illustrated Notes of an Expedition through Mexico and California (New York, 1852). Only the first part appeared, with four beautiful plates of Mexican scenery. Many of Audubon's sketches remained in California in the possession of a friend and were lost when the Central America sank off Cape Hatteras in 1857. Audubon's fragmentary journals were published in Cleveland, 1906, edited by Frank Heywood Hodder as Audubon's Western Journal: 1849–1850. Thirty-seven pencil drawings and water-colors which had survived, presented to the Southwest Museum in 1912, were reproduced with notes by Carl Schaefer Dentzel in a 1957 publication of the Book Club of California, The Drawings of John Woodhouse Audubon Illustrating his Adventures through Mexico and California 1849–1850.

The diary of J. H. Bachman, one of Audubon's companions, is quoted at length by Jeanne Skinner Van Nostrand in two articles in the California Historical Society Quarterly, December, 1942–March, 1943; and further details may be found in the letters contributed by John E. Durivage to the Picayune, especially from Brazos Santiago in March, 1849; see Ralph P. Bieber, ed., Southern Trails to California in 1849 (Glendale, 1937), pp. 159–255. These travelers took Perkins' route as far as Parras.

At Fort Brown all our preparations for the long journey were made; wagons, harness, mules and horses bought; the party thoroughly organized, offices and employments distributed, and a Captain chosen by vote, according to the invariable American practice; the unanimous voice honoring me with the command.

For two hundred leagues of the journey we had two enemies to guard against, the Indians and the cholera. The latter was making fearful ravages on all parts of our route as far as Monter[r]ey, and the former were out on their annual excursion of pillage and bloodshed at the expense of the defenceless Mexicans. We were witness to many a heartrending scene of entire households perishing from the cholera, and many a sickening scene of ravaged *haciendas,* and mutilated corpses, the work of the Indians. Caution and vigilance, however, preserved us from both dangers. We only lost one companion, who died of cholera the day after our arrival at Monter[r]ey,[5] and the Indians did not succeed in robbing us even of an animal, although they were several times in large force about us.

The war between the United States and the Mexicans had just been brought to a close, and we found the latter, naturally enough, in an exasperated state of mind; but the uniform good behaviour and prudence of our party, of which, by the bye, I was the only Englishman, gained the good will of the people, and it was only at the town of *Saltillo* where our little army ran a risk of a collision with the natives; a collision which we were however, fortunately, enabled to avoid.

We had arrived outside the town on the morning of Good Friday [April 6], on which day, as well as the two following, it is the custom in Mexico to forbid any transit in the streets with horses or carriages. This prohibition is very strictly enforced, and foreigners have been stoned by the populace or punished by the authorities for infringing it.

The rule in itself is all very well and proper, but might be susceptible of modifications on certain occasions. Saltillo is situated in a gap between two mountains, and the only highroad passes directly through the *plaza,* and in front of the Cathedral, and we thought it rather unfair to detain a large party of travellers for three days on such a frivolous pretext.

I sought counsel of some foreigners, resident in the place; they advised me by all means to lay over and not risk offending the people,

---

[5] See Perkins' further reminiscences of the death of Corse, in chapter xv; and compare McNeil's account in the Introduction.

apt enough at all times for a row, and more so at this present time, from the recent presence of foreign conquerors in their country. I sought the Military Commander, and, describing our position, demanded a pass. He answered it was out of his power to give me one, but that I might apply to the *alcalde*. I sought this functionary, but he purposely kept out of the way.

There was no remedy but either to delay our journey for three days, or risk the danger of a collision with the populace. We chose the latter alternative.

Placing the wagons in the centre of our little troop, with our rifles unslung and carried across the pummel of the saddle, we entered the town. The people scowled on us as we passed, and a few deep emprecations were hurled at us, to which we paid no attention. On reaching the great *plaza*, we found it full of people, evidently in commotion and apparently too ready to obstruct our passage. Here I ordered a momentary halt, directed every man to dismount and take off his hat, and then we proceeded slowly through the *plaza* and past the cathedral, each man with his rifle in one hand and in the other his hat and the reins of his bridle. The natives were taken by surprise, and pleased with our simple act of devotion and consideration for their religious feelings, were quite desarmed of their anger, and even cheered us heartily as we marched on; many little girls came running up to us, offering us bouquets of flowers, and the women smiled graciously on us as we passed. Once across the plaza, we all remounted, and the rest of our route through the town was a species of ovation, such was the enthusiasm inspired amongst the women by the mark of respect we had shown for their religion.

Our route through Mexico [had] led us past the towns of Monter[r]ey and Saltillo; Buena Vista, a famous battle field, where Gen¹ Santa Ana, with twenty thousand men sustained a desperate conflict with the small American Army, under Taylor, and where he came very nigh vanquishing the latter; Parrás; Quinquemay [Cuencamé]; Durango, all lay in our route. At the last named place, a town of some forty thousand inhabitants, situated at the very foot of the Cordilleras, we sold off our animals and wagons, and hired mules for the passage across the mountains to Mazatlán.⁶

---

⁶ Those who kept on to California by land, making their way north to the valley of the Gila, separated from the Mazatlán route west of Parras, going via

Durango is the principle town of all the Northern part of Mexico; it is the seat of a Bishopric, has a University, and a Governor, who is a species of viceroy. The buildings are very respectable, the streets paved, handsome *alamedas*, or public walks, delicious *quintas*, or gardens and pleasure grounds, and its Arena for Bull fighting is second only to that in the City of Mexico.

We were received with the greatest hospitality by the *Duranguenos*, and Gen[1] [José] Urrea, the Governor, called on us in state, accompanied by *Aide de camps* glittering in gold-laced uniforms. He afterwards invited me, with half a dozen more of the party, to dinner, when we were regaled with *nineteen* courses, and drank English porter out of champagne glasses.

The distance between Durango and the sea-port of Mazatlán is fifty leagues, and is entirely taken up by the Cordilleras and their numerous spurs. The road, or rather mule track, is exceedingly rough and dangerous; and the ascents and descents something awful to remember, but exceedingly grand and picturesque. The day's journey at times was not more than five or six miles, on account of the fearful work the mules had to do.

The northern slope of the Cordilleras at this point and at this season, is barren and cold. The summit however is well timbered with large pine trees, and we often had to spread our blankets for the night on the snow, and build up large fires with the plentiful resinous pine wood lying about.

We passed over vast plains covered with obsidium, a mineral of the color and appearance of black bottle glass, and extremely hard and flinty. The Indians work it up into beautiful and deadly weapons, such as lance and arrow-heads, with wonderful ingenuity.

There are many little hamlets and farm houses interspersed in the deep valleys of the mountains. One village, almost extensive enough to be called a town, is completely surrounded with mountains at least ten thousand feet high. It was a day's work to get down to it and another to surmount the heights on the opposite side. There has apparently been no effort to lead the road into practicable, or more facile passes. It is like the Chinese Wall, running butt up to almost inaccessible mountain

Chihuahua or taking a more westerly road through Ures and Altar. John E. Durivage traveled the Chihuahua route; the younger Audubon and J. H. Bachman describe the other road.

fastnesses; scaling dizzy heights, dashing through torrents and burying itself from daylight in the cavernous valleys. Within a couple of miles from Durango, there is a place which the loaded mules have to surmount by actually making prodigious leaps up the slippery faces of a huge mass of granite, and where I had some difficulty in scrambling up on foot.

As I have said, the northern face of the Cordilleras is cold and barren, with a climate similar to that of the Alleghanies in April, but on descending the southern slope the scene changes as if by magic into beautiful forms of tropical vegetation. The road led through groves of cocoa-nut trees, banana orchards, date and other palm-trees, immense cactii and *cereus,* five and twenty feet in height, interspersed with trees of all dimensions, covered with parasitical flowers as big as a dinner plate.

I think I never saw anything more fascinating than the southern half of the rugged road between Durango and Mazatlán. Every night we feasted on corn *tortillas,*[7] wild honey and the flesh of game and armadillos. Our camping ground at times would be in the midst of banana trees loaded with their huge bunches of luscious and golden fruit, wooing the palate of the tired traveller; sometimes beneath the ever rustling plumes of the cocoa-nut tree, to be awakened at early dawn by the chattering of myriads of gorgeously plumed parrots, and the hum of innumerable bright-winged insects. From sleeping in the snow, in two day's journey we found ourselves revelling in all the beauties of a tropical climate.

Mazatlán is situated on the gulf of that name, at the entrance of the gulf of California. It is a pretty Mexican town, and important in a commercial point of view, as being the port of entrance for the introduction of foreign merchandise destined for all the north Pacific Departments of Mexico. There are heavy importing houses in Mazatlán, mostly foreign, and they do an extensive business with Durango and Sonora, Guaymas and Lower California.[8]

The heat is oppressive at Mazatlán at all seasons of the year. The

---

[7] Perkins explains in a footnote that tortillas are "Corn cakes."

[8] By "Lower California" Perkins perhaps means here not southern California, as on later pages, but the peninsula, Baja California. With the exception of the seaport of Guaymas, in Sonora, he is naming Mexican states, not cities. Mazatlán was and is a principal city of Sinaloa.

latitude is well north, twenty three, but being completely surrounded by the lofty ranges of the Cordilleras, and with a southern aspect, it has much more of a tropical character than places in the same latitude on the Atlantic coast.

We had no difficulty in finding a ship for San Francisco; there were more than a dozen in port. We chartered the "Johanna and Oluffa," a Danish brig, each passenger paying one hundred dollars.[9]

The voyage occupied twenty one days, five of which we were becalmed off Point Lucas. Then occurred a storm that well nigh sent us all to the bottom, as the brig was any thing but seaworthy. But the hardest blow is preferable to being becalmed in a tropical sea, the ugly feature in our case being enhanced by a short supply of water.

Let any one unacquainted with a calm at sea imagine a burning brazen sun looking down through the yellow air on a sea smooth as a mirror; the lazy sails flapping listlessly as the ship rises and falls on the heaving ocean; for the immense body of water seems endued with gigantic life, and rises and falls continually as if in the act of breathing, although the surface may be unbroken by a ripple. Then, the unutterable loneliness of the sea, sky and air becomes oppressive almost beyond endurance. The feeling that there is no means of escape from this oppression; that the ship and all that is in it are chained to one particular spot of the vast ocean, and that all human exertion is futile, becomes by degrees unbearable, and a torpor and helpless listliness seize on every one. The deck soon becomes too hot for the bare feet of the sailors, and the sun brings out the pitch and tar of the deck seams in long black lines, while the paint rises up in large blisters on the sides of the vessel.

For five days we lay thus, the current which in this region sets down the coast towards Acapulco, carrying us to the south until we found ourselves in latitude twenty.

The captain had not laid in sufficient supplies of food and water for such a large number of passengers (there were upwards of a hundred

---

[9] Perkins should have said that he and his companions took passage in, rather than "chartered," the *Johanna and Oluffa*. The *Alta California* of June 14, 1849, noting her arrival at San Francisco on Saturday, June 9, speaks of her as "Danish schr Johanna & Oluffa, capt Engers, 23 days from Mazatlan, cargo to Huttmann, Miller & Co—100 passengers," thus correcting Perkins in various particulars.

in this little two hundred and fifty ton brig), and we became apprehensive of the results of a longer continuance of the calm. We therefore put ourselves on short allowance of water.

The "monsters of the deep" became very intimate with us during the calm. Whales, sharks, dolphins, flying fish, and porpoises surrounded the ship in vast numbers. Sea-birds of various kinds peculiar to these latitudes, were in abundance, the Booby, a fowl of the Pelican genus, (*Sula fusca,*) being the most notable. This name has been given it by the sailors because of its stupidity in allowing itself to be easily caught. The stormy Petrel, or Mother Carey's chickens, were very numerous, and presaged, in the minds of the seamen, a coming tempest, which sure enough came soon afterwards.

Sharks are held in horror and detested by all sea-faring people, and no pains are spared in order to capture, torture and destroy them. Sailors have a superstitious dread of them, and believe that when they follow a ship it is because some one aboard is doomed to die, and they are waiting for the body to be thrown overboard. The truth is these voracious monsters seek the vessel in a calm in order to pick up the offal, bones, etc. that are thrown over the side. Other larger fish flock to a ship becalmed to rub themselves on the hull, to detach the parasitical animals that fix themselves in large numbers to the skin of various fish and cetacea.

An enormous shark had accompanied us for some time, and the sailors had not been able to find the large hooks which all vessels have on board, called sharkhooks, and which had been mislaid. At last I overhawled my fishing tackle, and, picking out two salmon hooks of Limerick manufacture, I bound them back to back with strong iron wire, with which I also wound a fathom of halliard line; then baiting my pigmy trap with a piece of raw pork I got astride of the taffrail and threw the line overboard.

It was seized at once by a Booby. I hawled the foolish bird in, ballasted the hooks with a bit of lead to sink them out of reach of the water-fowl, and again threw them over. The line had scarcely touched the water when I had the satisfaction of seeing a huge blue mass darting towards it; then a flash and gleam of dazzling white as the monster partly turned on his back to seize the tempting morsel. He swallowed bait, hooks and two or three feet of the line.

I had him fast, to my great delight; but the difficulty was to bag him with means so ridiculously inadequate, apparently. However, in great excitement I sung out for assistance. The huge creature, not yet suspicious of the "dose of fishooks" it had just swallowed, kept cruising about the stern-post on the look out for another mouthful, when a short turn took him by surprise, and he leaped completely out of the water with pain and rage. We hawled in until we got him half way up the side, and fearful that the small hooks (all honor to their maker!) might break, a sailor was slung overboard who passed a strong rope round the tail of the brute, and we soon had him flapping on the deck. His head was chopped off and nailed in triumph to the mast. He measured seven feet six inches.

A shark is shaped something like a pike; the head is more rounded, and the mouth placed underneath, like that of a catfish, which peculiarity obliges it to turn partly over in order to seize its prey. This it does however, with the rapidity of lightning. Its appearance belies its terrific voracity, it being a handsome, elegant-looking fish; none of your clumsy porpoise-shaped bodies, but long, lithe and slender. On the back it is of a brilliant blue, and the belly is dazzlingly white.

The sailors cooked some of the flesh and ate it, on the same principle I suppose that led our forefathers to swallow the blood of an enemy. I tasted the flesh but found it insipid and tough; uneatable in fact.

After being heartily sickened by several days' calm, we were roused one night by unusual sounds in the air. The wind-spirits were giving us warning, and the Captain and crew were tramping about with unwonted activity getting the ship in trim, and before ten o'clock in the morning we were driving before a bang-up gale. There was no help for it; we had to run, and that too considerably out of our course. The storm lasted two days, during which time we had to subsist on biscuit and salt pork as it was out of the question lighting the galley fires.

The "Johanna and Oluffa" complained mightily, and the Captain was something more than anxious, as he afterwards acknowledged to me. However the little pug-nosed brig contended bravely with the big waves; when she could not get over them she went *through them,* without much consideration for the live cargo on board, and then we had to handle the pumps. The gale abated at last, and a slight change of wind enabled us to get into the oceanic high-road, that is into the path of the trade wind, on the eighteenth day out. This blows directly for

San Francisco, and on the twenty first day we had the satisfaction of sighting the mountains of the Californian coast, and in a few hours found ourselves inside the "Golden Gate" the name given to the narrow entrance to the Bay of San Francisco. And it was high time, as our supply of water had dwindled down to five pipes, and the last barrels of beef and biscuit had been hoisted from the hold.

CHAPTER II

It was in the "merry month of May," in the year 1849, that we arrived in California.[1] The coast in the vicinity of the Bay of San Francisco is rugged and bare of vegetation. The coast range of mountains appears here to project into the sea, forming a dangerous lee shore; and the entrance to the bay is so narrow, and hidden by great masses of rocks, that in dark or foggy weather, the vessels have to lay well off, and wait for it to clear up.

The general character of the Californian coast is mountainous and dangerous, with few harbors, the principal of which are San Diego, Monterey, and San Francisco. The latter is perhaps the finest in the world.

The Golden Gate, as the entrance to this magnificent harbor is poetically denominated,[2] is about a mile wide at its narrowest part, and about four miles long. In the centre, just before entering the inner harbor, stands a solitary naked rock, like a sentinel guarding the

---

[1] As observed in chapter i, note 9, the *Johanna and Oluffa* arrived from Mazatlán with her 100 passengers on June 9.

[2] John Charles Frémont originated the term Chrysopylae or Golden Gate in his *Geographical Memoir upon Upper California* (Washington, 1848). The name was applied, he says, "on the same principle that the harbor of *Byzantium* (Constantinople afterwards) was called *Chrysoceras* (golden horn). The form of the harbor, and its advantages for commerce (and that before it became an entrepôt of eastern commerce) suggested the name to the Greek founders of Byzantium. The form of the entrance into the bay of San Francisco, and its advantages for commerce (Asiatic inclusive) suggest the name which is given to this entrance."

gateway. Passing this rock, which commands the entrance and the bay, the harbor opens out to the right and left, into a broad expanse of water seventy miles long by ten to fifteen wide.

Immediately on rounding the point to the right, the town of San Francisco comes in sight, beautifully situated on the inner slope of the coast heights, fronting the bay, and with its rear to the sea, from which it is separated by a neck of highlands, five miles wide.

At the extreme right, the stream which waters the valley of San José enters the bay. In front the low fertile coast is backed by a lofty range of mountains, spurs of the coast range. To the left the bay, full of lovely islands, stretches up to the Sacramento river, which is, for sixty miles, so broad and deep that it may with propriety be called a continuation of the bay itself.[3]

Many of the islands, and the highlands surrounding the bay, are covered with a handsome growth of heavy timber, and at the epoch of our arrival, by large patches of brilliant flowers.

The coasts, harbors and inlets of this part of California appear to have been a favorite resort of Cetacea and marine amphibia. The family of seals is here fully represented. Huge sea lions, sea cows, walruses etc. are at any time to be seen gambolling by hundreds on the craggy shores; while out at sea, frequent white jets of water indicate the presence of the larger cetacea.

The day was gloomy, windy and cold, when we rounded the inner point of the passage; and I confess that the feeling of satisfaction at having safely accomplished a long and perilous journey, was somewhat mingled with regret and disappointment.

The scene that presented itself was not calculated to inspire a cheerful feeling. The town itself, as seen from the deck of the vessel, was wretched enough. The anchoring ground was crowded with vessels of all sizes, and apparently deserted by their crews. This we found to be actually the case. The greed of gold was too powerful an incentive for the sailors; and in many instances a ship has been left by her crew, captain and officers at anchor in the tide without a soul on

---

[3] The name Sacramento River is not applied below its confluence with the San Joaquin, the combined river broadening as Suisun Bay, connected with San Pablo Bay by the Straits of Carquinez. The river Perkins mentions, entering southern San Francisco Bay past San Jose, is the Guadalupe, not visible from San Francisco.

board to take care of her; and sometimes even with valuable cargo on board. But the mines offered greater temptations even than robbery, and, strange as it may appear, captains have returned to their deserted ships after three or four months absence, and have found every thing intact on board! with no loss or damage more than had been occasioned by neglect and the weather.

At the epoch of my arrival there were upwards of one hundred and fifty vessels in port, many of them with valuable cargoes. A large proportion of them had been deserted by all their crew, leaving the captain alone to take charge, and to wait with what patience he might, the return of his men. In other cases, as I have just stated, the captains themselves were not able to withstand the temptation which the bags of gold-dust of returned and fortunate miners offered to their bewildered imagination, and, taking the best measures for the security of their ships, have left the rest to chance.

As sailors are not the most steady people of the world, the fortunes of this new class of miners were none of the most brilliant. Some who were fortunate enough to find "rich pockets," generally squandered their gold at the gaming table, or at the drinking bar; and nearly all, lucky or unlucky in their search after gold, soon grew heartily tired of their new occupation and returned, one by one, to their more legitimate employment. Thus, after the lapse [of] a twelve month or so, it was not a difficult matter to man a ship.

In 1849, San Francisco presented a strange aspect. The old town was composed of some scores of poor adobe huts, with four or five houses of a better class. The plaza or square [Portsmouth Square], situated at that time within a hundred yards of high water, had on its upper side two old-fashioned buildings, the principal ones in the town. One was the alcalde's house, the other a government building, occupied at the time I am speaking of, as a post office.

Here and there, without much regard to regularity, were scattered the mud houses or rather huts of the natives.

But these were features completely thrown into the shade by what we may call the New town, which, not as yet offering any buildings as solid even as adobe, monopolized notwithstanding the attention, on account of its lightness and gaiety.

Tents of all colors; light wooden structures; deck cabins from the vessels; brush houses lined with cotton cloth, were placed wherever an open space was to be found near the sea.

The slopes of the hills presented the appearance of a military encampment on a spree; the tents pitched without regularity, and piles of merchandise scattered about in all directions.

The "Parker House" had just been erected; the first American house perhaps in California. It had been brought out ready framed, and was placed on the lower side of the plaza. Already its spacious rooms were full of gambler's tables; and the gamblers themselves were even at this time the aristocracy of the place.

The price of a bed and two meals in the Parker House was ten dollars; but few lodged or eat in the house except the gamblers, as all had their tents, and did their own cooking at home. The great profits of the Hotel proceeded from the rent of the tables for the purpose of gambling. These rented from ten dollars to an ounce of gold per night. Great gains were also made from the enormous sale of liquors at the bar, at half a dollar a glass.[4]

The streets were full, piled up in places, with merchandise of every kind. Boxes of tobacco and kegs of nails formed a pavement from the sea to the plaza. Valuable goods outside of all the tents and houses were strewed about, apparently uncared for.

This waste and loss is easily accounted for. At the first news of the wonderful discovery, vessels, loaded with every conceivable description of merchandise were dispatched to San Francisco. When these arrived, they found, instead of a large market, a few thousand miners, who had brought out with them every thing necessary for the first year at least. Few thought of building; still fewer of agriculture; and so it was found that with the exception of certain class of provisions, there was no want left to be satisfied, and the rich cargoes of wines, preserves, knic knacks,

---

[4] A letter by a correspondent of the New York *Weekly Tribune*, August 18, 1849, dated San Francisco, June 20, says: "It is true rents here are enormous, and the price of most necessaries greater than in New-York; but nevertheless the condition of the laboring man is much improved. As an illustration of rent, take the 'Parker House,' the new hotel recently erected by Robert A. Parker, Esq. This house yields an income to its proprietor which Croeusus never could have claimed. One small room on the second floor, used as a *monte* room, rents for $1,800 per month, and two rooms on the same floor for $2,400 per month. The billiard room rents for $1,000 per month, and the offices from $100 to $200. The net revenue of the whole house is at least $150,000 per year.

"A friend of mine, no later than yesterday, paid $200 per month for a sleeping apartment. Board is $21 per week; a game of billiards costs $1; and those who indulge in gin cocktails and brandy smashes must be ready to pay 25 cents per glass."

clothing, from Europe and general cargoes from the United States, were without demand.

It was only when business became systematized, and regular demands poured in from the mining regions, and towns sprung up in the plains, that these goods met with sale, and by that time many thousand dollars' worth had perished through mere carelessness. The eagerness of the new arrivals to proceed to the mines was a species of frensy, and hundreds had left valuable property, thrown away, given away, or left in the streets, in order to make their way to the mines, where their sanguine hopes painted the precious metal lying in brilliant heaps awaiting them.

I have not exaggerated the fact of the pavement being in places composed of kegs of nails and boxes of cavendish tobacco, which were well embedded in the mud of the street which led from the bay to the plaza.

The tide rises about six feet, and at low water about a hundred acres of the bay becomes a muddy morass, and made the landing extremely disagreeable and even difficult. Two years after my arrival, this space contained the finest streets of the city.

The good brig "Johanna and Oluffa" was deserted by passengers and crew within three days of its anchoring in the harbor. Even the worthy captain, a Dane, and a famous cook, who had insisted during the voyage from Mazatlán, as much in feasting his four [fore?] cabin, as in starving his hundred steerage passengers, also deserted his vessel, after taking, it must be said to his credit, every precaution for the safety of his craft; and the security of the little she still contained.

The second day after our arrival we got our traps ashore and, putting up a tent in a vacant spot near the water, E——, H——, B—— and myself separated ourselves for good from our three months' companions, the original company having kept together in the best harmony during the entire trip from the United States; a fact which speaks highly for the respectable elements of which it was composed.[5]

Having arranged our traps, I strolled up towards the hills, and had

---

[5] Here we learn, Samuel McNeil notwithstanding, that the company from Ohio broke up only after reaching San Francisco. E. and H. are clearly identifiable as D. A. Enyart and Charles Hyde; B—— might have been one Brent, first mentioned on the passenger list of the *Maria Burt* as remarked in the Introduction, note 2, but is probably L. Baker, one of the original Ohio contingent.

not proceeded far when I heard my name called out in tones of surprise. I turned towards a person standing at the entrance of a large blue tent surrounded with boxes, bales and barrels.

This was evidently the person who had hailed, and now strode rapidly towards me, and grasping me heartily by the hand, dragged me towards his tent. I strove in vain to recognise my new friend. I saw before me a tall, loose-made, bony individual, with an emaciated, yellow complexion, and hair and beard in which white was certainly the predominating colour. He appeared to be a man of about fifty-five years of age.

"Let's have a drink, first of all," said my new friend.

He opened a bottle of liquor and, pouring out its contents into two tin cups, he gave me one.

"Success, old fellow!" said he.

"The same to you, my boy," said I.

I was completely puzzled. I could [not] remember having seen the man in my life, and he was evidently enjoying my bewilderment.

"And so you do not remember me, P——," said he at last. "Well it is no wonder; I do not recognise myself, when I happen to look into the glass, which is seldom enough, now that I have eschewed that cursed operation of shaving. I am what was once H. C——."

I was thunderstruck. It was not six months since I had seen Mr. C——, a dandy of the first water in one of the Atlantic cities, with rosy complexion, brown waving hair, and with an imposing *embonpoint,* that really made him a handsome fellow of some twenty eight or thirty years of age.

"And is the climate of California so deadly?" I asked.

"No, my dear fellow," returned he; "but I will let you into my secret, that is a secret no longer. For twenty years I have lived the life of a martyr in order to wear the appearance of youth. I kept up the deceit until I arrived at Panamá where a severe sickness prostrated me for two weeks. Since then I have thrown off all disguise, and really feel younger at this moment than I did twenty years ago. Thanks to California, I have broken my chains. I am fifty two this year and I don't care who knows it!"

"And those magnificent rounded legs, and gentlemanlike signs of good feeding about the region of the waist; and the broad well-filled chest?" I enquired.

"Padding, my son, padding. I have made the fortune of half a dozen tailors. I was made up artificially, from the foot to the head."

"And the brown glossy hair, the full rosy cheeks?"

"Hair dye, paint and a gold apparatus inside the cheeks to fill them out," he answered. "Oh, my friend, what tortures I have suffered! What a fool have I been! And how happy am I now!"

I congratulated the pseudo-beau heartily, and after an other tin cup of wine, we parted.

I met Mr. C—— several times during my sojourn in California and must say that he appeared to be growing younger every day.

As every one appeared to be possessed with the idea that the mines were the goal to be attained, and seemed to look upon San Francisco only as a starting point, after a short recruiting, my little party commenced making preparations to follow in the general wake.

My observations were not favorable to the idea of establishing a house of business in San Francisco, according to my first intentions. At all events I desired to see the mines; so we laid in a barrel of pork, and another of beef, with two or three of biscuit, at New York prices, engaged [passage upon] a small schooner at an inconscionably extravagant figure, got our things aboard early one morning, and, after waiting half the day for a fair wind, we set sail for the southern mines, or in other words steered for the rising town of Stockton.[6]

---

[6] See Introduction for the distinction between the Northern and Southern mines. A letter signed Freaner, published in the New Orleans *Daily Picayune*, August 5, 1849 (and reprinted in the New York *Weekly Tribune*, August 18, 1849), written from San Francisco on June 30 after a three-week tour of the Southern Mines, estimated that four-fifths of the people arriving in the country shaped their course to the Sacramento and its tributaries, that is, the Northern Mines.

CHAPTER III

The large stream which carries down the waters of the Sacramento, San Joaquin, and their numerous tributaries to the bay of San Francisco, is navigable for the largest class of vessels as far up as the San Joaquin on the south, and some distance up the Sacramento to the north. Both of these rivers, but particularly the latter, are navigable for some hundred miles for good-sized steamers.

The lower stream, below the junction of the two last-named rivers, may almost be called an arm of the grand bay below, as at Benecia, sixty miles from San Francisco, there is a harbour large enough and deep enough to hold a thousand of the largest class of war vessels. At the time of my arrival the American Admiral had made it the head quarters of the Pacific fleet; and, for a long time, there were strenuous efforts made by the Admiral and some other influential men to make Benecia the port of entry for California and thus neutralise San Francisco entirely. But the scheme failed. The position of the latter was too obviously advantageous, and after a contest which lasted two years, the vast progress made in San Francisco destroyed the hopes of the ambitious Benecians of a successful rivalry.[1]

On our right, after entering the river, was the high chain of mountains that reach the height of four thousand feet in a peak called Bear Mountain, close to the bay. This is part of the coast range. To the left the land, though broken, is low comparatively, and undulating into long hills, covered at this season of the year (spring), with vivid green grass and immense patches of yellow and of purple flowers.

Within the coast range, extending to the foot of the Sierra Nevada, or snowy mountains, is what is called the valley of the Sacramento and the San Joaquin, watered by numerous rivers, and extending north and south for five hundred miles.

Benecia [2] is situated on the right bank of the river, in a fine commanding position. The largest man of war can move alongside the bank. There were already a few shanties and some frame houses belonging to the naval station erected, and some half dozen vessels, besides the government ships. On the opposite side of the river is a little Californian hamlet called Martinez.

The San Joaquin is narrow, very tortuous, but of a sufficient depth for vessels of two hundred and fifty tons. It is a sluggish stream, winding through extended marshy grounds, called the *Tulari* plains, which in the spring floods are covered with water.

In the dry season these plains are the resort of herds of the large

---

[1] The origins of Benicia are discussed in chapter xxiv, note 6.

[2] In a note Perkins says: "Venecia is the proper orthography; but Spanish Americans seldom distinguish the B from the V, and the Americans adopted the spelling from the way they heard the name pronounced."

Californian Elk; and sometimes the Grizzly Bear, coming down from the mountains, finds a secure retreat amongst the dense vegetation. It is the grandest hunting ground I have ever seen, and will remain so until the ingenuity of man converts it into rice or cotton fields.

A tedious and painful voyage of eight days, in which we were obliged to eat raw pork for want of fuel to cook with, and after loosing each pint of blood as a tribute paid to the ravenous myriads of mosquitos, brought us to Stockton.

Stockton is one hundred and sixty miles from San Francisco, and situated on a deep slough a few hundred yards from the river, on a plain, level as far as the eye can reach. It was by far the busiest place I had yet seen in California.[3]

Here we were brought in *rapport* with the gold mines. We began to smell the precious ore. Here were even real live miners; men who had actually dug out the shining metal, and who had it in huge buckskin pouches in the pockets of their pantaloons. Men who spoke jestingly, lightly of chunks of gold weighing one, five or ten pounds! Of "pockets" where a quarter of a bushel of gold-dust had been washed from! These men were awful objects of our curiosity. They were the demi-gods of the dominion of Plutus. Their long rough boots, red shirts, Mexican hats; their huge uncombed beards, covering half the face; the Colts' revolver attached to its belt behind, the *cuchillo* stuck into the leg of the boot—all these things were attributes belonging to another race of men than ourselves; and we looked upon them with a certain degree of respect, and with a determination soon to be ourselves as little human-like in appearance as they were.

I left my friend E[nyart] in Stockton in charge of a hulk for storage, that we jointly purchased, and started in company with H[yde] and

---

[3] Founded by Charles M. Weber in 1847 as Tuleburg, Stockton began to flourish only after the discovery of gold. The town was laid out in the spring of 1849, resurveyed by Major R. P. Hammond, and named for Commodore R. F. Stockton. In the *Appendix* to his *Map of the Mining District of California*, William A. Jackson remarked as of December, 1849: "Stockton is situated on a slough of the same name, three miles from San Joaquin River, and seventy miles from New-York of the Pacific. The slough is navigable for steamers and barges of four hundred tons. The location is excellent, embracing the peninsula between the two principal sloughs, and extends south to Mormon Slough. Population about 3,000. It contains some good buildings, and presents the appearance of considerable business activity. It is the great depot for the southern mining region, and is destined to be a place of much importance."

B——, my servant boy, and some Mexican companions, to walk to the mines, a distance of about seventy miles, our luggage etc. being put on an ox-cart, at the moderate rate of one dollar per pound.[4]

The weather was cool and agreeable in San Francisco, but on the plains we found the heat intense. The vegetation was already burnt up, and the flowers that still bloomed near the coast had of course disappeared on the plains.

We barely made some twelve to fifteen miles a day, as it was quite out of the question walking during the heat of the sun.

The plains are covered with a luxuriant vegetation, except in the summer, when the oppressive heat, unallayed by rain, which never falls at this season, dries up everything except the evergreen oaks [live oaks], which, growing singly here and there, give a park-like aspect to the plains, very similar to what I have remarked in Texas.

A fearful casualty overtook me on this journey that makes me shudder as I call it back to my memory. One day we were resting ourselves by the road side, and I fell asleep with my head under the poisonous plant known here as *yedra* (ivy), and in four and twenty hours my face, arms and legs were frightfully swollen.[5] The day afterwards I was quite blind and so remained for three days, still travelling on with my companions, as it would have been certain death to have lagged behind.

I was fortunately enabled to procure a mule, and my Irish boy, who had remained faithful to me through all, led the animal, and at night would sling my hammock between a couple of oak trees, and lead me to it. God knows how I got through that fearful journey! The sensation of blindness was overwhelming to the imagination, but my strength never failed me, nor my courage neither.

On the evening of the third day of my blindness, after having dismounted at our camping ground, I found I had regained my sight. Taking the bandage from my eyes, a blessed ray of light entered them,

---

[4] Perkins does not here say what route he traveled, but in chapter xxxiv he recalls that in 1849 he took the "river road," which crossed the Stanislaus at what was then known as Taylor's Ferry, at present Oakdale. A somewhat more direct road would have been by way of Knight's Ferry, or "Nye's Ferry," as shown on Jackson's *Map of the Mining District of California*, which was published early in 1850. This map interestingly depicts Wood's Diggings, Jamestown, and "Sonoranian Camp" on Woods Creek.

[5] Poison oak was the bane of the miners; many describe its ravages.

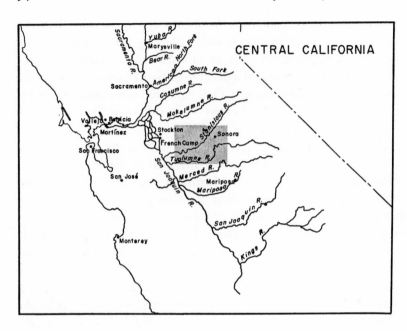

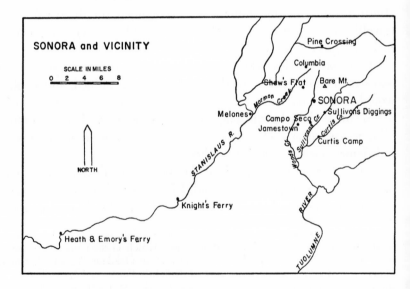

and I had a dim glimpse of a lovely spot, a dell surrounded with oak and pine trees, with a river running by. Our party had been augmented during the journey, and I could discover picturesque groups distributed under the trees, and preparations going on for the evening meal. With an indescribable feeling of gratitude to Providence I retired that night to my hammock.

On the seventh day we reached the first *placers,* called James' Diggings.[6] Here we found about four hundred men at work in the bed of a stream, and all the claims already occupied. We proceeded to Sullivan's Diggings,[7] some four miles further, and there put up our large tent, and I was enabled to enjoy the quiet which was so necessary to my health. My companions set to work at once, but were not very sanguine, as the place seemed pretty thoroughly worked already. My first and almost only experiment in gold digging, was made here. Infirm as I was I got down into a pit, and with a knife picked out several dollar's worth of gold, and had I been able to continue, I might have made from twenty to thirty dollars a day; but what was this in a country like California in 1849?

I had been in Sullivan's Diggings only a few days, when I heard that in the camp of the *Sonoraenses,* a distance of six miles, was an old friend, who had preceded me to this country some three months. I hastened to join him, finding him snuggly ensconsed in a handsome brush house, and exercising the honorable profession of *Alcalde* in a camp of Mexicans that had already grown to the dimensions of a town.[8]

Scarcely had I settled myself in Sonora, when I was seized with a

---

[6] The origins of Jamestown are discussed in the Introduction, note 10.

[7] See the account of Sullivan's Diggings in chapter xix.

[8] As appears in the next paragraph, Perkins is talking about James Fraser, who reached San Francisco February 28, 1849, one of the passengers brought by the steamship *California* on her famous first voyage. He must have come to Sonora soon after. The first alcalde (magistrate) there is said to have been R. S. Ham, who was not elected but simply assumed the duties and privileges of the office. When a man was to be tried for murder, the point was raised that the alcalde should be a man regularly elected and possessed of better qualifications than Ham, who is described by T. R. Stoddart, *Annals of Tuolumne County* (Sonora, 1963), p. 55, as "a rough, illiterate man, and formerly a teamster in the U. S. Army in Mexico." Fraser was "pitched upon and elected, as, not only the most influential man in the camp, but also the best educated, and one altogether suited to the office. He was then keeping a large store on Sonorita Gulch."

fearful nervous attack, the result of neglect and bad treatment of my poisoned limbs. For nineteen days I lay between life and death, suffering strong convulsions every half hour, until my strength, no longer able to sustain the shocks, left me entirely, and for days I lay in a state of catalepsy that could hardly be distinguished from death, by observers.[9] In this state, with an acute perception of hearing but unable to move or open my eyes, I have heard comments on my supposed decease and Mr. F[raser] actually wrote down to Stockton acquainting E[nyart] of my death, and the latter actually wrote a letter to my friends at home informing them of the fact. I fortunately got possession of this letter before it could be sent.

A big fat Mexican woman—she was an angel enveloped in the humanity of Falstaff—took compassion on me. She said I was like a son of hers she had left at home. She brought me clean sheets, and would sit beside me for hours tending me with as much care as if I had really been her child. It may be I owed my life to her attentions, for although I had an excellent physician attending me, there was a total absence of all the comforts and appliances of civilized life.

When I look back to that fearful trial, I acknowledge a Divine Power that saved me under circumstances that made perhaps all human efforts idle and futile.

F[raser] was very kind, and I remember on one occasion, when he was sitting beside me, I took the opportunity of requesting him, in case of my death, to have my body transported to the sea shore, and to bury me within sight of the great ocean. He burst into tears and rushed from the apartment.

The disease from which I suffered was very peculiar, and, as I have never met with a similar case, I note it down here for the benefit of the Faculty.

---

[9] Samuel McNeil, not exactly an admirer of Perkins, made a brief tour of the Southern Mines before departing California in the *Panama* on September 2. His narrative says: "When I was in the Macallemy river, I had the honor of seeing the lordly Mr. Perkins, of Cincinnati, who had acted so aristocratically towards me while passing through Mexico, so poisoned by the poisonous oak that he was bloated and full of sores. Knowing the virulence of the disorder, and seeing how greatly he had been poisoned, I judged that he afterwards died. Should I see him again it will seem like a resurrection from the dead." Perkins went nowhere near the Mokelumne, so McNeil must have encountered him at Sullivan's Diggings or Sonora.

A few days after the swelling caused by the poison had subsided, and I was convalescent, I felt one day a peculiar stinging sensation at the extremity of the little finger of the right hand; this feeling, which was not painful but very disagreeable, commenced travelling slowly up the hand, following the muscle of the little finger, to the wrist, then along the bone called *radius,* by anatomists, to the elbow; then along the *humerus* to the shoulder blade. From the shoulder the sensation passed into the cavity of the chest, on the right side. The moment this happened I was thrown into convulsions, and had to be forcibly held down by two or more persons.

For nineteen days, and sometimes at intervals of half an hour, I was afflicted by this extraordinary attack, which baffled the science of two first-rate surgeons. The convulsions generally lasted but a few seconds, but left me at times in a state which was often mistaken by my friends for death.

The twentieth day, one of the surgeons made an experiment, and whether it was the effect of this, or that the disease had worn itself out, I know not, but the next day I was well!

He made me indicate the path of the pricking sensation from the little finger to the chest, and drawing a chalk line along the sensitive parts, he placed round vesicatories of catharides of various sizes along this line, from the tip of the little finger to the point I indicated in the chest. I never had another attack from that hour, and in three days I was walking about perfectly well, and my friend E[nyart] arriving post haste from Stockton to attend my funeral, found me swinging in my hammock, reading a novel! [10]

Mr. F[raser] had been three months in the country, and had had a hard journey by the way of Panamá. He had made his way up to the Camp of Sonoraenses in company with a young officer of the regiment which was sent to take possession of California. [11] Mr. T[heall] had

---

[10] It would appear that Enyart was at Sonora as early as August 1, 1849, for he is one of 98 residents of Sonora who voted in the general election that day. See Stoddart, *Annals of Tuolumne County,* pp. 91–93. Because he was a foreigner or because he was sick, Perkins did not vote.

[11] Hiram Washington Theall had come to California in 1847 as a second lieutenant in Company D of the New York Regiment, commanded by Colonel Jonathan Drake Stevenson. He was stationed through much of 1848 at San Jose in Baja California, but by November was at Monterey, as shown by letters in

brought up a barrel of rum, from the proceeds of which he procured sufficient funds to put up a small store. F[raser] was named alcalde, and as every decision brought him from one to six ounces, he had filled already a few buckskin bags with gold, and had besides a lot of land in the *plaza* and a good brush house lined with red calico.

The Alcalde was the only authority, and as the bulk of the settlers was Mexican, the decisions of this authority were willingly respected. F[raser] knew little of Spanish, and the business of his court was carried on by the aid of interpretors, who were also well paid by the litigants. My knowledge of french used to bring me in sometimes as much [as] a hundred dollars in one day.

Brave times, that unfortunately did not last long; for the simple and effectual, if arbitrary, mode of procedure in the alcalde's court, was soon replaced by blackguard judges and venal lawyers.

F[raser] did not care to witness the change. T[heall] and I bought his lot for six hundred dollars, and his small stock of goods at proportionate prices, and, leaving his mantle of alcalde on the broad shoulders of my worthy partner, he dug up from the ground under his bed sundry bags and tin boxes of *dust*, and enjoining us to search for a bag of ten pounds which he said "was somewhere about," he left for San Francisco, with the intention of taking a cargo of goods to the Southern seas.[12]

---

the papers of Henry M. Naglee in the Bancroft Library. Theall briefly succeeded Fraser as alcalde at Sonora, was Perkins' partner at least into 1852, and apparently was living at Sonora as late as 1854. By November 6, 1855, as shown by another letter in the Naglee Papers, he had moved to Forest City in Sierra County as the representative of a gold-buying concern. He died at Hamilton, White Pine County, Nevada, about 1869. A street in Sonora is named after him.

[12] Fraser may have departed Sonora in September, 1849. Papers of Dr. John S. Griffin in the Bancroft Library include a letter from him dated San Francisco, 26 Oct. 1849:

Dear Doctor,
    Since your departure I found that the Barque 'Mary Frances' could not get her necessary papers as she had sailed under the Hawaiian flag, consequently she could not get an American Register and I threw up the purchase & withdrew the sum. On Monday I purchased 2/3ds of the 'Sarah M Fox' as she lies Young Mr Fox taking the remaining 1/3—her cost is $10,500 and she can be sent to sea for about $300. i[n] addition—this is the same vessel that I had offered $12,750. for previous to your arrival, including the stores;

CHAPTER IV

The Mexicans from the northern provinces of Chihuahua, Sonora and the Gulf, were of course among the first to take advantage of the gold discoveries in California. Particularly from Sonora came a large immigration. This Department of Mexico, already coveted by the North Americans, is advantageously situated on the gulf of California, with an excellent port, called Guaymas. Here large numbers of Sonoraenses with their families and stocks of native merchandize, embarked in small vessels, and arrived at the southern *placers* before

---

the owner had, after my first offer, removed a large part of her provisions, the value of which I deducted from the first offer, and then made the amount $10,500. I consider the 2/3^{ds} of this Vessel more valuable, and certainly with the prospect of realizing a freight, than the *whole* of the Bark. Fox goes with me to the Islands.

Brown turned over to me for you $456. in gold at $16. [per ounce] and I suspect he must have some of this back to purchase a Sextant with, which as Master he must have; of course as the amount bears to your whole amount to risk his proportion that he will receive from you be. Yours of 19. I received today and as I waited for it relative to the disposition of the money left for The[?] Robinson, I will act on your letter and retain it, leaving you to remit him the amount. As this vessel has cost more than the other I want all I can get.

I have bought some *bread* for ballast and hope to get to sea tomorrow. With kindest wishes believe me My dear Doctor

Very truly yours
James Fraser.

The *Alta California* of November 1, 1849, lists among vessels in port the American schooner *S. M. Fox,* Mason, which had arrived September 18, 162 days from New York. The *Alta* did not record the sailing of this vessel, but on December 31 reported the arrival on November 15 of the *"Samuel Fox"* at Lahaina from San Francisco. Most of what is known of Fraser's later history is recorded by Perkins.

The property purchased from Fraser by Theall, Perkins & Co. was Lot 68 of the later-surveyed town plat, south of Sonora Creek on what became South Washington Street. The Sonora Inn now (1964) occupies the site.

any one else. Thus when F[raser] reached these mines, he found a large settlement composed almost entirely of Mexicans, who had transported their families and effects to this place, and which received the name of the Camp of the Sonoraenses, afterwards changed to Sonora.[1]

This place soon became famous, and not only attracted the people of South America, but large numbers of Anglo-Americans; the latter principally gamblers; and when I arrived, the camp was in its glory, with a population of some five thousand people; and as it presented an appearance rarely witnessed, I shall try and describe Sonora as it was in the spring and summer of 1849; and I have no doubt there are some who may read my work in this country (South America) and will call to mind many items of my description with pleasure.

Sonora is situated in a valley of about two miles and a half in length, and about half a mile in breadth, some twenty five miles from the plains from which it is divided by isolated groups of mountains that do not attain a height of more than a couple of thousand feet, and round the bases of which a good level road runs.

A water course [Woods Creek], dry in summer, but a torrent in the wet winter months, divides the town into two parts. This water course, the same which passes by Jamestown, the first *placer* we reached on our way up, had been very thoroughly worked when I arrived, and was full of pits and diggings, already deserted, the miners having dispersed in search of richer workings, but leaving their families and establishments in the town, to which they were accustomed to return on Saturdays.

When I say the water course was thoroughly worked, I mean in appearance; we shall see what was done in the way of work, at a later date, when gold no longer was to be found on the surface, or picked out of the loose gravel with the point of a knife.

The town is surrounded by lofty mountains, and is about twenty five miles from the snowy range of the *Sierra Nevada*, whose glittering mantle shines brilliant and cold in the rays of the setting sun.

About three miles off, rises a huge round hill known by the name of Bear or Bare Mountain; whether from its bald summit or from the

---

[1] See Introduction. Contrary to Perkins' implication, relatively few Sonorans came to the gold fields by sea. As seen by the next paragraph, Perkins was writing retrospectively, after settling in Argentina in the 1860's.

grizzly bear frequenting it, I am ignorant.[2] It abounds with deer, or did at the time of which I am speaking; and I have had many a successful hunt amongst its pine-clad slopes. This mountain forms the most conspicuous feature in the landscape about Sonora, over which it looms to the height of four thousand feet. As late as the month of June, snow lies a foot thick on its northern ascent, while in the valley at its base the grass grows bright and green. The town is about three thousand feet above the level of the Pacific ocean.

Out side the line of tents and houses, and along the edges of the creek, the ground is delved, and dug, and thrown up as if some gigantic and mighty Behemoth had been rooting it up with his snout! Work that would have taken hired laborors years to accomplish, the thirst for gold, and the excitement of the search, has consummated in a few months; and what is more wonderful still, by men wholly unaccustomed to this description of toil.

When I arrived, at the commencement of June [July?], 1849, I thought I had never seen a more beautiful, a wilder or more romantic spot. The Camp, as it was then termed, was literally embowered in trees. The habitations were constructed of canvas, cotton cloth, or of upright unhewn sticks with green branches and leaves and vines interwoven, and decorated with gaudy hangings of silks, fancy cottons, flags, brilliant goods of every description; the many-tinted Mexican *Zarape,* the rich *manga,* with its gold embroidery, chinese scarfs and shawls of the most costly quality; gold and silver plated saddles, bridles and spurs were strewn about in all directions. The scene irrisistibly reminded one of the descriptions we have read of the brilliant bazaars of oriental countries. Here were to be seen goods of so costly a nature that they would hardly be out of place in Regents' Street. But what article was too costly for men who could pay for it with handfuls of gold dust, the product of a few hours labor!

Here were to be seen people of every nation in all varieties of costume, and speaking fifty different languages, and yet all mixing together amicably and socially; and probably not one in a thousand moralizing on the really extraordinary scene in which he was just as extraordinary an actor.

---

[2] Present Bald Mountain, about 8 miles north of Sonora. It has an elevation of 3,342 feet as compared with Sonora's 1,796 feet.

Here was a John Chinaman with his quilted jacket, his full blue cotton breeches reaching to the knees, and meeting the stocking-shoes with their soles an inch thick; his head covered with the peculiar cap like a small beehive, then scarcely known by Europeans, but since become a fashionable *tile* for both sexes. Under this head covering, coiled up and safely stowed away, lies the inestimable and dearly cherished pig-tail. This pig-tail is only suffered to grow from two or three inches of surface; the rest of the head is regularly shaved.

Here was a Lascar, known at once, and distinguished from the chinaman, by the more oval contour of physiognomy, the bright Madras handkerchief wound round the head, and the long *Kreese* stuck in the girdle.

And here was a *Kanacker*, or Sandwich Islander—small eyes, coarse face, and an immense shock of hair. A bright-colored calico shirt is bound about the waist with a gaudy silk sash. He wears no shoes, and his pantaloons are nothing but a pair of cotton drawers. There is a vacancy and stupidity of look about him, that contrasts unpleasantly with the intelligent-looking East Indian.

There were plenty of native Indians strolling about, many with a military jacket on, with a shirt barely covering their haunches and without pantaloons or drawers; their huge bushy head enveloped in a red handkerchief, their coarse matted hair always allowed to fall in front to the eyes and there kept cropped in a straight line.

Amongst the Mexicans, some wore only cotton drawers, a shirt and *zarape*, with a huge *sombrero* hat, black outside and lined with green; the crown decorated with large patines of silver, round and convex. Others wore the *vaquero* dress: a leathern jacket, double, with the outer surface scolloped out into fantastic patterns, showing red or blue figures on the under leather; half-tanned leathern trousers open down the leg on the outside, and adorned with rows of silver buttons; inside a pair of white cotton drawers, very wide and loose, and the leg encased to the knee in *botas* ornamented in the same manner as the jacket. In these *botas* is stuck the knife, the handle of which projects alongside of the leg, and, when the man is mounted, is most conveniently at hand. A pair of silver spurs, with rowels having the diameter of a good sized saucer, with the hat already described, complete the picture of the Mexican *vaquero* or Herdsman, (from *vaca*, cow). Others are entirely enveloped in a rich *manga*, which is a *zarape* made of fine cloth, and the space in the centre round the slit for the head to pass through, heavy with gold and silver embroidery.

The dress of the South Americans was something similar to the Mexican; but instead of the long *zarape* of the latter, they have a short one, which is called *poncho*, put over the shoulders in the same way, by means of the slit through which the head is passed. The Peruvian *poncho* is generally of thick white cotton, with colored bands along the edge; the Chilian is black, or some dark color, of thick woolen material, with red, blue, and yellow bands. The Peruvians and Chilenos, as well as the Argentinos, who appear to be the most civilized of them all, wear a heavy leather belt about six inches wide, and divided into various pockets, and in which they carry their money, their stock of tobacco, cigarrito paper and *Mechera* or tinderbox. These belts are fastened by buttons composed of silver dollars and often of gold ounces.

The dress of the saxon race was generally uniform as to shape. A pair of thick pantaloons, heavy boots worn outside the trowsers, a red or blue flannel shirt also worn outside, and gathered round the waist by a chinese *banda* or silk scarf, or a black leather belt, perhaps both; and in which a Colts' revolver was invariably stuck. As for the styles of covering for the head, their name was legion. It is scarcely possible for the imagination to conceive of any shape of hat or cap that had not its representative on the *caput* of some rough unshaven saxon, with the sole exception of the chimney-pot, black beaver; that abominable, ugly, inconvenient and yet indispensable "tile" of all civilized countries.

At the time I speak of, Sonora was probably the only place in California where numbers of the gentler sex were to be found. I have mentioned that the camp was formed by an immigration of families from Sonora, in Mexico; this accounts for the presence of women in the place.

The men had constructed brush houses and, leaving their wives and children in charge, separated in all directions in search of the richest diggings, where they would work all the week, to return to the camp and their families on Saturday, when they generally commenced gambling and drinking, and continued both until Monday, never thinking of sleep.

When Peruvian or Chilian women arrived in San Francisco, they soon found out that Sonora was the only place where their own sex were congregated in any number, and at once found their way to this vicinity. We have consequently always had an abundance of dark-skinned women amongst us, but white—none; except when some South American without much indian blood in her veins, made her appearance. These were generally *china-blancas, mestiza-claras* or *quinteras,* and they formed our aristocratic society. A lady's social position with the white gentlemen was graduated by shades of color; although we would sometimes give the preferance to a slightly brown complexion, if the race was unmixed with the negro—pure white and pure Indian. Thus the *mestiza* is a child of a white father by an Indian mother; rather dark; preferable however, to a *china-blanca,* who is the child of a white father, the mother being born of an indian father, and a negro or mulatto mother. The *quintera* is perfectly white, but comes from negro blood, through the *cuarterona* and mulatto. As for the *Zambas, Zamba-claras, chinas-oscuras, indias-mestizas* etc, they were not admitted into refined society at all!

It is evident that an intimate knowledge of ethnography was requisite to enable one to move in our society without soiling his dignity.

The dress of the women, all of them being of the spanish race, was much alike in form; the materials differing according to taste, and the ability of the person to purchase rich apparel. On Sundays, however, it seemed that the women, either Mexican or South American, white or black, all possessed the richest description of dresses. The Mexican beauty wears a rich skirt trimmed with laboriously worked flounces, satin shoes, flesh-colored silk stockings and a gloriously bespangled shawl, glittering with all the chinese arts of embroidery and colors. In the street the shawl is drawn over the head and thrown over the left shoulder, very gracefully. In the house it is worn more negligently, and the bosom is very freely exposed, as they wear no body to their dresses. In the week-days the shawl is carefully put away and a *rebosa,* a dark silk or mixed scarf, used in its stead. A Mexican woman is never seen without this universal article of costume, except when she exchanges it for a shawl.

On Saturdays and Sundays the old camp used to wear, night and day, an almost magic appearance. Besides the numberless lights from the gaily decorated houses, all of them with their fronts entirely open to the streets, the streets themselves were strown with lighted tapers.

Where there was an open space, a Mexican would take off his variegated *zarape*, lay it on the ground, put a lighted wax or sperm candle at
each corner, and pour into the centre his *pile* or stock of silver and gold.
The *zarape* would soon be surrounded by his countrymen, who, seated
on the ground, would stake and generally loose their hard-earned
weekly wages.

It would have been difficult to have taken a horse through the
crowded streets. As for wheeled carriages, they were not known as
yet.

Tables loaded with *dulces*, sweetmeats of every description, cooling
beverages, with snow from the *Sierra Nevada* floating in them, cakes
and dried fruits, hot meats, pies, every thing in the greatest abundance.
One could hardly believe in his senses, the brilliant scene appeared so
unreal and fairy-like.

On either side of the street were ranged the gambling tables,
generally covered with a rich scarlet gold embroidered cloth, in the
centre of which would be displayed a *bank* of perhaps a thousand
ounces, in silver dollars, gold doubloons or small bags of gold dust.
Coin of both metals commanded a premium of ten, fifteen and
sometimes twenty per cent, for gambling purposes in these times.

The tables belonged to the different habitations outside of which
they were placed. They were made of rough planks hewn out of logs
with an axe. There was no lumber; the head of a box a couple of feet
square was worth five or six dollars. The tables, as I have remarked,
were covered with rich cloths, thus hiding their rough material, and
would rent to a gambler for twenty, up to thirty two dollars, or two
ounces, according to their situation, per night; a table in any out of the
way place, readily commanding a nightly rental of an ounce.

Behind the gambling tables were the counters, made in the same
rough manner, and on which were ranged all kinds of liquor, which
was retailed at half a dollar per glass; and it was nothing uncommon to
see a Mexican enter, call for a bottle of brandy, which was worth an
ounce, and taking a wine glass, deliberately pour the whole contents of
the bottle into it, spilling of course all that the glass would not contain.
The bottle being empty and the wine-glass full, he would swallow its
contents with all the pride and satisfaction accompanying an ostentatious act.

The game always played was *Monte,* the great national game of

Mexico; and the Yankees soon became expert hands at it, and made such immense sums by it that it became a temptation too strong to be resisted, and hundreds of young men of respectable families, men who in their own home, would never have dreamed of entering a gambling house, became in California gamblers, then black-legs and soon ruffians and murderers.

There is no path of rectitude or virtue open to the gambler; he is like the unfortunates of the other sex; always descending; continually sinking lower in the slough of degradation. His very occupation makes him a Pariah, and he soon comes to look on all mankind as his natural prey, until the community he so often outrages takes the law into its own hands and rids itself of the nuisance by violence. Such is the history of most of the gamblers of California.

To return to my description of the town. Almost every house had its band of music, such as it was. Some of the Mexicans display considerable talent in the art, and some bands, composed of a clarionet, a harp and a base guitar, did much credit to their members.

Mission Indians, with scarlet bandanas round their heads, a richly colored *zarape* over their shoulder, a pair of cotton drawers, and bare-footed, would push their way through the crowd, carrying pails of iced liquor on their heads, crying in the shrill falsetto voice peculiar to most of the savage tribes, *"agua fresca, agua fresca, cuatro reales."*

Behind portable kitchens, were Mexican and Indian women, in their picturesque costumes, their head covered with the omnipresent *rebosa* occupied in making the national dish of meat and chile pepper, wrapped within two *tortillas* of wheaten flour, a delicacy for which the Mexican *peon* would sell his birthright.

Tortilla is the Spanish name for pancake, or thin cake of any material, but in Mexico a *tortilla* is a peculiar and delicate corn bread, which in my trip through that country, I learnt to appreciate.[3]

---

[3] Perkins explains: "A *tortilla* is made from bruised maize in this manner: A quantity of corn is washed and placed in a wooden trough in a strong solution of ashes, where it is allowed to remain for twenty hours; it is then taken out and washed repeatedly in clean rain water. Its color is now a brilliant yellow, and it is quite soft. It is then mashed between a large stone and a smaller one, worked by the hands, moistened occasioned [occasionally] with water, and as the paste works off fine enough, it is taken and patted into thin cakes, and placed on thin iron plates over live coals. The cakes must be eaten hot, as they become tough when cold."

An infernal noise was kept up all night, both by instruments and voices. The Indians are very fond of singing, and will sit in a circle for hours, chaunting the most unearthly music, and keeping their throats moist by constant draughts of *aguardiente*.

The noise of drums, guitars, fiddles, and the ringing metalic thrum of the little Mexican lute, never for a moment ceased from Saturday to Monday, but never disturbing however, for an instant the absorbing occupation of the ruffian-looking American gambler, or the easy, careless Spanish player, who puts down his four, five or ten ounces on a card, and looses or wins with admirable equanimity of temper.

In some less crowded spot, might be witnessed the national dances of the Spaniards. That of the Mexicans is simple but energetic. On a board about six feet long and ten or twelve inches broad, you may see a couple, fronting each other; the man with the perspiration streaming from every pore, executing the genuine "hoe-down" of the Virginia nigger, but with even more energy (if not with so much skill), than his more joyous rival of the States. It soon becomes a matter of competition between the dancer and the musicians, as to who gives in first; and there is often a lively vitality in the former's legs, when the latter's arms and lungs are in a state of complete exhaustion. The movements of the woman during all this time, are tame, and unexcited, being nothing more than a mere shuffling of the feet, and a piroutte now and then.

CHAPTER V

Such as I have endeavoured to describe it in the last chapter was the camp of the Sonoraenses, afterwards called Sonora, when the town became organized under American laws.

The winter months set in, and the scene changed as if by enchantment. Most of the Sonoraenses, fearful of the cold in these high latitudes, comparatively speaking, either returned to their country or made their way to diggings farther south, about *Mariposa* and King's

River.[1] The Yankees now poured into the town, and God knows they soon destroy every thing in the shape of romance.

The *ramadas* or brush houses, and the gay tents were all pulled down, and ugly *adobe*, or rough-hewn log huts were erected in their stead. The fronts of the habitations, once gay with streaming flags, and decorated branches, were changed to gloomy looking architecture, and the place changed its aspect of an Eastern encampment or bazaar, to that of a dirty American country town.

Some time after my recovery from the dangerous attack I have mentioned, and made arrangements with my friend T[heall] to enter into business, I was obliged to take a trip to the Estanislao river,[2] to see after a lot of goods that we had purchased.

I took my Irish boy with me, and provisions and coffee for some time, as in those days there was no such thing as road-side inns. The usual plan was to picket out the horses or mules, build a fire, make a cup of coffee and roll oneself up in a blanket, with the saddle for a

---

[1] These diggings were discovered in the spring of 1849, as related by J. H. Carson in the Introduction. In a note Perkins says concerning Mariposa: "This word means butterfly in the spanish language; and the district received the name from Col. Fremonts people, who found there, besides rich gold quartz mines, numbers of large blue and gold butterflies. Col. Fremont afterwards got a large grant in this district from the U. S. government; a grant that has caused great troubles in Mariposa, as it was said to interfere with what, with laughable impudence, were termed 'miner's rights.' "

The Mariposa area was granted in 1844 to Juan Bautista Alvarado, governor of California from 1836 to 1840. He never actually occupied the grant; and it had not even been formally located and surveyed when Alvarado sold it to Frémont in February, 1847. By the time Frémont returned to California, early in 1849, gold had been discovered, and he was influenced by this circumstance in determining the bounds of his grant. Prolonged litigation ended with the confirmation of the grant in 1855. See C. G. Crampton, "The Opening of the Mariposa Mining Region, 1849–1855" (doctoral dissertation, University of California, Berkeley, 1941).

It is interesting that Perkins does not mention as one factor in the departure of Sonorans from "the camp of the Sonoraenses" the rising feeling in the gold region against foreigners.

[2] In his book, Perkins consistently calls the Stanislaus River the Estanislao. History is on his side, for the river acquired this name during the 1820's through identification with a runaway Mission Indian known to the California authorities as Estanislao, whose rancheria was in the vicinity of Knights Ferry on the Stanislaus. After his death, José Jesus became the principal chief, surviving into Perkins' time. For an informal account, see Edna Bryan Buckbee, *The Saga of Old Tuolumne*, pp. 1–16.

pillow; and to tyros I would add that no pillow can be more comfortable. All sublinary cares are soon forgotten after a hard day's ride.

The atmosphere of this country is so exquisitely pure; the nights so entirely free from moisture, that no possible harm can arise from exposure: that is, no sickness, no colds, no rhumatism. True, I have been at times obliged to drive away two or three *Tarántulas* from the spot I desired to spread my blankets on, and sometimes I have found out in the morning that I had been sleeping all night on a nest of centepedes. But one easily accustoms himself to these petty dangers, and I have never met a man as yet, who had been bitten by the above named venemous reptiles.

Two days journey brought us to our place of destination; a wild and beautiful spot, miles and miles away from any human habitation, although on the direct route from Stockton to the rich mines of Mariposa, south of King's River.

I found here the goods I had come to look after, in a good strong brush house, open however to the road, or rather track. Here I lived in perfect solitude, save when travellers past, for two weeks, selling off the stock to the miners in the mountains. At night the hut used to be surrounded by prairee wolves [coyotes], and I had often to get up and drive them off by building large fires, and firing my pistols repeatedly at them. Their yelling is most intolerable. Two or three of these animals will make such an infernal noise, that a person not accustomed to hear them would suppose he was listening to a pack of at least twenty.

On two occasions we were visited by grizzly bear, which had been probably drawn to the spot by the smell of the jerked beef hanging from lines extended between trees. These visitors we were glad enough to let have altogether their own way, without disturbance whatever on our part, and I acknowledge to a considerable fright on each occasion.

For three days we had a tribe of the Mountain Indians [3] encamped in front of the house; so that what with these, and Mexican cut-

---

[3] The Indians who frequented this country were a linguistic group known as the Interior Miwok, for the most part a foothill people living on the slope of the Sierra above the San Joaquin Valley, from the Cosumnes to the Fresno. The central division occupied the drainage basins of the Stanislaus and Tuolumne rivers; see A. L. Kroeber, *Handbook of the Indians of California*, Bureau of American Ethnology Bulletin 78 (Washington, 1925).

throats, who had already appeared in the country, the grizzly bears and the wolves, my nightly slumbers were none of the most peaceful; and I was glad enough to make a present of the last few ounces worth of goods and return to Sonora.

I was fated to have another interview with a member of the Bruin family. The first night we camped in a beautiful little hollow, clear of underbrush, and with evergreen oaks growing here and there.

We tethered our mules out with our long lassos, made a fire and a strong pot of coffee, and after our frugal meal, spread our blankets in the centre of the hollow, in the light of an unclouded moon.

The night was deliciously calm and balmy. My boy had fallen asleep and I was still enjoying the fumes of some genuine Virginia leaf, when my attention was drawn towards the entrance of our little hollow by a peculiar sound. Gently raising my head, I saw at the distance of about fifty paces, a huge bear; at least he appeared as huge, to me, as an elephant, but perhaps fear put a pair of magnifying glasses on my nose. However, there was a grizzly, scraping away energetically at an ant-hill, and licking up mouthfuls of the savoury insects with great apparent gusto. My heart beat rather painfully. I knew what fearful brutes these are when brought into immediate contact with man, but I knew likewise that they seldom go out of their way to attack a man, unless in the case of a she-bear with her cubs. I did not wake the boy, but gazing quietly round, I singled out a tree into which we might easily climb if the bear, after finishing his meal, should make his way towards us. I waited in sufficient trepidation, I must confess, for more than half an hour, which appeared at least five to me; at the end of this time the bear quietly walked off in a direction opposite to where we were camped. I did not sleep much that night, I can assure my readers.

Two weeks after I left my rancho in the mountains, it became the scene of a terrible catastrophe in which one of my acquaintances, a grizzly bear, was the principal actor. The following are the circumstances.

Three hunters, arriving one evening at my deserted brush house, made themselves comfortable there for the night. The next morning one of them, on going outside, discovered a bear in the bushes on the opposite side of the level ground in front of the hut. The men all took their rifles, and, creeping quietly to within a couple of hundred yards of the animal, each got up into a tree to wait for an opportunity for a shot. The bear was a female, and accompanied by a pair of cubs, and consequently excessively dangerous; for under these circumstances these brutes will attack any thing with a blind and terrible fury. On other occasions, as I have said, they will rather shun a man, unless brought to close quarters, when they become formidable antagonists to any number of assailants.

One of the men, becoming impatient, cautiously descended from his perch and, making signs to his companions, acquainting them of his intentions, crept into the bushes and gained a position in closer proximity to the animal, but where there was no friendly tree at hand to fly to in case of peril. His companions now fired, to draw the attention of the bear towards themselves, and she immediately rushed out of the brushwood, followed by her two cubs. She was slightly wounded and, savagely sniffing the air, seemed seeking the quarter whence came the blow. At this instant, the man in the bushes, pushing his way gently towards the open space to get an opportunity of firing, drew the attention of the enraged brute, either by the scent or by the movement of the branches, as the hunter cautiously pushed his way through them. With a sharp growl she rushed on him. A yell of horror from his companions informed him of his peril. His only hope was in his rifle. In an instant he was out on the edge of the plain, and had only time to raise and fire his piece. Vain shot! The next moment he was seized and literally torn to fragments by the infuriated beast. The bear seemed to take a savage delight in lacerating the body. She would sometimes retire twenty or thirty paces, pause, and then suddenly returning, attack the body of her victim with fresh fury. This she did repeatedly, seeming anxious to improve the opportunity of giving her young brood a lesson.

The two survivors state that during this scene the bear was out of the range of their rifles, but the probability is they were so shocked and scared by the awful fate of their companion, that they were glad to remain concealed until the animal, tired of mutilating the body, should retire. This she did at the end of a couple of hours, followed by her interesting offspring, with their muzzles red with their sanguinary pastime.

The men made the best of their way to a settlement, leaving the remains of their unfortunate comrade where he met his fate. A company was immediately formed, which set out in pursuit of the bear; and, burying the poor hunter's body, the men followed the animal up, and finally succeeded in killing her, capturing one of the cubs alive. The grizzly when skinned, was found to have received seventeen rifle bullets in its carcass, proving the thickness of skin, and the extraordinary tenacity of life, of these monsters of the *Sierra Nevada*.[4]

---

[4] Annals of the Sierra Nevada during the 1850's are replete with tales of the grizzlies. The California grizzly has now for many years been extinct, though the State still supports a considerable population of black bears.

CHAPTER VI

From this epoch, my reminiscences will take the form of a Journal, as by this means I shall be better able to depict the daily, weekly and monthly events which checkered my life in California, and which I shall take from the copious notes I jotted down under the influence of the actual circumstances.

I must premise by stating that my experience in actual digging has been very limited, and what little work I have performed in that line was more for amusement than profit. I had no sooner arrived in the mines, than I decided to turn my attention to commerce in preference to mining, which entailed an amount of labor and personal suffering I was entirely unwilling to encounter.

To commence then with my Journal.

JANUARY 1850. Our house is built of *adobes*,[1] and is surmounted by a large sign-board, painted by myself. The house boasts of two glazed windows, the sash of which is also of home manufacture, made with no other tools save a saw and a pocket knife. No other building in the town can boast of such luxury, and they are the envy and admiration of all our neighbors. It is consequently a pardonable vanity of T[heall]

---

[1] "The Mexican *adobe*," says Perkins in a note, "is a large sun-dried brick. Its usual size is eighteen inches by ten or twelve, and four inches thick. A house built of these bricks and protected from the rain by lime plaster lasts as long as stone."

and myself, if we spend half an hour daily outside the store in admiring our handy-work. The shelves, counters and doors are all made with our own hands. A tin, or rather sheet-iron stove, with copper sheathing pipe, stands in a corner, and I, at least, have the right to look with complacency on the treasure. The history of the copper pipe is worth relating.

The rains had set in early in November, and so much water fell that the roads became entirely flooded and cut up. It was impossible to traverse them even on horseback, for the virgin soil became so saturated and spongy that a horse would sink to the belly in almost any part of the route between the mines and Stockton.[2]

Two of our teams had been weather-bound at the river, a distance of forty miles, and, as there was no hope of getting them through until spring, I had to walk down to where they were, and dispose of their contents.

The tin stove we had already received at a cost of one hundred dollars. The pipe was in the unfortunate waggons, stuck in the mud at the river.

I managed to dispose of the merchandize to the Ferry boat company, and the copper pipe I shouldered with my blankets. My first Christmas in California I spent up to the knees in mud with ten feet of stove pipe strapped to my pair of blankets. I could not help laughing at the figure I cut, and at what the good folks at home, rejoicing in all the festivities of the season, would have said, had they had a glass of such majic power as would have presented me to their eyes. Lord! how tired and jaded I was after walking some forty miles with my load, between daylight and nine o'clock at night. I thought, on arriving home, that Sonora was the most charming place in the world; one of the peacefullest of resting-places for the *heavy-ladened.*

Alongside the stove, to keep them dry, is a large pile of blankets, for our bedding. These we spread on the earthen floor of our house, as lumber is not to be had to make bunks or flooring. The roof is of canvas and, I am sorry to say, not quite water-proof, which puts us at times to no little inconvenience; but we are so comparatively comfortable that it would be a downright shame to complain.

---

[2] In 1849 the rains set in November 12. A hard, wet winter followed. Sacramento was beset by a historic flood in January, and all the lowlands had the quagmire character Perkins describes.

I will note down here the prices current at this epoch, premising that goods of all descriptions are much cheaper than they were at the time of my arrival in June, last year. Flour, seventy five cents, per pound; Pork or Bacon, one dollar; Sugar, one dollar; Nails, two dollars (these nails, by the bye cost us in San Francisco five cents per pound, and for freight, thirty cents more, leaving a pretty decent profit). Butter, four dollars per pound; a pair of shoes, twelve dollars; Rice, seventy five cents; Nutmegs, half a dollar each; Champagne, eight dollars the bottle; Salt, one dollar per pound; Sperm candles, six dollars per pound; Lard, three dollars; Writing-paper, one rial per sheet; A bottle of Lemon Syrup, six dollars; a tin pint cup, one dollar and a quarter. The cost of carriage on most of these articles has been from thirty to forty cents per pound.

Once the winter has set in we have had few days without rain. The natives say it is an extraordinary season, and believe it is because of the presence of the Yankees in the country.

It is wonderful the amount of good order there is in the mines, and the almost perfect security with which people leave merchandise exposed night and day. But I fear that as gold becomes more difficult to procure, or when what is produced will have to be divided into smaller portions, the state of society will become very bad. At the present time, however, the precious metal is too easily earned. People have not yet commenced to jostle each other in any of the various paths to fortune, and there is no incentive to petty crime and apparently no disposition for great ones.

The average of rows is not so numerous by any means as upon any line of canal or rail-road in the United States. True there is greater loss of life; this is because the weapons differ. In settled countries men do not, in general, carry deadly weapons about their persons; in fits of rage they either pick up the first object that meets the hand, or else use their fists; in either case the probability is that life is not endangered.

Here, every white man is armed, and, I may say, every one; for those who do not carry pistols, the Mexicans and natives, always have formidable knives; so that when a row takes place, the aggregate of injury is not so great perhaps as in similar cases in other countries, but individual instances are more fatal.

Since my arrival here, three Mexicans and one white man have been killed in street-fights; but we have not yet heard of a single cold-blooded murder having been committed, and considering the strange heterogeneous crowd we have on these "diggings," and the many temptations offered by the hoards of gold possessed by so many miners, this absence of crime, when so much might be gained by crime, is wonderful.

The laws, such as they are, have been respected. The Government is an Alcalde, an official that the Mexicans are taught from childhood, to respect and such a fair character does Sonora possess for equal distribution of justice to Spaniard as well as to the white man, that this town has always been the favorite resort of Mexicans, Chilenos, Peruvianos and Californians.[3]

The office of Alcalde is elective, and he is Judge and Jury in civil as well as in criminal cases. This office will, of course, be abolished when the Government shall be organized on the United States' system.[4]

---

[3] "When I make use of the term 'Spaniard' in contra-distinction to that of 'white man,'" Perkins writes, "I must be understood as referring to the lower orders of Mexico and South America, who being a mixture of indian and spanish races, are generally very dark; the better classes of the same people are often as fair as we are; and amongst the Spaniards proper, red hair, blue eyes, and fair complexion are by no means rare; and there is no reason they should be, when we remember that spaniards [several words lost from manuscript] with Moorish blood has only been partial."

[4] Sometime in the autumn of 1849 H. W. Theall, who had succeeded Fraser as alcalde, gave way to Charles F. Dodge, who served until the organization of Tuolumne County on May 13, 1850. According to Heckendorn & Wilson's *Miners and Business Men's Directory*, pp. 37–38, "On the 7th, of Nov. 1849, the citizens of Sonora organized themselves into a town government, mainly with a view of providing a Hospital for the sick. . . . The first Town Council consisted of C. F. Dodge, Joshua Holden, C. Labetoure, Peter Mehen, E. Linoberg, J. B. Litton, Wm. Perkins, and ———

"They ordered a survey of the town into lots and streets by Cooper and Galledge, whose map was, for a long time, the official chart by which all disputed lines were settled. When it was decided at San Jose that Sonora was to be the county seat, Col. Freaner immediately dispatched a letter to Joshua Holden informing him of the fact, and advising him to confide the secret to only a few who should take up as many lots as possible in order to speculate on them, as he supposed they would soon become valuable. Instead of complying with his advice, Mr. Holden laid the matter before the Town Council that same evening, and they passed a resolution unanimously that no one should be permitted to take up vacant lots, but that all unoccupied lots should belong to the Town as

At this moment there is a great amount of sickness among the Mexicans. Intemperance and exposure in a climate so much colder than their own, added to a total ignorance of medicinal remedies, are carrying them off in great numbers.

On the ninth of this month, the principal people got up a public meeting to take into consideration the state of the indigent sick of Sonora. A thousand dollars were subscribed for at once, and an Hospital has been erected, and the sick of all nations are tended by nurses and a good physician.[5]

The common complaint is an ulcerating of the legs, and is the most obstinate disease I have ever witnessed. It is a species of scurvy, but seems to disappear with warmth of temperature. There were no cases

---

such, and be sold to the highest bidder. The money derived from the sale of lots was devoted partly towards paying for the survey, and the rest towards defraying Hospital expenses."

The second issue of the *Stockton Times*, March 23, 1850, reports in this connection: "The common council of the town of Sonora (formerly the Sonorian camp) have accepted the proposal of Mr. Cooper, to survey the town lots unoccupied within the limits of the said town. We understand that the common council will sell the above at public auction as soon as possible, for the improvement of the town. The following named gentlemen are officers of the town of Sonora:

"C. F. Dodge, 1st Justice of Peace, and chairman of the council; J. Holdings; E. Linoberg, J. B. Litlen, Labator, Williams Prendis [*i.e.,* William Perkins], councilmen."

Carlo M. De Ferrari has pointed out that although a legal document of February, 1850, shows that a "Common Council of the town of Sonora" then existed, Mehen and Perkins do not appear as members.

[5] According to Heckendorn & Wilson, as quoted in the preceding note, also quoted by T. R. Stoddart in his *Annals,* the sickly state of the camp was the reason for organizing the town on November 7, a date Perkins gives as the 9th. Stoddart says that a total of $779 was raised—"a small sum to build up a Public Hospital for those days. Yet small as it was, the [Relief] committee did not despair, but began to carry out this noble work. It soon became evident that the building was totally unsuited to the exigencies of the time, and measures were at once taken to erect a better building for the accommodation of the sick. Nor was it a w[h]it too soon, as numbers were brought in daily, many of whom died from sheer want of the necessaries and comforts of civilized life. Laws were therefore passed, among which was one making provision for raising money for the accruing expenses by ordering the town lots to be sold; but this not proving sufficient to defray the bills, a few citizens generously stepped forward and paid heavy sums out of their private purses, in order that this humane institution should not be closed for want of funds." Stoddart prints some of the hospital bills, dated between January and March, 1850.

during the summer. The disease is not caused by debauchery of any kind; it appears to be more the effect of exposure of the naked limbs in stagnant and putrid waters, the blood becoming tainted in this manner; and probably caused in part too, by the want of fresh vegetables. The only food to be had in the mines is fresh beef, salt pork, and beans at least a couple of years old. The Americans make a kind of tough bread, or rather say, fried dough. We are somewhat more fortunate. The good Captain [Engers] of the "Juana and Oluffa," who had commenced his sea-life as cook, taught me, during the voyage from Mazatlán to San Francisco, to make an excellent bread with a little carbonate of soda and tartaric acid; and as my medicine chest contains the necessary ingredients, I make, two or three times a week, a batch of bread that would not disgrace the table of an English farm house.

Apart from the disease I have mentioned, there is not much sickness except that produced by intemperance. The most common and fatal result, however, of drunkeness is falling into some of the thousands of deep pits, dug during the summer by the miners, and now full of water. Scarcely a week passes that two or three bodies be not fished out of these holes; a fact not to [be] wondered at when we remember that the Mexicans and Indians spend the Saturday night, Sunday and following night in a continual state of inebriety.

I was out the other day with a party of five, in chase after a grizzly bear, that had come down from the mountains and was seen in the vicinity of a Rancho, about two miles from the town. We saw nothing of the brute, *fortunately* (?) He was tracked the day after by a couple of Americans, who did come upon him, *unfortunately,* for the beast attacked them after having received two rifle balls in his carcass, and wounded and lacerated both of the men in a shocking manner. One of them is since dead, and the other is maimed for life.

On the twentieth we weighed our stock of gold-dust; found just a quarter of a hundredweight; and we lent out two thousand five hundred dollars at the rate of ten per cent interest per month; a pretty good business, *if we only had enough of it,* but nothing compared to similar operations last year. We then used to lend specie dollars at two per cent *a day, with gold dust for security.*

But those times have gone, never to return. It is not much more than eight months ago, when a man by the name of Savage, one of the early settlers in California, had a whole tribe of mountain Indians at work in Jamestown, a few miles from Sonora. The rule that he adopted reminds one of the story of the old Pennsylvania Dutchman, who used his hand for a pound weight. Savage used to put his raisins and other delicacies in one scale, and make his workmen balance them with gold dust! The latter was then worth eight silver dollars the ounce; now it is worth fifteen.[6]

JANUARY 20. Today, a piece of pure gold, weighing twenty two pounds, two ounces, was dug out by three Mexicans a few yards from our house. They sold it immediately and divided the amount. For one whole week without intermission, will these poor devils drink and gamble, at the end of which time it is highly probable none of them will have a cent left. Mexicans believe, as a general rule, that gold was created for gambling, silver for dress and women, and copper for food.[7]

---

[6] James Savage was a turbulent character, who came overland to California in 1846. Although he frankly exploited the Indians, it was not an Indian but a county judge, Walter Harvey, who shot him to death in August, 1852. A summary sketch of his life is provided by Annie R. Mitchell in *Jim Savage and the Tulareño Indians* (Los Angeles, 1957). His experiences from 1847 to 1850 merit fuller investigation.

[7] In its first issue, March 15, 1850, the *Stockton Times* gave an account of "The Sonorian Lump of Gold": "We have seen the eighth wonder of the world! We have held in our hands the Sonorian lump of gold, weighing 22 lbs. 6 oz. . . . During the month of January . . . , three Sonorian Mexicans were following their mining pursuits in the arroyo of the town of Sonora, and discovered this 'pile'; but they (possessing rather erratic tempers, being flushed with their wonderful success, and stout devotees of the rosy God) in a few days had squandered the whole amount in 'riotous living.' The piece afterwards fell into the hands of our worthy friends, the firm of Linoberg & Co., of Sonora, who sold it again for a considerable amount to Messrs. Alonzo Green and Joshua Holding [Holden], Merchants, of the same place, for a very high premium. To our own knowledge, these gentlemen have again been offered $2000 for it above its intrinsic value. It is estimated that there are about 4 lbs. of common quartz mixed up with the precious metal, as is generally the case in large specimens." For further comment by Perkins, see his first letter signed "Leo," reprinted in the Appendix from the *Stockton Times* of March 30, 1850.

John S. Hittell, *Mining in the Pacific States of North America* (San Francisco, 1861), p. 48, gives an admittedly incomplete list of nuggets found in the Sonora area between 1850 and 1858, his information derived from the columns of the *Alta California*. Sonora, as he says, "was the richest place in California for nuggets," though Columbia and other nearby localities come within his definition of Sonora.

When gold is found pure near the surface, it is nearly always blackened, as if by strong heat, and would be passed by without notice, as an ordinary black stone, were it not for its weight.

When it is found at greater depths, and in the beds of streams it wears its true color, a shining yellow. In quartz it is still more bright. The difference in the color of gold found in distinct districts is curious. The Sonora gold is dullish; the Calaveras gold is almost black, while that from Tuolumne and Mariposa is in brilliant and thin scales.

27TH. The weather has changed; from the cold, rainy and wretched temperature of a wet winter, we have suddenly the agreeable change to warm and beautiful sunshine.

Who has not experienced the glorious exhilaration of a bright, balmy spring morning after weeks of chills and damps?

The appearance of the country is by no means wintry. The hills are covered with pine trees and live oaks, that retain their verdure all the year round; and the grass in the valleys is green and bright. In a few more weeks the shrubs, and trees, and flowers will be coming out in their spring holiday attire. The sun has brought out the lazy and invalid greasers,[8] who with their dirty and variegated *zarapes* have stretched themselves in the warm sunshine where ever the street offers a dry spot of ground. Mexican girls are tripping about with white and yellow satin shoes, but have not yet ventured to display their silk stockings. Satin shoes, on otherwise bare feet, is half dress. For full dress the indispensable flesh (white flesh) colored silk stockings.

This evening a call was made upon my medicine chest for a bottle of hartshorn, to find out if life still existed in the body of a drunken Mexican, who had just been taken out of one of the man-traps of water, I have mentioned in another place. I went at once to see the poor fellow, and found him with life completely extinct.

31ST. After a couple of days of cheering weather came suddenly a storm of rain that threatened in one night to carry off the whole town. Ye Gods! how it did come down; something in the fashion of the young deluges I have heard mention tumble down in Central America. T[heall] and I were sleeping in a tent behind the house, and we were

---

[8] "A nickname the Americans, during the war with Mexico, gave to the half-breed lower orders" (Perkins).

awakened by being actually washed out of our beds by a torrent that had made its way through a neighboring house.

CHAPTER VII

FEBRUARY FIRST. A party of Mexicans, well armed, passed through the town today in pursuit of some Indians who have committed several outrages in our vicinity lately. If the belligerents meet, I expect the Mexicans will get pretty well "licked" for they are the most cowardly wretches I know of. They will butcher in cold blood, but any thing like resistance always scares them.

SECOND. Last night a small party of Indians came down from the mountains and actually entered the town, broke into a *corral* and, after murdering a Mexican in charge of the animals, escaped driving off seven mules. This is temerity to be visited with swift vengeance, if we desire to sleep in security; so a call for volunteers was made at once, and there being three stout men in our establishment, we felt in honor bound to send one, and although a tramp up into the snowy mountains at this season of the year is not to be envied, with magnanimous loyalty, I volunteered. I put my blankets and a bag of provisions on a mule, provided myself with lots of ammunition and a "Mississippi yager," stuck a heavy bowie knife in the leg of one of my boots, put a plug of cavendish in my pocket and a short pipe in the bosom of my thick red flannel shirt, and was ready for a start.

We were all on foot, with three mules to carry the blankets and provisions, as we should be obliged to climb mountains, when any weight would necessarily impede our progress. We struck the trail of our Indian marauders about three miles from town; here we found it broad and well marked, and about twelve hours old. About ten miles further we came up with our Mexican friends who had passed through Sonora the day before. They had also struck the trail, some hours before us, but were too timid to follow it into the mountains. However, on seeing a company of eighteen well armed white men, they were inspired with a new and wonderful zeal, and followed us with a great show of courage.

The first night we encamped in a romantic and beautiful little valley, where an American by the name of Lewis[1] had put up a tent and had commenced the cultivation of a small patch of garden land; which promises to furnish us with a few vegetables this summer, of which we stand so much in need.

The Indians had passed about two hundred yards to the north of Lewis' garden, and here one of the mules had got away from them and was caught by Lewis the following morning, and secured in his *corral*.

He told me how he managed to catch the animal, and how in doing so he had received a kick in the face, which *en passant* I noticed was considerably swollen, and added seriously:

"It was fortunate for me that the wet had softened the hoof of the brute; otherwise I should have been killed."

The first time I ever heard of such a case of self-congratulation.

The next day we were off at daylight, and struck at once into the mountains; not into the passes, but following the trail step for step, through the most difficult route, the snow being in many places up to our knees.

About twelve o'clock, ten of our Mexican companions gave up, and took the "back track." We kept on and in a couple of hours came upon a deserted Indian rancho. The trail here crossed a mountain stream, swollen by the late heavy rains. How the savages had got the mules across this torrent is more than I can say. We were obliged to make a bridge. The mountains beyond this stream were very difficult to surmount, and the Indians seem to have taken the most inaccessible passages, in order to evade pursuit. It was tremendous work for Christians, but we trudged along bravely.

We camped that night on the north fork of the Estanislao, in a dell so deep and overhung with such mighty piles of nature's masonry, that at mid-day the sun's rays could only have made a sort of twilight.

---

[1] James R. Lewis voted in the Sonora election on August 1, 1849. M. Lewis at Sonora joined in signing a petition to the California legislature in the spring of 1850. Lewis' garden would seem to have been about three miles east of Sonora, on the upper end of Sullivans Creek, an area now covered by Phoenix Lake.

Long after the moon rose, and the heavens above us were bathed in light, our camp was lighted only by the huge fire we built to keep off the bears and the cold.

Here we discovered the disagreeable fact that half of our party had started without provisions, and those who had been more provident had to share with all, and there was very little left for the journey. At the time, this did not alarm us, as we hoped to be able to kill venison enough for the party. In this, however, we were entirely disappointed, on account of the utter impossibility of following the deer up the steep mountains.

The next morning we were again on the march by daylight, and were four hours climbing the mountain that bordered the river. Once on the top we found the trail running along the ridge, and as the Indians generally place their towns on the highest ridges, we surmised that the ranch belonging to the marauding party we were in pursuit of, could not be very distant. We therefore sent out our best men as scouts in order to discover the town and bring us word, so that we might take it by surprise.

After a six hours march one of our scouts brought us the welcome intelligence that the town we were looking for was only half a mile distant. We halted and made the necessary preparations, and then marched on in the strictest silence.

Suddenly on turning an abrupt angle of a huge pile of rocks, we came upon a large *Rancheria*, consisting of more than a hundred well built huts in the shape of beehives. In the centre was the council house, also used as a sweating or *medicine* house, about fifty feet in circumference.

On the opposite side was a sloping hill at the foot of which ran a stream of water.

The alarm had been already given, and the hill was covered with men, women and children, the latter running like deer, while the men with their bows and arrows stood their ground; but the first volley of rifle bullets was too much for them. The affair did not last more than five minutes. I did not fire my rifle more than three times. We were too much fatigued to follow the agile rascals. Some of the most active of the scouts followed the enemy for two or three miles, and the reverberation of their rifle shots was heard now and them; some time after we were in quiet possession of the town.

The tribes of Indians inhabiting these mountains, are called Root-Diggers, and are the most wretched of all North American Indians. They are about four feet high, with very large heads and huge shocks of hair, coarse and black. Their limbs are very small; their legs are no larger than the arm of a moderate size man. Their feet are ridiculously small, and their hands and fingers long and exceedingly thin and slender. They go entirely naked even in the severe region in which they reside, and subsist on roots, acorns, berries and the small edible part of the pine cone, which is found in great abundance in all the mountains of California.[2]

These Indians are not the depredators on the white settlements; but they harbor, in large numbers, the "Mission Indians," of the lower country, who are much more daring, and are physically rather a fine bodied race. They have been, and are, very prejudicial to the settlements, robbing mules and horses and even murdering the solitary miner. They carry their plunder to the almost inaccessible fastnesses of the Root-Diggers, with whom they share, receiving in return hospitality, and the coarse provisions of their allies.[3]

In our conflict with the Indians even in the heat of the combat, we were anxious to avoid killing the Root-Diggers; aiming only at those Indians whom we noticed with dresses on, as the lower country Indian always wears some piece of clothing or finery, if it be only a red handkerchief round his head, or a colored calico shirt.

I know that for my part, I was very much shocked and pained on seeing two or three bodies of these poor wretched Root-Diggers, who had probably been shot by the Mexicans, who are not scrupulous in the matter of bloodshed.

The meat of the six mules was already hanging on the branches of the trees along with that of others stolen before. It is something strange

---

[2] Perkins' ethnology is rather shaky. The term Digger, or Root-Digger, was applicable to most Indians living among the mountains and in the deserts of the West. Usually Diggers were Indians of Shoshonean linguistic stock; but here they would have been Miwoks, as noted in chapter v.

[3] By "Mission Indians" Perkins refers to the Indians who had been kept in a condition more or less of peonage at the various California missions until secularization in 1831. There had been many runaways even before that time, leading to periodic military expeditions by Spanish and Mexican authorities into the San Joaquin Valley. The lot of the Indians was not improved by the secularization of the missions; many were simply taken over by the California land owners, along with the mission lands.

that these Indians prefer mule flesh to any other, as the Pampa Indians of Buenos Aires prefer that of mares.

We had eaten nothing all day, but a few berries picked from the bushes on the way; so it may be believed we were a hungry "crowd." I roasted a piece of mule flesh but found it as tough as an old shoe. On looking about, however, I found the hind leg of a dog, skinned, and ready for the spit, with the hair left on the paw. This *was* a prize. I roasted it and had a repast fit for a Canadian, or a King.

Dog-flesh is delicate and has very much the flavor of veal to which it is nothing inferior. To me it was not new, as I had eaten the delicate flesh of the Sandwich Island dog, reared on purpose for the table.

We found in the *Rancheria* a large quantity of stolen clothes; plenty of handsomely made baskets; immense quantities of acorns and pine cones, with bread made from the pounded flour of the two latter. This bread we tried to eat, but found it exceedingly disgusting to the palate; bitter, and with a flavor that was nauseous in the extreme.

Collecting every thing moveable, we piled all in the ranchos, and set fire to the whole town, in imitation of the warriors of the middle ages.

After the excitement of the fray had subsided, I could not help asking myself the question, as to how far we were warranted in destroying life and property to such an extent; for although the value of property destroyed probably did not amount to much, still it was the whole amount of worldly goods possessed by the tribe. The houses, we may readily believe, have as great a value, comparatively speaking, to their owners, as ours in Sonora. Their baskets, and above all their supply of provisions, may certainly be placed on a par with our household goods. And we had invaded and destroyed the lives and property of these poor, miserable people, to chastise what in their eyes is no crime.

To say the truth, I was not entirely satisfied with myself. For the loss of life amongst the Mission Indians I did not feel much compunction; for they are a bad set, and the indisputable law of self-preservation, if not entirely a satisfactory warrant, suffices at all events, to pacify the conscience. But in this case, not only did Root-Diggers fall in the conflict, but the women and children suffered from the loss of their homes and necessaries of life.

Stern necessity of pioneer life! We invade a land that is not our own, we arrogate a right through pretense of superior intelligence and the wants of civilization, and if the aborigines dispute our title, we destroy them!

We camped in a meadow some few hundred yards from the burnt Rancheria; and gathering a quantity of dried grass I made a comfortable bed. We had to keep a strict guard, as the Indians surrounded us in great numbers all night, but did not dare to attack us. Notwithstanding the dangerous position we were in, after I had stood my guard, I wrapped myself in my blankets and slept like a top.

The next morning the first dawning of day saw us in march. Taking a fresh trail, after four or five hours travelling, we came upon another large Rancheria. The inhabitants had received intelligence during the night of the invasion and had decamped, taking off every thing moveable. We burnt all that remained, that is to say, the houses.

The Indians were in great force on the ridges of the mountains but did not venture within rifle range. We found nothing to eat, and began to suffer from hunger. The air was so subtle and rarified at the great height we found ourselves in, that it sharpened our appetites wonderfully.

We now turned towards home, and on the way came across another Rancheria, deserted by its owners. This we also burnt. Towards the evening we struck the main branch of the Estanislao, which we had some difficulty in crossing, augmented as it was by the late rains and the melting snows. This day we climbed mountains that tested our locomotive powers to the utmost. Often we were obliged to crawl on our hands and knees; and the Indians on the ridges above us kept up a continual attack on us with bows and arrows, and immense boulders which they rolled down the face of the mountains. The noise of these falling rocks was heard at the distance of fifteen miles by the people of the first encampment on the river. We had one man seriously wounded, and others slightly.

We managed to keep the savages from close quarters with our rifles, but they harrassed us greatly.

We encamped on a knoll out of danger of the falling rocks, and very soon the surrounding ridges were covered with hostile tribes, who kept up a continual yelling of rage and defiance. The nearest group was on a hill, as near as I could judge, about twelve hundred yards off.

There appeared to be some twenty or thirty, and one of the party, with a bright red shirt on was conspicuous even at that distance. Knowing the great range of the weapon called Mississippi yager, which I had with me, I drew the charge and put in a double charge of powder, and resting the rifle on a stone I aimed at the group, in the centre of which was the red shirt. The bullet evidently whizzed in amongst them. We had no means of ascertaining if it struck any of them, but the way the whole party tumbled head over heels down the rocks, and made off as fast as possible was proof of a pretty good scaring. This shot had the effect of clearing the vicinity, and we passed the night quietly, but with woefully complaining stomachs.

Deer were in abundance about us, but the mountains were inaccessible; and our best marksmen, men who at five hundred yards would be sure of their prey, had not been able to bring down a deer.

The next day we toiled along, but much weakened by hunger and fatigue I had almost given up half a dozen times; but the certainty that if I did lag behind, I would be butchered by the Indians, kept up my failing strength, until towards night we struck the "Pine crossing," on the south fork of the Estanislao, where a party of Americans were encamped.[4] I shall never forget our joy when, after having struggled up the river range, we looked down, and at the depth of between four and five thousand feet, we discovered, nestled among the trees, half a dozen white tents, with a graceful and beautiful column of white smoke rising straight up from the midst into the quiet and transparent air.

We all with one accord, gave a shout that drew the tired miners to the doors of their tents. Short work was it descending to the river, the which, crossing on a bridge formed with two immense pine logs, we were hospitably welcomed by the sturdy pioneers, who were well pleased to learn the success of the expedition, as they had suffered repeated losses of cattle, stolen by the Indians, who had lately become so daring that the miners had to work with their rifles at hand.

They mentioned having heard the noise of the falling rocks,

---

[4] Perkins' "Pine crossing," also known as Paso del Pino or Pine Log Crossing, was situated on the South Fork of the Stanislaus north of Columbia, near Experimental Gulch.

thrown down upon us by the Indians, and which they supposed was caused by earthquakes in the mountains.

Ye gods! what a supper we had! Venison, fresh bread, pork and coffee. Never did any repast taste more delicious; and after a fast of eight and forty hours, in continual danger, jaded and fatigued, it may be imagined how delightful was our present position, and with what satisfaction, after a soothing whiff from our black pipes, we rolled ourselves in our blankets along side of a huge fire of pine logs.

"Pine crossing" is only ten miles from Sonora, in a north westerly [northerly] direction, while we had struck into the mountains in a north easterly direction. Our route consequently had described two sides of a triangle, and we had probably travelled some sixty miles, and undoubtedly had penetrated farther into the domains of the Indians than any white man had done before; and it is to be hoped that the severe lesson the savages have just received will enable the miners to work in peace in future.

The following morning I walked into Sonora before breakfast.

Intelligence was received from San José on the fourth [of February], that Sonora has been made the capital of the county of Tuolumne. With the news however, came the disagreeable addition that the name had been changed to "Stewart"; no doubt the underhand work of our member of that name. But the gentleman will be disappointed as we are all determined that the name shall not be changed.[5]

---

[5] What the California legislature had first thought to name Oro County was renamed Tuolumne in the act on county organization approved February 18, 1850. In that act Sonora was renamed Stewart, for the Assembly member from the San Joaquin District, Malcolm M. Stewart. Carlo M. De Ferrari has printed as Appendix A in editing the Stoddart *Annals of Tuolumne County*, an undated petition filed with the Assembly April 13, 1850. This interesting document, of which William Perkins, D. A. Enyart, and Theall & Perkins are the first signers after Alcalde Charles F. Dodge, deplores the change in name as "undesirable and undesired by the Citizens of the said town [of Sonora]," and asks reconsideration on the basis that "more than a year since the present cite of our town was encamped upon by numerous Mexicans from the State of Sonora," soon becoming, "the most populous, prosperous and extensive encampment in all the Southern Mines," by universal consent taking its name from the character of its first settlers, "and from then nearly to the present period" known as the Sonorian or Sonoranian Camp. "From the spring of 1849 to the present the population of our town has most rapidly increased—its limits have widened—its tents have been superseded by substantial houses—and it has grown into the

SEVENTH. The weather is still lovely, and we have strong hopes of spring setting in, and have already begun thinking of our new buildings which we intend putting up. Provisions are falling in price, although the roads are still impassible for waggon or mule.

Gamblers are finding their way into Sonora in large numbers, to be in readiness for the spring and summer campaign. They are the curse of this country; disreputable scoundrels who are ready for any act of atrocity. Nine tenths of the murders commited in California, up to this time, have been perpetrated by these ruffians; many of them once respectable members of the communities whence they came, but brutalized by their habits and associations in this country. They form the most blackguard and dangerous phase in the society of California.

Today I bought the first "chispa" for the collection I intend making of gold specimens. It is a handsome piece of gold and quartz weighing four ounces, and cost sixty four dollars.

Another party of Americans which started up the mountains after us, in pursuit of Indians who had murdered a miner, has just returned with a pair of scalps. I think that Sonora will be free from their depredations in future.

I had no idea that these mountains contained so many tribes of aborigines. Within a circle of a hundred miles, I am told there are at

---

most important point in the San Joaquin region:—In population, in the richness of its surrounding placers, now filled and worked by many thousand miners, in commercial activity and geographical position it is unsurpassed. With the improvement of the place and its increasing importance the name of the Sonorian or Sonoranian Camp was slightly changed into that of the town of 'Sonora,' and as such it is now known throughout the State of Sonora, in Chili and Peru—to a large portion of our countrymen in the Atlantic States, and throughout the State of California—To *Sonora* our friends and kinsmen in the old states direct their letters—To *Sonora* our foreign and Atlantic commercial correspondents send us their advices—To *Sonora* our merchandise, our provisions and letters of every discription are sent—" If the name Stewart or any other name were substituted for Sonora, the change would be attended by great inconvenience, annoyance, and injury to the citizens of the town and the miners of the vicinity. "In the present bad and imperfect condition of the Postal Arrangement, no foreign or Atlantic communication directed to 'Sonora' would ever reach 'Stewart'—our business transactions would be impeded and our present poor facilities for correspondence with our distant friends for a length of time utterly distroyed. . . ."

This petition was favorably reported by a committee which included Stewart himself, and, on April 18, 1850, the legislature changed the name Stewart to Sonora.

least a hundred rancherias, some of them with a population of five hundred. In all of them are to be found large numbers of the lower-country or Mission Indians, who as I have said, form the bad element, the others being comparatively inoffensive. It is to be deplored that in the necessary castigation inflicted on the first, the others often become the innocent victims. However, it is by no means improbable that the "Root-diggers" and "Snakes," opening their eyes to the danger of harboring an enemy to the white man, will separate themselves entirely from the Mission Indians.

SUNDAY, TENTH. This day is usually the busiest of the week. Little do we respect the day that most Christians look forward to as one of rest and devotion. And what is our excuse? To make a fortune more rapidly so as to be able, it is to be hoped, the sooner to return to a Christian country where, at least, the observances of propriety and morality are retained. Gods! to what base uses do we devote our faculties in the pursuit of gold!

I have said that Sunday is the great business day of the week here. I must however, in part, do justice to ourselves and explain why it is so. The population of our country has been always largely foreign and Roman Catholic. With Frenchmen, Mexicans, Peruvians and Chilenos, Sunday is not so much a day for devotion, as it is a day set apart from the others, for the purposes of rest and amusement. These people work outside, some several leagues distant, and never approach the town except on Saturday nights, when they come for a two-fold purpose: to amuse themselves and make their weekly purchases, which they carry out to their camps on the Monday morning.

These camps are situated, generally speaking, miles from the town, in the deep *gulches*, ravines and *arroyos* of the mountains, sometimes ten or fifteen miles from the settlements. These miners amuse themselves in their own fashion from Saturday night to Monday morning; the Frenchmen conversing, quarrelling and singing; those of Spanish origin, drinking and gambling. Their purchases are all made on Sunday; and it often happens that those of the Mexicans are gambled and lost on the Sunday night.

As the warm weather is approaching, and outside amusements become practicable, the streets on Saturday and Sunday nights look quite lively. Last night and today, so many gay dresses are to be seen, so many drunken men, so many noises of all kinds of instruments, and of singing, that we are put forcibly in mind of the gay and extraordinary scenes of last summer.

Today a lot of ground opposite our store, fifteen feet wide, was sold by auction for one hundred dollars per foot, when land at the distance of four hundred yards, ay, two hundred and fifty, may be occupied for nothing. One hundred dollars per foot, for lots in a mountain town in California where two years ago, the wandering tribes of Root-Diggers were its only and occasional occupants!

Prendez, a chileno merchant, returned from below on the eleventh; he reports that the roads are improving rapidly, and that if the fair weather continues, they will be passable for waggons in another week.[6] Many citizens who had left Sonora last fall, to pass the winter in San Francisco, are returning. Truly, when the rain set in last November, the prospect for any comfort during the drearily chilly days and nights, seemed very unpromising.

We have just received the news that our friend F[raser], the first Alcalde of Sonora, was dangerously ill in the Sandwich Islands, at Honolulu. My partner [Theall] at once started for San Francisco to inquire into the report. Mr. F[raser] has made a considerable amount of money, and if any thing happens to him, it must be secured for his wife and children. However I trust the report is exaggerated.

Received an offer of one hundred and fifty dollars for my four ounce "chispa," but would not part with it.

A pleasant night with a party of excellent young men, fellow passengers from Mazatlán. During this voyage we got up a respectable glee club, with the aid of this party; but on arriving at San Francisco we all separated. They have also found their way to these mines, and are established at Wood's camp, some four miles from Sonora, and we have recommenced our musical *soirees*.

We shall be inundated by women this season. They are pouring in like a general immigration. Every man may have a wife if he chooses. As yet however, we have no *wives* in California. Thousands of women there are, but they are all mistresses, or independent. This state is so common that it excites no remark. The mistress occupies here the same position that the wife does in other countries, and most of the women are of a class that think it no disgrace. Mexican and Frenchwomen

---

[6] Manuel Antonio Prendes was one of those who signed the petition quoted in the preceding note.

here, in fact, prefer this temporary union to the one blessed by the priest. Both have their reasons. The first will not *marry* a *heretic*, but will live with him as his mistress. This is general in all parts of Mexico. The latter does not care to bind herself by ties that she knows she will soon find irksome, and that her natural temperament will soon force her to break.

Both the Mexican and Frenchwomen make faithful, happy and contented helpmates, as long as they are well treated, *or until they desire a change.*

CHAPTER VIII

My only excuse for this chapter is that I find it in my Diary. It was written under a profound impression caused by a strange case of somnambulism in the person of a young man, resident of Sonora, and also a strange psychological phenomenon which occurred in my own proper person. Those of my readers who feel no interest in the supernatural, may skip this chapter.

Diary, February twelfth. I witnessed last night a very perfect and interesting case of somnambulism, Trance, or sleep walking, and as I shall describe the circumstances with some minuteness, and shall further go into some probably lengthy dissertations on the subject, and shall bring in the contents of several scraps I have already written and collected on incomprehensibilities, I forewarn any future and unwary reader, so that he or she may not be swindled into reading what follows, unknowingly.

The subject alluded to is a Bolivian, and a man of rank in his own country; his name is Don Nícanor, and the title of *Marques de* la Plata, is or was, before Republican institutions knocked the aristocracy on the head, in his family. A young Argentine friend of mine, Ocampo [Cupertino Scampo?], came to me last night and asked me to go to his house, as I would witness something strange. I went and found the Marquis in a perfect state of somnambulism. He was writing; his eyes were perfectly closed, and he was breathing heavily and regularly, as a man does when in a deep sleep.

He spoke now and then in a calm conversational tone; but it was evidently a communion with some imaginary companion; for apparently, he would have questions put to him by this invisible personage, which he would answer.

At times he became, naturally, in *rapport* with some person actually present, and would sustain a conversation in a rational, and at the same time, quite animated manner, until the unknown power would again withdraw the connecting chain of thought, or perception, or knowledge, and he would immediately become insensible to the presence of the people in the room.

Any object that the busy spirit thought of would apparently become instantly visible, and as soon as another image presented itself to the mind, the former would vanish.

In writing, there is no hesitation; he writes correctly and his caligraphy is very beautiful. He will sometimes pause as if concocting a fresh sentence, and if, during this period, the paper is removed, the fact appears to be ascertained by the touch. The fingers are run over the blank page left in the place of the written one, and the difference appears at once to be known. This perplexes him. When the written page is returned to its place he is again made sensible of the fact by the fingers, and, without displaying any feeling of surprise, he quietly commences to write *precisely where he had left off*, and, strange to say, without breaking the thread of thought or the sense of the sentence.

This is a more extraordinary case than that of the young french Curé (mentioned in the Reports of the Royal College of Surgeons), who generally wrote his sermons in a state of somnambulism, but was not capable of distinguishing his written paper from a blank sheet put in its place.

Where is the sense sight placed? This is a question not easily answered. I remember reading in the above mentioned authority, where the hypothesis is sustained that, in a state of somnambulism, or natural *clairvoyance*, as well as the artificial one of magnetic sleep, the patients have the power of *physical* vision placed in the upper part of the forehead.

This opinion was deduced from the fact that with several subjects, in various experiments, they usually saw more clearly by holding the head low down, or approaching the object to their forehead, their eyes being closely bandaged at the time.

In one instance the patient, a young girl in a deep magnetic sleep, stated that she saw plainly certain objects placed before her, from her forehead, and indicated the precise place of vision, just where the hair meets the brow. It must be remembered these are experiments stated on the high authority of the College of Surgeons, in London, whose Reports are to be taken with the utmost confidence.

The cases I have personally witnessed makes me incline to the opinion, however, that the organ of vision is not confined to any one particular part of the body; but that, according to the profoundness of the artificial or natural magnetism, the power of vision is extended to the whole body, or, in other words, the power of sight is communicated to the nerves; and that that power is greater or less according to the graduation of spiritual or physical existence, and as one or the other predominates.

Don Nícanor is certainly the most extraordinary somnambulist I have ever heard of. He will in a state of Trance address people correctly, will listen to their answers, and acts, apparently from outward sensations as well as from mental or spiritual promptings. Last night he wrote a letter to a friend in Stockton, and, not being able to remember the address of his correspondent, he walked to the store of Señor Prendez, and enquired. On being informed, he asked for a pen and ink, and wrote the address on the envelope, sealed it and requested it might be forwarded to Stockton; all this time, being in a deep sleep. This is a wonderful combination of physical and mental powers and instinct in a somnambulist.

He afterwards sat down for some time in the house of Señor [Luis G.] Elordí, a gentleman from Buenos Ayres, where some ten or twelve other persons, including myself, were congregated. Don Nícanor seemed only conscious of the presence of the master of the house. With him he conversed freely, but did not seem to hear any observation made by others of the party; and when he got up to leave he took no notice of any one in the room except Elordí.

The night was perfectly dark, there being no moon, and the heavens obscured with clouds. Several of us accompanied the somnambulist with candles. He walked slowly, like a man in a fit of deep musing, one hand across his breast supported by his buttoned coat, the other hanging by his side; his breathing was deep and regular, and through the nose; his mouth and eyes closed.

He walked very much as a man would do who was passing over a well known road, in deep thought. He went along confidently over the unobstructed part of the street, but reaching a spot where the carpenters had left some logs of wood, he stopped for a moment, and then avoided the logs by going round them, and so walked on, completely insensible of our presence, but apparently seeing every thing else, until he reached the *arroyo*, or stream which runs through the town.

Here the street falls some feet in crossing the creek, and a large squared log is thrown across, for the accomodation of foot passengers; alongside, from two oak trees, is stretched a hide rope for security.

Over the rough part of the street before arriving at the crossing, the somnambulist stepped carefully, pushing his foot forward and feeling the inequalities. This appears to prove that the spiritual vision was somewhat affected by the obscurity of the night. He did not however, alter the position of his arms, which he would have done, had any doubt or perplexity existed in his mind in reference to the road.

When he arrived at the bridge he disengaged his arm from the breast of his coat, and took hold of the rope, and feeling with his foot for the log, stepped on to it and walked over without hesitation. When about the middle, he stopped for a moment, and put one foot over the side, and let it fall a few inches, seemingly in a playful manner, for there was no appearance of uncertainty in the action.

Now, crossing this log at night is by no means an easy matter for a man with his eyes wide open, and his physical senses all awake; and every step has to be taken with caution. Many people prefer taking the centre of the street, when a stream of water flows, to crossing the narrow log at night.

Don Nícanor walked straight to his canvas house, entered his bedroom, took off his coat, folding it carefully up, sat down on his bed and pulled off his boots; and then placing his hand over his eyes appeared to drop into a fit of musing, or perhaps repeating a prayer. He lit a cigarito, smoked it, and then, completing his undressing, got into bed, and lay perfectly motionless as if in a sound natural sleep.

On questioning him this morning, I found him perfectly uncon-scious of the night's occurrences, but he is aware of his proclivity to sleep walking, and tells me that he has been a somnambulist for many years, and he often finds that he performs things in his sleep which are entirely impossible in his waking hours. I found him a very gentlemanly, refined and educated man, and somewhat reserved on the subject of his extraordinary propensity to somnambulism.

I have been rather minute in the description of this case, as I believe it is one of the strangest we have any knowledge of; and as every one of the circumstances passed under my own observation, I can certify to their strict truth and correctness.

How are we to account for the phenomena of somnambulism unless we acknowledge that we possess two existencies, each independent of the other? Wonderful thought! And yet, we are approaching perhaps the age when it will be no longer a mystery. The metaphysical researches of the Germans, although very little more than a fanciful medley of incongruities, yet have undoubtedly warmed into existence the germs of many vast truths, some of which may take ages to develop, that now glimmer upon the mental vision like the first star that shows itself in the twilight of a summer sky.

Are we to turn to what Philosophers term Animal Magnetism, for a solution of the many strange mysteries we at times witness? for Trance, for somnambulism, spirits, second sight, dreams, vampyrism, clairvoyance, the Divining rod and supernatural appearances?

No one can deny that many things that not long ago were termed transcendental, are now received as truth. It has been proved that something very like an apparition may be obtained through chemical means, and the action of a deseased imagination over the physical sense of sight is well known to most medical men.

But there are many phenomena that completely baffle our scientific knowledge as well as our rational intelligence.

The phenomena of Trance and dreams are, considering our familiarity with their recurrence, a mystery to philosophy.

Catalepsy, Epilepsy and somnambulism are the three phases of Trance. The first is a state where the physical system is, to all intents and purposes, dead. The ordinary functions of the body cease their activity, and no signs are visible by which the most practised anatomist may discover the existence of the principal of life, except that the body does not decay; and yet in the inert mass the mind or soul is active, observant and sensible of surrounding events.

Catalepsy, though rarely witnessed, is still recorded in the annals of Medicine as a known fact; and who may tell how many cases have occurred when, mistaken for its brother death, it has consigned living beings to the tomb to awake to the horrible certainty of an awful and actual dissolution!

Since the year 1830, in France, upwards of two hundred cases are known where it has been discovered that victims have been buried alive. And how many remain undiscovered! Particularly in Spain and in Latin America, where it is the custom to inter the dead within a few hours after dissolution.

Catalepsy has undoubtedly been the cause of a large proportion of these cases. Well may it be said to be the most terrible of all the porches to the spirit world!

Epilepsy is more of a nervous disease, weakening and destroying the functions of the body; but the connection between the mind and body is not broken.

Somnambulism presents the extraordinary spectacle of the mind directing the body in the absence or temporary suspension of the physical senses belonging to it. Somnambulism is defined by Dr. Abernethy as "a state in which the mind retains its power over the limbs, but possesses no influence over its own thoughts." The case I have mentioned of the young Bolivian seems to disprove the latter part of the sentence. How far its influence may be over its own thoughts, is difficult to prove, for the memory when the body is awake may not be, and I am convinced is not as perfect, as when the body is in repose, and the mind is in full exercise of its wondrous powers, as in trance, and often at the moment of death.

How little do we understand dreams; and yet how strange, how wonderful is this same faculty of dreaming!

In Germany there was a man who, becoming disgusted with the world, secluded himself from society. In a short time he discovered that he possessed the power of controlling his mind while in a state of slumber, and soon his dreams not only attained an extraordinary vividity, but became *continuous;* and a spiritual life of such wondrous beauty was presented to him, that real life became burdensome. This man was always unhappy, miserable, during his waking hours, and longed with impatience for the hours of night, when, in sleep, his unreal existence would commence *where it had left off the night before.*

A Vampyr is a dead-alive being:

> "The nightmare Life-in-Death was she
> That thicks man's blood with cold."

This horrid myth is said to live in the grave, where it has been buried after a supposed death, but which it leaves, however, by night, for the purpose of sucking the blood of the living, whereby it is nourished and preserved in good condition, instead of decomposing like other buried bodies. The person bitten by a vampyr soon dies and in his turn becomes one. The mark left by the bite of a vampyr is very small and has a bluish appearance. The popular remedy is to eat a handful of dirt off the grave of the vampyr.

Such is the vulgar superstition prevalent in many parts of Germany as late as the middle of the last century in reference to vampyrism.

Now I will state some circumstances, which, as their existence was placed beyond all doubt by a government investigation, give this mith of vampyrism a very sinister and terrible consistency.

In 1727 a disbanded soldier, by the name of Arnod Paole, returned to his native place Meduegna, near Belgrade. He was betrothed to a young girl by the name of Nina. A few days before their marriage, observing him very melancholy, the young girl enquired the reason. After much urging, he at last expressed an unwillingness to marry her, saying that he had been bitten by a vampyr, while with the army in Italy, and that he would soon die. Nina, who it appears was a girl of simple and strong mind, laughed her lover out of his mood, and in course of time they were married.

A few weeks afterwards Paole actually died, praying forgiveness of his wife, and firmly convinced of his vampyr existence. Nina then related to her family the circumstance, and in a short time she died, and was followed by member after member of her family.

Soon after, some of the villagers were taken off; all without any apparent disease. The people become greatly alarmed. The terrible cry of vampyr, stupified them with horror.

At last the grave of Arnod Paole was opened after forty days, and the evidence of the persons present was that the body was found perfectly fresh, with liquid blood on its lips. This satisfied all doubts. A stake was driven through the body, which, the witnesses state, was heard distinctly to groan.

This process, however, only stayed for a few days the epidemic. The people implored the Government to interfere, and a commission of three army surgeons arrived on the spot, with orders to institute a strict investigation of all the circumstances from the beginning to the end of the strange affair.

The report of this commission is still in existence. They ordered all the graves of those persons suspected of vampyrism to be opened, and they found upwards of a dozen bodies in the so-called vampyr state; that is with the flesh perfectly preserved and with fresh blood in the mouth or on the lips.

Francisco, an author of the eighteenth century, mentions the case of a man by the name of Grande, in France, who after being buried some time, was exhumed on suspicion of vampyrism. The body was found to be warm, with fresh blood on the grave clothes. The head was cut off, and the body showed unmistakable evidences of life by violent contortions.

Colonel Townsend is a proof that it is even in the power of some individuals to put themselves voluntarily into a deep sleep or trance resembling death.

The case of the Indian in Hindostan is well known, and vouched for by evidence beyond any suspicion. This man would, after some slight preparation, allow himself to be buried in the usual manner, six feet under ground, with the compact that exactly at a stated hour he was to be disinterred. He would remain buried, in a voluntary cataleptic state for several days, and recovered without apparent injury.

Here then are facts that may be of service in clearing up the mystery of vampyrism, that at one time, and that, little more than half a century ago, created so much terror in different parts of the Continent.

Why may not the terrible disease of catalepsy, about which so little is really known, and that undoubtedly exists to an alarming extent; why should not this disease be contagious? And in the case of the villagers of Medeugna, have been communicated by some hidden and subtle means, or by simple fright? Or say, by the principle known, but not understood, by the name of Animal Magnetism?

A reasoning man must come to the conclusion, that when the graves of Arnod Paole, his wife and so many of the villagers were opened, and the bodies found in the so-called vampyr state, that these bodies were actually *alive,* and in a cataleptic fit; and might have been brought to life and health with little difficulty; and the barbarous ignorance and superstition that caused the commissioners to drive a stake through each body were really the cause of so many murders.

The case of Grande is conclusive. The body showed actual evidences of life when the head was being cut off; yet such was the ignorance of the people, that this fact only proved to them the truth of their superstitions and barbarous belief.

On dreams and apparitions or spectres, much has been written, and we are not much wiser, if infinitely less credulous than our forefathers. The difficulty however of disproving the many circumstantially evidenced cases of so-called supernatural appearances, has set the wits of scientific men to work to prove them the effect of natural and physical causes.

One rather startling experiment was the result of the researches of a Russian physician, whose name I can not recall to mind. By the aid of a chemical mixture, I think it was chloride of Barium, placed on a metal dish, and held on the open hand in a dark moist place, he succeeded in producing a natural spectre. The warmth of the hand acting on the plate and the mixture, and aided by an atmosphere adapted to the experiment, had the effect of producing a perfect spectre of the hand that was under the dish, in the air immediately over it, where it hovered in the shape of a luminous emanation like the vapor of phosphorus.

This singular experiment is attended with difficulties; the atmosphere in which it is to be made requires, it appears, certain elements and requisites that are rarely to be met with.

The great German chemist Baron von Reichenbach labored hard to prove that this flame is a natural emanation from all animal bodies. He had a patient, a Mad^{lle} Rachel or Reichel, whose nervous temperament was so exquisitely sensitive, that this flame or phosphoric emanation was distinctly, and at almost all times, visible to her. The Baron took her to a thickly populated graveyard; and here she described herself as if walking up to the waist in lambent and waving flames.

The german philosopher Pfeffel, in whose word great faith must be placed, avers that in his garden on several occasions he remarked the apparition of a vapory flame hovering above the ground in a certain spot. He also states that it took the outlines of the shape of a human figure. On digging, the bones of a human skeleton were found.

Similar to the above is the well authenticated relation of the luminous appearance of a child hovering over the hearthstone of a house in Scotland, and under which human bones were found.

A student at Oxford was very much alarmed one evening, on returning from a ride in the country, by an apparition of an exact counterpart of himself and horse, riding alongside of him. This, it appears, is an instance of a species of sensorial illusion, which is by no means uncommon, but which nevertheless baffles our scientific knowledge. The extraordinary apparitions of Nicolai, the illusionary angels of Swedenborg, the appearance of saints to Joan of Arc, and finally the many authenticated cases, familiar to medical men, of patients who were afflicted with the sensible presence of apparitions; all these are sensorial illusions which science assigns now to natural causes; whether satisfactorily or not, is not my province to argue.[1]

In my opinion, the most extraordinary occurrance of a so-called supernatural nature, and which cannot easily admit of a scientific solution, was the apparition of Mr. Wynyard to his brother. The latter, General Wynyard, was sitting conversing with his friend, Sir John Colebrook. (This occurred in England.) Mr. Wynyard was at the time in the East Indies. Suddenly the General drew the attention of his companion to a figure standing beside the door. It was recognized by *both* as the brother of the General, and both started up to receive the unexpected guest. On approaching the spot, the vision disappeared. Mr. Wynyard, it was afterwards verified, died in India at the same time.

---

[1] Perkins adds in a note: "The disciples of Swedenborg believe to this day that these illusions were genuine revelations. (What if after all they are right?) Swedenborg states, not with the deceptive tongue of a Mahomet, but with all the apparent calmness of truth, his co[n]versations with St. Paul, with Luther, with St. John, even with Moses; and also that he was in daily communication with angels; which last, he remarks, 'often travel in the shape of a large luminous globe, composed of a number of angels, forming that shape, in order to bound with more facility from planet to planet, as well as to allow a reciprocity and identity of feeling."

A sturdy, unpoetical Dane, a captain of a merchantship, whom I had in my employ for some months, and whose name was Adolph Lorenzen, mentioned to me a similar circumstance. On one occasion, on a voyage between London and the Baltic, he was awakened without apparent cause, when he saw the apparition of his mother, sitting on the bunk at the head of his berth. He was so frightened that he cried out, and the spectre vanished. On arriving home he found his mother had died that same night.

Heinrich Zschokke possessed the singular faculty of being able to reproduce in his own mind the exact history of any person with whom he conversed. It seemed to him as if a "flash of memory" spread out to his mental perception, the private history and life of such person without any effort on his own part and without any anterior knowledge of his companion. This is only to be accounted for by Magnetic Agency. Zschokke was never known to have erred in the exercise of this wonderful gift; neither could he give any explanation or account for the existence of a power so strange.

We also may remark here that in the instances of young boys who have astonished the world by their extraordinary faculty for mental calculation, not one has been able to explain the process by which the most difficult problems were solved, apparently without mental effort.

It is needless to mention any instances of what the Scotch call second sight. We may possibly trace this as well as other curious, but little understood, phenomena to *Animal Magnetism,* an agent that may be fated to enlighten us on many subjects that are now shrouded in the mantle of ignorance and superstition.

By magnetic influence, Zschokke's mind was probably thrown into direct communication with that of the person he was brought in contact with, whose mind became enveloped or absorbed and identified, by the superior powers of Zschokke's will.

It is not impossible even, that the mind of Arnod Paole, as he lay in his grave *alive,* in a fit of deep trance, may have drawn into communion the minds of others above ground, already exalted and excited by fear and superstition.

I will now describe a strange case of psychomachy which occurred to myself a short time ago, in Sonora. It made a great impression on me at the time, and I wrote down a relation of the circumstance, and it happens that in this chapter I find a ready mode of preserving it.

On the fifteenth day of December, in the afternoon, after a ride of some miles, and somewhat fatigued, I went up stairs and threw myself upon the bed with my face to the wall. I immediately fell asleep, and slept until I thought that Enyart came into the room. The opening of the door disturbed me, and experiencing an uncomfortable feeling, tried to awaken myself more thoroughly, but unsuccessfully. I then requested Enyart to shake me to drive off the lethargy which oppressed me; his efforts were equally futile, and I at last requested him to desist and leave me. He did so, and I strived by strong mental efforts to awaken myself. Many people undoubtedly have experienced this feeling when suffering from nightmare.

At last I succeeded, and, finding myself perfectly awake, I turned round, and there by my bedside, close to my head, in a chair, was sitting the *counterpart of myself*. I rubbed my eyes; I gazed round the room, noting the different objects all in their accustomed places, and felt convinced I was thoroughly awake. I turned again to my second self, and, without any feeling of terror, stared at the figure, which seemed to be intently gazing at me. This must have lasted some ten minutes, neither of us speaking a word.

Now commenced the most extraordinary part of the vision or illusion. A transfusionary change began and I felt distinctly, sensibly, palpably, my identity transferring itself to the figure by my side. It is impossible for me to describe this curious process; I only knew I went through it, as we see two clouds advancing towards each other, apparently mingle and then separate distinct and unchanged.

When the transfusion was completed, *I sat on the chair by the bed side*, gazing on the form lying before me with the same impression of non-identity with which I before regarded the figure into which I now appeared to be changed! This difference existed: whereas before I felt a physical existence, I now existed in a spiritual form, but possessing the outward form and the same mental faculties of my former self.

I rose and leaving the *body asleep* on the bed, walked out. Nothing was changed. I noted the same objects where ever I went that I had daily been in the habit of seeing, but no one appeared to remark me, and I felt that I no longer belonged to humanity.

After some time I returned to my room. *The body was still lying on the bed.* I sat down in the same chair but what occurred afterwards is very indistinct. I began to feel the same transfusionary process recommence, but soon became insensible. When I returned to consciousness I found myself on the bed awake and refreshed.

Had I been in a trance, or was it only a dream or nightmare?

CHAPTER IX

I was standing, the other night, among a crowd in the large café opposite our house, listening to a funny fellow who, from the top of a barrel, was giving a ludicrous political speech. Suddenly a Mexican, wrapped in his *zarape,* who was standing by my side, dropped down, like a man dead drunk. Thinking that the man was really intoxicated, I took no further notice of him until the speech was over, and I was about to retire. I then gave the fellow a kick, with a *"levantate, borracho"!* He did not move. Two or three then proceeded to lift him up. He was quite dead, with a knife still sticking in the body, where it had been driven right through the heart! The poor fellow had not uttered a groan. The perpetrator is unknown, and no cause can be assigned for the cold blooded act.

The streets of the town are full of lazy lounging "Greasers," as the Mexicans are commonly denominated here. They are a singular people, and it is difficult to say which race they assimilate with, their Spanish fathers or their Indian mothers. They are all *Mestizos,* except those from the lower parts of Mexico where the negro blood has been introduced from the West Indies, and has helped to degrade the race still lower.

The "Greaser" has all the characteristic vices of the Spaniard; jealous, revengeful and treacherous, with an absorbing passion for gambling; and he has a still greater likeness to the inferior tribes of Indians; the same apathetic indolence; the same lounging thieving propensities; never caring for the morrow, and alike regardless of the past as of the future.

Strictly believing in the power of the Church to remit all sins without the disagreeable necessity of repentance, and never meeting with any difficulty from their priests in the way of absolution for even the most atrocious crimes, they are ready at any moment to rob and murder, if they can do so without fear of detection; for they are cowardly to a point of degradation. Their principal, in fact only, delights are gambling, sitting on their haunches all day in the sun and dancing all night to the unmeaning music of *Jaronita* and cracked voices.[1]

FOURTEENTH. Valentine day. I wonder what made me remember this. Probably because I took out one of my black cloth coats from the trunk to air, and the sight of it put me in mind of a civilized country.

With the exception of once at Monter[r]ey at the funeral of poor Corse, and for some days in Durango, I have not worn a coat since I left the Gulf of Mexico. Here, my dress is a check shirt over which for all top covering, I wear a brown, blue or red flannel shirt, worn outside the pantaloons and bound round the waist with a silk sash, in which a revolver is always placed as an indispensible part of the outfit.

SUNDAY. What a noise and racket! About three hundred Indians are in the town, drinking, fighting, singing and dancing. As they are otherwise inoffensive, they are allowed to do very much as they please. They are what are termed Mission Indians. Most of them have been employed on the Mission farms on the coast, when the Jesuits [Franciscans] were the only civilized people in the country. Since the settlement of the North Americans in California, a large number of these Indians returned to the hills and to their old savage course of life. Those who remain among the white people, are not dangerous or inimical to civilization.

At the Missions they learnt the spanish language which they have engrafted on their own, and they were also taught the church

_____

[1] "A Jaronita, the Mexican name for a small guitar strung with double cords of brass wires" (Perkins).

chaunting, which seems to be the only species of music they indulge in, but disfigured by barbarous words and actions.

They are fond of display like most savages, and I have seen one of these fellows with a rich military jacket, and devil a ha'porth of other clothing on.

The tribes of Root-Diggers I have already spoken of. They go entirely naked and are not often seen in the settlements. They are very short, large head, long and very thin limbs, delicate hands and feet, and with chests and shoulders fully and often disproportionately developed. The women are nearly the same height as the men; perhaps an inch lower. I have seen women of these tribes with feet well shaped, and not over four inches long. Their arms are not as long as the men's, but their legs and particularly the thighs, are larger than those of the other sex; but they have narrow hips, and their legs are thrown out from the lower part of the body very much in the fashion of the legs of a stool. The breasts are flat and pendant and the chest is not developed like the males. In features it would be difficult to distinguish the sexes apart. The eyebrows of both are nothing more than a delicate black line, like a thin pencil mark. I could never satisfy myself that this peculiar feature, which is universal with the Root-Diggers, is the result of art or that it is natural. I have been assured, however, it is the latter.

The women of these tribes do not appear to be so subject to the despotic will of the husband as in the higher tribes. The Lower-country Indian scorns to assist his wife in any work; and I have seen the latter with a burden that made me shudder, while her lord and master walked ahead with no other weight about his person than his bow and quiver of obsidium-pointed arrows.

FEBRUARY 18. A singular feature in the climate of California is the entire absence of electric storms. We never hear thunder; we never see any lightning. It is consequently difficult to imagine that the upper portion of California will ever become important as an agricultural district. On the coast there are rich pastural lands in abundance, and the immense plains lying between the coast range of mountains and the spurs of the *Sierra Nevada*, or snowy cordillera, are very far from being barren. But the dry and rainless summer withers up every thing except the stunted live oaks.

It is true a grand system of artificial irrigation is practicable, but this must be the work of another generation. In the mean time California, within the coast range, will be essentially a mining and manufacturing country. In a few years more, as an agricultural immigration settles down in the fertile plains bordering the Pacific, California will produce her own food, but in the mean time, must draw its necessary supplies from foreign ports. Oregon, the western coast of South America, the Sandwich Islands and Australia, all are within hailing distance of the "Golden Gate." [2]

All the luxuries of the world may be commanded from the trade of the Pacific Ocean; And San Francisco must become the New York of the western side of the continent.

This era is almost as important in the history of Nations, as that of the discovery of what was then called the New World.

A few months ago the trade of this immense portion of the globe was confined to a few whaling ships, and one other, that used to make an annual trip to San Francisco and the lower coast exchanging calicos, sugar and tea, for hides and tallow.

Now, the extensive area of the Indian Archipelago will be opened up and developed to commerce. The resources and products of the Sandwich Islands will become valuable; the trade of the numerous Republics of the southern seas will be fostered and increased; and the wheat growing and timber producing regions of Oregon and British Columbia will receive such benefits as will confer instant prosperity on those splendid territories.

The cramped up masses of the Old World will here find means of life, health and prosperity.

The discovery of the auriferous wealth of California will have done this. The passion of gold then, in this instance will have been the inglorious means of opening a New World to the enterprize of the nations of the Earth.

This fact cannot but strike one as being part of a wonderful scheme of Divine Intelligence. Without the lust of wealth, so ignoble in itself,

---

[2] Here Perkins appends a rather arch note, again indicating that he wrote his book about 1862: "The march of events in California has been even more rapid than the author imagined, and the country, that he, very naturally, denominates essentially mining, has become in twelve years, the greatest agricultural region in the Pacific, and actually exports cereals to the places mentioned in the text—*Printer's Devil.*"

the continent of America might have remained undiscovered, certainly unpeopled by the Spaniards. The same incentive is peopling an immense tract of waste territory, which otherwise would have remained useless and unknown, perhaps for ages, in California and Australia.

TWENTIETH. Two men came in today with the intelligence that, of a party of five, all Texans, attacked in the mountains by the Indians, they only escaped. They left their companions dead, and are themselves badly wounded. Here then is the commencement of a warfare that seems, from past history, to be inevitable in every country where the Caucasian race comes in contact with the aborigines of the soil. The result will also be inevitable—the total destruction of the native races.

TWENTY SECOND. The birthday of George Washington. The American citizens have erected a huge flagstaff on which floats the banner of "Stars and Stripes" for the first time in the wild mountainous district of Sonora. The sight was so exhilerating, and inspired so much enthusiasm, that many of our townsfolk deemed it only an act of patriotic justice to themselves, their country and the Diggings, to get gloriously drunk on the occasion.

Merchandize is coming in from below. The greater part is brought up on mules. These are a really valuable animal in a country like this, and it is surprising the load they will carry; three or even four hundred pounds over mountainous routes.

The Mexican is probably the best muleteer in the world, if we except the Spanish *contrabandista*, and the celerity with which they load an *Atajo*, is wonderful. An *Atajo* generally consists of from thirty to forty mules. Sometimes as many as a hundred form one *tropa*, but such a large number is more or less unmanageable, and the muleteer likes to have his troop *in hand*, no one animal being too far off to hear his voice.

Each mule has its own packsaddle and cloth, with its name embroidered on the latter in large bright letters. At the head of the *atajo* is invariably a *madre*, mother of the mules; This is a mare, generally, although in fault of a mare, a horse answers the purpose. A bell is put on the neck of the *madre*, and the mules never leave her. On the road as long as the animals hear the tinkling of the bell, they trudge along quietly and patiently, but the moment it is out of hearing, they become restive and uneasy. At night the bell keeps the whole *atajo* together, so that the *arriero* has only to tether the mare, and he is sure to find all his mules congregated about her in the morning.

In Mexico the price of freight by mules is generally about one dollar per hundred pounds for a distance of one hundred leagues. Here the price varies from seven dollars to seventy five, from Stockton, a distance of seventy miles, according to the state of the roads. When freight is at the latter price, it may be imagined how dear provisions must be.

A long hiatus occurs in my diary at this date, caused first by sad intelligence from home, where death has been busy, and secondly by a trip to San Francisco.

I found the city wonderfully changed in the nine months I have been in the mines. Between Stockton and San Francisco, there is already a small steamer.[3] It does not contain any berths, and one has to roll himself in his own blankets on the deck. However, this is a great improvement on the wretched little schooners, and being devoured by mosquitos. San Francisco has already assumed the appearance of a city, with fine closely built up streets, and some handsome and large houses.

The plains at this season (the middle of April) are literally covered with flowers. No garden can compare in beauty to the banks of the Estanislao. I think I never witnessed such a profusion of colors, and such brilliancy of hues; and this, not confined to small and isolated spots, but the whole country is one immense flower bed. The hills look like gigantic bouquets, and the *llanos* like a huge Persian carpet.

The air, as we pass through this gorgeous display, is so delicious, so etherial that the senses acquire a buoyancy only to be equalled perhaps by the intoxication of the opium smoker.

APRIL EIGHTEENTH. A disgraceful row took place in town today. Two drunken gamblers with loaded pistols in their hands, *"ran a*

---

[3] The *Alta California* of April 4, 1850, contains an advertisement for the *Wm. Robinson,* Capt. James Devoe, which was scheduled to leave on Monday, April 8, at 10 A.M. for Stockton from Central Wharf; the steamer was to leave regularly on Mondays and Fridays. Similarly, the *Stockton Times* of May 11 advises that this steamer regularly leaves, from Stockton every Tuesday and Friday at 2 A.M.

muck" through the crowded street. They shot a poor Mexican before they were secured.

Sonora is being built up rapidly, and with good houses. Our new buildings will cost us twelve thousand dollars; the walls of *adobe* bricks, and two storeys high. An adobe wall, with overhanging roof to shelter the unburnt bricks from the rain, will last almost as long as stone. In Mexico it is with few exceptions, the only material used in building.

The most expensive item in building is lumber. Many people have been employed during the winter in sawing boards by hand, but lately there has been established a steam saw mill, so that lumber is to be had in abundance, but it is very dear; five hundred dollars the thousand feet, for inch and a half boards.

The rainy season lasted five months, and the winter has been more than usually severe, according to the old settlers; but putting aside the inconveniences and sufferings proceeding from incomplete shelter, the winter has been favorable to merchants and miners. Our daily sales for weeks were from three to four pounds of gold and several other mercantile establishments average the half of this amount. Now that fresh goods are pouring in at comparatively low freights, the necessaries of life have fallen considerably in price. Most articles of provisions are selling at three rials; sugar is worth five rials, and flour two rials, or one shilling sterling per lb.

The abundance of water enables the miner to work to advantage in what are called "Dry Diggings"; that is, in places where there is not a supply of running water as in the flats, and the brows of hills.

CHAPTER X

MAY NINTH. Am just returned from a second trip to San Francisco, where I witnessed the great Fire of the second [fourth] of May.[1]

The town of San Francisco, or rather the city, for it begins to merit

---

[1] The *Alta California* for Monday, May 6, 1850, reprints from an evening edition of Saturday an account of this "Devastating Conflagration!" in which three hundred buildings were burned, with an estimated loss of nearly $4,000,-

the latter name, is, as I have said a little way back, greatly improved within the last year. Twelve months ago there were only two or three of the old adobe houses of the ancient port, and one timber house, the "Parker Hotel," which I have mentioned at the beginning of this work. The rest of the town was composed of the mud huts of the natives, and thousands of tents, canvas and brush houses, of the new comers.

Now, a space of about forty acres is completely built up with good houses, some of adobe, some of brick, some of iron, but, unfortunately, most as yet of wood.

A favorite speculation, from the beginning of the gold fever, has been the sending out of ready made wooden houses, and there is scarcely a point on the river where they are not to be seen. Half of San Francisco at this epoch is composed of these inflammable tinder boxes.

The fire of the second of May commenced in one of these light frame buildings used as the "United States Restaurant," on the lower side of Portsmouth Square, or the Plaza, and spread down to Clay street, and Montgomery street, destroying the whole square. It then

ooo. "About 4 o'clock, this morning, the alarm of fire was given in Portsmouth Square, and flames were seen issuing from the building known as the United States Exchange. Before many persons had collected the entire building was enveloped in flames, which communicated with lightning-like rapidity to the Phoenix Exchange, toward Washington Street, and to the Empire House upon the Clay Street side. Alarm and confusion pervaded all sides, and all the efforts which could be used to check the flames were utterly fruitless. The scene was animated beyond expression, and hundreds were seen hurrying to and fro endeavoring to clear their stores of goods, and convey them to a place of safety. The flames spread across Washington street and caught the building upon the opposite corner, and also the S. A. Wright Hall. What little assistance could be offered toward checking the flames was of no avail, and the huge flakes of burning materials, which were wafted by the breeze and fell upon the surrounding buildings, rendered their destruction inevitable. The entire block between Kearny, Clay, Washington, and Montgomery streets, was entirely destroyed, with the exception of Dubois's Banking House, and Burgoyne & Co.'s. The books, money, and valuable papers, in almost all the mercantile houses were saved. Upon the north side of Washington street nearly all the buildings were consumed to Montgomery, including the large brick building occupied as the National Theatre. Taking a backward course the flames spread across Washington street and destroyed the Bella Union, Haley House, Washington Hall, St. Charles Hotel, *Alta California* Printing establishment, Frazer's building, and all the edifices up as far as Dupont street, sweeping through to Pacific, and going down again to the lower corner." On May 7 the *Alta* reproduced a diagram of the burned district.

ignited the square to the north, burnt it completely, and spread upwards to the north side of the Plaza destroying also the whole of this square.

I was lodged in an hotel, one square from the upper part of the Plaza, and, consequently, two squares from where the fire originated; and seeing the direction the flames appeared to take, away from us, and towards the bay, we were under no apprehension.

It was a fearful sight to see the flames spreading from house to house with gigantic leaps, and a helpless crowd looking on with no means of arresting them.

When the whole square of the plaza fronting the bay was gutted and the square to the north ignited, we remarked to our consternation that the conflagration instead of proceeding towards the water was returning towards the plaza, the north side of which was built up with some of the handsomest houses in town, let to female adventurers, and full of women of ill fame from New York, New Orleans, and New South Wales.

This whole square was soon in flames and completely burnt down, most of the women taking refuge in the hotel where I lodged, which being on high ground was considered safe. Vain hope! In half an hour more, I commenced moving my light baggage to the open square and in another half hour the fire consumed the hotel, where however it stopped.

Three entire squares and part of a fourth were completely swept, and the loss of property must be enormous, for very little was saved. In fact no efforts were made to save any but personal property.

I was fortunate in having shipped all my purchases the day before.

The next day I was enabled to judge of the extraordinary elasticity and vigor of the American mind. With very few exceptions, the burnt out people were at work amongst the ruins of their establishments, clearing away the hot rubbish, and even burning cinders, and putting up edifices of every description. One man in particular, deserves notice. He had a general store in Clay street, about a square from where the fire originated. He saved a quantity of his goods. The next morning at daylight, he, with one assistant, was at work, clearing his lot of ground. By night he had a handsome canvas house erected, his goods stored in it, and making sales as if nothing uncommon had happened!

The weather in San Francisco was cold. In fact it is cold there nearly all the year round. It seems to be a speciality belonging only to this particular spot. A little further down the coast, or a few miles up the rivers, and the climate has a difference of thirty degrees.

While in San Francisco I bought a superb Californian mare; price two hundred and fifty dollars. She is jet black, large eyes and nostrils, legs like a deer, and small ears cut out of black silk velvet.

The breed of horses in Lower California appears to be very superior to that which we meet with in Mexico. The *Mustang* is a valuable animal, compact, strong and tireless, but he is small and devoid of beauty. The California horse, on the contrary is thin flanked, delicate, small limbed, and with a symmetrical head; all evidences of an Arabic origin; so we must suppose that the first breed brought over by the Spaniards, has not been deteriorated by crosses with inferior animals, as has undoubtedly been the case in Mexico.[2]

The flowers are disappearing from the *llanos,* and the grass is already turning brown and crisp. What a pity it is that the summer in this country should be so dry! Were it otherwise, California would be a paradise, in beauty of scenery and salubrity of climate. But by the commencement of June nothing green is to be seen except the leaves on the trees, and these are blackened by the dust and the constant sun.

Quite a domestic tragedy occurred here the other day. A Mexican was unfortunate enough to discover a brother *paisano* under very suspicious circumstances, which left no doubt at all of the fact, that the wife of the first had ceased according to her lord and master that love, honor and obedience she was bound by her vows to do. The enraged husband, with his eyes "In fine frenzy rolling" pulled out two pistols and made instant use of them; killing the man on the spot and severely wounding the woman.

The male delinquent was sentenced to ten years imprisonment. A great pity for the poor devil of a husband, that it was proved clearly that the wife was a very frail wife indeed, and not worthy of such a roman display of jealous revenge. So thought the Jury at least, and punished

---

[2] Perkins observes: "The Spanish adventurer Cobrillo discovered California in 1542, and probably left a breed of horses in the country at that time, for when the Spaniards colonized the lower part in the eighteenth century, they found the present breed of horses existing in a wild state." Juan Rodríguez Cabrillo sailed up the California coast in 1542, but he left no horses in the country, and none seem to have existed in California in a wild state when San Diego was colonized in 1769.

the crime because it appeared more an act of revenge than proceeding from the sudden anger caused by outraged honor.

The callousness of the Mexicans in reference to shedding blood is scarcely to be credited. The men seem actually to delight in murder. No *moral* power restrains them, and a Mexican is as ready with his knife as the Irishman is with his shilaley. The mere act of murdering a man, to a Mexican is nothing more than the butchering of a calf or a sheep.

During my absence in San Francisco the authorities of the town have been organized. We are now governed by Municipal laws, a town council, Recorder and Judge.[3]

MAY SIXTEENTH. I received today my travelling trunk from Stockton where it has remained ever since my arrival in California. I found all the things just as I had packed them nearly eighteen months ago, at home. Not one of my linen shirts have I worn since I embarked at New Orleans. I then, over a silk under shirt, put on one of fine flannel; and over this a thick sailor's flannel shirt, and nothing else, and I believe this dress was the principal cause of my uninterrupted good health on the journey.

MAY NINETEENTH. A foolish act passed by the Legislature, obliging all foreigners to pay a tax of twenty dollars a month for the privilege of working in the mines, is operating badly against the commercial interests of the southern district, where are congregated the greatest number of aliens.[4] Yesterday was a day of fearful excitement, and we made every preparation for converting our adobe house into a citadel. During the day most of the better class of women sought shelter under our roof.

---

[3] Perkins' notation on the further organization of Sonora is backed up by the *Stockton Times* of May 4, 1850: "There was an Election at Sonora on Saturday the 27th ult. for three members for Town Council to fill vacancies; the following gentlemen were duly elected: Chas. J. Dodge now Alcalde, whose term of office expires on the 20th inst., Joseph Jackson, and W. H. Mintzer."

Heckendorn & Wilson's *Miners and Business Men's Directory*, p. 38, says that "This first organization [described in chapter vi, note 4] not being based upon any Act of the Legislature, became null, of course, as soon as the County was organized under the Laws of the State, in the spring of 1850. From that time there was no Town Organization until May 1851, when, in accordance with a charter from the Legislature, Sonora became a city." Stoddart's *Annals of Tuolumne County* repeats in substance this erroneous information.

[4] See the Introduction for a fuller account of the events Perkins relates.

It was the advent of the Tax Gatherer [L. A. Besançon], with a *posse* from below to enforce the law, that commenced the alarm. Large bodies of armed Frenchmen, Chilenos, and Mexicans assembled outside the town, from all parts of the country, and were holding meetings and consulting on the best means to evade the payment of the tax. Not much notice was taken of these demonstrations, for the citizens of Sonora have so uniformly treated the foreigners in a friendly manner, that we could hardly entertain any fears for the peace of the town.

About noon, however, the whole foreign population of the town assumed a threatening attitude. Two deputations came in from the assemblies outside the town. At first they were moderate enough. They wished to know if any action of the authorities might arrest the consummation of the contemplated tax. They asserted that it was impossible such an amount could be paid; that they would willingly pay four or five dollars per month, but that it would be out of the power of more than half of the miners to pay the sum required, as many were hardly getting more gold than sufficed for a mere livelihood.

During the discussion, an American who wished to get out of the crowd, began elbowing his way from the place where he stood, when a Chileno or Mexican drew his pistol on him. In a moment the row began. The foreigners were driven out of the town and every thing promised a serious conflict. Our peace was threatened by about five thousand armed foreigners outside, and the actual amount of American citizens and Englishmen who sided with them was not more than a couple of hundred.

We all armed ourselves, and expresses were sent to Mormon Creek,[5] and Sullivan's Diggings, and Jamestown, and were answered in less than five hours by the arrival of five hundred riflemen, who marched into the town like disciplined soldiers. This demonstration was sufficient; the crowds in the vicinity dispersed and quiet was restored. The only thing to be feared is the misguided zeal of the Americans, who, although generally sympathizing with the discontent occasioned by the impolitic tax, are incensed that the foreigners should presume to take the law into their own hands, and these men may not be willing to allow the affair to rest where it is.

---

[5] Mormon Creek rises near Columbia and flows into the Stanislaus below Melones. Apparently the name dates from the fall of 1848, but it is not known who the Mormons may have been.

A serious affray on a small scale took place this afternoon in which a Mexican lost his life. A man was noticed parading the street with two or three pistols and a knife in his belt. The man was intoxicated, and the Sheriff after some trouble secured him, and took from him his arms. In doing so a Mexican came up behind the officer, and made a stab at him with a large knife. The murderous intent was frustrated by a bystander, who cut down the assassin with his bowie knife.

MAY TWENTIETH. A guard was kept up all last night, but every thing was quiet, and I believe the danger has passed away. But the excitable feelings of the hundreds of Americans now under arms had to have an outlet or safety valve, and hearing that at a camp, mostly composed of foreigners, situated about seven miles from Sonora, they had torn down the American flag, and hoisted in stead those of France, Chile and Mexico, a large party started to the camp in question to chastise the insult. In the evening this party returned; they found every thing quiet and had the good sense to refrain from any wanton aggression.

The foreigners are acting under a strong excitement occasioned by this sudden and unexpected call for a heavy tax. Few, if any of them have heard even the Collector's name, and are not aware who are authorized to collect the tax. They complain, and most justly to my thinking, that they have never received the slightest intimation to prepare them for this action on the part of the Government.

The passage and action of this law is a subject that will become one of earnest discussion. That it is illegal, men who are acquainted with constitutional law, will not question. No territory or incipient state has a right to interfere with the proceeds of public lands. No state has the right to set aside the treaties between the Federal Government and foreign states. By these, the natives of other countries have the same right to labor as the citizens of the United States.

Notwithstanding my opinion of the illegality of a tax on foreign miners, I was in favor of a moderate sum being raised from them, in exchange for a legal (as far as the state could make it legal) warrant to dig. The miners themselves desired this, for the license would have protected them from many an outrage and indignity.

Our foreign working population in Tuolumne county numbers at least ten thousand. Supposing twenty dollars per month to be collected from each one of them, and we have an income from public lands, placed at the private disposal of a state or territory, of two hundred thousand dollars a month, or nearly two millions and a half per annum from one county alone.

It is not to be wondered at if the Federal Government deem this is a little too large a bite for our State to indulge in.

Again, the Collector, I understand, has a commission of three dollars on each license. This would be an income of thirty thousand dollars a month or three hundred and sixty thousand dollars per annum!

This simple statement of facts is conclusive proof of the recklessness of the legislators in San José.

A respectable portion of the foreign population held a meeting in order to memorialize the Governor on the subject of the tax. I translate a portion of this memorial to show the moderation of these people. After stating their conviction (which is also ours) that the tax will destroy all their interests along with the commercial interests of the southern mines, causing thousands to leave them, they go on: "Without doubting for a moment the power of the present government to make a difference between American citizens and those of other countries, we humbly draw your Excellency's attention to the fact that it is altogether contrary to the institutions of the free Republic of the United States to make such a difference as amounts in reality to a prohibition of labor. Without assuming any tone other than that of the deepest respect for the government under which we live and are protected, we beg humbly to suggest to your Excellency that a larger state income might be raised, and that too, without causing the slightest dissatisfaction, by the imposition of four or five dollars instead of twenty."

I have written letters containing the above views amplified, to all the Journals of the state, and we have no doubt of being able to knock this absurd law on the head.[6]

Five hundred Sonora Mexicans have left the country for their own country.

---

[6] See Perkins' letter of May 19–22, 1850, signed "Leo," reprinted in the Appendix. Stoddart's *Annals of Tuolumne County* records that an agreement to contribute for testing the law was signed in Sonora by Joshua Holden, who offered $25 for preliminary measures and $125 for counsel fee if successful; Theall, Perkins & Co., $25 and $100; Charles F. Dodge & Co., $10 and $40; G. S. Evans, $10; and Charles Bruce, $10. As Carlo M. De Ferrari observes, "All of the subscribers were merchants or dealing in services to the miners."

CHAPTER XI

JUNE FIRST. The flowers have disappeared from the fields, but the trees are clothed in luxuriant spring drapery, and the cool night air of the mountains has as yet, kept the grass bright and green. The weather is delightful, and while we are enjoying balmy days and cool nights, the unhappy folks on the plains and in Stockton are sweltering in heat.

We have one great advantage in the climate of the mountains: although the days are often intensely hot in the summer, the nights are always delightful. Not cold, nor even cool, but with a delicious feeling of the entire absence of heat; a temperature that woos one from the house to pass the night in a hammock outside.

The atmosphere at night is so calm, so intensely pellucid, so free from moisture, that the moonlight and starlight flooding the heavens is something to wonder at. I never witnessed anything like it. The starlight is almost as brilliant as the moon is in Canada; but when this is at three quarters or full, the light is so vivid, that lamps or candles become unnecessary, and we read or write outside by its rays, with the greatest ease and convenience.

The diggings have been good about the town. Another "chunk" of pure gold weighing twenty three pounds, was taken out yesterday near the *arroyo*, and a few hundred yards from our house; and also a large number of *"chispas"* weighing from one to five pounds.[1]

O, for a camara lucida to enable me to delineate some faithful pictures of mining life and scenery! I thought thus, as I sat watching a party of Mexican women, who, in a little stream behind the house were busy in the occupation of washing clothes. There they were, all squatted on their haunches, and naked to the waist, for they are obliged to disembarrass their arms and shoulders from the folds of the *rebosa*, and, as under this they wear only the loosest drapery, the upper part of the body is entirely exposed. In justice to them however, I must say that

---

[1] See chapter vi, note 7.

the young girls, that is, those from twelve to sixteen, are more modest. As they wash the finer articles, they place them, folded up, on the head, so that in a short time each has a headdress of the most picturesque character. Around a group of washerwomen are always to be seen a number of lazy *Greasers,* with their dirty *zarapes* thrown over their still dirtier shoulders, lounging upon the bank, and keeping up a continual clatter of not the most chaste conversation with the dark nymphs.

On the twenty seventh, we had a large, public meeting in order to take into consideration the necessity of active measures for the repeal of the Tax Law. We determined to fee the best counsel in the country to argue the legality of the law before the Supreme Court.[2]

I have finished painting a goodly signboard, twelve feet long, and with letters at least a foot long. I believe if money was to be made in no other way, I could make a decent living by painting. It is good to have a genius for mechanical jobs in a country like this. The window sash I made for our house last year has been removed, of course, to be replaced by more artistic work; but we do not view the latter with half the complacency and pride that we did the former, when it was considered by ourselves and the whole camp, as a *chef d'oeuvre* of skill and ingenuity.

A word about my companions in the mines. Mr. Theall, the eldest of the three, but yet quite a young man, is from New York, and came out as one of the officers of the small United States force, sent to take possession of the country in virtue of the treaty of *Guadalupe Hidalgo.*[3] He is the handsomest man in the mines and, what is still better, an honorable upright man, and with a happy disposition that enables him, like Mark Tapley, to be jolly under any circumstances. Mr. Enyart, the junior, is from Cincinnati, and came out with me. We have never

----

[2] In his notes on Stoddart's *Annals of Tuolumne County,* p. 140, De Ferrari observes that Solomon Heydenfeldt, a North Carolinian who came to San Francisco in 1850, was employed as counsel. He was unsuccessful in getting a writ of *quo warranto* to prevent the collector, L. A. Besançon, from exercising his duties. "Later, Heydenfeldt appeared on behalf of the California Attorney General in 'The People *ex rel* the Attorney General vs Naglee' in an equally unsuccessful attempt to have the statute creating the tax on foreign miners declared to be unconstitutional, *I Cal 2d* 85, 232."

[3] Theall was already in California with Stevenson's regiment when the Treaty of Guadalupe Hidalgo was signed on February 2, 1848.

separated, and mutual appreciation has made us more like brothers than associates in business. When I add that neither of my companions is addicted to any of the vices so rife around us, it may easily be comprehended the harmony and good feeling that has always existed amongst us, giving birth to a friendship that, in whatever position we may afterwards severally occupy, will never be wholly obliterated.

Speaking of my partners puts me in mind of a funny incident which occurred to us a short time ago. The driver of one of our eight mule waggons, rejoices in the name of Coe. One day we received several bills, containing items to the value of some hundred dollars against the firm from various establishments on the road between Sonora and Stockton. On making enquiries we found out that our friend Mr. Coe, had passed himself off generally as the "Co" (as the word *company* is abridged in mercantile firms) which appears in the name of the house; and he had found people ignorant enough to believe in the imposture. The rascality was so *spirituelle,* that we forgave the man.[4]

SUNDAY, SECOND. Another tragical row took place today. Two men, one an American, the other an Englishman by the name of Mackay, quarrelled over a Monte table about a bet of half a dollar. This occurred last night. This morning the American armed himself with a double-barrelled gun, and walked towards the large tent where Mackay was playing. Some of the latter's friends informed him of this, and, getting up, he drew his revolver and sallied out to meet his antagonist, followed by a large crowd.

The American, as soon as he caught sight of his adversary, turned and ran, but suddenly stopping, in front of my door, where I was standing at the time, he fired. Mackay was standing in front of a crowd of people, yet, whether from chance or skill, the ball struck him in the chest, and in a few minutes he was a dead man. The assassin was taken at once, but I suppose he will be absolved on the plea of self-defence.

It is surprising how indifferent people become to the sight of violence and bloodshed in this country. Here we have almost daily rows, attended with loss of life, and we look upon these scenes with the greatest callousness of feeling, at the same time being well aware that

---

[4] Presumably, this teamster was Alex M. Coe, who voted at Sonora on August 1, 1849, along with Theall and Enyart.

in any of these rows, one's own life is just as much in danger as another's. A man now fires his pistol on the slightest motive for quarrel, with the same readiness that in another country he would strike a blow with his fist.

A somewhat comical scene followed the one I have just related. We have in town a man who once held a high position in the Southern states, as a talented, brave, though somewhat reckless gentleman. Since he has been in this country, he has thrown himself completely away. He is always drunk; for he has become so saturated with liquor that a twelve hours sleep will not sober him. He is generally goodnatured and inoffensive, and is more amusing than otherwise when in his cups, for he is keen-witted and quite eloquent when drunk. His name is David Allen, or *Dave* as he is always called.[5]

Being in Mr. Holden's store one day, the colonel (who is an old Texan Ranger)[6] turned him out, telling him he was a drunken loafer. Dave's dignity was deeply wounded; so getting his pistols ready, he prepared to avenge the insult.

In the mean time Holden was informed of Allen's warlike intentions, and, loading his rifle, he sat down on the porch of his house. Dave was soon seen approaching with a revolver in his hand, and as he was crossing a small bridge over the *arroyo*, Holden cocked his rifle and bringing it up to his shoulder, as if taking "sight" of a deer, sung out: "Dave, if you come nearer by another step I will blow your d— brains out!"

Dave stopped, drew himself up, scratched his beard for a moment, seeming to cogitate. At last his face broke out into a broad smile, and turning round he walked off. Brave as he certainly is, he was sober enough to appreciate the inevitable fate which awaited him had that "step" been taken.

---

[5] According to the "1850" census enumeration for Tuolumne County, made at Sonora in May, 1851, David Allen was 36, a miner, born in Virginia.

[6] The census cited in the preceding note lists Joshua Holden, aged 48, born in South Carolina, with real estate to the value of $20,000. His wife Eliza, aged 38, was from Massachusetts. De Ferrari prints some biographical notes on Holden, including the fact that he "came overland to Mazatlan as a member of the Texan Company under the command of Major Richard C. Barry." He had killed a man at Austin with a bowie knife on January 1, 1847. Holden died at Sonora June 27, 1853.

On another occasion, Dave got into a quarrel with a gambler at a Monte table. The man got up and, drawing his pistol, fired it at Allen. The shot missed. A second pistol was fired, and again Allen escaped. He did not stir until both shots had been fired. He then got up quietly, went to his room, got his pistol, followed the gambling scoundrel until he found him, and, holding his pistol within a few inches of the man's head, was about to fire, when his friends around him seized his arm and prevented the consumation of his innocent desires. The gambler, however, was ignominously expelled from the town.

JUNE TENTH. The times are dull. The "B'hoys" amused themselves today in dressing up two superannuated donkeys in regimentals and straw hats, and parading them through the streets.

This incident may appear puerile and unworthy any notice; but there is an important significancy in it. It proves that we are already loosing the aspect and character of a border and pioneer town; that we are approximating to the life of older states; that we have *Idlers*. Not drunkards; those we have always had; but they were laborers at the same time. Their sober hours were occupied with digging, the hardest kind of work. But idlers are those lazy beings that are to be seen in every town, village and hamlet in all settled countries; loafers who are averse to any steady work; who have no future; no ambition beyond satisfying the wants of the hour. In pioneer life there is no room for such men.

There are large numbers of Mexican women now in Sonora, and many of them rather pretty. I have already described their Sunday appearance. Like the men they are all addicted to gambling. Last night I sat down beside a couple of young girls, richly dressed, who were playing at a Monte table in one of our handsome saloons. They commenced with one dollar each, and had such an immediate run of luck, that in a half an hour they were possessors of a considerable pile of silver dollars. They continued betting, flirting and smoking cigaritos, winning almost always, when the devil tempted both at the same moment to stake all their money on one card. The card lost! But the *sang froid* of this people is sublime. Not a sign of discontent was to be noticed in the faces of the olive beauties. Rising from their seats, they gracefully drew their *rebosas* over bosoms that had heretofore been somewhat exposed in the excitement of the game, and with a soft and sweet *buenas noches, Señores* they glided away. Yes, *glided;* that is the word. A Mexican woman never *walks;* she floats rather, over the ground, such is their natural grace.

Our new house is entirely finished, and I have just put the finishing coat of varnish to a handsome desk, made by myself, and on which I am now writing, while Enyart is busily engaged whitewashing the front of the house, which now presents an appearance that would pass for respectable in a more settled country than this. The house consists of a large front store and store-rooms and living rooms behind, with two large rooms up stairs; all surrounded by a handsome wooden awning.

The good folks at home fancy they work hard if, getting up at eight o'clock they work in their offices until four or five, and then go home to dine, and to amuse themselves, either in society, or at the theatre, at concerts or at balls. *We* have no amusements. We work at all hours and at every thing; from washing the dishes, making bread, cleaning horses, chopping wood, to selling in the store, keeping accounts and writing journals. So true it is, we never know what we are capable of doing until Mother Necessity gives us a kick from behind.

The hardest work I ever had to do in this country was driving a team of six mules with a loaded waggon from Stockton to the mines. Fancy a man whose hardest work at home was driving a quill, a ride on horseback, a polka or a fencing match, seated *en postillon* on the left leader, in a dirty red shirt and blackened face, yelling to a lot of obstinate mules! I did not recover my voice for a week afterwards.

When I think of that job, I wonder how I ever surmounted alone the difficulties that beset me. I had never driven any thing but a pair of horses in a carriage; the roads were wretched, the rivers high and no ferry boats, so that at the Estanislao I was obliged to hire Indians to carry my goods across a foot ford while I swam my mules with the empty waggon across in another place.

On this occasion I had bought the team in Stockton on speculation for eight hundred dollars, and, having already sent all my purchases ahead, I took a load to deliver in the mines for five hundred dollars, and hired a huge, brawny down-Easter Yankee to drive the team. At the end of eight or ten miles the rascal collapsed, gave up, refused to move a step further. I was accompanying the team on horse back. I urged the brute not to leave me in such a "fix"; but he was obdurate; he was scared at the work before him, and was determined to return to

Stockton. I was so exasperated that I pulled out my revolver and marched straight up to the fellow, intending to frighten him, and he did put on such a comical look of alarm, that I burst out a laughing, and giving him a hearty cursing ("our army swore a great deal in Flanders") I pitched his traps from the waggon, tied my horse behind, mounted the driving mule and in four days was in Sonora, pocketing the five hundred dollars, net profits.

On my way up one evening, I had tethered my mules out, built a fire and had cooked my dinner and tin of coffee, and had stretched myself on the grass enjoying a pipe, when I heard a loud gee-wo! proceeding from an ox establishment; and soon as rough a looking individual as I was myself, stopped his team under my oak tree, set his cattle loose, came up and politely asked permission to make use of the fire I had built. We camped together, and I found out he had been Professor in Yale College, and had left his wife and children in Boston. He told me he made more in each trip of his ox cart, than he earned in a year with his Professor's chair in Boston.

I was last night at a *Fandango* in the house of a Chileno, and saw for the first time the great national dance called the *Samacueca*. It was danced by Elordí, an Argentino, and a young girl from Valparaiso. The steps, movements and music are all very exciting. The music is generally a guitar accompanied by a song, with words not always of the chastest. A drum accompaniment is made by some one rapping with his knuckles on the body of the guitar. How gracefully these Spaniards dance, men and women! On this occasion we had lots of music, lots of dancing, lots of fun and lots of brandy and water.

The *samacueca* is the national dance of Chile, although it is also general in some parts of Peru, and the Argentine Republic. It is a kind of minuet, danced by two, and may be made very graceful, and pretty, and chaste; but the way it is generally danced is any thing but chaste; although it may be graceful. The dancers have white handkerchiefs in their hands, which they wave around each other in a coaxing manner, as they sway and bend to the exciting music.

CHAPTER XII

JUNE 20TH. A couple of days ago, an Irishman by the name of Magher, caught cold and died very suddenly. He was married, and the wailing and shrieks of the widow were piteous to listen to. Magher was a fine, stout, hearty man, and his death was much regretted, particularly to his countrymen, whom he was ever ready to befriend.

Amongst our heterogeneous population a certain individual, also an Irishman, and called Peter M——; an exceedingly vulgar, ignorant and pompous little personage. He is one of our town curiosities. His vanity is always getting his ignorance into scrapes. He can neither read nor write, and the efforts he continually makes to conceal his want of education, have, as might be expected, an opposite effect, that is, of exposing the fact.

This person, it was observed, took upon himself the charge and trouble of attending to the burial of the body of poor Magher, and sent out notes of invitation to the neighbors and friends. I of course attended, and found the wife in a violent paroxysm of grief, apparently. She held the head of the deceased to her bosom, kissing repeatedly the cold blue lips, and at the same time emitting the wild lamenting gutteral sound, peculiar to the Irish on these sad occasions. It was with great trouble she was separated from the corpse, and when at last removed, she fell down, as if in a fit. This creature was a coarse, ugly and vulgar Irishwoman; a kitchen scullion looking wench; but had her grief been sincere, it would have made her respectable and interesting.

Well, Peter M—— took the lead, walking in front of the coffin, and General Besançon and I walked behind as chief mourners; a duty that the respectable men of the town have made it a practice to perform, on the death of even the humblest of our white citizens.

The next evening, Peter was married, by the catholic priest, to the disconsolate widow! The priest, shocked at the indecency of the affair, refused at first to perform the ceremony, but on second thoughts he considered it the safest plan to prevent a still greater scandal.

On the same night the boys got up, for the benefit of the "happy couple," a most horrible *charivari*, which they kept up until daylight, making the "night hidious" with noises by no means of a musical character.

Today, Master Peter is strutting about the streets with all the importance of a freshly made Benedict, and with a happy consciousness of having made himself the butt for the ridicule of the town. Long life to him and his sensitive spouse![1]

It is cheering to hear the stage horn, and to see a coach, yes, a coach, rattle up the street and draw up in front of our house. Why should we not call it a *coach?* It carries the mails and passengers, and has springs! In reality, however, it is a large, commodious, covered waggon, with a fiery team of six spanking *mules!*

What should we do in this country without these patient hardworking animals? With the exception of a few ox-waggons, they do all the packing from the lower country to the different mining regions. Very few horses are used as yet except by gentleman travellers. The price of a mule now is from seventy five to a hundred and twenty five dollars.

SUNDAY, JUNE TWENTY-SECOND. Today, for the first time, a load of veritable hay was brought into town, and bought by us for twelve dollars per hundred pounds. It created some curiosity. Heretofore we have been obliged to feed our animals on barley, and the coarse green grass brought from the mountain valleys, and during the great heats of summer on barley alone, in which grain there has consequently been an immense trade; the whole of it up to the present time coming from Chile. The first eight or ten months of my life in California, we had generally to pay a dollar a pound for horse feed, and, for many a day since, I have spent ten dollars for barley and grass for my mare "Kate." Barley is now worth fifteen cents a pound, and this with hay at twelve cents, is not very expensive. In future we shall be regularly supplied with this hay, which is now cut in great quantities on the *Tulare* plains,

---

[1] According to a family Bible in the possession of a descendant, John Magher married Margaret Loler in Melbourne on November 22, 1845. He died June 10, 1850, and she married Peter Mehen at Sonora six days later. The marriage may have seemed precipitate, but the situation of women in California during this era was such that rapid remarriages were the rule. Mehen was a member of the provisional town council and a prominent member of the community; Stoddart's *Annals of Tuolumne County* makes frequent reference to him. For further comment, see chapter xv, note 3.

bordering the San Joaquin river. I have mentioned these plains in another part of my Journal.

This evening old Coe came up with our waggons, and brought us a *cat*. Never were cats in such demand since the days of the renowned "Tom Whittingdon, Lord Mayor of London." The whole town is overrun with mice, and they destroy a deal of property for us. The advent of Grimalkin the First is consequently a subject worthy of commemoration, particularly as we were at once offered an ounce of gold dust for every pound the cat weighed!

The list of murders in our vicinity for the last week is as follows:

On Friday night [JUNE 19], two peaceable Americans were murdered in their tent, a few hundred yards from the town, in a most shocking and cold-blooded manner. The perpetrators of this horrible act are not known, nor is any trace left of them but the bloody deed. The murdered men were from the state of Massachusetts, and were respectable quiet hardworking men. One of them had kept a journal of his travels, and it was very well written. They were comrades; ate together, slept together and worked together. They must have been attacked at night, while they slept, for evidences of ill directed aim were apparent in the position and nature of several of the wounds, which must have been made with a heavy bowie knife, or with the murderous weapon belonging to the Mexicans and called a *machete*. The head of one was nearly severed from the body, and the hand was nearly cut in two, from the victim having grasped the naked instrument of death. The circumstances are of the most attrocious character, and have created an intense excitement amongst us, notwithstanding our familiarity with bloodshed.

Last night a Chileno was killed. He quarrelled with an American and, with a gun in his hand, threatened to shoot him. In a moment the American had his revolver out and commenced firing, accompanied by another white man, who probably thought it a good opportunity to give his pistol some exercise! Between the two, six or eight shots were fired at the Chileno, who stood firm and did not return the fire until he received a ball in the face, which broke his jaw. He then raised his gun, and lodged its contents in the arm of one of the Americans, and fell a few moments after with four bullets in his body. The Chileno having been the first to threaten to shoot, the others are of course exonerated!

Early this morning a Frenchman and a Mexican quarrelled, and from quarrelling got to fighting, and the former stabbed the latter, killing him instantly. The verdict (that is, had we such an institution as a Coroner's Inquest here) *accidental death.*

We have Bull-fights every Sunday, and they are sure to draw the Mexican population into town from all the *cañadas* and camps for fifteen miles around. The procession has just passed by the door. First comes the *Matador,* dressed in great finery and painted. He rides a prancing horse and carries a drawn sword in his hand, as emblematic of his office, which is to slay the poor bull after he has been well tired out by the *Picadores.* Next to him comes the clown, *el Payaso.* He prances about with great agility, sometimes on his feet, sometimes on his hands, gesticulating violently, and describing in rapid sentences, the delights of the Bull-Ring. He is not very delicate in his language, and comes out every now and then with a broad and coarse witticism, which the women are by no means the last to laugh at and applaud.

Following the *Payaso* comes a band of Mexican music, a violin, clarinet and bass horn. Then come a few gawdily dressed men representing the *Caballeros,* or horsemen, and after these the *Picadores,* the principal actors in the Ring.

The actual sport in the Arena is not worth going to see; the cattle being tame and spiritless. It is a butchery, nothing more.[2]

JULY THIRD. Since writing the above we have had five or six fresh murders. They are becoming so common that I hardly think of putting them down in my Journal. The times are becoming dangerous, and the roads particularly so; yet I shall have to go down to the coast in a day or two. Scarcely a day passes but some murderous atrocity is committed. It is next to impossible to say who are the guilty parties in the numerous cold-blooded murders we have had lately. Most likely they are Mexicans, for I do not think white men could be so

---

[2] "At Durango in Mexico," Perkins says in a note, "I saw some splendid Bull fights, in a magnificent Arena, and felt profoundly disgusted; particularly at the excitement and evident enjoyment with which the beautiful girls and women would gloat over the agonies of the poor dying brutes. I used to go to watch *them,* and not the sports or cruelties of the Ring. I was interested in what appeared to be a strange phase in human nature. The Mexican women are kindhearted and tender, and yet put them in a Bull Ring, and one would think them tigresses, or as bad as the Roman women, who seldom hesitated in making the fatal signal for the death of a conquered Gladiator."

bloodthirsty, and yet take such pains to conceal all traces. The Mexicans, as I have before remarked, are actually *fond* of butchering the white men, but they are also very fearful of incurring the penalty if found out, and only kill when they are confident of being able to do so with impunity. When this opportunity occurs they show no mercy, but butcher with all the savage cruelty of wild beasts. I do not know any race of people, except the *Thugs*, of India, to compare them to.

Individuals living alone in their tents are being murdered in all directions, and people are only safe in crowds, or being constantly on the alert, and well armed. Something must be done, for this state of things is by no means pleasant.[3]

The heat for four or five days past has been excessive. Cold water and lime juice are all the rage. Notwithstanding the great heat, however, we do not suffer from it to the degree of lassitude, I have experienced in other countries, with the thermometer at a lower figure.

---

[3] The *Alta California* of July 8 remarks that the *Stockton Times* of the 6th "is filled with accounts of murders and robberies in the mines, showing a most disturbed and dangerous state of things. The *Times* contends that the foreign miners tax law has contributed to and brought about this unhappy result." Several of the atrocities are detailed. George E. Jewitt, mining at Pine Crossing on the Stanislaus, wrote in his diary on June 15: "There have been several robberies & some murders committed within a few days by Mexican desperados. There have but few of them [been] caught." Again, on July 4: "Scarcely a day passes but our ears are shocked with the account of some horrible murder. The people begin to reflect on the officers thinking they do not do their duty & talk of taking the law into their own hands. If they do there is no telling where it will end."

Perkins later mentions the fact, expanded in the *Sonora Herald* of July 13, 1850, that on July 3 a public meeting was held, he himself acting as secretary, at which it was resolved that "a company of 25 good men and true" be appointed, to "immediately proceed to such portions of the county as have been the scenes of the late brutal murders, and also such other places are likely to prove the hiding places of the murderers, and . . . use all lawful means to bring them to justice." It was further resolved that a committee of three apply for a company of U. S. Dragoons to be stationed at Sonora, and that the citizens of Sonora and Tuolumne County be requested to contribute funds for carrying the resolutions into effect. "Messrs. Tuttle, Marshall, Luckett, Perkins, Holden and Mehen" were appointed to press for the measures, Captain J. B. Litton was named captain of the volunteer company, and Justice F. C. Whitehead and Constable C. G. Stanley were requested to accompany him. See Stoddart, *Annals of Tuolumne County*, pp. 147–150.

The air is so pure and elastic, that I have been riding on horseback, when the mercury has stood at 110, under an oak-tree.

Our town is a little scandalized by another domestic incident. Mr. and Mrs. Lyons came up some time ago from Stockton, and established a boarding house in Sonora. They are English people and appeared to be quite respectable. To our astonishment however, Mrs. Lyons after having enjoyed the reputation of being a lawfully wedded wife, no small credit in this country, made known to the public that she is not married to Lyons; that she is nothing more than his mistress. Her reasons however soon came to light, and cleared up the mystery. A Mr. W——, another Englishman, and Editor of a newspaper, had gained the affections of the pseudo Mrs. Lyons, and giving her up his own heart, accompanied by an offer of his hand (and pen) he succeeded in inducing her to expose her real position, in order to be made a real and genuine "honest woman," which act was duly and truly consummated, much to the discomfiture of the deserted Lyons, who was left to mutter: "Frailty, thy name is Woman."

Mr. W—— has not proved himself to be very fastidious in the choice of a wife, but as Shakespeare says: "For to be wise and love, Exceeds man's might; that dwells with gods above." [4]

WEDNESDAY, JULY TENTH. We have had more murders, and still more of excitement. About six miles from Sonora, a party of Yaque [Yaqui] Indians and Mexicans were discovered burning a tent. They were surrounded by a dozen Americans and captured, when it was found that inside the burning tent were two human bodies amongst the flames and ashes, and partly consumed. The captured men were

---

[4] Perkins concentrates on human interest, sometimes to the neglect of more mundane history. His Mr. W—— is clearly John White, who, with John G. Marvin and Dr. Henry H. Radcliff, began to publish Sonora's first newspaper, the *Sonora Herald*, on July 4, 1850, using the famous Ramage press brought to California in 1834, which was also used when California's pioneer newspaper, the *Californian*, commenced publication at Monterey in 1846. White retired as editor in September, 1850, after the twelfth issue appeared. Later he edited or published newspapers in Stockton, Sacramento, and San Francisco. See Helen Harding Bretnor, ed., *A History of California Newspapers, 1846–1858, by Edward C. Kemble* (Los Gatos, 1962), pp. 109, 153–154, 172, 179–180. The bereft Lyons may have been James B. Lyons, who voted in the Sonora election of August 1, 1849. On April 28, 1850, he joined with L. D. F. Edwards in staging a widely advertised horse race at Sonora. (His horse won.)

doubtless the murderers, at least such seemed the belief of all, and that they were taking this means of concealing their crime.

They were brought into Sonora by a large number of Americans, who swore that although they would allow the villains to be regularly tried, yet "Judge Lynch" was to attend to their instant punishment, on conviction.

The excitement was intense; I could not help joining in it. The murders daily committed are heart-sickening, and leave no room for a feeling of mercy in the breast.

The authorities were alarmed and could do nothing at first. The Magistrate who was to try the men, and take the evidence, after a vain attempt to empannel a Jury, gave it up in despair. A party then of some two hundred men bound the criminals, and, putting halters round their necks, led them outside the town, where they formed a "Lynch Court," and after convicting the men with all the due forms, they made preparations for carrying the sentence into execution. A large oak tree was chosen, and the prisoners,—there were five of them—were placed under it, while some men climbed the tree to pass the ropes over the branches. Two of the ruffians during this operation were smoking cigaritos. They did not appear to be at all concerned, although they certainly could have had no hope of evading their fate. When their hour *does* come, these Mexicans and Indians display more equanimity than the Saxon.

At this moment the county Judge and three Sheriff's officers, all on horse back, rushed through the crowd, and, dashing gallantly up to the fatal tree, seized the ropes attached to the necks of the prisoners, and, telling them to follow, dashed away at full gallop towards the jail.

The act was done so suddenly that there was scarcely any resistance; but when the party had cleared the crowd, a yell of disappointment rung out from the multitude. A number of shots were fired, and a most exciting chase commenced. The prisoners knew they were running for their lives, and each one taking hold of the rope, one end of which was round his neck, and the other lashed round the pummel of the officers saddle, to ease the strain on his throat, kept pace with the rapid flight of the horses. The "Law" won the race, and the prisoners were safely housed in jail to await a legal condemnation; which means that in a week or a month, they will escape from jail and recommence their crimes. The crowd, hungry for blood, threatened and swore, but finally they were all pacified, and returned to their diggings.[5]

---

[5] Here Perkins relates a famous incident in the history of Sonora, described in Herbert O. Lang's *A History of Tuolumne County California*, pp. 39–44, and in the *Daily Alta California* of July 19, 1850. In each case, the original source was the *Sonora Herald* of July 13. The account in the *Alta* reads as follows (with corrections in brackets from Lang):

"On Wednesday last [July 10], three Mexican Indians, and a Mexican, named Pablo Martinez, Domisio Ocho [Dionisio Ochoa], Gabino Casias [Gabino Jesus], Rinz [Ruiz] Molina, were brought to Sonora, in the custody of four Americans, named Thomas Shirley, J. B. Owen, George Hudson, and Thomas Hill, and the report immediately became current that another horrible murder had been committed at the Green Flat Diggings, about eight miles from this town. The entire population of the town immediately crowded to the court house of the Justice of the Peace [R. C. Barry], and a thousand inquiries were made relative to the particulars of the affair; and as the horrible details were related, the observer could see in the angry exclamations and flashing eyes of the people a settled resolve to avenge the crime that had been committed upon their countrymen. The prisoners were arraigned before Justice Barry, and then commenced a scene of confusion and tumult that baffles description. The universal cries were 'String 'em up,' 'Hang them,' 'We will have no mistake this time,' and a rope was actually prepared with which at once the people might hang the prisoners. The officers of the court did their utmost to calm the passions of the people, but with little effect. Our active and worthy sheriff, George Work, declared that the first man who interfered with the prisoners, while they were in his charge, should do so only at the peril of his life. Judge [John G.] Marvin, who was listened to with great attention, in a forcible address, begged the multitude to allow the law to take its regular course, assuring them that justice would be done, and urging them to consider the solemn responsibility that would attach itself to them if they took the law into their own hands. The evidence of the four Americans was then taken down in writing by Justice Barry, and it was to the following effect:—They stated that they resided about a mile from the tent where the murdered men were found.

"On the previous evening a Mexican boy informed them that two Americans had been murdered at the Green Flat Diggings, but they took no notice of the report. In the morning, however, another Mexican called and corroborated the report of the boy. Witnesses immediately proceeded to the spot indicated, and there found the four prisoners in the act of burning the tent and the bodies of the two men. They were immediately taken into custody, and brought to Sonora. It also appeared in evidence that a shovel and a pick axe, the property of the deceased were found in the possession of the prisoners. The defence set up by the prisoners was that it is a custom of their countrymen to burn the bodies of their dead: that the bodies had been lying dead several days, and had become offensive in consequence of their rapid decomposition. The demeanor of the prisoners was calm and becoming to an extreme, which, amidst the tumult, excited in some minds a sympathy that was most marked. The personal appearance of three of the prisoners was very uncouth, but this is a peculiar attribute of their race. The Mexican's countance was a pleasing one; he has a fine head

We cannot live much longer in this way. All over the State the prisons are mere shells. No prisoner is secure in any of them; and criminals of the worst description are continually escaping. We want a court that will try, sentence and execute a man on the same day. By no other means shall we be able to rid the country of the thousands of ruffians who now commit their crimes with impunity.

---

and well formed features. By the time that the evidence was taken, the excitement of the crowd was so great, that it was proposed that the matter should at once be brought to an issue, and a jury of citizens be empanelled. This was done, as the best alternative that could be adopted. But Mr. M'Alpin and others objected to serve upon it, wishing that the law should take its course. Another tumult occurred, and the court retired to consult. During its absence, the people elected a judge from among themselves, and Mr. Peter Mehan was, with acclamation, proposed for the office. A rope was then passed around the necks of the prisoners, and they were led in this manner to a hill in the immediate neighborhood of the town, where the trial was commenced anew. Several hundred persons were present.

"A second jury was empanelled, the prisoners found guilty and sentenced to be hung. The Mexican was to be the first victim, and the cord passed over the limb of a tree. He knelt down, kissed a cross he had in his bosom, muttered a few words in prayer, and with the calmest resignation, resigned himself to his fate. His body was actually dangling in the air, when Judges Tuttle, Marvin and [Charles M.] Radcliffe, and others arrived on the spot.—Judge Tuttle begged the people to stop these violent proceedings, and in a powerful, feeling and eloquent address urged them to respect the laws. The crowd became incensed, but Mr. Wm. Ford throwing himself into it, was of the most material assistance in saving the lives of the prisoners, who were then again seized by the officers, and taken to the prison. The fate of these unhappy men will be decided on Monday next.

"We may be allowed to urge the public to calm the excitement in which they are now involved. Far better would it be that a hundred guilty men should escape than the lives of four innocent men be sacrificed. Let us do to others as we would they should do unto us. Let no blind passion determine them to hang a man before he is proved guilty. There appears to be some mystery in this case. The coroner states that the deceased have been dead several days; that he found maggots in their skulls. Let every circumstance be calmly considered, and justice be done."

On July 24 the *Alta* quoted the *Stockton Times* of the 20th: "We are informed that the four Mexicans apprehended on the supposition of having murdered two Americans whose bodies they were burning, are acquitted; it being evident from the state of the remains of the bodies that death had occurred upwards of eight days prior to the time at which they had been discovered. We are happy to state that the excitement in Sonora and vicinity, although still great, is on the decline, and in the absence of fresh causes of stimulus will soon subside. Large bodies of men are under arms, and in nearly all the camps night watches are kept."

We have held a meeting in order to raise a body of twenty five men to protect the town, and have sent down a request to the Government to station a company of U. S. Dragoons in Sonora.[6] The roads are quite dangerous to travel. The party going down with me tomorrow consists of ten men, well armed, and we think we can withstand an attack. It is feared that there are organized bands of Mexicans headed by white men; the former warring against the Americans for revenge, the latter for plunder. We have plenty of bad characters from Sydney, and doubtless many of the late murders are by them. It is easy to distinguish a murder committed by a white man from one perpetrated by a Mexican. If by the former, the deed is done in the shortest and most simple manner, and the body left where it falls. In the latter, the corpse is disfigured and mutilated, evidently after the fatal stroke has been given.

[6] It does not appear that the requested company of U. S. Dragoons was sent to Sonora. The meeting was held on July 3. See note 3, above, and compare page 329.

CHAPTER XIII

JULY, TWENTY FOURTH. I have just returned from San Francisco, where I spent a pleasant week with several old friends, amongst whom was my good friend F[raser], the first Alcalde of Sonora, who had lately returned from a trip to the southern seas, in one of the islands of which he had the boatswain of his vessel eaten by cannibals, and he himself narrowly escaped the same fate.

He proposed that I shall raise all the money I can by the first of next May and meet him in San Francisco. Thence to the southern seas and islands to trade; after that to China, to lay in a stock of Indian goods; send the vessel to New York by the way of Cape Horn, and return ourselves by the way of Europe to be in readiness to receive her. I like the idea, and accepted it conditionally. *Mais l'Homme propose et Dieu dispose.*[1]

[1] The contemplated mercantile adventure with Fraser did not work out.

A couple of days before my return to Sonora, a fatal affray took place in our house. A young man of education, but sadly tinctured with the vices of California, had come up from Stockton on business. He, with several others, was standing at the door of the warehouse, "chaffing" in high spirits with Theall, and a person called McElroy, also from Stockton. They soon commenced playing practical jokes which, amongst men, are sometimes any thing but innocent. McElroy received a thumping blow on the shoulders from Marshall, and, taking it in good part, laughingly swung a great coat he had in hand, and brought it down on the others head. Unfortunately in one of the pockets was a heavy slung shot, and this struck Marshall just over the eye inflicting a slight but painful wound.

He became, unjustly, very much enraged, and, notwithstanding McElroy expressed his regret at the accident, it was with difficulty Marshall was pacified. In the back room they again got into an altercation, Marshall insisting that the other had hurt him intentionally, and becoming again greatly excited.

At this time they were alone in the large back room, Theall being busy in the front store. In his anger, Marshall at last grasped his pistol. McElroy said: "Don't shoot me Marshall, it was only in play." But the other pulled his pistol from the belt, when McElroy, to save himself, and not giving Marshall time to fire, drew his own pistol and put a bullet through his adversary's body. Marshall's pistol was in his hand when he fell, which appeared to be conclusive proof of McElroy's assertion that he only fired in self defence. This, with the fact of Marshall having tried to fasten a quarrel on McElroy, exonerated the latter from the charge of intentional homicide.[2]

---

[2] The *Stockton Times* of July 27, 1850, reports on "the recent rencounter at Sonora, in which Mr. [George] Marshall was shot by McElroy." The facts are given as sworn to in the trial of McElroy by Judge Tuttle:—

"I saw the prisoner and Mr. Marshall in the store of Theall, Perkins & Co. Mr. Marshall tore one of the skirts from the prisoner's coat, whereupon McElroy tore off the remaining one and playfully struck Marshall with it. Shortly afterwards Marshall became aware that blood was droping from his head upon his shirt, whereupon he spoke in a sharp tone to McElroy, who said that he did not understand how he could have been the cause of it, but at the same time, if he did it at all, it was done quite unintentionally. This appeared to be satisfactory to Marshall. Shortly afterwards they met again in my presence. The first remark I heard proceeded from the prisoner: it was, 'I do assure you, sir, most positively, I had no intention of hurting you; it was purely accidental; if I did

AUGUST FIRST. The country is in a state of great confusion on account of bands of marauders, who are committing the most wanton outrages on the Mexican and other spanish population, in order to drive them out of the country. Under the supposition—probably too well founded—that Mexicans are the principal agents in the numerous, we may say daily and nightly, murders, the American mining population is aroused and is intent on driving all foreigners from the mines. In doing this, the white men are committing a greater aggregate of crime and outrage than that for which they are inflicting such summary vengeance.

AUGUST SEVENTH. Poor Jack is dead at last! Jack was one of those good-natured, good for nothing fellows who have a prototype in nearly every town. He was no man's enemy but his own; always ready to do a light job for a glass of grog, and depending upon chance for his daily food, and on the liberality of his numerous acquaintances for coats and pantaloons. He was a sailor and had seen better days, but strong drink, that has floored many a better man that Jack, counted him as one of its numerous victims.

We tried on many occasions to break Jack from a habit that was slowly killing him, and sometimes kept him for a fortnight without liquor, until in fact he became haggard from desire. He could not live without the stimulant, and it was just as evident it would kill him. And so it has, poor fellow!

We buried him, and I read the funeral service over his remains, and it was listened to by more people than Jack himself could have dreamed would have attended his humble obsequies.

Last night a poor Indian lost his life through an ill-timed and cruel jest. A party of young men, rather the worse for liquor, seeing the

---

it, I ask your pardon.' The prisoner's hand was on Marshall's shoulder, in a friendly manner, while he said this. Marshall angrily said, 'Take your hand off me,' and immediately, with his left hand, grasped McElroy by the bosom of his shirt, who begged the former not to let any difficulty grow out of it. Marshall still retained his hold of McElroy with his left hand, while with his right hand he drew a pistol, but before he had a chance to use it, McElroy drew his pistol and fired. Marshall fell, the ball entering his left breast, passing through his lungs.

"McElroy was acquitted, it being satisfactorily proved that he shot in self-defence.

"Marshall has since stated in the presence of Judge Marvin that he did not blame McElroy for what he did. He was still alive on Thursday morning."

Indian intoxicated, commenced amusing themselves at his expense. One of the party, remarking that the Indian had a sinister looking face, offered to wager that he could be induced to commit a crime. The bet was taken, and the young man put a pistol, unloaded in the Indian's hand, and told him to go and rob a man whom he pointed out walking up the street.

The Indian, taking the pistol, marched at once up to the man and presenting it said: *"Deme su dinero, o le mataré.* Give me your money or I will kill you!"

He had hardly time to finish the sentence, when the man addressed pulled out his pistol and shot the poor devil down. The young man (a lawyer from the state of Kentucky) who had incited the Indian to commit the assault, was arrested; but it turned out that he had, for the last four or five days, been actually a maniac, from the effects of liquor himself.

The Mines are still rich, and large quantities of gold are continually being taken out of *placeres* where the ground has already been worked over two and even three times, proving, how very imperfect has been the manner of extracting the precious metal.

All the machines sent out from England and the United States have turned out to be humbugs; constructed on theory without practical knowledge of the work necessary to be done with them. The Miners themselves have made the only improvements. At first, a pickaxe, a knife and a tin or wooden pan, was all the Miner had to work with; and among the Mexicans, they stick to this day to their *barreta* and *batella;* the latter a pan scooped out of a section of a log of wood, and on account of its lightness and body, much easier to handle than the tin pans in general use.

Soon the American and English miners, not satisfied with the slow process of washing by hand, invented the *cradle,* and with this machine did ten times the work in a day than by the old method. The *cradle* was placed near a supply of water; one man worked it; another baled water, and others supplied it with auriferous dirt.

But the greatest improvement is the "Long Tom," which is as yet the perfection of washing machines. A trough ten or twelve feet long is placed in a slanting position; in this are slats to receive the gold, and a stream of water is brought either by canal or by canvas pipes, and falls in a constant current into the machine, which washes enormous quantities of dirt, with no other labor than that required for supplying it.

With this machine, the mountains of waste dirt, once or twice worked over in the primitive fashion, have been made very productive; the second and third working of a *placer* often proving more profitable than the first. For this reason, although the diggings immediately in the vicinity of Sonora have been worked incessantly for eighteen months, there are still thousands of miners at work within the circumference of five miles.

In the Southern Mines, gold is found every where. It is not, as is generally the case in the Northern Mines, confined to *arroyos* and beds of streams and "gulches," but is found in plains and in beautiful valleys; on the sides of mountains and on hill tops, and in all the rivers. The *Mocalumne,* the *Estanislao,* the *Tuolumne,* the *Mercedes* and *King's River,* are all full of gold, and the supply seems to be inexhaustible.

Where it all comes from is a mystery. How is it formed? What is its matrix? When gold is found in high grounds, it is always coarse; and at times in lumps varying from an ounce to many pounds. When found in the plains and rivers, it is fine; either in grains or in flakes. This proves clearly enough that it originally comes from the mountains, where it has been manufactured by nature in vast beds of quartz; for quartz seems to be the only rock in which gold appears to be indigenous. I saw a piece the other day weighing ninety pounds and in which the gold was sown in a most beautiful manner. In some specimens the gold and rock are so mingled that they appear to be one substance.

As heavy rains have laid bare the auriferous veins, the action of the air and water, and probably of earthquakes, has broken off masses, and these have been carried away by the torrents, and broken up, and ground into fragments, the finer portions carried to the flooded plains and rivers, to undergo still further trituration; while the coarser ones, sinking into the crevices of the rocks and ravines, have remained more [or] less intact. And who can say how many thousands of years this operation has been going on? And how many generations of races now forgotten, have taken out the glittering treasure? In the county of *Calaveras,* there is a deep pit evidently the work of human hands, and of great antiquity. In it there has been found working tools of obsidium and flint. Who were the antique laborers in these regions, and how has all knowledge of their existence become extinct? Were they of the great peoples who built up the wonderful monuments whose ruins have been found in Mexico, Yucatan and Central America, and who probably worked, at the same time, the copper mines of Lake Superior? For there too we have evidences of ancient labors. The spaniards found no gold mines in America. In Mexico, although the Kings possessed the metal, it was not in abundance. These mines must have been worked long before the time of the Aztecs, for even in their time the existence of the workers had been forgotten.[3]

On the twentieth of November, the rainy season commenced, later by some days than last year. I have neglected my Journal sadly, but what with trips to San Francisco, journeys throughout the mines, and work about the store, getting ready for the winter, I have had no time to attend to literary labors.

I am writing now on the second day of December 1850, and on this day the first snow of the season fell, melting as soon as it reached the muddy ground.

During the last three months, Sonora has increased in size surprisingly. A large number of good houses have been put up. Ours is now by no means the finest building in town. We have however, excellent arrangements for the winter. Our store is large, and we have made additions behind for storehouses and kitchen, and in the latter we have a good cooking stove. How different to our uncomfortable position last winter, when with difficulty we kept our beds out of the rain, which came dripping through the roof in a dozen places. And yet I remember all these inconveniences were borne not only without complaint, but with jokes and laughter, and on one occasion with uproarious demonstrations of enjoyment by the *non-sufferers*, when Theall and I were washed out of our blankets by a sudden torrent of water. But we are becoming particular, forsooth, now. In a short time I suppose we shall be wanting sheets in our beds and white shirts to wear!!

A few days ago the circuit court opened its sittings; the first regular court we have had in Sonora. A large number of gentlemen of the black robe attended. Notwithstanding the existence of this court, the depredations and murders still continue. No hand but the hand of the people, once aroused, can put a stop to them, for although we have

---

[3] Archeology lends no support to these speculations about prehistoric gold mining in California.

Judges and juries to convict criminals we have no secure places to keep them in before or after trial.

A very handsome chilena woman, the mistress or the wife of a South American merchant here, for some reason best known to herself, swallowed the other day *an ounce of arsenic*. As I am as yet the principal medical man in town, in virtue of my *medicine chest,* I attended her, and exhausted my stock of hydrated peroxide of iron. Fortunately the amount of poison of such a nauseous character as arsenic, was so repugnant to the stomach, that nature herself assisted in getting rid of such an unwelcome guest. The woman's life was saved but her beauty is gone for ever.

We have taken shares in a company formed for working a vein of auriferous quartz, on the river Estanislao. Whether it will turn out a profitable investment or not, it is difficult to surmise. We have as yet no means of separating the gold from the pulverized quartz, and until a machine is invented that shall do this thoroughly, quartz mining will, in the aggregate, be a loosing operation.

There is no doubt that a large quantity of gold exists in the numerous auriferous veins in the mountains, but until we shall be able to separate it by the aid of competent machines, the results will be doubtful. It is true, however, that "leads" are sometimes discovered, in which are large masses of native gold, which may be separated from the quartz with the aid of a hammer; but this is mere luck or hazzard.

A german physician, Dr. B——[4] has just established himself in Sonora. I mention him to preserve his name, even in astericks, in my memory. He is a superbly handsome man; but it is not for this quality he is best known. He is the greatest *liar* I have known in my life, and have seldom read of one equal to him. Mariatt's [Frederick Marryat's] Captain Kearney must have been a *cousin german* to the Doctor. I believe that he often is convinced himself that the lies he is continually telling are nothing more nor less than truth; so natural it is that what one is always repeating comes to be an established fact in the mind. The Doctor's lies are often amusing, for he has considerable talent. His account of his apocryphal marriage with a commodore's daughter in New York is worthy the *Thousand and One Nights;* and as for his wonderful and hair-breadth escapes from fearful dangers in Mexico,

---

[4] Possibly the Dr. Burns mentioned in chapter xvii, note 1.

they are simply stupendous. I was aware he had crossed Mexico, for I met him in Mazatlán; but he crossed in a lower latitude than I did, and where there could have been no dangers to encounter of starving, and Indians. On one occasion he was attacked by Indians in the night, and all his party scalped but himself, his presence being so imposing, when he drew himself up before the fire, that the Indians were awed! On another, a Mexican lady offered him a million of dollars if he would divorce himself and marry her. Unfortunately the Doctor's lies are not always so harmless as the above. He has induced many people to enter into speculations with him that have turned out to be nothing more than barefaced and impudent swindling.

CHAPTER XIV

The Grizzly Bear has come down from the mountains, and [they] are pretty abundant in the vicinity of Sonora, and make our deer hunting dangerous sport. An old hunter was attacked some days ago by a couple and nearly killed. He succeeded in climbing a tree after being badly torn. Yesterday (fifteenth) another hunter was attacked by a number, he says eight, and left for dead. He recovered, however, and managed to crawl to a ranch. Day before yesterday a father with his two sons were out hunting, and were attacked by two bears, and the old man was torn to pieces; one of the sons is also badly hurt; all this with in two and three miles of Sonora.

We have become so familiarized with murders, bloodshed, terrible accidents etc. that unless my Journal happens to be at hand, and I note down an occurrence at once, in an hour or two something else equally startling happens, and drives the first from the memory. There is not a day passes without its deed or deeds of crime, and although I am generally cognisant of the circumstances at the time, they are almost immediately rubbed out of the memory to give place to some new impression.

Within the last few days, four parties have been attacked by the

Grizzly Bear, the most ferocious and dangerous, as well as the most powerful animal in North America. Some of these encounters have had fatal results. One however was of a ludicrous nature. An Irishman, Jemmy Fagan, was chased by one of these monsters, and his yells brought some other men with their rifles, from a gulch near by. When Jemmy felt the bear near him, he fell down as if in a fit, and thereby saved his life, for the animal rushed head long over him and precipitated itself into a little gulch or ravine. The Irishman, if he really was in a fit, recovered mightily quick, and scrambled up the hill to where his friends were. When he found himself safe, the poor fellow did go off into a real fit, and it was half an hour ere he could be brought to. Master Bruin was shot the same day, and Jemmy bought the skin for two ounces of gold, and he vows he intends to sleep on it every night, "to get accustomed to the taste."

It is not known what has brought the bears down in such numbers from the mountains; and it is not only about Sonora they are numerous. In other parts of the mines, north and south, they are more numerous and dangerous than they are here. Many miners and hunters have been killed or maimed for life. "Bear stories" here, are just as truthful as they are wonderful, but I refrain from noting any thing that I cannot vouch for.

Large numbers of Mexicans with their families have left the town, some to return to their own country, but the greater part to the mines south of King's River. Their departure has been caused by various reasons. The sufferings of last winter frightened many; the greater difficulty of finding the precious metal, and lastly the hostility of the American Miners, who, as I have already said, believing the Mexicans to be the authors of the numerous murders in the district, have treated them on several occasions with great cruelty.

The result of the departure of so many of these people, is that the town is dull and quiet; little gambling, which is an advantage; the mexican has always been the *bonne bouche* of the american Gambler. The nights are comparently quiet; no *fandangos*, music, noise nor dancing. Even Saturday nights and Sundays are becoming staid members of the week.

DECEMBER, SEVENTEENTH. A poor young man by the name of Browning, a Canadian I believe, was accidentally shot this evening. He was passing by where a man was showing a revolver; the weapon went off, and the ball passed through his body. He only lived for a few minutes, long enough to give the address of his mother. Poor lad! and poor Mother!

At the same moment that this mournful accident happened, a negro who was in the street just opposite our door, was shot dead by some person unknown. As an evidence of the *sangfroid* with which people view these occurrences, where Browning was shot there are a number of gambling tables, round which were grouped men and women. Not a game was stopped! Some of the players got up to have a look at the dead body, and returned to their game quite unconcernedly. Even the women become brutalized by the constantly recurring scenes of bloodshed and violence. People get accustomed to the sight of blood, let it be that of a calf or that of a human being.

CHRISTMAS DAY! but why mention it in this country! It makes me sad to write the words, for they bring memories of home, and civilization and household affections.

Young Groff, a brother of a friend of mine in Canada, has made his way to Sonora in a destitute condition. He found me out, and I gave him what he required to commence work with. He is in good health and will do well. He started from the Atlantic with the famous or rather infamous Captain French, who managed to swindle his whole company, and left them in the lurch before half the journey was made. Many of his men were nine and ten months getting to California, ragged, penniless, and hungry, and all stigmatizing the said Captain French as a most infernal scoundrel. In Mexico, this fellow swindled not only his own men, but many mercantile houses, by drawing fraudulent Bills of Exchange on New York etc. Groff was one of his victims, and has suffered great hardships in reaching California; but he is in good spirits, and happy to have at last found a friend.[1]

---

[1] Here Perkins refers to one of the celebrated episodes of Gold Rush history, the misfortunes of the Parker H. French company, which sailed from New York on May 13, 1850, broke up at El Paso in September, and straggled across the southern reaches of the continent by detachments. A principal source of information is William Miles, *Journal of the Sufferings and Hardships of Capt. Parker H. French's Overland Expedition to California* . . . (Chambersburgh, Pa., 1851); additional details were recalled by Charles Cardinell in the San Francisco *Courier*, 1856, reprinted as "Adventures on the Plains" in California Historical Society *Quarterly*, July, 1922, Vol. I, pp. 57–71. Members of the company reached San Francisco December 14, 1850. Perkins' "young Groff" presumably is the "M. Grouff" listed in Miles's "Roll of Passengers."

Sonora has just been honored and beautified by the arrival of a bevy of fair and frail damsels, who have come up with the laudible design of easing the miners of their hard-earned gold-dust. They are a bad set, and last night a serious row took place in the house where they are lodged, and some men were badly hurt.

Up to this date very little rain has fallen and it is to be feared we shall have as dry a season as the last was a wet one. The weather is beautiful, and, in proportion as the skies grow brighter, the prospects of the miners and the merchants grow darker. Without abundance of water the mines in this region cannot be worked to advantage, and the miners will move off to the rivers and thus damage the business of the town.

We have finished a large and handsome Masonic Hall, and St. John's day was celebrated in a very creditable style. The procession numbered over five hundred, in which there were not a few Royal Arches and Knight Templars in their rich regalia. I was chosen Orator on the occasion, and delivered the first Masonic discourse in the Southern Mines. The Order is highly respectable here; surprisingly so, when we consider the state of society. There is more care taken to exclude unworthy men than I have remarked in the United States and Canada.[2]

Now that I have brought my Journal to the end of 1850, I shall devote a chapter to the discovery of gold in California, and to a sort of retrospective view of the condition of things during the year, as far as they have passed under my observation. The statements in reference to the first discovery of Gold and its immediate effects on the then scanty population in the country, I make on the authority of people with whom I have conversed, and publications of eye witnesses. The country had only just been militarily occupied by the United States troops, and only a few civilians had as yet found their way into the

---

[2] The *Stockton Times* of May 4, 1850, reported: "The first Masonic Meeting was held at Sonora on the 28th day of April, 1850; a Lodge is about to be organized immediately, working under dispensation of the Grand Lodge State New York." According to Lang's *A History of Tuolumne County*, p. 85, the Tuolumne Lodge, F. & A. M., No. 8, was chartered at Sonora on November 27, 1850. Perkins' name appears on the list of members. He was orator of the day when cornerstone ceremonies were held on June 24, 1851, for a Masonic Hall about to be built. This date would seem to conflict with Perkins' journal entry, but the *Sonora Herald* of September 20, 1851, mentions that the new Masonic Hall is rapidly approaching completion.

ceded territory. The whole of the gold region contained only tribes of wandering aborigines.

CHAPTER XV

It was in the month of January, 1848, that two men, whose names were [James] Marshall and [Charles] Bennett, were engaged in the erection of a saw mill for John A. Sutter, on the south fork of American River, at a point where oak, pine and cedar trees covered the surrounding hills, and where Indian labor was to be procured in abundance and at a nominal price; these of course being the motives that prompted Sutter to establish a mill and trading post in this, at that time, wild and savage region. Little did he imagine or foresee that, in the hands of a great overruling Destiny, he was to be the instrument of disclosing to the world riches, of which the wildest imagination had never dreamed, and of opening out an immense field for the enterprize of the crowded population of the old world, covering the hitherto virgin Pacific with the white sails of Commerce and Industry!

One morning, Marshall, while inspecting the tail-race of the mill, discovered, much to his astonishment, some small shining particles in the sand at the bottom of the race, which, upon examination, he became satisfied were gold. Not content however with the result of his own investigations, he sent some specimens, by Bennett, to San Francisco, where all doubt was removed of their nature and purity. The discovery was kept a profound secret while Bennett proceeded to Monterey, then the Capital, and tried to obtain a grant of the land on which the gold was found, from Colonel Mason, then Military Governor of the Territory. The Colonel however informed him that he had no power to make such a grant, and Bennett returned to San Francisco, where he exhibited his specimens to Mr. Sam Brannan, Mr. [Lansford W.] Hastings and others.

A number of persons visited the spot and satisfied their curiosity.

Chapter VI

From this epoch, my reminiscences will take the form of a journal, as by this means I shall be better able to depict the daily, weekly and monthly events which checkered my life in California, and which I shall take from the copious notes I jotted down under the influence of the actual circumstances.

I must premise by stating that my experience in actual digging has been very limited, and what little work I have performed in that line was more for amusement than profit. I had no sooner arrived in the mines, than I decided to turn my attention to commerce in preference to mining, which entailed an amount of labor and personal suffering I was entirely unwilling to encounter.

To commence then with my journal.

January 1850. Our house is built of adobes,* and is surmounted by a large sign-board, painted by myself. The house boasts of two glazed windows, the sash of which is also of home manufacture, made with no other tools save a saw and a pocket knife. No other building in the town can boast of such luxury, and they are the envy and admiration of all our neighbors. It is consequently a pardonable vanity of J. and myself, if we spend half an hour daily outside the store in admiring our handy-work. The shelves, counters and doors are all made with our own hands. A tin, or rather sheet-iron stove, with copper sheathing pipe, stands in a corner, and I at least have the right to look with complacency on the treasure. The history of the copper pipe is worth relating.

The rains had set in early in November, and so much water fell that the roads became entirely flooded and cut up. It was impossible to traverse them even on horse-back, for the virgin soil became so saturated and spongy that a horse would sink to the belly in almost any part of the route between the mines and Stockton.

Two of our teams had been weather-bound at the river, a distance of forty miles, and as there was no hope of getting them through until spring, I had to walk down to where they were, and dispose of their contents.

* The Mexican adobe is a large sun-dried brick. Its usual size is eighteen inches by ten or twelve, and four inches thick. A house built of these bricks and protected from the rain by lime plaster lasts as long as stone.

A leaf from William Perkins' manuscript, in his own hand.

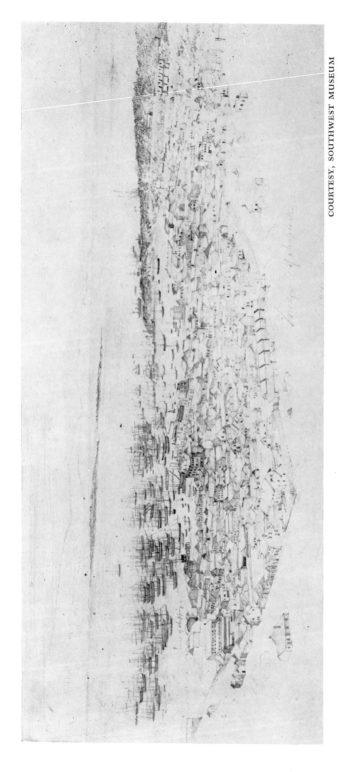

San Francisco. Sketched in pencil from Nob Hill on May 30, 1850, by John Woodhouse Audubon. At center, Long Wharf extends into Yerba Buena Cove.

Wood's Creek.

Wood's Creek in 1849. A lithograph from William M'Ilvaine, Jr.'s *Sketches of Scenery and Notes of Personal Adventure in California and Mexico* (Philadelphia, 1850). The artist mentions traveling from Wood's Creek "through the Mexican (Sonorian) encampment, the most beautiful one in the mines, boasting many ladies . . . where the dry-goods and other stores had quite a city look . . . even ice creams could be procured."

Stocktow.

Stockton in 1849. A second lithograph by M'Ilvaine. He describes Stockton as "situated on a slough which empties into the San Joaquin River. The scenery . . . is entirely different from that of the Sacramento—immense Tulárè (bulrush) marshes extending on both sides as far as the eye can reach. . . . The Sierra Nevada . . . were too distant to enter into the scene . . . though their snowy summits could sometimes be discovered."

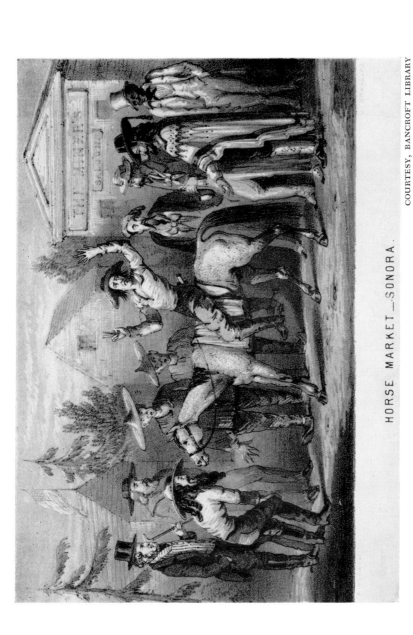

HORSE MARKET—SONORA.

Horse Market, Sonora. Colored lithograph by Frank Marryat, one of
William Perkins' Sonora acquaintances, from his *Mountains and Molehills*
(London, 1855).

THE BAR · OF · A GAMBLING SALOON.

The Bar of a Gambling Saloon. A second colored lithograph from Marryat's *Mountains and Molehills*, perfectly illustrating Perkins' journal.

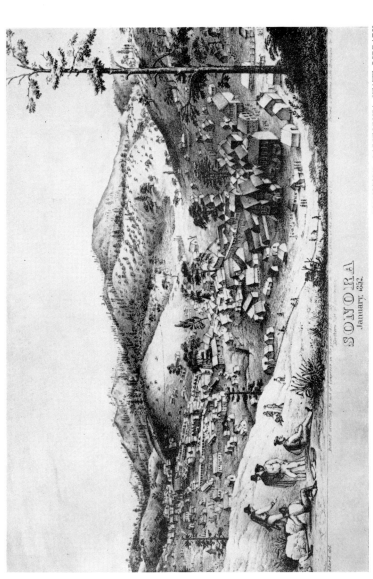

Sonora in January, 1852. Lithograph by George H. Goddard made six months before the great fire of June 17, 1852. The view is north toward Bald Mountain. The large building under the pine limb at right is the Masonic Hall. The structure with the three gables, a little to the north on South Washington Street, may have housed Theall, Perkins & Co.

Lower (Southern) Californians. A vaquero and his lady, sketched in pen, pencil, and crayon by William Perkins. See his comment in his journal, p. 294.

Captain Sutter himself went to San Francisco and confirmed the statements of Bennett, and about the first of April the fact became public property.

Of course the news spread with velocity, and in eight or ten days, about a thousand people were on their way to the gold region.

The more staid and would-be sensible men affected to, and possible did, view it as an illusion, and cautioned others against the probability of ruining themselves in the pursuit of a chimera; yet many of these, who would boldly pronounce the discovery a humbug, and the gold hunters maniacs, might have been seen on the morrow stealthily wending their way, with a tin pan and shovel concealed beneath their cloaks or *zarapes,* to the boats about proceeding up the golden Sacramento.

By the middle of July, the whole lower country was depopulated. *Rancheros* left their herds to revel in delightful liberty upon the hills and plains. Merchants closed their stores; lawyers marched off side by side with their clients; doctors deserted their patients, and soldiers and sailors took "french leave" of their regiments and ships. Col. Mason, the governor, was himself seized with the prevailing mania, and started off for the mines with his adjutant and an escort, in order, he said "to be better able to make a report to the Federal Government at Washington." [1] The Alcalde of San Francisco stopped the wheels of Justice and followed the current. Every idler in the country who could beg, borrow or steal a horse, a pan and a shovel, was off, and ere the first of August, in the principal towns, none were left but the aged, the sick, the females and the children. In San Francisco, the headquarters of all the business done in California, there were, at the time I am speaking of, but seven male inhabitants left, and only one store open.

In the meantime the most extravagant stories were in circulation. Hundreds, and even thousands of dollars were mentioned as being the general result of a day's labor. The reality was wonderful enough. All

---

[1] As noted in the Introduction, Colonel R. B. Mason first visited the mines in June and July, 1848. His celebrated report authenticating the gold discovery and the extent of the deposits was dated August 17, 1848, and, when released with President Polk's Message to Congress, December 5, 1848, did much to touch off the Gold Rush.

kind of liquor was sold at an ounce a bottle. Indians greedily gave ten or twelve ounces for a blanket; and provisions sold almost for their weight in gold.

Fresh discoveries were made at "Mormon Island," as far north as the Yuba River, and as far south as the Estanislao, and the mining population had swelled to about three thousand.[2]

The reports that were in circulation at this time, although some were highly colored, were, in the main, true. I have seen many persons, whose word I had no reason to doubt, who have assured me that in the early times of the mines they have taken out for days and days, fifty ounces of gold, and then stopped from actual surfeit of the glittering treasure! And I will vouch for the truth of the latter part of the above sentence. I have myself seen dozens who have worked for a week, made one, two or three thousand dollars, and have then thrown up work until the whole of the amount was spent. I have seen men invent the most extravagant means to get rid of their dust. The pouring a whole bottle of liquor into a wine glass, which I think I have mentioned before, was a common *gracia*—in fact the foolish bravado of the English sailor, eating a five pound note with his bread and butter, has been parodied in a hundred different ways, during the first gold fever.

One would naturally suppose that, under these circumstances, the merchants or traders would have secured immense fortunes. No such thing! They were just as improvident as the miner; and at this moment there is probably not one out of ten of those who enjoyed such wonderful opportunities for money making, but that is now a poor man. A Mr. Belt, of Stockton,[3] when I arrived there, had a business that was

---

[2] To this point in chapter xv Perkins has closely paraphrased E. Gould Buffum, *Six Months in the Gold Mines* (Philadelphia, 1850), pp. 67–69. Again in chapter xix Perkins relies upon Buffum for information relating to events of 1848.

[3] George G. Belt had come to California in 1847 in Stevenson's regiment. Later he was the partner of Peter Mehen in a Sonora mercantile venture which broke up in a lawsuit. Carlo M. De Ferrari relates that the courts decided against Belt on grounds that Mehen was an illiterate man who defrauded his partner of $5,000 through ignorance; Belt, as an experienced business man, should have checked over accounts more carefully. Mrs. George Eastman points out to the editors that Mehen came to be highly respected in the Sonora community, being given by the citizens of that town on June 18, 1860, "a magnificent gold watch, as a token of their appreciation of his services as a public servant, in various

giving him a thousand dollars a day profit. He used every morning to fill his buckskin bag with gold-dust, and by night it would all be spent. At the time I am writing, he is in difficulties. Teamsters would get from fifty cents to one dollar a *pound* for carrying freight to the mines, and would return with empty pockets. Traders in the mines would sell their goods at a profit of four or five hundred percent, and would scarcely have enough left to pay the first cost. Where all the money went to is a mystery, for it is plain that if one man spent it another must have received it, and yet none returned to the States with large fortunes in those days.

As a sample of what a breakfast cost, even after my arrival, I copy a bill which I paid one morning, riding from one camp to another.

A small box of Sardines	$5	
Sea biscuit, ad lib	1	
a bottle of English ale	8	
8# Barley for horse	12	*Total Twenty-six dollars*

But with all this, as I have said, people did not seem to grow rich. The fact is that gold became a drug, and the class of people then in California did not value it. In those days almost every miner made what is called a "strike" every week or so, that gave him a small fortune, and he then seemed to be on thorns until it was spent.

Were I to set down the tithe of the number of "strikes" made by the miners, that I am cognisant of, the account would astonish the reader. The extraordinary treasures found in unthought of places; the "pockets" filled with shining gold, the large "chunks" found by lucky individuals, all would sound like a fairy tale, or the effect of Aladdin's Lamp. But my own adventures, my own experiences and my own reflexions are what will form the most appropriate subjects for a work of this description, where daily events, jotted down in the unsophisticated language of a common place book, will convey an accurate idea of the reality.

It is difficult for a people who lives in a level country, to understand the tremendous labor of traversing the mountainous parts of California, in the so-called Gold Region. This auriferous region lies among the spurs of the *Sierra Madre,* or Cordilleras. The mountains are not in

capacities, in that city, for the past ten years" (*Columbia Times,* June 28, 1860).

regular ranges, but in groups varying from five hundred to six and eight thousand feet in height, and are of the most rugged character. No animals but mules can cross them, and in the early days of the mines, when a mule was *worth its weight in gold dust*, the miner, in moving about from place to place "prospecting" had to pack his provisions, his implements, such as spade, pick axe and washing pan, with a pair of blankets, on his shoulders, and make his weary way on foot over these gigantic rocks.

The descents to the different rivers are fearful. From a dizzy height you look down, down, and there amongst titanic boulders of granite, of awe-inspiring magnitude, you may see what appears to be a thin thread of silver, winding its way like a ray of light amongst the awful and mysterious looking abysms and the wilderness of piled up rocks, that look as if some mighty fiend had stood on the mountain tops of the *Sierras*, and had cast the huge masses promiscuously and headlong down the steeps.

"How fearful

And dizzy 'tis to cast one's eyes so low!

The crows and choughs, that wing the midway air,

Show scarce so gross as beetles: half way down

Hangs one that gathers samphire; dreadful trade!

Me thinks he seems no bigger than his head!"

On getting "half way down" the encampment of the white tents of the miners becomes visible. Once at the bottom you find yourself in another world. The "thread of silver" becomes a broad and rapid stream. Extensive plains spread out among the mountainous boulders, and you find hundreds of busy miners at work, who were entirely invisible from the summit. The air is sensibly darkened by the towering walls of the valley; the temperature is much higher, and the intense quietude of Nature, broken only by the rush of waters, is almost overpowering. You look towards the heavens and fancy that the river's walls are mingling with, and embracing the clouds.

I have seen and felt what I have so tamely and inadequately described. There is a grandeur about these scenes that requires abler pens than mine to do justice to.

Notwithstanding that I run the risk of repeating something already written in this work, I will describe the various positions in which the gold is found, and the numerous ways of procuring it.

At first it was supposed to exist only in fine particles in the mountain streams, and miners for a length of time "prospected" in these localities only. But it was soon discovered that the precious deposits were in the plains, far away from running streams, on the brows of hills, in the banks of rivers and creeks, in slate formations on the Yuba, in quartz, and in the earth even on the tops of high mountains; in fact everywhere. The gold found on the top of high hills has puzzled people considerably. It is found on or near the surface in coarse grains. The earth has to be brought on the backs of donkeys to where there may be water, and washed in pans, *batella* or cradle. It is not often, however, that gold is found in this situation.

For a long time the existence of the precious metal in quartz veins was unknown. It was discovered one day by a man in Mariposa, who, curiously examining a vein of snow white quartz that cropped out of a hill of granite, was agreeably astonished to find it rich with gold. He considered his fortune made. The news spread rapidly and hundreds commenced prospecting for quartz veins.

The discoverer, of course, set to work on his *veta*, and the first quartz blasted out was so rich that the gold was separated from the stone with hammers. But this richness soon disappeared, and when it became necessary to pulverize the quartz and separate the gold by means of amalgamation with quicksilver, it was found the operation was not remunerative. In fact to this day this description of mining has proved ruinous to nine out of ten of those who have tried it. By and by, with the aid of capital, science and proper machinery, it may become profitable.

It is generally denied that gold is to be found in any other matrix but quartz, and I am of this opinion. It is true large quantities of the metal has been found in the slate range on the river Yuba, and I have found it in slate formations near the river Estanislao. I have also in my possession a specimen where the gold is imbedded in a piece of limestone. I do not consider these as proofs however, of the falsity of the theory that quartz, and only quartz, is the true matrix of gold.

When the gold is found in any other rock than quartz, there is pretty evident proof of its having been imprisoned or embedded accidentally, while in quartz it appears to be a part of the stone, as felspar is a part of granite; proving that the deposition or creation of gold has been simultaneous with that of the quartz.[4]

The great slate formation of California extends to some distance about the river Yuba in the northern mines. The gold has undoubtedly been precipitated on this range by great floods and the lamenated upright rocks securely imprisoned the grains and flakes, which in some places have been found in large quantities. The manner of extracting the gold from these rocks is either by picking the flakes out, or by pounding the slate and washing it.

When it is supposed that the bed of a river or stream is rich, the waters are, when practicable, diverted from their channel, the loose earth scraped up, and washed in cradles. Many such speculations have turned out very well, while others have returned nothing. The fact is, unless the gold finds a secure hiding place at the bottom in narrow clefts, or on beds of clay, the continual action of the rushing waters and the grinding process of the ever rolling pebbles soon reduce the metal to impalpable flakes, in which state it is carried along by the current and finally into the ocean; for in the alluvial bottoms of the lower rivers, it would find no resting place.

The largest deposits of gold have been found in the banks of streams, where it has been lodged in clefts or "pockets" as they are technically termed, and in clay beds, by extraordinary floods, and where it has probably lain undisturbed for thousands of years. It is in such situations that the greatest "strikes" have been made; pockets having been found which contain *half a bushel* of gold. I have seen a thousand dollars washed out of a single panful of dirt.

But after all, the surest digging in California is in the plains or valleys of the mountains. The only difficulty is the scarcity of water. This drawback has to be remedied by bringing the necessary element by means of canals and often by canvas pipes to the spot. In these level places the gold seems to have been very equally distributed, and resting

---

[4] These views on California gold may be compared with the monograph of Adolph Knopf, *The Mother Lode System of California* (U. S. Geological Survey, Professional Paper No. 157, Washington, 1929). The Mother Lode was created by the same forces that brought the Sierra Nevada into being; gold and other metallic deposits were originally in the form of veins, but erosion widely scattered them to create the Calfornia gold fields.

upon the same stratum at an uniform depth. Here labor is always certain to be repaid, not perhaps extravagantly, but with profit. The miner digs a square hole about eight or ten feet in diameter, and throws up the dirt until he reaches the auriferous earth, which a little experience soon enables him to recognise. This he carefully collects in hide bags, and carries to the washing machines. When this auriferous earth is reached, it continues more or less rich, until stopped by the first rocky formation or by a bed of clay.

This fact seems to indicate that gold is of more recent formation than any of the metamorphic group; and I have not been able to find any instance of its being found *under* any considerable stratum of clay slate, primitive limestone or protogine, all of which belong to the Primary formation. In fact we find that the blue clay in the Tertiary and superficial formations forms a bed through which the gold seldom penetrates.

The veins of quartz running through the ranges of trap, granites, and gneiss, and which seem to be the cradle of gold, all apparently demonstrate a more recent existence than the Plutonic, or even the Volcanic formations.

Near Sonora there is a rich digging in a small valley, where the deposits of gold lie immediately under a transition or Granwacke formation; but the miners themselves, without knowing the difference between the Plutonic and the Tertiary groups, and having no theory in reference to the production of gold, consider the circumstance of its being found in such a situation as something extraordinary. The gold is not found intermixed with the rocks, but in the loose earth underneath.

I had some interesting fossils brought me from this place, consisting of leaves of fern etc. An interesting volume might be written on the geological structure of the mining region of California; yet I question if it shall ever be in the power of that science to elucidate the mystery of the production of gold. And in this we must acknowledge a higher wisdom than we possess; for should we by any means get possession of this secret of Nature's Laboratory, and find out the origin of gold, we should probably render it comparatively valueless, and would thus destroy one great incentive to colonizing the wastes and deserts of the world, all of which, it is undoubtedly the Will of the Great Intelligence, shall, at some time or other, be made subservient to the wants and happiness of mankind.

CHAPTER XVI

NEW YEARS DAY, 1851. Twelve months have flown rapidly away since I commenced this Journal. Will it be written up to the close of the present year?

Fearful and yet exciting has been my life in this country, and it seems a special dispensation of a good Providence that I am at this moment in life, and health. Yes, an eventful year the last has been to me, and a general summing up would probably form a picture that might well startle me in after years.

We will let it pass. I have escaped, and uninjured in mind and body so far. But this day makes me sad; it makes me think of the quiet home, and domestic fireside that might have been mine under other circumstances. Am I then unhappy? No; far from it. I have been light hearted, "jolly" and industrious. My life in this country has not been an unhappy one. All that makes up the enjoyment of a bustling life has entered into mine: dangers, labors and excitement of every kind, success in worldly affairs, good friends, a free spirit and a clear conscience.

It is ungrateful of me to be sad. I cannot look back upon any former equal period of my life and see in it fewer weary hours, fewer unhappy ones. Then, to complain, is ingratitude to Divine Providence for the *enjoyment* of such a life as I have been obliged to lead in California.

But still, there are days in the year when sweet homelike thoughts take possession of a man's mind to the exclusion of all others. These are days hallowed by the memory of times gone by, when, as children, we celebrated them with children's joy, and children's games. When ever such a day comes, wherever the Wanderer may be, his thoughts spring back to home, for he knows that on that day he is in the hearts and memory of his early and dearest companions. Then if the Wanderer is in my situation, he will commence to draw comparisons between the enjoyments of the great world, the adventurous excitements of a wild life, the unsympathizing communion with strangers, the continual contest in the whirlpool of Fortune-making, the rough scenes through which both mind and body have to pass—to the quiet of a home, the peacefulness of communion with those who are near and dear to the heart; the happiness of a domestic hearth; the cheerful smile of a loved wife, the prattling welcome of children, the calm—Halloo! where am I running to! Any thing in the shape of sentimentality sounds so strange in this matter-of-fact country, that I am *almost* inclined to laugh at my little ebullition of sensibility.

This time last year, we were ensconced in a miserable adobe hut, (we thought it magnificent at that time!) with very few goods, and those few with difficulty sheltered from the rain; sleeping on the damp ground with a saddle, or perchance a log of wood for a pillow; our clothes almost always wet, and at times drenched by sudden torrents breaking through the doors, or the canvass roof of the house. Yet for all that we were as merry as crickets, and a hot arrack punch would set all to rights. Now we have a large establishment, and a good house, and I may say gratefully, we ought to be very well satisfied with the years business. If I am not quite as lighthearted now as I was, it is because I have naturally more cares upon me, in the control of an increasing business, and in the position which I occupy in the community.

But if some sad thoughts will naturally force themselves upon one at this epoch of festivity in other lands, they must be bravely combatted.

"Frank! make me a huge champagne cocktail."

"Si Señor."

"Here's to the New Year! Frank, is dinner ready?"

"Señor, *the banquet waits!*"

Frank, short English for Francisco, is our Mexican boy; and the above phrase is all he knows of the language. That scamp, Enyart, taught them to him; and he astonishes the San Francisco folks, when we happen to have any of them in the house, by the serious and *bona fide* manner in which he enunciates the pompous summons, the absurdity of which will be better understood at seeing our bill of fare—a piece of beef and a plate of beans.

JANUARY EIGHTH. Enyart received letters from home that have induced him to return to the States. He started for San Francisco today. His absence causes a blank in my every day life, that one not acquainted with the intimacy between us could scarcely believe, for our characters are entirely distinct. He was my steady companion from

Cincinnati to California, and we have together gone through scenes that try men's characters by a severe ordeal. He ever proved true as steel.

In the company that I commanded through Mexico, there were four of us who, from the sympathy caused by the similitude of education and habits, formed a little set apart from the rest; that is, we messed together, made up our beds together; smoked and chatted together, with more freedom than with the others of the party.

Hyde and Corse, from Maryland, Enyart, from Ohio, I, from Canada. Poor Corse, who had left a young wife at home, was seized with the cholera in Monter[r]ey. Hyde, Enyart and I were the only members of the party who dared remain with him. The rest encamped some twenty miles the other side of Monter[r]ey. All that was to be done we did for our poor friend, but the attack was fearfully violent, and the same night he died in my arms. We buried him in the beautiful cementary of the American Army, at Walnut Springs, a few miles from town; and we were accompanied by most of the foreigners, residents of Monter[r]ey; Gen.[1] Miñon, then in command, sending his Aid-de-camp, as a mark of respect. It was a sad day for us, and dampened our spirits for a long time.[1]

Mr. Hyde's history is as mournful a one as the preceding. When I first came up to the mines, he accompanied me, and the unlucky incident which I have mentioned in a former part of this Journal, my being poisoned, brought me to Sonora. Otherwise I should have accompanied him to the *Mercedes* river. However, we separated, and on the occasion of my trip south to look after a lot of goods, finding myself near to the Mercedes, I rode over to see him. I found him in his miner's dress, and strong and robust as a bear. He had not been successful, and spoke of going down to San Francisco, and there enter into business.

In November of 1849, I went down to Stockton to see if I could send up a few loads of goods, although the rain had already set in heavily. There were no hotels in those days. Every man carried his own bedding with him, and got the shelter of some friend's house or tent. I went to lodge in a large canvas house belonging to a young man by the

---

[1] See Perkins' remarks in chapter i, and Samuel McNeil's account of Corse's death quoted in the Introduction.

name of [A. A. ?] Brinsmade. Here I found Enyart, who as yet had not been to the mines,[2] a Dr. Clements, whom I had met in New Orleans, and Mr. Hyde; the latter with a bad cough, but otherwise apparently healthy and strong. It was a joyous meeting for us all, and we passed a jolly night.

The next day, the rain poured down without intermission; and about one o'clock I saw Hyde put on his india-rubber coat to go out. I remonstrated with him. However, he went, but returned in a few minutes. At six o'clock he was lying on his bed coughing and gasping. I became alarmed, and sent out to seek Dr. Clements who had not yet entered. Hyde treated it all as a trifle, and said he would be up and well by tomorrow.

Alas! his tomorrow was Eternity!

At ten o clock the Doctor came in. I asked him at once to examine Mr. Hyde.

He went into the little space canvassed off from a corner of the house. He was absent about ten minutes, and when he returned, his look startled me. He took me aside, and said:

"You and Enyart are the most intimate friends that Mr. Hyde has here; one of you had better go in and break the terrible fact to him, that he cannot outlive the night."

I was thunderstruck; for although my limited medical skill had informed me that Hyde was more seriously ill than he thought himself, yet I had no idea of the existence of immediate danger.

"Good God! Doctor," said I, "what do you mean?"

"What I say"; replied he, in a low tone. "His pulmonary complaint has reached that awful climax, when, in the space of a few hours, his lungs will melt away like wax before a strong fire."

"And no hope; no chance of a favorable turn; no remedy?"

"His death tonight is as certain, as is yours or mine at some future period," said the Doctor. "No human power or skill can avail him. And his time is so short, that it is a duty you owe to him, to acquaint him at

---

[2] Mistakenly or not, Perkins consistently holds that Enyart remained at Stockton during the summer of 1849. Compare chapter ii, note 10. The doctor in whose company Perkins found him was Dr. J. B. Clements, who, with Dr. Jno. W. Reins, was proprietor of the Stockton Drug Store, advertised in the *Stockton Journal,* November 6, 1850.

once of his certain fate, so that he may make immediate preparation."

The Doctor was right; it was a painful duty, but one we had no right to shrink from.

Enyart and I walked softly into the chamber of the unsuspecting, but doomed man. In as firm a voice as we could command, we did our errand. Great God! it was a fearful message to deliver a man who still felt the healthy and hot blood coursing through his veins!

He started up in his bed, and glared upon us with a wild and terrified look.

"What, die tonight! Impossible! Why, I feel quite strong! call the Doctor; oh God!" and he fell back on his pillow.

The Doctor came; Hyde interrogated him with a look; it was enough!

"Get me pen and ink, quick," said he. "I want to write to my wife. Enyart, you write for me; quick, quick!"

And we left Enyart alone with him, receiving his last wishes and writing down his last words.

When the letter was written, he called us all in; he was about to sign his name himself. He did so; *Charles Hyde,* in almost illegible characters.

He then requested me to read the prayers for the dying, from the Common Prayer Book. He responded in a distinct voice; then requested the Profession of Belief, and as with dim eyes, I commenced it from the Communion Service, he cried:

"Not that one, P[erkins]; the other; the short one!"

This over, he bade us farewell; shook hands with all of us. I took his hand; it was clammy, but warm.

"God bless you, dear Hyde" I sobbed: "do not fear."

"P[erkins]" said he calmly, "you have known me for some time; have I been wicked? Have I used bad language? Have I ever injured you or any one? Tell me."

"My poor Hyde," I replied; "I know of no sins that can at this moment lie heavy on your soul; to me, and to those who know you here, you have ever been a Christian gentleman." And I said nothing more than the plain truth. Hyde was a highminded, pure and honorable man.

He spoke no more. In a few seconds, he suddenly raised himself upon one elbow, seized a glass of water standing on a table by his bedside, and carried it tremblingly to his lips. His teeth chattered fearfully against the edge of the tumbler; he could not drink; he set the glass again upon the table, and without a groan or struggle, fell back on the pillow, *dead.*

Thus died the second of our quartette; and by a singular, shall I say providential, chance, both Enyart and myself by his side to attend to the last sad offices we are permitted to pay to humanity.

I am not sorry that I have been led into this digression, as it has enabled me to record the names and melancholy fate of our two poor friends. In penning the account of Hyde's death, it appears to me, even at this distant period, that every scene, every word has flashed upon my memory with a vividness and clearness almost extraordinary.

We buried him in the burying ground of Stockton, about half a mile from the town, Enyart, Brinsmade and I being the sole companions of his last earthly journey. The day was dark, and the rain pouring down in torrents, and it was with difficulty we could find a wretched cart with one mule to carry the body. For this we paid an exhorbitant price; six ounces, I think; six ounces more for digging the grave and four ounces for a poor deal coffin, which however, we covered with black cloth.

CHAPTER XVII

SUNDAY, TWELFTH. As yet we have had no winter. The weather is lovely, warm and balmy. Since the first fall of rain in November, the skies have been cloudless, and the miners have moved off to the vicinities of the rivers.

The Indians are becoming more mischievous than ever. A party of five men has just been attacked by them, a few miles from Sonora and all the five are badly wounded with arrows. A body of hunters immediately started in pursuit, and, overtaking the savages the same day, a smart fight ensued, the result of which was a booty of twenty Indian scalps. The rest escaped up the mountains.

What surprises me is, that the Indians have not attempted to fire the town at night. It might be done with the greatest ease and impunity, for there is never any guard; policemen, watchmen or sentinels are not known here, and the town, within a days journey of a dozen, probably a score of Indian *Rancherias* full of our mortal enemies. Really we are superbly careless of our lives in this paradoxical country.

TWENTY SIXTH. We have just received intelligence from Curtiss' Camp, a *Placer* eight miles from Sonora,[1] that a fatal affray has taken

---

[1] The catalogue of violence Perkins here begins also provided subject matter for a letter by Robert Wilson to the *Alta California* of February 10, dated Near Castoria, February 7, 1851:

"MESSRS. EDITORS—I am indebted to Mr. [Emanuel] Linoberg, a merchant of Sonora, for the following items:—

"During the week ending on the 1st instant there were five violent deaths in the region of country within 6 miles around Sonora.

"At Curtisville, on Sunday the 26th ult., a young man named Boggs, of Maryland, was shot through the head by another named Bowen, of Missouri. Bowen was immediately seized, a lariat was thrown around his neck, and he was hung upon the spot.

"On the same day, at Shaw's Flat, two men quarrelled about four dollars, and one of them, named Fowler or Fuller, shot the other. The murderer is in prison.

"At York Town, a man named Kelley, and a Mexican, had a quarrel. The Mexican killed Kelley with a club. He was arrested.

"A Chilano, near Sonora, in loading a pistol, shot himself through the head.

"A German doctor, named Burns, has been working a very rich gold vein, in Sonora, for the last month. He has already taken out an immense 'pile.'

"Mr. Linoberg thinks the population of the town of Sonora is about five thousand. Business had improved a little, but was still very dull. Stock of goods heavy and prices low. The winter supplies laid in by many of the miners were nearly exhausted.

"Buildings are still going up in Sonora. A saw mill in the neighborhood, worked by water power, is making money. There are three auctioneers in the town, three apothecaries, eight doctors, five lawyers, and not a single priest or preacher. The Freemasons have a lodge, and fifty members.

"Mr. Linoberg met, on this side of the Stanislaus, a drove of seven hundred cows, most of them with calves, just arrived from the lower country. The price asked for a cow and calf was sixty dollars."

Curtis' Camp, or Curtisville, where the lynching occurred on January 26, was situated on Curtis Creek, an affluent of Sullivans Creek, south of Sonora. The *Sonora Herald* of February 1 gives the names of the principals in the affair place in which a gambler killed a man in a most brutal manner. The miners immediately secured the murderer, tried him in a Judge Lynch's court, and, finding him guilty, strung him up on an oak tree; the best action I have heard of in the mines. The example will, I hope, be followed every where.

FEBRUARY FIRST. Four murders have been committed in our vicinity this week. A gambler shot a miner, and he in his turn was executed by the people. This however may well be termed a legal murder, as the man was tried and condemned fairly by a jury. We want a few more of such examples. When the constitutional law is powerless, the people must protect themselves.

Another murder took place on Sunday at Shaw's Flats, three miles from Sonora.[2] Two American miners quarrelled, and commenced fighting. They were comrades, worked, and lived together, in the same tent. The fight took place in front of the tent, where a large fire was burning. In the contest, the combatants grappled and fell near the fire, when the one who was uppermost, scraping up some hot coals and ashes threw them into the others face and bosom. The tortured man screamed in agony, and begged for quarter, reiterating that he "gave up." His antagonist let him rise; but no sooner was he on his feet, than he rushed into the tent, and seized his rifle. The other took to his heels across the plains, but the enraged and suffering man took deliberate aim at his flying comrade, fired, and shot him dead. The murderer gave himself up to the authorities; but it was properly considered that the provocation was so great, that for the time being he was a maniac, and not responsable for his actions. He own conscience will be his most unforgiving judge. He has killed his dearest friend, and the man is

---

there as Elander or Alexander Boggs and William Bowen. The *Stockton Times* of the same date prints a Sonora letter by "Alpha," January 28, which recounts the quarrel between Bowen, a monte dealer, and Thomas D. McMasters, during which Bowen drew his revolver but was prevented from shooting by Alexander Boggs, a friend of McMasters. The quarrel was amicably settled and the parties drank together, but next morning, Sunday, Bowen killed Boggs and was hanged. The same correspondent tells of the quarrel at Shaws Flat between Tindall Newly and Andrew J. Fuller. At the time of writing Fuller had been arrested and jailed; Newly was still alive, with hope entertained of his recovery.

[2] Shaws Flat lies northwest of Sonora, between Woods Creek and Mormon Creek. As seen by the preceding note, the murderer was apparently named Fuller.

even now almost wild with remorse. No punishment can be as severe, as the letting him live.

Near the same place, a poor Irishman was murdered at the same time, by some Mexicans two or three of whom it is believed are in custody, but nothing can be proved against them. The Irishman's throat was cut, and he was buried the same night. The next day he was missed, and his friends, suspecting his fate from a quarrel he had had with a Mexican, made search for him, and soon found the body, half buried.

The Indians are still committing outrages around us. Several murders have lately been perpetrated by them. They seize every opportunity of attacking isolated miners, and, unfortunately, the latter give them too many occasions. In the spirit of adventure, and impatience of ill-success in the old *Placeres*, there are always plenty of miners, who, strapping their blankets and mining tools on their shoulders start out alone for the mountains, "prospecting"; that is, seeking some new *placer*, valley, gulch or ravine hitherto unknown, and that may turn out rich in the precious metal. Here in their solitary labors they are set upon by the Indians, and murdered.

How many must have lost their lives in this manner, that we know nothing of; whose friends, whose relatives will never hear of them, and whose actual fate we shall remain ever ignorant of. The number of these victims must be already considerable. Poor wretches,

> "Unhousel'd, unappointed, unanel'd
> No reckoning made, but sent to their account
> With all their imperfections on their head."

FEBRUARY TENTH. Last night there was a grand *Fandango* in the Ball room in the second storey of Lecoq's new house, and all the Mexican women were dressed in their best. I sauntered in during the night, as a "looker on in Vienna," and stood with my arms folded, in one corner of the room, watching the voluptuous movements of the *Samacueca*. At this moment a scuffle took place on the balcony in front of the house, and a young gambler by the name of [William] Anderson rushed into the room with his face covered with blood, followed by another gambler, notorious as a scientific "bruiser" and dangerous villain, who had already killed several people in quarrels and fights.

Anderson passed out of the room, but a few minutes later, as

Mulligan was explaining how the quarrel commenced, a great uproar was heard below, and Anderson rushed into the room with a revolver in his hand. Mulligan's pistol was out at once, and here, in a room full of people, most of them women, did these two ruffians commence firing at each other. The confusion was terrible. As there was more danger in trying to make my way out of the crowd, than remaining inside, I kept my position without stirring, in the corner. The scoundrels fired *nine shots* with their revolvers. One took effect in Anderson's knee, shattering it completely; another killed an old Mexican in the street, and a third wounded a Mexican girl in the room slightly. It is a miracle there were so few casualties.

SEVENTEENTH. Just returned from Stockton, which town is filling up rapidly with respectable people from the States; and the magnificent plains which surround it are being cultivated in a regular manner. Many of the merchants have sent home for their families, and, for the first time in California, I have enjoyed the society of respectable women, and romped with white curly headed Saxon children. I actually put on a white shirt and a black coat, and escorted the lady of a Captain in the U. S. army to the theatre!

On the twenty fourth, the French population gave a dinner in commemoration of the declaration of the Republic in France, in 1848. One hundred and fifty people sat down to the table, and the whole affair was something that has never before been seen in the Southern Mines. How Louis and Lecoq, our worthy Restaurateurs,[3] managed to set such a table, up here amongst the mountains, puzzled me greatly. There were delicacies which, although common enough in New York, I was ignorant were to be procured in this country. The feast cost upwards of two thousand dollars.

I have a little pride in saying that I am a great favorite with the

[3] Perkins alluded to "Lecoq's new house" on February 14. According to the U. S. census enumeration made at Sonora on May 20, 1851, Louis Le Coq, aged 25, and Louis Ville [*i.e.*, Vielle], aged 45, both born in France, were tavern keepers in Dwelling No. 1026. Le Coq owned real estate to the value of $10,000, Ville to that of $5,000, which might indicate that the former had a two-thirds interest in the enterprise. Their "French Coffee House, Restaurant & Table D'Hote" was advertised in both English and French in the *Stockton Times* from April 6, 1850, as also in the *Sonora Herald* after that paper commenced. The festivities of February 24 mentioned by Perkins are recorded in the *Sonora Herald*, March 15, 1851, a feature of the occasion being toasts by himself, Tuttle, and H. P. Barber.

foreign population. The French call me, *L'ami des Etrangers;* the Spaniards *El Amigo de los Estranjeros,* a title that I am proud of, as it has been acquired by continued exertions on my part to defend the rights of these people against the sometime brutality and injustice of the Yankee lord of the soil. I will do the latter the justice to say, however, that as a general rule the Americans have behaved nobly and generously with the foreigners in California. But there are many exceptions; and the character of the Americans often leads them into errors in reference to people from other countries.

To the South American, the arrogance or rather the quiet contempt of the North American must be very galling. The Yankee has in a preeminent degree, the Saxon vice of looking down, as upon an inferior, on all those who may happen not to be able to converse with him in his own native tongue. Now, amongst our Spanish population there are numbers of gentlemen of family and education, particularly among the Argentinos, from whose country the vulgar tyranny of Rosas has driven the greater part of the aristocracy to seek a shelter in foreign lands; and the situation that these men, with all their pride of race, find themselves placed in with reference to an overbearing and vulgar class of Americans, must be painful in the extreme; and I will venture to say, these people will carry with them, when the[y] leave the country, a very lively and perhaps unjust feeling of intense hatred to every thing pertaining to, or claiming kindred with, Brother Jonathan.

A novel sight was witnessed yesterday in our streets—a huge living turtle that had been brought up from San Francisco. But the creature died this morning. The length and fatigues of the journey were too much for him. Visions of turtle soup and green fat that had entered into our dreams last night, vanished with his untimely end.

MARCH SEVENTH. William Anderson, the young gambler, shot in the knee, the other day, died last night. He was one of the unhappy many in this country who have forsaken respectable associations, and disgraced respectable connections, by adopting gambling as a profession. Anderson's fate undoubtedly awaits nine tenths of the crew in California.[4]

I meet with so few of my countrymen in my travels, that it is always a pleasure to find one. In the Collector for the county of

---

[4] As detailed in the *Sonora Herald* of March 8, William Anderson died on the 6th, three weeks after being shot in the leg by William Mulligan.

Calaveras, I found Harry A[skins] the son of Col. A—— of London,
Canada; jovial, contented and industrious like most of the Canadians.

THURSDAY, THIRTEENTH. High doings today!

There is living in Sonora a Texan, by the name of [Joshua]
H[olden]. Report gives him but a very equivocal character. She says he
had to fly from Texas for murder, and that while there he was neither
more nor less than a common gambler. However, be that as it may, he
is one of the oldest citizens in the place, and has helped to build up the
town, and has conducted himself here as a respectable man. There is
nothing refined about him, but that is of little consequence in this
country. He is a great friend and patron of gamblers; that is, the better
sort, or aristocracy of the *Monte* table, and although he does not gamble
openly himself, he suffers it to be done in his house.

So much as a preface to what follows.

At the north end of the town there is a valley of about a mile in
extent, and a perfect plain. Mr. H[olden] had fenced in some twenty
acres of this valley, and had sown barley and vegetables in the
enclosure. In process of time most of this valley had been "prospected,"
the miners always respecting the ground enclosed by H[olden].

A few days ago, however, a company of down east Yankees, the
most unbearable, if they are the most honest of our population,
commenced working on the confines of this land and found the earth at
the depth of ten or twelve feet, rich with gold. Without the least
respect (when did a down easter ever respect any thing?) for the rights
of the owner of a fine field of barley, these independent gentlemen at
once staked off the whole field, destroying the grain and vegetables.

There can be no doubt that the miners had certain rights, but they
had no right to destroy property. They should have compounded with
the owner of the crop, or have waited for its removal.

Mr. H[olden] raised a party, proceeded to the field in question,
drove the miners off, and severely whipped the President and secretary
of one of the Yankee companies.

Although the impudent disregard of the rights of property deserved
chastisement, the act was imprudent to the last degree. H[olden] is
looked upon as the head of the gamblers, and the idea of these
disreputable scoundrels overawing the miners, was not to be borne.

Yesterday the latter assembled in force, set to work on the disputed
territory, and defied opposition. This morning H[olden] got together a

large body of his friends, and, well armed, marched down to the attack. A number of us followed, to see the fun. Bravely the attacking party rushed on, and bravely the Miners lay awaiting them behind their dirt intrenchments.

As soon as H[olden]'s party got within range, the miners opened fire with one general volley. A gambler, named [Leven] Davis, dropped dead, and some others wounded. The distance was too great for more deadly execution. The attacking party only waited to give one volley, wounding a miner, and then turned and ran. It was laughable to see them. But the affair is no laughable one.

The blood of the whole mining population is up. They are assembling in vast numbers, and swear that either they will have H[olden]'s blood, and the lives of every gambler in the town, or they will burn Sonora to the ground. H[olden] swears he will not be taken alive, and he has some desperate men with him. I fear that in their blind rage, the miners will commit outrages on innocent people.

I am writing this, after having loaded all the firearms in the house, and prepared for the worst. Our house, being of adobe, strongly built and ball proof is the refuge of most of the women of this quarter of the town. There are at least twenty of them now in the back room, and warehouse. I suppose I shall be obliged to give up my bed to some dark-eyed senorita; it is to be hoped she will not have the conscience to exact the whole of it!

Nine o'clock. Lord! how these women chatter, and what a row there is outside in the street. Without any reason whatever, we appear to be in hostility with the miners, who seem determined to consider Sonora as the abettor of the gamblers.

FRIDAY, FOURTEENTH. We have been up all night. In fact, I believe not an eye was closed in the whole town. Every moment we expected to see ourselves engaged in a deadly conflict; but, thank God, the danger has been turned aside. We have effected a reconciliation between H[olden] and the miners; the former making all the concessions in his power; offering to take care of the wounded miner at his own expense, and giving himself up to be examined before the Magistrates, where, no one appearing against him, he was discharged. A number of his friends, the gamblers, have been obliged to leave the town.

Thus our fearful forebodings of yesternight have disappeared in the calm and security of today, and many a breast is lightened of a weight of well justified apprehension. We have every reason to be thankful that the affair has ended so well. Only one life has been lost, and that of a man belonging to a class, whose entire destruction would be considered in any other light than a misfortune.

A number of young gentlemen from the Southern States, established at Mormon Gulch, hearing of our danger, came over in hot haste to our assistance. They had been told that our house was to be attacked, why, I do not know, and like stout men and good friends, were determined to stand by the first adobe house in the mountains. Instead of powder, we opened a case of prime old Arrack, and, aided by our friends and some of the chiefs of the formidable League, now convinced of their error, left it as dry as a tinder box.[5]

---

[5] For Joshua Holden see chapter xi, note 6. The incident Perkins relates, also recounted in the *Sonora Herald* March 15, 1851, and in the *Alta California*, March 17, 1851, is described as a "memorable riot" in Lang's *A History of Tuolumne County*, pp. 55–60. The "Holden Garden War" was fought near the site of the Sonora Union High School; his antagonists termed themselves the "Washington Company." According to the *Herald* for March 29, George Dangley died on March 25, 1851, of wounds received in this affray; thus there were two fatalities.

CHAPTER XVIII

APRIL TWELFTH. I have been twice down to Stockton since closing the last chapter; on one of the occasions, having the hardest ride I ever had in my life; seventy five miles in eight hours with the same horse. The reasons for these rapid journeys was, that heavy rains threatened to close the roads, and we were in want of merchandise.

The rain did not continue for many days; it is already too late in the season to hope for more water, and we must content ourselves as we best may. The spring foliage is coming out. The trees are budding, and the grass on the plains, making its way through the recently moistened earth.

A Duel *very nearly* came off a day or two ago between two

prominent gentlemen of our town, one a merchant Mr. P——
[Francisco Paria?], the other, the town Magistrate, Major [R. C.]
B[arry]. I believe the latter entered the Lodge in a state of entoxication
and was severely reproved by the former.

The Major's dignity was hurt, and, advised probably by some
over-zealous friends, and before the fumes of the liquor he had taken
could evaporate, he penned a challenge, which he immediately sent to
Mr. P—— by the hands of Major C——.

The challenge was of course accepted, and the weapons stipulated
were double barrelled guns loaded with a single ball.

The next morning at half past five P——, his second H—— and
Dr. Charneaux [Leon Charnaux] a french surgeon, mounted on
mules, were on their way to the place of meeting. This was the top of
a picturesque hill, about a mile from town. On arriving at this hill, the
party was to proceed until an appropriate place for the combat should
present itself.

P——'s party reached the top of the hill and dismounted to wait for
the other. By some culpable ignorance or carelessness on the part of
Major B[arry's] second, his party was on foot; the consequence being
that the principal, a rather stout short man, was completely blown, on
reaching the top of the hill, and was obliged to rest a considerable time,
to recover himself.

The belligerents then quickly walked down the slope of the hill,
and soon reached an open level spot, where forty steps could be measured off fairly for both parties.

In tossing up for choice of position P——'s second won, and he
placed his principal, giving him a very slight advantage of the sun, that
was now peering over the lofty mountains.

The *modus operandi* of the two seconds was ludicrously in
opposition to each other.

H—— made his principal take off his coat and vest, and slip on
over his cloth pantaloons others of white linen. There he stood all in
white, as if ready to be popped into a coffin; but it must be confessed,
offering a very wavering and uncertain mark in the sun's rays for his
adversary's aim.

The latter was placed on his ground by his second, all in black. He
did not even divest him of a voluminous great coat, probably considering it in the light of a shield.

The moral difference between the parties was as great as the physical. The White side was gay; Dr. Charneaux, an old army surgeon, kept up a chatter of reminiscences, that even the staid Mr. H——, the second, could not resist now and then laughing at. The Black side appeared to be more impressed with the seriousness of the affair.

When the men were placed, Charneaux stationed himself a few paces to the right of his friend, who advised him to move a little further off for his own safety; but with a Frenchman's levity he said he was certain, from a mental calculation he had made, Mr. B[arry]'s ball would pass on the other side.

In this critical position, and just as the seconds were about to separate, to give the word, down thundered a posse, the Judge [John G. Marvin?] and his officers, and arrested the combatants; that is, passed through the form of arresting them, for to have offered to carry them off would have been dangerous. As soon as the Judge had thus accomplished his duty, he gallopped off, as if fearful of hearing the reports of the guns.

White, now insisted on proceeding without loss of time, but Black, being an administrator of the laws, thought it incumbent to show his respect for them, by obeying their mandate. In other words Major B[arry] chose to consider himself under arrest, and retired with his second from the field.

He had made the matter public since the night before, and was even followed to the field by several individuals, who however kept at a respectable distance. In this way the Judge got scent of the affair and, being a well meaning man, a friend to both the belligerents, and withal very timid, he tried his best to put a stop to the duel.

But it happens that Mr. H—— is one of those quiet, determined men, who only require to be placed in difficult circumstances to show what stuff they are made of. The challenge had been given, without sufficient provocation, in a partial state of intoxication, and it had been accepted. The natural conclusion was that the parties had to fight, or the challenge had to be withdrawn. Mr. H—— in behalf of his friend, presented this alternative, proposing a spot out of the county for the next meeting, and stipulating that the principals should be kept in ignorance of the time and place, until the moment of starting. Major C—— on behalf of his friend, accepted the new arrangement, and every thing appeared favorable to the consummation of a gentlemanly homicide.

However, Major B[arry] had the good sense to acknowledge that he had acted somewhat hastily, and, early in the morning, when the seconds had already prepared mules for the occasion, he sent a note, withdrawing his challenge, and so the affair ended, after having kept the community in a twenty four [hours'] ferment, for, as I have said, the persons implicated were amongst the most prominent people in town.

APRIL FIFTEENTH. Two more unfortunate miners have been murdered. There are suspicions on the man [McElroy] who killed young Marshall in our house some time since. Since that event he has become a disreputable character, and a dangerous man; thus it is: "C'est le premier pas qui coute."

And from that, the path of guilt is like a rushing torrent. How many thousands of honest young men have been led into dissipation, and by an easy gradation, to crime, by being tempted to stake a few dollars at the Monte table! Were it not for this cursed love of gambling we should be comparatively free from crime in California, or at all events we should be able to guard ourselves against vulgar and petty villains. The two murders mentioned above were the result of quarrels at a gambling table.

SEVENTEENTH. Yesterday the rain came down in buckets full, to use a homely expression, but today the heavens are clear, and the air dry and warm.

A wretched murder was committed in town this morning by a villain of a gambler. He has fled, but there are strong parties out after him.

TWENTY THIRD. Today a party of the murdered man's friends brought in the ruffian, who committed the cold blooded murder, mentioned above. They were accompanied by a number of miners, who insisted on the authorities immediately trying the criminal; if not, they stated their determination to take the law into their own hands.

The Court had to meet, to satisfy the public will, and singularly enough although there is not the slightest doubt of the man's guilt, no witness was to be found who could or would swear to the fact.

It was with great difficulty that the officers of Justice prevented the people from seizing the prisoner and executing him at once. They have compromised the affair by loading the man with irons, and a guard of miners are to watch the prison night and day until witnesses can be found, and the fellow convicted.

It may appear strange that people under these circumstances should be so culpably negligent of their duty as citizens; and it is scarcely credible that the ends of Justice are continually thwarted by the witnesses of crimes being too careless, or too indolent to come forward and give evidence against the criminals.

Here we have a murder perpetrated without provocation (at least at the time), in open day, in the presence of a score of people, and yet when a couple of witnesses are wanted to swear to the fact, none present themselves.

But the fact is the people know that the Authorities will not, or cannot, execute the law. They know that a trial by the constituted tribunals is little more than a mockery. By some means or other the murderer is sure to escape, and the witness becomes the next victim. Up to this date I am not aware of one judicial execution having taken place in California.

This I repeat cannot last. The people, who have delegated the execution of the laws to Judges, Sheriffs etc. must for their own safety, repossess themselves of the authority, and administer the laws until the elements of our society acquire a healthier tone.

Already in San Francisco, they have organized what they call a "Vigilance Committee," and most of the influential men of the city have enrolled themselves as members. They profess to aid the officers of justice, with this proviso: that when a known murderer and dangerous character is secured, instead of handing him over to the Authorities to be confined in a prison, whence, either by bribery or force, he is certain to escape, he shall be tried in the Committee Rooms, and on the delivery of a verdict of "guilty," he shall be immediately executed.[1]

---

[1] The affair that provoked Perkins into making these remarks was the murder of George Palmer by John Wilson, alias Thornley, at the Arkansas Hotel in the northern part of Sonora, April 18. The murderer was brought back to Sonora on April 22 by Sheriff Work, having been arrested at Green Springs. A mob gathered that day, and another the next, but with all the excitement there was no hanging: So reported the *Sonora Herald*, April 26, 1851. On May 31 the *Herald* detailed the sequel: Thornley had escaped from jail.

As early as 1849 a vigilance committee was organized in San Francisco, first

Other towns in the State are following the example of San Francisco. The Authorities are not powerful enough to weed the country of the legion of cutthroat villains that invest every corner of the land. A few terrible lessons, such as have already been given in San Francisco, will suffice.

Better that gentlemen should for a short period act the part of hangman, than live longer in the state we are in, surrounded by continual and deadly perils.

If ever self-preservation warranted acts of violence, the justification of the precept in this country is undoubtedly as clear as day.

APRIL TWENTY NINTH. A young friend, Ramon Navarro, an Argentino—much to my gratification, for the times are mighty dull—came up today accompanied by a Reverend french Abbé; the latter to cleanse the consciences of the sinners about here, and, a secondary object, to make a collection for the purpose of building a catholic church in Stockton.[2] He appears to be a jolly old Abbé, with a good, open, honest face that wins a man's sympathy at once; mine particularly, as I pique myself upon a belief in Phiziognomy; for as Mecaenas, who was something of a worldling, and knew the tricks of mankind, says:

"All mens faces are true, whatsoe'er their hands are."

The Abbé is clever, good humored and sociable, and puts me much in mind of some of the good parish priests of Lower Canada. But I do not envy him the entering upon the Herculean labor of listening to the confession of those of his faith in this vicinity. They have been so long without a spiritual guide, that each one has accumulated such a

---

called the Hounds Association, later the Society of Regulators. By early 1851 robbery, incendiarism, and other crimes had risen to such levels as to arouse the populace, but not until June was the first formal Committee of Vigilance organized in San Francisco. For a fuller account of the vigilante era, see H. H. Bancroft, *Popular Tribunals* (San Francisco, 1887), 2 vols.

² Perkins' "French abbé" would seem to have been Abbé Reynaud, who with a party of French emigrants sailed for California from Le Havre in the ship *Grétry* on February 27, 1850. He is recorded to have performed a marriage in Stockton the following December; see Robert Eugene Bonta, *The Cross in the Valley* (Stockton, 1963), index. The phonetic similarity suggests that Abbé Reynaud was the Father "Arnault" said by Herbert O. Lang, *A History of Tuolumne County*, p. 21, to have ministered in Sonora during 1850–1851. Father Henry Alric was assigned to the Sonora pastorate in May, 1851, and remained until 1856.

pile of sins, that the poor innocent Abbé will be scared out of his five wits. Such a conglomeration of vice, wickedness and crime will he have to chastise, give penance for and absolve, that the task of cleaning the Augean stables was a labor of love compared to what his will be.

Two men, sleeping in fancied security last night, in a small canvas house, within a hundred yards of us, had their throats cut. There is no clue to the party or parties who did the deed. Robbery was undoubtedly the object, as every thing in the room was turned upside down in search of the gold dust that it was supposed the men possessed.

Whether they had gold or not is not known, as the victims were newcomers—miners who had moved into Sonora from some other *placer*. I cannot find out their names even.

This barbarous murder looks very much as if it were the act of Mexicans, for the bodies bore the marks of unnecessary violence. The murderers must have crept in cautiously, and first wounds were probably those nearly severing the heads from the body. All the others must have been given in pure wantonness of cruelty. These fellows are true bandits. It is next to impossible to get hold of any proof against them, their work is so silent and secret. Sleep facilitates and night covers their atrocious ruthless acts. And it is useless offering rewards. One Mexican will never inform on another.

CHAPTER XIX

This first of May is like what all Firsts of May should be; balmy, warm, sunshiny and joyous. The air is full of pleasant sounds and sweet perfumes, and the "far depths" of the azure heavens are so clear, so transparently blue, that the eye never tires of gazing. The air too, is so elastic, so inspiriting, that the very act of respiration is a species of intoxication. In such an atmosphere one wishes for wings as the only appropriate means of locomotion.

What a climate! Those who are accustomed to the coarse air of the Atlantic side; the foggy atmosphere of England, the oppressive heat of the countries adjacent to the gulf of Mexico, cannot conceive, cannot form an idea of its loveliness. There is no fitter word to apply to the atmosphere, than that often misused one of *intoxicating*. Here one comprehends the strict applicability of what generally looks more like a poetic exaggeration. The effect of this mountain air in spring in this country is, of course in a less degree, the same as inhaling Protoxide of Nitrogen.

The leaves are expanded; the flowers are covering the hills, as if each particular mount and each shady vale were the favorite gardens of Persian Peris. The mountain sides are clothed in green, and the dark, lofty pines are grimly and enviously frowning upon the more brilliant colors of the spring clothed oaks. But, "All thats bright must fade," and soon the summer's sun will banish the winged zephyrs to the mountain fastnesses of the *Sierra Nevada;* dry up the gold and purple mists of the valleys; shrivel up the brilliant flowers on the plains and hill sides, and tan to an olive brown, the now vivid green of the waving trees.

M. l'Abbé has a bed in my room. Over the toilet table hangs a picture of Turkish Ladies in a Bath, very finely engraved and beautifully colored, and, as a work of art, precludes any idea that prudery might suggest, of its being unchaste. Without, however bringing prudery into the question, the picture is certainly not one to place before a priest, whose vow exacts an abstention from all carnal doings and desires.

The first night after the arrival of the Abbé, Navarro was out visiting his friends, and I retired to bed a few minutes before the priest. As I lay awake he came in and prepared himself for his couch; then went to the table, and kneeling down commenced his nightly orisons.

For some time the good man kept his head bowed down, but, as his petitions became more empassioned, he clasped his hands and raised his head and eyes in the manner perhaps he had been accustomed to do, praying before a crucifix or an image, and his gaze of course encountered the laughing glances of my beautiful, naked and not over-bashful nymphs, apparently much edified and gratified by the Abbé's involuntary adoration. The poor priest immediately moved gently to the other side of the table; but it would not do; the saucy eyes of the voluptuous bathers were still upon him, and he arose from his knees. I could not restrain a little smothered laugh.

"Pardonnez moi, mon cher Abbé," said I, doing my best to disguise the ludicrous impression the scene had made on me.

"Ah, mauvais sujet," said he, smiling. "These are the saints you pray to, are they?"

A small chunk of pure gold, weighing twenty pounds avoirdupois, was taken out of a gulch behind the town, yesterday. It was found near the same spot from whence was taken the lump of twenty two pounds, mentioned in another part of my Journal; and again a company of three mexicans were the lucky finders. They sold it at once, and divided the proceeds. Last night one of the Mexicans lost every dollar of his share at *Monte*. A second has been drunk ever since, and in a few days his share will also have evaporated. The third has wisely gathered together his other worldly wealth and intends starting for home, although it is highly improbable he will ever consummate his intention. It is next to impossible to keep a Mexican from gambling when he has money. This one will go down to San Francisco, and there, while waiting for a vessel to take him to Mexico, he will commence to play, and undoubtedly loose every cent he has in the world.

This brings to my memory a singular instance of rashness, strength of mind and good luck, that occurred about a year ago; and although my general plan in this work is to write nothing that has not actually passed under my own observation, and at the risk of repeating a "thrice told tale," I will note down the following incident, that according to the authority of an eye witness, and friend of the individuals concerned, took place in San Francisco.

Two young Americans came out together, and worked together in partnership in gold-digging. They were fortunate enough to realize, in some few months, ten thousand dollars apiece. With this sum one of the companions expressed himself satisfied, and announced his intention of returning home, to settle down on a little farm. The other determined to remain and increase his store.

The homeward-bound man started for San Francisco, and was accompanied by his chum, to see him off. On their arrival at the Bay, they found that the Steamer would be delayed some days, and the same night, after securing the bag of gold in the hotel, they sallied out to amuse themselves, and naturally entered one of the gorgiously fitted up Gambling Saloons so numerous then, as now, in San Francisco.

Here the spirit of Play entered into the head of the man about to leave, and he said to his companion:

"I have ten thousand dollars; that is not enough for me to do what

I desire to do in the United States. I intend fetching the bag, and shall bet it on a card on *Monte*. If I win, I shall be satisfied; I shall have enough. If I loose, there are two or three hundred dollars, loose change, with which I will recommence in the mines."

His comrade tried hard to dissuade him, but fruitlessly. He fetched his heavy bag of gold from the hotel, and, going up to one of the largest *Monte* tables and putting it down on the rich cloth, asked:

"Will you let me stake ten thousand dollars on one card?"

The gambler glanced at his bank, reflected a moment and answered:

"Yes."

To those who have never seen the great spanish game of *Monte*, I will explain shortly the *modus operandi*. When the pack of cards is well shuffled, the dealer holds it with the faces down, and from underneath draws out two cards, which he places with the faces uppermost on the table. The bystanders make the election they please, placing their money on the card, or if the bet is a large one, calling the amount. When the bets are made, the dealer turns the pack up [and turns over one card after another, until one matches one of the two open cards]. If the first card shown, corresponds with one already on the table, the dealer only loses half the stake, while he wins the whole amount bet on the other card. This is the only advantage the game has, and even this is waived at the option of the parties by "barring the porte," that is, placing the dealer and the better on equal terms.

The money was staked, and the gambling dealer turned up two cards; the young man chose one; all the bystanders suspended their play. Slowly, very slowly, the dealer turned over card after card. By the Lord Harry! I should not like to have been in that young fellow's shoes! If his card is first matched, he wins, if the other, he is ruined! We can fancy the agonizing suspense of the one, in contrast with the cool, hardened, imperturbable face of the other, whose profession accustoms him to all the vicissitudes of fortune. Slowly and more slowly does he slip the cards off the pack. The lookers-on scarcely dare to breathe. The practised dealer knows the under card the moment that the smallest part of its surface is exposed by the removal of the upper one. Why does he drop his hands? A general hah! is heard as each breast is relieved from its volume of pent up air. The Miner has won! He eagerly takes up the stakes that the baffled gambler counts out to him in adobes,[1] gives half to his comrade to carry, rushes out of the saloon, and in half an hour he is on board of the Steamer. And on board he remained, never putting his foot on shore for an instant.

Sonora is improving daily, and large numbers of people are immigrating to this country. Gamblers are as "Thick as leaves in shades of Valambrosa." Some decent fellows among them, most are infernal scoundrels. Wherever there are plenty of Mexicans, these blood-suckers are sure to reap a good harvest. The poor wretches, after working all week in dark holes in the mountains, or up to the middle in water, in the bed of some stream, dress themselves in their best on Saturday to come into town to get drunk, and loose all the gold dust they have collected during the week.

But why commiserate them? They have no other idea of enjoyment. It is impossible to make them understand that money might bring them more comforts than those they have been accustomed to. They are not to be induced to purchase warm clothing in the winter, or make their habitations more decent and comfortable. Whatever may be the amount of money they possess, they use the same miserable dress, live in the same filthy manner, and eat the same wretched fare. Pence and *clacos* they keep for food and clothing, silver and gold for dissipation and gambling. They are a people like the wild Indians; they never can be civilized according to our ideas of civilization.

Looking out of the window, I see before me a group of five *Greasers* sitting in the middle of the street on their haunches, with their dirty *zarapes* about them, sunning themselves, like dogs, in the warm rays of the sun.

"Sullivans Diggings," a *placer* some three miles to the south of Sonora, after having, as it was supposed, been exhausted by repeated workings, is now again the scene of busy labor. The whole *cañon* is being rewashed, and, with the aid of "Long Toms," the ground is paying richly.

This is one of the first *placers* worked in the Southern mines, and a fabulous quantity of gold has been taken from the spot. It was

---

[1] In a note Perkins says: "*Adobe* is the vulgar but general name given to a rough octagonal shaped coin made in California, of the value of fifty dollars. It was made from the ordinary gold without refining or alloying it."

discovered by an Irishman of the name of Sullivan, in 1848. He was an ox driver, and in three months took out twenty six thousand dollars worth of gold. The same man has purchased property in San Francisco, and is now quite wealthy.[2]

The camp has always retained the name of its first discoverer, and is famous for the number of large lumps which have been extracted from its workings.

This was my first stopping place on my arrival in the mines, and had I not been prostrated by the accident from poison, I should probably have turned gold digger there, for the average labor of a man in these diggings brought him from sixteen to twenty dollars a day.

All the gold in this portion of the Southern mines is very coarse, different from the shape it is generally found in amongst the Northern mines. I remember, on the day after my arrival at Sullivans, half blind, lame and with one arm in a sling, I descended into a deserted pit, and with my knife scraped out several pieces of gold, one of which weighed two dollars. Who knows how much I might have collected had I had strength to dig and wash the dirt!

However, every thing is for the best. I do not think I could have stood the severe manual labor and exposure, consequent and necessary, to success in digging. Poor Hyde, had he taken to trading instead of mining, might have been alive now.

The labor and hardships a miner has to undergo, are of the most severe and arduous nature. Prying up and breaking huge rocks; shovelling dirt from deep pits, work requiring strong sinews and great

---

[2] Perkins derived this information from Buffum, *Six Months in the Gold Mines*, p. 126: "John Sullivan, an Irishman, who, when I first arrived at San Francisco [March, 1847], was driving an ox-team, some time in the summer of 1848, discovered a *canon* near the Stanislaus River, which proved so rich that ere the winter was over he had taken from it twenty-six thousand dollars worth of gold dust. With this he established a trading post, purchased property in San Francisco, and is now on the highroad to a large fortune. The *canon* he discovered has ever since been called Sullivan's Diggings, and has been celebrated for the 'big lumps' which have been taken from it."

According to an obituary in the San Jose *Pioneer*, August 5, 1882, Sullivan was born in Limerick County, Ireland, in 1824, voyaged to Canada in 1830, and eventually made his way to St. Joseph, Missouri. He came to California in the Stephens-Townsend-Murphy party of 1844, established himself in San Francisco in 1846, and for a time engaged in business with William A. Leidesdorff. Later he was one of the founders and first president of the Hibernian Bank. He died in San Francisco in July, 1882.

strength; washing the auriferous earth in a most uncomfortable position, with feet wet all day; sleeping on the damp ground all night under a thin canvas covering, or probably with none at all; with coarse and unwholesome food; when we consider that all this the miner does and undergoes, we do not wonder when told of the great mortality among the young men, who have commenced this description of life without any preparation, and often without ever having been accustomed to manual labor that might have hardened their muscles and strengthened their limbs. The exchange of the pen for the crowbar does not always prove salutary.

The labor of gold digging may be compared to a combination of canal digging, ditching, plowing, planting potatoes and carrying logs; so it may be readily conceived there is more of reality than poetry and romance in the work.

Notwithstanding this however, a man with a good constitution and a *light and cheerful heart,* who will not despond under disappointment and suffering, is worth perhaps more than one who has only strength and experience in hard labor. The eager hope, and expectation of great gains, keep a man's courage up and induce him to perform labor that he would shrink from attempting for any specified wages, even were those wages double what the probable result of his mining operations may turn out to be.

On the same principle I have known in the Southern States of North America, a party of gentlemen sit playing "poker" for three days and three nights, without sleep or rest, when not one of them but would have been half dead with fatigue by the end of the first night, had he been called upon to sit up with a sick friend.

CHAPTER XX

MAY THIRTEENTH. The weather is lovely beyond description. At night the air is so pure and delicious, that it is impossible to remain in the house, and it is positively an effort to retire to bed. When there is a moon, the night is as light as a cloudy day is with us in Canada; and when the stars only are to be seen, even then, every object for the distance of a couple of hundred yards is distinctly visible.

"Contarino Fleming," who speaks so rapturously of the delights of a fragrant cigar in the groves of Italy, would have acknowledged a greater bliss, had he enjoyed the experience of a *pipe* in the Sierras of California; and all the Odes to the moon that have ever been written, are tame compared to the one which *might* be inspired by a Californian moon.

I have often to chronicle the continued arrivals of fresh batches of the fair sex. We have them of all colors and of almost all nations. There are some "honest women" amongst them, but, veracity obliges me to add, they are few, and certainly the least propossessing in a physical point of view. Some few miners and farmers have brought their families, but that article of head dress ycleped a bonnet, which would indubitably prove the wearer to be a Saxon and a decent woman, has not yet been seen in the streets of Sonora.

It is true that many couples pay a nominal tribute to virtue by giving out that they are married: Mr. and Mrs. So and So; Monsieur et Madame Pierre; el Señor y su Señora Fulano. All this is very well and very proper; for although we are aware that no legitimate or legal ties exist, yet it makes our society apparently more respectable. For instance I am introduced to a Madame Wharton; I find a well behaved, handsome and intelligent woman living with a person who calls himself by the above name, as his wife. What absolute necessity is there for me to know that Mrs. W. is a Parisian *Lorette,* an adventuress, who has attached herself to Mr. W. from interested motives, and who will probably leave him some fine day and become Madame X instead of W? The same rule obtains throughout our society. Each one strives to cover the nakedness of reality with the mantle of illusion; and there are enough of respectable men in Sonora, whose good opinion and protection are desiderata of sufficient consequence to induce a strict observance of all the exterior rules of respectability on the part of the better class of women.

The Frenchwomen are monopolizing the business of the Lansquenet tables and the liquor Bars. There is now no decent place where liquor is retailed, but there is a pretty and handsomely dressed Frenchwoman behind the counter. This of course draws custom; for even a staid and sedate man like myself will at times spend a few quarters for the enjoyment of a genial smile from a pretty face, or perhaps the still greater stimulus of a flirtation, for which latter a Parisienne is always ready; and as the tongue under these circumstances requires more or less *oiling*, a double object is attained by the fair damsel.

The fatal fires that have devastated San Francisco and Stockton, have created serious apprehensions up here. A conflagration in Sonora, where the buildings are of the most combustible materials, would be very disastrous in its effects. On Theall's last trip to San Francisco, the great fire of the sixth of May occurred, and he had a large stock of goods destroyed.[1] It is true we did not loose much, as the merchandise had not been delivered. All up country merchants take the precaution to place all the responsability of the safety of the purchases on the vendors, until the goods are actually taken out of their stores to be shipped. On this occasion, had it not been for this necessary precaution, we should have been completely ruined, as Theall had already purchased a heavy stock. We were nevertheless great sufferers, as it was found impossible to purchase the same stock, and every thing in the shape of merchandise rose from twenty five to fifty per cent.

We have had for some time lots of amusements; Circuses, Theatres, Model Artists and Concerts. The mountain town of Sonora is progressing! The Circus is a poor affair, got up in Mexico, and the horses and men are about on a par, both being sorry brutes. The Theatre is only occasionally opened, sometimes by Spanish Players, and sometimes by French Amateurs. The exhibition of the Model Artists is a vulgar affair that will be prohibited by the Authorities; and it does not speak amiss for a certain species of morality in the mines, the fact, that these indecent shows are very little patronized.[2]

---

[1] Perkins has trouble dating his San Francisco fires; the one referred to here broke out on May 3 but is known as the great fire of May 4, 1851. He himself had witnessed the conflagration of May 4, 1850. For further comment on San Francisco fires, see chapter xli, note 2. A fire said to have occurred at Sonora in November, 1849, is not mentioned by Perkins. He left there before the great fire of June 17, 1852.

[2] As a footnote to morals, Lang, *A History of Tuolumne County*, pp. 81–84, remarks that after the Common Council of the City of Sonora was organized on May 26, 1851, early ordinances were passed prohibiting within the corporate

The Concerts are the only amusements worth the entrance money. Among the French population there are numbers of artists in every line, and many excellent singers. These have formed an Amateur Company, and give weekly concerts that would do credit to more civilized communities than ours.

MAY THIRTEENTH. [sic] M. l'Abbé returned to Stockton to day with his purse well lined with offerings for his new Church. The largest contribution, he told me laughingly, but with a good deal of feeling, was from a *mauvais sujet,* a "heretic." I bid the good priest farewell, with a cordial grasp of the hand.

Ten o'clock at night. Returning from a pipe and a glass of brandy and water, I stumbled over what I thought was a drunken man, by our door. I entered and fetched a light, and found a white man, a stranger, lying murdered with a deep wound made with a knife in the breast. We brought the body inside; it was warm but life was quite extinct. If he had money, it was stolen, as his pockets contained nothing. Who the poor fellow is, or where he comes from, we have not been able to find out. Something startling this, even in Sonora! A man killed at the very door of the principal house in town, at nine o'clock, on a clear night, and we may say in a crowded street; for the theatre, gambling saloons and drinking houses are all in this vicinity.

MAY TWENTY FOURTH. I have returned from San Francisco, accompanied by Enyart, who arrived in the last Steamer from the United States. As may be easily imagined we were all very glad to have him back, and he is besieged night and day with questions, congratulations and invitations to drink. The idea of a *live* Californian *returning* from home! People can hardly believe the fact. Leaving the civilization and comforts of home for a second time to plunge into our wild life, appears to all of us to be something wonderful. There must be a fascination after all in the dangers, hopes, and labors of Californian

---

limits "The game known as 'French Monte' or 'Three-card Game,' or the game of 'Loop' or 'String Game,' or the game known as 'Thimbles,' or the game known as 'Lottery,' or the game known as 'Chinese Puzzle' or the 'Lock Game,' or any game having in its tendency deception or fraud." Another ordinance provided for licensing "every faro bank, monte bank, roulette, or other gaming table, or game of chance," these apparently having a more respectable character. Yet another prohibited "entertainments devoted to the display of the human form, particularly the exhibitions known as the 'Model Artists,' " under penalty of a fine not less than $500.

existence, to have induced Enyart, a young man of good family and respectable position, to come out a second time.[3]

JUNE THIRTEENTH. A fearful row took place at "Melones"[4] last night. Two men, an American and a Mexican, quarrelled about their women, who had had a small private fight on their own account. In separating the women the men came in contact, and, after some words, the Mexican made a pass at the other with his knife, or short sword. The row, thus commenced became general; the first thing done by the Mexicans was to steal as many revolvers from the belts of Americans as possible. By this means they got possession of five Colt's pistols, and with these they fired volley after volley, and drove all the Americans, many severely wounded, out of the house.

The latter soon returned with reinforcements and arms, and a bloody fight commenced, which terminated in the defeat of the Mexicans (there were also Chilenos), with three of their party killed and almost all wounded. I believe no American was killed, although three are badly wounded. Some of them I have just seen with three, four and five bullet holes in their clothes.

The Mexican who commenced the attack received three bullets in his body, and was then *pinned to the dirt floor* with his own sword, and in this position kept yelling "Mata, mata a los C—— Yengis"! Kill kill the d——d yankees!" until he was knocked on the head and silenced for ever.

They tell me that this man was a Mexican, but I can hardly believe it. From the courage he displayed he must have been a lower

[3] Since Enyart was a successful merchant, his 1851 return to California could be regarded as a special case. However, by 1852 many returned Forty-niners were finding that California had charms not apparent to them when on the Golden Shore; they began thronging back to the tawny land west of the Sierra, bringing wives and families with them.

[4] Melones Diggings on the Stanislaus now lie beneath the waters of Melones Reservoir. The row Perkins describes was reported in the *Sonora Herald*, as reprinted by the *Alta California* of June 16, 1851: "A terrible affray took place at Meloney's Diggings, on Thursday evening last [June 12], in which one or two Americans and three or four Mexicans were killed, and a number mortally wounded. The fight commenced about two women in a gambling saloon. The Mexicans drove the Americans from the house, and the latter in turn drove off the former and regained possession. The melee became general, and an express was started for Angel's Creek for assistance. About 100 persons came up and order was partially restored. We have heard several accounts of the excitement, but owing to their conflicting nature we forbear giving them."

Californian, if a Mexican at all; but I am inclined to think him a Chileno, who when their blood is up are very devils. The generality of North Americans never dream of specifying the nationality of a man of spanish race. With many of them, all spaniards are *Greasers,* Mexicans; and in this manner they mislead themselves, and do great injustice to many excellent foreigners of the spanish race.

For instance: the immigration from the Argentine Republic is composed almost exclusively of men of education and family. The reason is simple. Rosas, the Tyrant of Buenos Ayres, is governing with the half savage masses, and has driven more than half of the aristocracy from the country. Large portions of these banished families are in Chile, others in Bolivia, in Perú, and Brasil. None of the lower orders of Argentinos have left their country, which is so far off, and presents so few facilities for leaving, that a poor man cannot get out of it.

Those Argentinos in California then, are almost without exception the exiles from Chile and Perú. They are proud, clean in their habits, fast friends and fonder generally of the guitar and poetry than hard work, but never meddle with any one, shun brawls and drinking saloons, and do not gamble as much as other south americans. They are ostentatious in dress, and are generally honorable in their mercantile transactions. Once a friend, an Argentino knows no bounds to his disinterestedness.

Such is the character of the Argentinos in California. What they may be in their own country I have no means of knowing.

The immigration of Chile is much more of a mixed character. Men of all classes have come from there; for Chile is not only a seaboard country, but its people are infinitely more enterprising than any other of the spanish Republics of South America; and they have a very respectable marine. It has consequently been no difficult matter for Chilenos, of even the lower class, to make their way to California.

The lower orders are sturdy miners, and the better classes, sharp merchants. The latter class is seldom seen at hard work, but have made large fortunes in commerce. In San Francisco some of the principal houses are from Chile. These people are noisy, quarrelsome, and with a sense of honor very obtuse; dirty, given to gambling and very lascivious, but seldom addicted to drink. This is the character of the better class.

The lower class is composed of strong industrious, well formed men. As I have said they are excellent miners, fond of gambling and drink, and are quarrelsome in their cups; ever ready to use the knife, and are not to be cowed by the insolence of the North American. Ferocious when engaged in frays, the Chileno is not vengeful like the Mexican. They are not assassins; if they strike it is in hot blood, and they are consequently to be trusted, although their ideas of honesty are extremely lax.

Of Peruvians and Bolivians there are very few, and none of the lower class.

The great bulk of Mexicans, on the contrary, are the dregs of that rich and debased country. There are very few of the better classes, and those few are engaged in commerce in the lower towns. The character of the Mexican, as often portrayed in this work, is cruel, revengeful, sanguinary and cowardly. In their habits they are filthy. They have no redeeming good quality and are, besides, inflamed with a bitter hatred of the Americans, who have, as they imagine, despoiled them of this golden country.

It will be evident by this description of the different spanish races in California, that the North American, when he places the south american on the same level with the Mexican, does great injustice to the former, and this injustice, proceeding from ignorance and misplaced pride of race, has, on many occasions caused serious conflicts between the lords of the soil, and a class altogether superior to the lazy and worthless Mexican.

Of these conflicts, as few if any have occurred in the vicinity of Sonora, I have not spoken; following my rule of noting down nothing that has not passed under my own observation. But I am aware that both Chilenos and Argentinos, who form a highly desirable immigration, have had many motives given them for discontent and even enmity, by ignorant and arrogant Americans; a circumstance that may tell disfavorably against the latter when they shall seek establishments in the Southern Republics.

A certain notorious gambler, known throughout the length and breadth of California, and by name Bill Owen, was the American hero of the affair at "Melones." This man is worth describing. He comes from respectable connections in the United States, and although soon after his arrival in this country he disgraced these connections by adopting the "profession" of blackleg, he has, notwithstanding, a good name for being honest and generous hearted. He is one of the bravest men in California. Nothing intimidates him; he will attack ten men with the same nonchalance as he would one. He has been in dozens of fatal affrays, and has always been victorious. On the late occasion his clothes were riddled with balls, and he escaped without a wound. This man is as ready to do a generous and noble action as he is to take part in an ignoble row.

It is a great pity to see a man, so evidently suitable for some respectable if not conspicuous position in society, in such a disreputable and blackguard mode of living; with the almost certain fate awaiting him of being slain in some disgraceful brawl, or in some drunken frolic. He is a handsome young man, rather effeminate in his appearance, with long black, silken, curling hair, which he wears falling over his shoulders after the fashion of the times of Charles the Second.[5]

---

[5] Perkins adds in a note: "William Owen afterwards distinguished himself in the unlucky expedition of Genl. Flores to conquer Ecuador. He returned to California, and if I mistake not, was killed in an expedition to annex Sonora, in Mexico."

CHAPTER XXI

My Journal is taking very much the style of a Newgate Calendar,[1] and yet I do not note down a third of the murders and deeds of violence which are almost daily occurrences. Those only whose impressions are a little more lasting than others, find a place in my Diary, to serve in after years as indications of the lawless life in California during the first years of its progress towards an epoch, not far distant, when the history of the present will appear like an exaggerated nightmare; and when the then industrious and peaceable inhabitants will perhaps read with wonder a work like this, which depicts only the scenes in a small corner of the state.

---

[1] The *Newgate Calendar* was a publication giving accounts of prisoners in Newgate, London, with details of their crimes.

On the tenth a very cold blooded murder was perpetrated in Dragoon Gulch,[2] about half a mile from town.

A party of four Mexican miners, all living together in a hut on the hill side, made a purchase from a respectable old man, an American, of a "Long Tom"; and on the morning of the tenth he was to go to the house of the purchasers to receive the amount, one hundred and fifty dollars.

In the mean time the scoundrels had agreed to murder him, and thus not only avoid the payment of the debt, but rob him of what he might have on his person. To consummate the crime in security, they had dug a grave inside the house and covered it over with raw hides. The grave was four feet deep and four feet long with an excavation in one end for the head of the proposed victim. Nothing could exceed the extreme coldbloodedness of the scheme. The murderers actually intended *to sleep on the body of the murdered man!*

Early in the morning Mr. Snow walked down to the house, and there, while one of the party pretended to be weighing the gold dust for the payment of the debt, the others set upon the old man with their knives. The moment that he felt himself wounded, Snow rushed to the door, stumbled over the threshold and screamed for help.

The Gulch is quite populous, and miners were at work within a couple of hundred yards of the hut where the murder was perpetrated; but it seems that no one heard the shouts and screams of the wounded man. Fear, however, took possession of the guilty wretches, and they fled without consummating, on the instant, the murderous deed.

Mr. Snow managed to crawl some twenty or thirty yards up the valley, and then fell insensible from loss of blood. In this state he was found a couple of hours afterwards, and lived long enough to give the above particulars, and describe the men, who are fortunately known. While alive, two Mexicans were brought in and taken before him for recognition, but they were not of the party and were liberated.

The consequence of this fearful act of atrocity, has been the immediate formation of a Vigilance Committee in Sonora, in which

---

[2] The name of Dragoon Gulch is said to reflect discoveries by a party of discharged U. S. Dragoons and artillerists on furlough in 1848 or 1849. As De Ferrari observes, Dragoon Gulch heads at the southwestern edge of Shaws Flat, draining into Woods Creek about a quarter of a mile north of the confluence of Woods and Sonora creeks.

fifty of the most respectable men in town at once enrolled themselves, and the Authorities, knowing their own weakness, have not interfered.[3]

The Vigilance Committee of Sonora will act in concert with those of San Francisco and other towns, and for the time being will take the law into its own hands. It is a terrible alternative and a terrible responsability, but the state of the country renders the measure imperatively necessary. For a time, as I prognosticated a little while ago, gentlemen must accept the office, and perform the duties of the hangman. And let us hope that this awful responsability will be characterized by Justice and temperate conviction! We have no other means of protection.

SATURDAY, FOURTEENTH. Theall went down to San Francisco today, and I rode over to "Melones." There are here a considerable number of Mexicans, and a very strong feeling exists in reference to the fatal affray I have described in another place, in which there were ten or twelve Mexicans killed and wounded. There fortunately are enough white men to neutralize any danger except that of midnight assassination, which occurs only too often.

SUNDAY, FIFTEENTH. Sonora was the scene of a pretty row today, but having a decent police force, the affair passed off without any serious damage to the general peace of the town.

At a public house, where were congregated about fifty Chilenos, two of these commenced quarrelling and finally set to work disfiguring each other with their knives. The fight soon became general, when the town Marshall, a tall, stout man, rushed into the crowd alone and attempted to separate the combatants. This drew upon himself the attack of a number of Chilenos, who fancied their liberties infringed upon by the interference. With some difficulty Mr. Work parried the thrusts of the knives, and extricated himself from the infuriated crowd.

---

[3] A long account of the murder of Captain George W. Snow, aged "about 31" (hence not an "old man"?) and from North Frankfort, Maine, is reprinted from the *Sonora Herald* by the *Alta California*, of June 16, 1851. Three Mexicans or Pueblo Indians committed the atrocity, "in a secluded part of Dragoon Gulch, about one mile from Sonora." Snow died about midnight on June 10. Lang, *A History of Tuolumne County*, pp. 74–76, describes the murder and its sequel, the hanging of two suspected men, Antonio Cruz and Patricio Janori, by a "People's Court" convened at Shaws Flat. The details were derived from the *Sonora Herald*, June 21, 1851.

Once outside he stopped, and turned round, and seeing a man advancing upon him with a knife, drew his pistol and shot him dead. The police coming to the assistance of the Marshall, a fight took place, in which, as one party had revolvers and the other only knives, the Chilenos, although more numerous, got worsted, three of them being killed outright, two mortally wounded, and several slightly wounded. One of the police was badly cut with a knife. Two of the rioters were lodged in gaol, the rest fled.[4]

The Vigilance Committee did not feel called upon to interfere, as it only takes cognisance of deliberate crime, and known criminals. Every crime committed in hot blood is beyond or rather below its jurisdiction.

This first serious resistence to the police, and the fatal result—it led to the death of three and probably five of the rioters—has had already a beneficial effect on the lower orders of the Spanish population, who had begun to fancy that liberty in this country is nothing more than a license to act according to individual caprice. Consternation is plainly to be read in the faces of all of them, and more particularly the Mexicans; a consternation partly inspired, too, by the knowledge of the existence already of a Vigilance Committee of whose force, authority and ramifications they are ignorant, but which terrifies them from its secrecy and unknown power. The members are not publicly known, and this adds to the general uneasiness. There are probably few

_____

[4] George Work, described by Perkins as the town marshal, was actually sheriff of Tuolumne County, first to hold that office. He married Gregoria Garcia, and their son, William Smith Work, born in September, 1850, is declared to have been the first white child born in Sonora. Work was killed, De Ferrari notes, "during a drunken quarrel with Early Lyon, or Lyons, at Adamsville, in Stanislaus County, on August 7, 1854." As a law officer, he was generally respected despite the prevalent lawlessness.

The *San Joaquin Republican* of June 18 prints a letter by a correspondent, "R," dated Sonora, Tuesday morning [June 17]: "Last night all was quiet. Nothing was heard but the tramp of the Police, who were called out for the occasion, and who kept up a strict guard. Much credit is due to Marshal McFarland for his selection of the Police. At night Mexicans were seen prowling about the outskirts, many of them being armed to the teeth, but everything passed off quietly until about noon, when, as the Marshal was coming down Wood's Creek with a witness, who was in the Sunday scrape, he was unexpectedly shot at six times, the bullets fairly taking his buttons off. He caught sight of the scoundrels, who were either Mexicans or Chilenos. Several hundred persons are kept constantly on guard. We fully expect a general attack tonight; all are making preparations for it. The town is upside down."

Mexicans who are not culpable of some crime, and now that they are
convinced of the existence of a Tribunal to punish them in a summary
and instantaneous manner, it is not surprising they should be somewhat
disturbed in mind.

WEDNESDAY, EIGHTEENTH. Two of the murderers of Snow were
taken yesterday. From the description of the scoundrels left by their
victim, there was no doubt of their identity, and if there had been it
would have been put to rest by the recognition of miners, and
afterwards by the confession of the prisoners, who after a long
examination, and with a conviction on their part that they were known,
stated that they belonged to the party who committed the murder, but
that they did not aid in the bloody deed. Snow's dying testimony
however implicated all the four. The prisoners described their companions and gave their names.

As there was no doubt in this case, neither was there any difficulty
in arriving at the conclusion. The men were taken to the spot where
the crime was committed. Just above the hut where the grave had been
dug for poor Snow, was a large oak tree. The wretches could not be
made to believe in their fate at first, and when the ropes were put about
their necks, and they were told to prepare for death, they showed great
consternation; not so much I am inclined to think at the idea of death,
for I have seen these fellows, cowardly as they are, meet it with all the
stolidity of an Indian, but because there was no priest to absolve them
before dying.

The ropes were passed over a horizontal branch of the oak tree, and
a body of twenty five or thirty of the Committee men ranged
themselves with the ends in their hands. On a given signal the
murderers were hauled up with a run that extinguished sensibility and
life almost at the same time. This is the system of the yard-arm
executions on board a man of war, which many people believe to be
more merciful than the *drop* system. I do not know. I have seen both,
and it has really appeared to me that there is less suffering in the
former. On the present occasion the criminals scarcely moved a
limb.

The Authorities did not interfere in any way. It is impossible to
confound the Committee with a vulgar Lynch Court, and as it is
supported by all the respectable part of the community the judges and

officers are not at all displeased to see that it is a power against which it is useless to contend, and they are thus exonerated honorably from all responsability.

Besides their confession of the murder of old Mr. Snow, the criminals stated that their two companions (and with themselves no doubt) murdered the two miners Burke and Doff some time ago. I believe I have mentioned the fate of these two unfortunate men, elsewhere.[5] They were killed so barbarously that the event created great excitement and horror at the time, and it is satisfactory to think that summary justice has overtaken a part of the murderous band. The Committee has sent out men to scour the country for the two Mexicans still at large, who, as they are known, it is hoped, may not escape.

FRIDAY, TWENTIETH. Yesterday the Committee was fortunate enough to secure another of the murderers of Snow, at Melones. This man is known to have been a bad character. The Committee went over in solemn procession. The man was positively sworn to, and accused also of many other crimes. He did not deny his guilt, but kept an obstinate silence. He was pronounced guilty, and shared the same fate of his companions.

The criminal displayed a dogged sullenness perfectly intractable. He would not answer a single question, but glared on the surrounding crowd with the savageness of a captured tiger. A few seconds before he was run up, he asked to have his hands partly unloosed in order to make up a cigarrito; a *paisano* gave him a light, and he was allowed to

---

[5] See note 3, above, for the execution Perkins describes. By his account the Sonora Vigilance Committee was in charge of these proceedings, though Enos Christman, as quoted in chapter xxiii, note 1, indicates that it was not until June 29 that the committee was formed. Perkins has not previously mentioned Burke and Doff, but a docket kept by R. C. Barry as Justice of the Peace and Coroner Pro Tem commences as follows:

"Wm. Doff, who was murdered with Buck, October 20, 1850, one mile from office. There was $13 found on body of deceased, which I handed over to J. M. Huntington, Public Administrator. Nothing more found to be his. . . . (No clue to murderers.)

"Michael Burk, Oct. 20, 1850; murdered one mile from town. No effects found on deceased." (See Lang, *A History of Tuolumne County*, p. 66, or Lang's source, Heckendorn & Wilson's *Miners and Business Men's Directory*, p. 4.) The *Stockton Times* of October 26, 1850, contains a Sonora letter of October 20 by a correspondent "H.," which describes the murder of Michael Burke, an Irishman, and one Dolf, said to be from Maine.

finish his smoke, when, throwing the stump away, he signified his readiness, and in a few moments, there was another villain the less in the country.

CHAPTER XXII

A few days ago, in examining a quartz out-cropping ledge on Bear Mountain, a short distance from town, William Ford discovered a very rich deposit of gold in the stone. He has been working it ever since, and from the labor of one week he has pounded out twenty five pounds of the pure metal.

This is one of the lucky "strikes" one hears of now and then; and another evidence that Dame Fortune is as blind as a bat. Ford is one of the worst characters we have in Sonora; a great bully and drunkard; and has created more disturbances in the town than almost any other man, narrowly escaping being shot on several occasions. Once only in California have I taken my pistol from my belt with the intention of using it, and it was Master Ford who was the object. It was in my own house too. However, he had enough sense left to retire precipitately, and saved me perhaps the commission of homicide. Of late he had become a town nuisance, and many of the keepers of hotels and gambling houses had threatened to shoot him if he entered their premises. Since his discovery, however, he has changed for the better, and has become a little respectable.[1]

I went into the *cancho* where Ford was pounding out his gold yesterday, and could not help being struck with admiration at the extraordinary beauty and brilliancy of the metal when preserved in all its purity in the matrix.

When gold is found in other rocks, it is always more or less tarnished, a proof they are not its original home, but that the metal has found its way into them by artificial means, if we may make use of the term in this sense.

---

[1] William Ford is discussed in chapter xxiv, note 1.

But in quartz it is different. With this rock the gold is intermingled as much as two metals of such distinct nature can be intermingled. It appears even at times to form part and parcel of the quartz to such a degree, that it requires some attention to note where the quartz ends and where the gold begins. The very color of the rock is at times auriferous, perhaps owing to minute and invisible particles of gold impregnating it. The brilliancy of the shining metal contrasts so admirably with the snow white stone, that there are few geological objects of such dazzling beauty; and I have seen brooches and rings made from fine specimens that equalled in lustre some of the precious stones.

Copper is the only metal that is to be found in the same matrix and in the same shape as gold. This combination is also very beautiful, but not to be compared to the former.

June twenty ninth. Twelve o'clock at night. We have had a fearful night's work, and I can scarcely believe in the reality of what has just occurred, sitting quietly as I am in silence, and alone, writing at my desk. I will try and give a detailed account of everything that has actually passed.

Among the men known throughout California as common cut-throats and villains of the deepest dye, was one who generally went by the name of Tom Hill; it was afterwards discovered that his real name was Charles May, and I think he was an American.[2] Of this however there are doubts, some saying that he came from Sydney, and was an escaped convict, of which class unfortunately we have too many in this country.

This man has committed several murders and extensive robberies, and was well known to the Vigilance Committee of San Francisco, which at this moment has several of its emisaries in the interior on the search for him.

In *Campo Seco*, five miles from Sonora, Hill broke into the house of a Mr. Martiss, a few nights ago, and with a companion robbed the contents of an iron safe. A young man in the place at the time

---

[2] There is some confusion about this man's name. Enos Christman in his journal for June 28, 1851 (*One Man's Gold*, pp. 189–190) gives the name as Jim Hill, as does Lang's *A History of Tuolumne County*, pp. 76–79. The *Sonora Herald*, as quoted in the Stockton *San Joaquin Republican*, July 2, 1851, declares, "The prisoner's real name was David Hill, and he was from Courtland co. New York."

recognized Hill, who is pretty generally known in the mines. This young man was Charles Lippincott, brother to the Senator of that name, a highly respectable man from New Jersey, and one of my earliest and best friends in California.[3]

The two ruffians debated in the hearing of Lippincott, as to whether they should murder him, he at the time feigning a deep slumber. They thought it the best policy however, to carry off the gold without further risk, and the young man may congratulate himself on a very narrow escape.

The sheriff and his officers were on the look out, and on the twenty eighth Hill was captured near Sonora, in a house of bad fame on the outskirts of the town.[4] Fearing the intervention of the Vigilance Committee in Sonora, Work, the sheriff, took his prisoner to *Campo Seco,* to deliver him to the authorities there, before the capture was made known here. But Mr. Work jumped from the frying pan into the fire, for when he arrived at Campo Seco, the Miners rose in a body and took forcible possession of the prisoner, determined not to loose the opportunity of ridding the country of one of its greatest pests.

They held a Lynch Court, and as no evidence was required more than identification of the man, and he did not attempt concealment, he was declared guilty, and sentenced to be hanged at once. A scaffold was erected, a grave dug, and a coffin prepared. All this however required time, and in all such cases time cools the passion of the crowd, which is not generally actuated by any high principle, but merely by the excitement of the moment, or impelled by a transitory rage.

The Sheriff was on the ground with two or three of his men, but

---

[3] The reference evidently is to Benjamin S. Lippincott, a New Yorker who came to California overland in 1846, was a member of the constitutional convention of 1849, represented the San Joaquin district as a senator in the first two sessions of the California legislature, and died at Red Bank, New Jersey, on November 25, 1870.

[4] Enos Christman says Jim Hill was 23 years old, "a man with a scar on his neck," and relates that he "went into a store at Camp Seco in the night and held pistols over the heads of the proprietors, while others of his gang stole the iron safe. Last night he was in Sonora. He went into a Spanish house of ill-fame, where Guadalupe, the keeper, is no doubt an accomplice. Hill took a pistol from a man, a stranger to him, struck him with it and then shot at him. The man ran out of the house, frightened, and gave the alarm, not knowing who had robbed and shot him. Hill then hid under a bed where he was found by the sheriff."

had hitherto been a passive spectator; fearing, without doubt, to draw the tide of popular indignation upon himself by interfering. But when he noticed that the ardor of the crowd had subsided somewhat, and a certain indecision had taken its place, he judged it a safe moment to assert the supremacy of the laws, and, rushing up to where the prisoner was standing, seized him, hurried him into a cart, and accompanied by his men drove off at full gallop with his prize. A few shots were fired, and a few oaths expended, but no regular attempt at a rescue was made, and Mr. Work was permitted to carry his prisoner off, taking the road to Sonora, there to lodge the murderer in gaol.

An account of these proceedings was brought to the Chamber of the Committee by one of its members, who, riding his horse at full speed over the mountains, by the short road, or mule track, reached the town a full hour before Work could be expected. A determination was at once taken. Hill was a well known criminal; one of those men who gloried in boasting of his crimes. His own confession damned him, in which he not only had admitted the commission of atrocious crimes, but implicated several associates, men who are eagerly sought for at the present time, by the Vigilance Committee of San Francisco.

A great public meeting was called in order that the Committee might be authorized on this occasion by the public voice. The unanimous verdict was, *he must die!* The Committee accordingly took the necessary measures. Bodies of men were stationed at the different points of the town where the Sheriff might be expected to smuggle his prisoner in. It was nine o'clock; the night clear; the stars giving sufficient light as there was no moon.

The arrangements were scarcely concluded, when the cart was seen entering the principal street by a narrow lane. The crowd raised a fearful shout. The Sheriff, in his confusion, ran the cart into a post, and could not extricate it. He then jumped down, and making his prisoner do the same, grasped him firmly by the wrist with one hand, while with the other he brandished his revolver, dashed through the crowd, running the gauntlet through a grove of pistol barrels. Up like a whirlwind he rushed towards the prison without appearing to remember that he was trying to save a man whom the next day he would have been obliged to hang, if the laws could be executed.

Now commenced a race of life or death. The night was clear as I have said, and the street was, besides, illuminated by the numerous

shops and saloons, so that there was light enough to see the principal
actors in front, and the dark, moving, thundering mass behind.

I was standing in front of the store when they passed. The form of
the prisoner I shall never forget. His body was bent, probably to escape
a bullet, and his head pushed forward as he strained every nerve in the
fearful race.

The people were deterred from firing, although a hundred revolvers
were in steady and determined hands, from a fear of killing the Sheriff,
who, after all, was bravely performing the duty of his office, and
nothing more.

One young man overtook the officer and threw himself upon the
prisoner, clasping him in his arms. Work raised his pistol, but a dozen
men were close upon him, and shouts of: "Don't fire, George, or we
will cut you to pieces!" made him drop his arm, and wresting the
prisoner from the grasp of his assailer, he redoubled his speed, and
gained the door of the gaol ahead of the crowd.

At the door of the prison, Work was brought to a stand, and he saw
that all his labor and efforts had been in vain. With his back to the
door, and a revolver in his hand, stood Colonel C[heatham], a determined, calm and fearless man. The Sheriff was greeted with these
terrible words:

"Stand back! George Work; advance another step, and you are a
dead man! Deliver up your prisoner!"

The Sheriff stopped; his first movement was to raise his pistol upon
this fearful obstacle in his path, but one of his men, "Bill Ford" a man
I have mentioned before in this journal, seized his arm saying: "It is
no use, George; we have done all we can. Give him up!"

A dozen men threw themselves on the murderer, and shouts of:
"We have got him! We have got him!" were answered by the satisfied
"hurrah!" of the immense crowd.

Shall I say who were the principal actors in this scene? No common
men! no blackguards! no gamblers! no rowdies—far from it!

In a few minutes a comparative silence reigned; the solemn
preparations were going on. The guilty man was led outside the town,
to where a large oak tree stood, whose huge horizontal branches spread
over a space of twenty yards. Here a large circle was formed with men,
each one having a large revolver in his hand. Outside a strong force was
stationed, for there are, at this moment, at least four hundred gamblers

and blacklegs in the town, friends of Hill and many of them just as guilty.

The prisoner asked for a clergyman; one was sent for. He then asked for water, but when a jug was brought, he did not drink. Fifteen minutes of breathless silence passed, awaiting the arrival of the clergyman. He came at last, but it seemed that the doomed man only wanted to gain time, hoping to be rescued, for he did not address a single word to the minister. The rope was put round his neck, the other end thrown over the branch of the tree. A couple of score of men ranged themselves alongside the long rope, each having hold of it; the words, *all ready! now then! hawl up!* and in a moment a black object shot up, and loomed in obscure relief against the bright starlit heavens.

The body spun round as its weight untwisted the coil of the rope, but no other movement was visible. Death, or at least entire insensibility, was almost simultaneous with the act of running the man up.

So died one of the most dangerous villains that plagued the mines, and it is to be hoped that the sternness, determination of thorough union of the respectible portion of the community in Sonora, in the punishment of the murderers of Snow, and tonight in the execution of Hill, in the presence of the authorities on one side, and of scores of desperate cutthroats, who would willingly have rescued the prisoner, on the other, will have a beneficial effect.[5]

To uninterested persons, and possibly to my own self in after years, the delineation of these scenes may present an aspect of horror; and I may perhaps come to think that the right of a community to protect itself has been or may be too much strained in California; but I question the probability of my opinion changing on the subject at a period, unless loss of memory supervenes.

At this moment, however, when the very air teems with the fumes of the blood of slaughtered men—when no man is safe in making a journey, nay, not safe in his own bed, from the midnight assassin—when, almost every day, we find some poor fellow barbarously murdered, often in a wanton and savage manner, and we congratulate each

[5] Enos Christman has an equally dramatic account of the lynching of Hill; Lang provides other details; and the *San Joaquin Republican* of July 2, 1851, further enlarges the record.

other and ourselves that as yet we and our nearest friends are untouched, reserving however in our own hearts, the conviction that tomorrow may be our turn; I say, that with all these feelings fresh and strong within us, it is no wonder if mercy and commiseration should be banished from our breasts, and the murderer, the assassin when caught, be treated in the same manner, as in other countries are destroyed mad dogs, wolves, and other noxious animals, not only without compunction but with the satisfaction attending the performance of a duty.

The only means of purging the country of the dangerous villains who infest every town and settlement, is to hang them. The gaols are insecure, and the gaolers ever ready to assist the prisoner who can pay him well; and there is never lack of gold for this object.

In San Francisco, the Judges traded almost openly with the criminals and bartered the honor of their position for gold, unblushingly and in open day. To such an extent was this iniquity carried on, that caricatures of individual Judges, receiving bags of gold from a convicted murderer in one hand, while with the other he opened the doors of his prison, were sold in the book-shops of the City, and hawked about the street.

Many men there are even at this present time, who occupy high positions, who openly and unscrupulously acknowledge that the acquisition of wealth, in California, is paramount to all other considerations; that in a country like this it is ridiculous to be hampered with ideas of honor that are only applicable to communities and societies of other countries, already civilized and governed by organized and acknowledged forms of Law; that man in this region should be accountable only to himself for his actions.

It was this open proflagacy and corruption on the part of the Judges of San Francisco, and the advocacy by men in power of the above pernicious sentiments, that led to the formation of the first "Vigilance Committee."

All the great criminals had either friends or money, and there was not an instance of one of these men having been punished, even after conviction in a legal form by a Jury. The reason is clear; the Judge, the sheriff and the jailor were his friends, or bought by him.

Was it possible, under these circumstances, for the people, the major part of whom are respectable, law-loving men, to submit, for an indefinite period, to such a state of things? Lynch law in such cases is not the unlawful rising of a mob, but the indisputible right of a community to protect itself in the absence or the weakness of delegated executive authority.

CHAPTER XXIII

JULY SEVENTH. The summary execution of Hill and a few Mexicans has had a more wonderful effect than could have been anticipated. May it be unnecessary [to have] a recurrence to such sharp remedies!

For seven days I have not had to record a murder, or even a row in Sonora. Almost immediately after the event of the night of the twenty ninth, the town was cleared of a large number of bad characters, among whom were many white men, gamblers and rowdies who had committed homicides, and who felt in hot water here. The behaviour of the balance is wondrously modulated. Many who strutted insolently about the streets with pistols and knives in their belts have quietly laid them aside, and walk about like decent people (for I think I have not stated that for some months, the custom of wearing a pistol continually, has been discarded by respectable people, who now arm themselves only when out at night or when on the road). A dread, a salutary dread, has fallen upon the spirit of evil-doers, and I sincerely trust that the people may not again be called upon to take on themselves the gravest responsibility of the Law.

The Committee has had enough to do in a minor scale however. There are numerous petty nuisances to be got rid of; some inveterate thieves, and many drunken blackguards, who in their cups have made it a practice to disturb the peace of the town, fomenting rows that have often ended with serious, and at times, fatal consequences. Of this gentry some half dozen of the worst were taken up, fair trials with counsel were allowed them, and the people themselves were the witnesses. They were sentenced to be whipped, their heads shaved, two of them were branded on the shoulder, and all were drummed out of town.

The signal for calling the Committee together, is the striking of a large gong. Whenever the members are required, a man takes this gong and, walking or running, according to the urgency of the summons, he strikes three blows and repeats them at intervals of thirty seconds. At the first three blows, dozens of men are seen hurrying from all quarters to the Rooms, buckling on their pistols as they run.

The effect of the booming, rattling sound of the gong, perhaps calling upon men to sit in judgment on a case of life or death, is solemn and fearful in the extreme; and more particularly so when the awakening din strikes upon the ear at night. As the brasen thunder rolls through the street, all other sounds are hushed. The gambler stays his hand in the middle of the deal; the fair Frenchwoman, serving out glasses of liquor from behind the brilliant bar, suddenly stops her occupation and turns pale; the noise of guitar playing and dancing in the Mexican and *Chileno Chinganos,* is hushed; the thievish and lazy *Greaser* hurries terrified to his hut, and a dead silence reigns interrupted only by whispered inquiries of "What is going on? Who is taken up?"

The Members of the Committee each pay a monthly sum into the treasury. This money is expended in paying the expenses attending the apprehension of criminals etc. Every thing connected with the proceedings of the Committee is carried out with as much publicity as is consistent with safety (from organizations of gamblers) and policy; a certain mystery being necessary to inspire a salutary fear in the breasts of the Mexicans, and make them believe that the power wielded by the Committees is more potent and omnipresent than it really is. By this means, an organization of a couple of hundred men has, in four weeks, overawed and cowed at least two thousand murderers, thieves, rowdies and gamblers in Sonora and its vicinity.

The *modus operandi* of the punishment by whipping is as follows: After the criminal has been found guilty in the Committee Rooms, and his sentence pronounced by an *unanimous* vote, he is then led out, and the people called together by the gong, struck in a peculiar manner. The sentence is then read by the crier, and, if any one objects, his reasons for doing so, are taken at once into consideration. The man is then bound and put in charge of the Committee Marshall. The members form in line and walk two and two, followed by the people.

The scene of punishment is on the top of a small hill which overlooks the town, and on which stands a single pine tree. To this tree the criminal is bound; a large circle is formed lined with the members of the Committee, one of whom stands in the centre to count aloud the lashes. At the end of every twenty five lashes a physician examines the man under punishment. When this is over, one side of the head is clipped close; a collection made on the spot of thirty or forty dollars and given to the man, if he wants it, and he is then liberated with the intimation that a similar castigation awaits him if he is ever found within ten miles of Sonora without a special permission.[1]

JULY TWENTIETH. I have just returned from San Francisco, and find everything quiet in Sonora, not a single murder having been committed within a circuit of ten miles. The severest punishment that the Committee has inflicted was two hundred and fifty lashes on a common scoundrel, who, if proof could have been obtained of his

---

[1] Enos Christman writes on June 29, amid remarks on the Hill affair: "In almost every camp and city in the country, the most respectable portion of the community have formed what are called 'Vigilance Committees' which appoint officers, organize courts, catch rascals, try them and, when found guilty, punish them by whipping, banishing or hanging. Frightful disorders prevail, for California has been scourged by as desperate bands of villains as the whole world could produce. For a long time they have preyed upon us, and our laws, on account of their loose administration and many technicalities, have been found inadequate to the protection of life and property.

"A large Vigilance Committee is being organized here and we shall soon have a full police of our best citizens standing guard all the while. Early this morning a meeting of the citizens of Sonora was held preparatory to forming this Committee. Major Ross was called to the Chair and myself appointed Secretary. The following resolutions were adopted:

"*Resolved*, That no members be admitted to this association except they be unanimously elected.

"*Resolved*, That ten gentlemen be selected to act as a police for the night.

"*Resolved*, That the police have a private watchword, 'Action!'

"*Resolved*, That three successive blows on a gong be a signal for the assembling of the committee, and at the sound thereof the committee should assemble opposite Mr. Holden's house. The central watch was instructed to procure a gong.

"*Resolved*, That secrecy should be observed as to the doings of this committee by the members thereof.

"*Resolved*, That if called upon by the People's Police of Camp Seco, this committee respond by lending their aid.

"*Resolved*, That a committee of five be appointed to draft constitution and by-laws and report tomorrow evening.

"*Resolved*, That we meet tomorrow evening at early candlelight."

crimes, would have been hanged. Several other notorious bad characters have been severely whipped and drummed out of town. The change for the better is something astonishing.[2]

The Vigilance Committee of San Francisco has complimented that of Sonora on its firmness and success, and the two bodies have made a treaty of reciprocity; an extra-judicial treaty it is true, but the people have determined to act upon the axiom that they are the fountain of the Law; and under extraordinary circumstances, such as exist at the present moment in California, it is undoubtedly a republican constitutional principle, that, the servants of the higher power, those to whom the execution of the laws is delegated, being incompetent from want of sufficient strength, not from want of energy or willingness, to protect society by the fulfilment of their duties, the People have an indisputable right to resume temporally the power of executing the laws themselves, responsable only to public opinion for their acts.

Without doubt it is at all times and at the best, a dangerous necessity. The power is very apt to be abused, and the principle can hardly be too severely condemned by writers and statesmen in order to prevent a frequent recurrence; but I think that even while condemming the principle they must acknowledge its occasional necessity.

But it must be well understood that, as I have before stated, the Vigilance Committees, although authorized and sustained by the people, are not a lawless mob. They are composed of the very men, who are the first in every country to sustain and obey the laws; men not actuated by momentary passions, such as have inspired the miners on several occasions to lynch a gambler, murder Mexicans and chinese, and commit many acts afterwards repented of. The Members of the Vigilance Committees on the contrary act under a painful personal responsibility; impelled by a disagreeable and imperative necessity, and take all the measures possible to give solemnity and equity to their acts; and as they are actuated by a calm sense of duty and not from passion, it would be unjust to designate their proceedings as Lynch Law.

---

[2] Enos Christman, under date of August 9, mentions that on Sunday, July 13, "the Sonora Vigilance Committee hung another horse thief. The following Sunday three Mexicans were tied to the whipping post, and each received twenty-five lashes well laid on. Another Mexican was found with a stolen horse in his possession, and sentenced to receive 150 lashes, to have one-half of his head shaved, and to leave the country in 48 hours under penalty of being hanged if he ever returned."

This phrase of *Lynch Law* gives rise to another and important observation. Had this peculiar institution of "Vigilance Committees" not been organized, Lynch Law with all its atrocities and violences would have become common in the mines and even in the cities, for the power of sufferance of the people had well nigh reached its terminus. We should have had then mob-law in earnest, and who may venture to guess the amount of outrage that would have been perpetrated, once aroused the evil and undiscriminating passions of the people at large?

Now, the Miners are comparatively tranquil with the knowledge that a powerful organization of the best people in the state has temporally charged itself with the security of the country, and there is no doubt whatever that the existence of the Vigilance Committees will not only have purged the country of crime in its worst form, but will have been the means of preventing anarchy and profuse bloodshed amongst the peacefully disposed of the inhabitants, who, once taking the law into their hands, would probably have become even more to be dreaded than the cutthroats and murderers now so abundant in California.

The incidents recorded in my Journal give an idea, though a feeble one, of the amount of crime in and about Sonora. I have not jotted down a tenth part, for reasons easily understood. My frequent trips to San Francisco prevented many things coming to my knowledge; as I have remarked before, crime became so common that the events of yesterday were obliterated by those of today, and we even became so accustomed to scenes of blood that they lost their power of interesting one, and a murder committed five miles off was scarcely spoken of in Sonora. In the Northern mines scenes of violence were even more common than in the south, and many more instances of Lynch law are known; but, as will be remarked, I have confined myself almost entirely to the delineation of life in Sonora, which, after all, will not be found an incorrect type of all the state.

I think it cannot be doubted then, that a fearful crisis was preparing throughout California, and this crisis has been avoided by the organization of the Vigilance Committees.

While I was in San Francisco the famous bandit Stewart was captured by the Committee, and brought to the City. The solemn clang of the great bell told us that something important was going on. In San

Francisco, the members of the Committee are called together by a bell, the largest in the City, and which is hung above their Rooms.

Stewart was found guilty, and was hanged in the plaza, most of the respectable men in the city having hold of the rope. There was a perfect *furor* amongst all classes to assist in some way in the execution, and participate in the responsability. The Authorities, from a conscious feeling of not having performed their duty on another occasion, when they suffered this same man, Stewart to escape after having been convicted, or possibly from lack of power, made no effort to interfere.[3]

---

[3] The *Alta California* of July 12, 1851, has a long account of the hanging of James Stuart by the San Francisco Vigilance Committee the previous day. He had been arrested by the Vigilance Committee about a week earlier, found removing some stolen trunks; he was tried for the murder of one Moore and a variety of other charges. By his confession, he had been shipped out of England at the age of 16, sent to New South Wales after being convicted of forgery, and had come to California via Callao and Panama. See also George R. Stewart, *Committee of Vigilance* (Boston, 1944).

CHAPTER XXIV

As a relief to the somewhat gloomy tenor of the last two chapters, I shall commence this gaily, with no less a subject than a *Ball*. Not of that class which has done so much havoc amongst us, a leaden one, but a regular civilized *Fandango* on a European scale, and given by the members of our house to our friends in exchange for the uniform consideration and friendship we have experienced from the foreign population. "Cards were issued" to the number of fifty, and not a single invitation was slighted. It is true that the society was not quite so select as it might have been in our own countries but, in exchange, it was probably much more jolly, and as far as propriety was concerned, was every thing that could be wished. The pretty damsels who nightly tend the "Lansquenet" and "Veintiun" tables, and the graceful nymphs who serve out beverages to the thirsty from crystals not half so bright as their own eyes, were there; and in toilets that would have passed muster any where. There was also a sprinkling of the better class of dark eyed beauties from the sun-embrowning climes of the tropics; one or two Mexican girls, some chilenas and the world renowned *Limeña* with her gazelle eyes, and waist the size of a bullrush.

These spanish women are much more elegant, graceful and outwardly correct in their deportment than the Frenchwomen. The latter are more brilliant, lively and talkative, but they are far more profligate. The spaniard, even in the equivocal position of a mistress, never for a moment, suffers it to be seen that she considers herself debased. She never looses her dignity; and for this reason we rarely or never see them keeping a gambling table or tending a bar of liquors.

The Frenchwoman on the contrary, has generally lost the inward sentiment of dignity which distinguishes the spaniard. Artificial in the extreme, she adapts her manners, as she does her dress, to circumstances. Fond of admiration, without which life has no charms for her, she is a lady, a gambler, a coquette, a fury, a bachante and a prude by turns, just as she finds it her interest to put on a disguise. She will avoid a scandal if possible, not from innate feelings of delicacy, like the *Española*, but because she thereby loses caste, and consequently suffers in her interests; for money to the Frenchwoman is the real object of her adoration, and to acquire it there is nothing she will not do. The spaniard never allows a glimpse of interested motives to be observed. She may be fond of money, for the purpose of dress, but she never shows it, and gold is viewed by her with indifference. The difference between the two may be summed up in a few words: The spaniard in all circumstances remains a *woman*, with all the feminine qualities pertaining to her sex, warm hearted, generous and unartificial. The Frenchwoman is made up of artificiality; profligate, shameless, avaricious and vain, she studiously covers these defects with a charming manner, fascinating conversation, and a deportment before the world, which is unexceptionable. She is the Apple of the shores of the Dead Sea enchanting on the exterior, within a mass of filth.

My readers must bear in mind that I am not making strictures on the sex in general, be they French or Spanish women, but on the peculiar class that has found its way to these shores. Of the English women from Sidney, and the loose American women from the States, I say nothing; vulgar, degraded and brutish as they are in their own countries, a trip to California has not of course improved them. But the women to whom I refer are adventuresses of a better class, some of them educated; all of them accustomed to the forms of society; many with innate feelings of delicacy and womanly decorum, even after virtue has been discarded as an unnecessary appendage to California life.

To return to our Ball. A stranger ignorant of the elements which compose our society would have been surprised to have found himself in the midst of half a hundred well dressed men and women, in a brilliantly lighted saloon in Sonora, at this epoch; and to have remarked the perfect behaviour, decorum and politeness that prevailed; as well as the beauty of many of the women, the richness of their toilet, the gracefulness of their dancing, and the correctness of their conversation. He would have felt convinced that the bevy of ladylike women in the room, were the most modest and chastest of damsels. At all events the illusion was complete, and that is saying a great deal at the present time. Ten years hence, perhaps, the standard of morality will have improved, and something more than a show of respectability will be required, but I question if a jollier *Fandango* than ours, will be then produced.

The music was a piano, a violoncello, a harp, a violin and a couple of guitars; the dances, all those fashionable in the old world, with now and then, the graceful *Samacueca,* which I have described already, and which, when performed correctly, is extremely elegant and fascinating. There was also plenty of singing in French and spanish; and the supper was something really wonderful for the mountains. Ices, creams, blancmange, pastry, cold ham and fowls, pheasant pies, quail pasties, formed a bill of fare that would have been by no means unworthy of a London Alderman's table. And then the wines! For be it known that cargoes of the richest wines produced in France and the Mediterranean were sent to San Francisco in the first excitement of the gold fever. What mattered the first cost of a liquor that sold here at an ounce a bottle! The result was a larger stock than could be disposed of, and for some months we have been purchasing exquisite champagnes, clarets, Burgundies, sherries, even Lachrymachristi, at half the original cost. I have bought "Chambertin" worth eighteen dollars the dozen in New York at five and six dollars, and the finest brands of champagne at seven and eight.

At the supper two dozen of claret, three dozen of champagne and one dozen of Burgundy were consumed; a very moderate quantity taking into consideration that Frenchwomen are proverbially tipplers; but then, on the other hand, it is scarcely possible to induce a spanish woman, above the common class, to finish even a glass of champagne. The men too, are not addicted to wine or strong liquors; sherbets, lemonades, ices, they are fond of, but not of wine.

It was broad daylight when the "women folks" were taken home, and we addressed ourselves to our daily duties, very well satisfied with our first Ball in California, and quite proved that our half savage life had not made us forget the steps of the Mazurka and Polka.

On the twenty fifth, I saddled my bonny Kate, and rode over to the "Estrella de Oro," the mine which my friends the Navarros are working, and which is situated about fourteen miles from Sonora. These fourteen miles multiply themselves into a couple of score on account of the mountainous region they traverse.

I found the "Estrella de Oro" situated in a lovely little valley, quiet and secluded, apparently hundreds of miles from human habitations. The solitude of an african desert could not be more profound.

I very much suspect that Navarro is losing time and money with his works in this place. He is working a mine here in the same manner that the silver mines are worked in Chile, expecting at a certain depth to encounter a golden vein. The expectation will prove fallacious, there is little doubt. The general positions of gold and silver are very distinct. The latter is hidden deep in the bowels of granite ranges, while the former appears to be encountered almost invariably on or near the surface and in alluvial depositions. In California, when gold has been found in quartz, it has in almost all cases disappeared at the depth of a few feet.

My visit proved unlucky to poor Navarro. On the morning after my arrival, as I was sitting smoking my pipe after breakfast, he jumped upon Kate, barebacked, and gallopped her round the valley, and then made her perform a variety of fantastic evolutions in front of the tents. He is a magnificent rider, as all Argentinos are; but the best horseman will sometimes meet with an accident. Mistress Kate unfortunately got her right foreleg into a hole and came down on her chest, throwing Navarro with such violence that he broke his collar-bone.

I carried him to the tent, bathed his shoulder with cold water, and set the bone as well as I was able, and placing him in as comfortable a position as possible, saddled Kate, who fortunately was not hurt, and galloped to "Melones"; here I left my mare, hired another horse, and was in Sonora by dinner time.

Amongst the late arrivals in town is a jolly little french surgeon, by the name of Lasvignes, a great friend of the Navarros. He has all the characteristics of the *Quartier Latin*, noisy, fond of good living, impertinent, intelligent, and good hearted. I at once sought him out, and found him at the Restaurant commencing his dinner. I pulled him from his chair, lead him to the door, made him mount the horse, gave him directions for the road, told him where to find Kate, and hurried the poor Doctor off before he well knew what he was doing. So completely taken aback was he that he had not time even to give vent to some energetic expletives with which his conversation is usually rather profusely garnished, and as he galloped off I sang out to him to bring his patient at once to Sonora.

The next day, somewhat to my astonishment, Lasvignes got back, and bringing Navarro with him; or, more correctly speaking, the latter brought the Doctor, who was so completely done up that he had to be assisted off his horse, while his patient, with one arm tightly bound to his breast, was quite strong and active.

The pursy little surgeon in his good natured zeal to serve a friend had strictly followed my directions, and had travelled all night without stopping, repeatedly loosing his way. He had slept a couple of hours at day light, half dead with fatigue and hunger, and got to Navarro's camp about seven o'clock, with his milk of human kindness necessarily a little soured.

Navarro had suffered a good deal during the night, and, after the first greeting was over, was anxious to have the bone set. But the little Doctor's patience was exhausted.

"F—— avec votre épaule!" said he; "Est ce que vous voulez moquer du monde? Caramba! Donnez moi a manger: l'épaule peut bien nous attendre, mais mon estomac m'importune. Donnez moi á manger, f——."

And not a step would he take until he had satisfied his appetite, and had drank a bottle of claret, when, in wonderfully modulated tones:

"Allons mon ami, mon pauvre Samuel, montrez moi l'epaule," and he set it so skilfully, and bandaged it so firmly, that the same day they set out for Sonora, where they arrived at night, but as I have just said, with the patient well and in good spirits, and the Doctor so knocked up that we were obliged to put him to bed.

JULY, THIRTY-FIRST [i.e., twenty-eighth]. An event long expected, occurred last night. Bill Ford was killed. I have mentioned this man's name on one or two occasions. He came out in Stephenson's regiment, in which my partner Theall, held a command, and has always lived in Sonora since its first establishment. When sober he was a quiet idle fellow, fond of gambling, and mortally disliking anything in the shape of hard work. But when tipsy or drunk, Ford was a very quarrelsome dangerous man; so much so that he was the terror of all the saloon keepers.[1]

His good fortune some time ago in discovering a quantity of very rich quartz, had the effect of making him careful, and of inducing him to lead a more respectable life for some time; but his gold vein gave out at last, and lately he had become worse than ever, and his nightly orgies disturbed the whole town. But the fact of his not being naturally a bad

---

[1] William Ford, who should not be confused with William H. Ford, the first Tuolumne County Clerk, is of unknown antecedents; Perkins' statement that he had come to California in the New York Regiment has not been verified, although it would seem he was a New Yorker. He figured in a stabbing affray at Jamestown in March, 1849, as related in Stoddart's *Annals of Tuolumne County*, and voted at Sonora the following August. According to Stoddart, Ford was a deputy sheriff under George Work for a time, but this also has not been verified.

The *San Joaquin Republican* of July 30, 1851, said concerning Ford's demise: "We regret to record the particulars of another unfortunate difficulty, which occurred at Sonora, on Sunday last [July 27]. At the El Dorado Mr. William Ford, of New York, (the owner of the rich quartz vein) and a Mr. Cardwell, had a difficulty and closed on each other. Subsequently, however, Ford seized his antagonist by the head, drew him towards him, and bit a piece out of his upper lip. Ford was intoxicated at the time, but Cardwell was sober. The latter left the room to bring a pistol, and, returning, shot Ford, the ball taking effect in the arm-pit and passing into the body. Cardwell then ran, but was seen by a police officer, who called on him to stop. Cardwell refusing, the officer shot at him but missed him. The ball hit one [Augustus] Kauffman, from Galveston, Texas, who was standing some fifty yards off, and killed him instantly. Ford died at 4 o'clock on Monday morning. It is said that Cardwell's act was justifiable."

The census enumeration of May, 1851, lists at Sonora Robert B. Cardwell, aged 21, a miner, born in Tennessee. The Barry docket refers to him as "Stud-Horse Bob," adding, "Arrested him and examined the case—no fault found." For additional information, see the *Sonora Herald*, August 2, 1851.

man except when in liquor, had up to last night, saved him from being shot or drummed out of town as a dangerous nuisance.

The circumstances of his violent end are characteristic and logical.

A certain gambler by the name of Cardwell, with a companion, an inoffensive youth named Coffman, [Kauffman], were playing Lansquenet in Louis and Lecoq's saloon, at the table of Mad"ᵉˈ Virginie. At this table was also Ford, standing opposite Cardwell.

Lansquenet is played in the following manner: Any bystander makes a bet or rather a bank, of any sum he pleases; say five dollars, which he places on the table. The keeper of the table "banks" on this amount, calling on those who stand or sit about the board to bet against it. Each person bets what he pleases of the sum until the five dollars are covered. But often one person bets the whole amount, when he calls out "banco." The proprietor of the first money then turns up two cards from a number of packs mixed together, one for the bank, the other for the betters, and the first card matched from the pack wins. It is the duty of the keeper of the table to see that the parties who bet against the bank have their money on the board, for the players look to the table for their stakes and not to the betters.

Should the first matched card be in favor of the dealer, the bank is increased one hundred per cent; that is, the five dollars become ten, and the players are again called upon to bet against this sum; for the dealer must win three times e'er he can withdraw his money, which doubles each time he wins. Thus the second time he wins, his bank consists of twenty dollars (supposing the original bank to have been five dollars), and the third time, of forty. He can now give his deal up, and draw his winnings, leaving the amount of the first bank for the profit of the table, or he may go on with the remaining thirty five dollars in the same way as long as he wins or finds people to back him, the fair owner of the table taking especial care to substract five dollars each time the dealer wins the third round.

I have seen some extraordinary runs of luck. On one occasion a man bet or made a bank of two dollars. He won nine times in succession, that means that he won nine hundred and forty eight dollars, and the table six dollars. Another, I saw bank on ten dollars, and win six times running, winning five hundred and ninety dollars, and the table twenty.

Cardwell made a bank of three dollars, and Ford called out

"banco," or in gambling phraseology, "tapped," it without however putting the money on the table. He lost; and the bank was supposed now to contain six dollars. Ford again called out "banco," and again lost. Twelve dollars was now the value of the stakes, and for the third time Ford bet the whole amount, and for the third time lost.

The dealer had now a right to call for his money, twenty four dollars, less the percentage of the table. Cardwell got up and demanded his money from the owner of the game. Ford immediately exclaimed, in an insolent tone:

"You have to look to me for that money."

"I do not know you in the transaction," said Cardwell; "I look to the table for my money."

"No Sir," said the other; "it is with me you have to settle, and if you behave decently, I may perhaps pay you."

"As for my behaving decently" retorted Cardwell, "I will allow people to judge which is the more decent of the two; but I repeat, I have nothing to say to you, and no account to arrange. The table is responsable to me. Settle you with Mdd¹¹ᵉ Virginie, as you please, but do not try and force a quarrel on me at this moment for you are armed and I am not."

Ford had his large revolver in his belt at the time, but he did not draw it, but walking round to where Cardwell was standing, seized him in his arms, and bending him down over the table, struck him severely in the face. After struggling together for a few moments, both fell; Ford uppermost, and in this position the savage scoundrel bit his antagonist's lower lip off.

Coffman and others at last managed to separate the combatants, and the former removed Cardwell and took him to the surgeon to have his face dressed.

Half an hour afterwards, as Ford was conversing with Lecoq, and slightly leaning on his shoulder, Cardwell and Coffman reentered the saloon, and marching straight up to where Ford was standing, Cardwell cried out:

"Bill Ford, I am come to kill you!"

Ford at once attempted to draw his pistol, but it was too late. He received his adversary's ball full in the breast, and fell in Lecoq's arms without a cry, and in an hour was a dead man.

This was not to be the end of the tragedy however. As soon as

Cardwell fired and saw that the ball had taken effect, he turned and ran out of the house, and up the street, accompanied by young Coffman. Some policemen were at hand and pursued, calling on the fugitives to stop. This, however, very foolishly they did not do, and several shots were fired, one of which struck Coffman, killing him instantly.

Cardwell then gave himself up. There will be nothing done to him. The provocation was not bearable, and no one blames him. In fact there is a general satisfaction that Ford has so easily been disposed of, thus saving some trouble for the courts or the Vigilance Committee. There is a sincere sorrow felt for poor Coffman, who was a quiet decent youngster. The two bodies were buried side by side this evening.

Immediately after the fatal occurrence I went to see Ford; he was speechless and appeared insensible. I then paid a visit to the beautiful Mdd¹¹ᵉ Virginie, whom I found calmly continuing her game, as if nothing had happened. She greeted me with a fascinating smile.

"Ah Monsieur, quel horreur!" turning up her brilliant eyes towards the roof, and dealing slowly the cards at the same time.

I made her describe the circumstances to me, which she did with all the calmness she would have evinced had she been relating a scene from a novel. To me, her delicate white hands seemed smeared with blood, and I left her in disgust, a feeling I had scarcely politeness enough to conceal.

CHAPTER XXV

AUGUST. We commenced the business operations of this month with the purchase of a lot of land opposite our house, and thirty feet in width, for seven hundred and fifty dollars, from a Mexican who desired to return to his country, and sold it a few days afterwards to Monsieur Planel for twenty two hundred and fifty. I mention this circumstance to give an idea of the value of property in Sonora at this epoch. The ground has nothing but a large canvas house on it, which we bought separately. Planel intends building a Saloon in front and a Theatre in the rear of the premises.[1]

The town has been very sickly. Many people have died. There is a species of epidemic raging, something like the "Black tongue." The physicians however are not unanimous as to what it really is, but it is becoming serious. Two Frenchmen died last night very suddenly in [Casimir] Labetour's house, next to ours; and a few days ago an American woman died, the first occurrence of the kind in the mines; but she was in delicate health when she arrived.

There are large numbers of women in town, some of them extremely handsome: the Italian singer with her unearthly beautiful eyes; Mad^{lle} Virginie; Madame Bremaire; Señora Abalos, once prima Donna in the Opera house in Mexico, and her little daughter Sophy; Señora Miranda, and some others, are all magnificent women in a *physical* point of view, and if their occupations, of bar tenders, gambling-table keepers and actresses, are not exactly what might be termed *respectable* in our "mighty particular" countries, it must be remembered there is no other way of making a living, and that there is many a gentleman of education in California at the moment, driving an Ox team, or serving out liquor behind a bar.

Eureka! we all exclaimed a day or two ago, on the arrival of the wife and family of our American Doctor.[2] But, good Lord! and I

---

[1] According to the Tuolumne County Record of Deeds, Vol. I, pp. 345–346, on August 18, 1851, H. W. Theall, Wm. Perkins, and Daniel A. Envart sold to L[ouis] T. Planel, for the sum of $2,250, a lot on the east side of Washington Street with a frontage of 32 feet, extending back 100 feet. On this lot stood a store known as "Mexico," between the Harmony Saloon on the north and C. F. Dodge & Co. on the south. On this same date Planel mortgaged the property to Theall, Perkins & Co. for $1,450; evidently Planel paid $800 down.

[2] Thus Perkins records the arrival in Sonora of the family of Dr. Lewis C. Gunn—his wife Elizabeth and their four children, who had left Philadelphia on January 30 in the ship *Bengal* and reached San Francisco August 9. In a letter written from Sonora August 24, 1851, Mrs. Gunn describes the journey from San Francisco and her new home; see Anna Lee Marston, ed., *Records of a California Family*, pp. 139–155. Picturing Sonora from the Gunn domicile, she writes: "On one side of us, about a square off, the village begins. The little houses and stores are as close together as they can be, and on the high hills which surround the village are many tents. On the other side of us, for about half a mile, it is open country, with a few tents under the oak trees. A Frenchman and his wife live in the nearest tent, and they dig gold together. She dresses exactly like her husband—red shirt and pants and hat. Almost all of the Mexican men wear two pairs of pants, white ones underneath, and over them a

confess my very pen is blushing while it writes the sentence, the comparison is any thing but favorable to morality. What chance has virtue in the shape of tall, gawky, sallow, ill-dressed down-Easters, in rivalship with elegantly adorned, beautiful and graceful Vice! The strife is unequal. Virtue must put on some more pleasing aspect to enable her to conquer the formidable enemy already entrenched so advantageously.

It is too much to expect from weak male human nature in California, that a man ever so correctly inclined, should prefer the lean arm of a bonnetted, ugly, board-shaped specimen of a descendant of the puritans, to the rosy cheeked, full formed, sprightly, and elegant spaniard or Frenchwoman, even with the full knowledge that the austerity of virtue accompanies the one, while the dangerous fascination of Vice lies hid under the exterior of the other.

AUGUST, TWENTY SECOND. We have just received important tidings from San Francisco. Some days ago the Vigilance Committee secured the well known villains, Mackinstrey and Sam Whittaker, two murderous ruffians, escaped convicts from Australia, and who have won an infamous notoriety in this country by a series of atrocious crimes.

The Committee took them to their Rooms, where they were condemned to be hanged. But at this juncture, the Governor of the state, Mr. [John] McDougal, quite unexpectedly assailed the Committee Rooms with a posse of constables, and took the prisoners off by force, and lodged them in the common jail. Now, as this, every one knows, is tantamount to setting them at liberty, the community of San Francisco feels very wrathy; for the proceedings of the Committee are authorized and sustained by nine tenths of the inhabitants of the City, and they will not submit to the authorities in cases like this. If the Government and the laws were powerful enough to protect the lives

---

pair of leather, open up the outside from ankle to waistband and trimmed with two rows of brass or steel buttons. If it is cold, they can fasten them up, but usually they hang flopping about their legs. A long red crepe sash with fringe is fastened about the waist, and usually over one shoulder a large blanket is thrown. It is red and black, or of many colored stripes, and looks very gay. They sleep in these blankets at night. I have seen a few Mexican women. They cover their heads with shawls instead of wearing bonnets. I have seen some American and French women who look just like the folks at home. One went past yesterday in a black silk dress, mantilla, bonnet, and kid gloves."

and property of the Citizens, then it would become the duty of the Vigilance Committees quietly and cheerfully to resign their assumed power; and when that time comes, such are the ingredients of these bodies throughout the state, that the duty would be at once fulfilled. But as yet, it would be dangerous to destroy the only power that is capable and willing to restore peace and security to the country; and it is to be hoped that the pride of officials may not interfere to obstruct this desired object.[3]

Among the many victims to the epidemic now raging in Sonora, were two Brother Masons. We laid them in the cold chamber prepared for all humanity, with the honors and ceremonies appertaining to the Ancient Craft.

The Masonic Burying Ground is a quarter of an hours walk from the town; a little valley sprinkled with live Oak trees, and carpeted in the spring time with millions of flowers. The place had been "prospected" in various parts and no gold has been discovered, and we consequently chose this spot, hoping that the bones of the dead may be respected by the unscrupulous seekers after the coveted metal.[4]

I am, thanks to Providence, strong and hearty amongst the numerous sick and dying. I never refuse to visit any of the afflicted, and sometimes am roused up in the middle of the night to jump upon "Kate" and ride out to some Camp to see and administer to some poor white man taken suddenly with the prevailing disease.

There is now no doubt that this disease is the *Black tongue*, and the patient is carried off by conjestion.[5] How the fatal malady found its

---

[3] Here Perkins describes the sequel to the hanging of James Stuart, whose confession had developed some of the malodorous history of these confederates. The man Perkins calls Mackinstrey, usually spelled McKenzie, in his confession said his name was properly Robert McKinney; he was an Englishman who came to California in 1849. The *Alta California*, in its issues of August 18 and 21, relates the events culminating in the seizure of McKinney and Whittaker by Governor McDougal (aided by Sheriff Jack Hays, a deputy sheriff, and half a dozen policemen), then, on August 25, describes the exciting happenings detailed by Perkins under date of the 27th, which occurred on Sunday, August 24.

[4] The "Masonic Burying Ground" described by Perkins has not been conclusively located, but Mr. Edward M. Jasper of Sonora has suggested to us the likelihood that it was south of town, about midway between the present Masonic and I.O.O.F. cemeteries. Excavations there have turned up bones, casket nails, and some crockery.

[5] Perkins' frequently-mentioned "Black tongue" surely cannot have been typhoid fever, then well known by its proper name?

way up into the mountains, and how it can exist in such a fatal form in
the pure air of the *Sierras* is difficult to imagine. I have often spoken of
the extraordinary salubrity of our atmosphere; and I have heard
Europeans say that no place in the world is equal to it except the shores
of the Gulf of Corinth. One may sleep with impunity in the open air
in almost any season, and yet here we have a malignant plague,
spreading rapidly and carrying off the people by hundreds. Sonora used
to enjoy the name of being the healthiest spot in California; at this
moment it is the reverse.

It may not be uninteresting to make a comparison between the
value of different articles of merchandise in this month of August 1851
and in January 1850, at which period I noted in my Journal the prices
of some things. The same articles are now selling as follows: Flour 9½
cents per pound; Pork 20 cents; Sugar 12½ cents; Nails 20 cents;
Butter 50 cents; Rice 15 cents; Salt 8 cents; Sperm Candles 62½ cents;
Lard 25 cents; a pair of shoes 1½ to 2 dollars; Nutmegs 25 cents per oz;
a tin cup 25 cents; Champagne 15 dollars per dozen; Writing paper 75
cents per quire; a bottle of Lemon Syrup 75 cents; Freight from
Stockton, 3 dollars per hundred pounds. It is true these are summer
prices, and if the winter season turns out to be a severe one, every
species of goods will of course become much dearer; but we never
expect to see the market in the same state it was in throughout the year
fifty.

California being so distant from the producing and manufacturing
countries, we often witness some strange phases in commercial speculation. Some petty article, for instance, may be a perfect drug in the
market, on account of over-abundant supplies, and this fact being
known in foreign places of shipment, no consignment of the merchandise in question is made. But by imperceptable degree the stock is
worked off, and suddenly to the astonishment of every one, the article is
in demand, and can only be had at an enormous price.

Thus, I remember at one time, the stores of San Francisco were so
glutted with wooden pails, that the Merchants did not know what to do
with them, without burning them. I have seen vacant lots of ground
piled up with them to the height of thirty feet. They could be bought
for four shillings the dozen.

Of course all shipments were stopped, and little by little the huge
stock was being worked off, when one day a shrewd fellow went round

and bought up every pail in town. The next day the up-country merchants looking over their lists of wants found: 5 dozen, 10 dozen or 20 dozen wooden pails amongst the items.

"Pails, pails! why bless me, I believe we are just out, we sold the last yesterday; but there's plenty of them in town I guess. Mr.——— has his yard full———we'll fill your order."

But Mr.——— had also sold out the last of his stock yesterday, and in a couple of hours it was found that the whole stock, and that not a very large one, was in the hands of one individual, who asked the moderate price of ten dollars a dozen for pails he had bought at one and one and a half.

The same profitable operation has been made in various petty articles of necessity, but too trifling to be taken much notice of in the bustle of Californian commerce. A man made a small fortune with corn brooms, in this way. When the market is once bare of any forgotten article, it will be remembered that many months must elapse before the fresh orders can be executed, despatched and received.

AUGUST, TWENTY SEVENTH. Day before yesterday in San Francisco, the Vigilance Committee proceeded in full force to the City Prison, demanded and received the two men, Mackinstry and Whittaker, rescued from the Committee some few days ago by the Governor of the state, and marched them down to the sea shore and hanged them from the third [second] storey of a merchants storehouse. The city papers express the clearest approbation of the act, and the unanimous opinion is that this act will do more to put a stop to crime in the state, than the whole moral and physical force of the government has been able to do in six months.

It is now just two months since the notorious Hill and a half a dozen Mexicans were hanged in Sonora. Some people, by and by, will undoubtedly qualify these executions as murders, for there is never a lack of sympathy amongst a certain class for criminals, when the same persons never dream of entertaining a feeling for the victims. Now if we turn to the pages of this Journal, for months before the date of the twenty ninth of June, we will find a most startling list of cold-blooded murders; and, as I have already said elsewhere, I have mentioned but a small part of them. Since that date, I have not heard of a single murder within ten miles of Sonora. These executions, in the persons of well known murderers, and perpetrated without the sanction of the law, have undoubtedly saved the lives of at least fifty innocent and useful members of society in this vicinity alone. Is it possible, with this stubborn fact staring us in the face, to doubt the legality, the morality, the justice of the proceedings of the Vigilance Committees?

TWENTY NINTH. An affecting incident came under my notice today. Early this morning, a man by the name of Ransome called on me with a letter from the President of the Vigilance Committee of Stockton, requesting me, if it were in my power, to aid the bearer, who was a worthy honest man. This is Ransome's tale: He left a wife and family in the United States in eighteen hundred and forty nine, and coming out to California, settled on a tract of land on the Tuolumne river. He succeeded in making his place valuable, and although he had some property at home, he determined to bring his family out and settle permanently in this State.

He consequently wrote to his wife, and the answer he received to this letter, he read to me; it was couched in affecting and affectionate terms of ready compliance with his desires.

In Stockton lived a man called Moore, a friend of Ransome's, and to whom Mrs. Ransome's letters were addressed. Moore opened some of these letters, and found out when the woman was to arrive in San Francisco, went down to meet her, and readily persuaded her that her husband had sent him down to take charge of his family. Mrs. Ransome unsuspiciously put herself under his protection and accompanied him up to Stockton. Here Moore hired two waggons, and, putting the children in one, he and Mrs. Ransome occupied the other. From the statement of one of the little boys that the father had got hold of, it appears that Moore by persuasion or force induced the woman to accede to his desires, and afterwards by threats compelled her to accompany him to the mines of the Stanislao, instead of taking her to the Tuolumne. They came up to the mountains, where Moore very shortly getting tired of his companion, took what money she had, and left her with a party of men, one of whom it seems took possession of her, and carried her off to parts unknown.

In the mean time, the husband, hearing of his wife's arrival in San Francisco, went down to meet her, and soon found out how she had left Stockton in company with Moore. From Stockton he traced her step by step up to the mines. At Jamestown he recovered his children, but lost all trace of his unhappy wife. After a vain search, he was informed that a woman answering the description he gave of his wife had been seen at a mining camp some four miles to the north of Sonora. He immediately posted here with his letter to me. He was anxious that the Vigilance Committee should take the matter in hand. Poor fellow! I pitied him; but told him, in such an affair as his, the Committee could not interfere, it being entirely out of their province; but that I would accompany him to the spot indicated, and should there be any resistence on the part of the violators I was prepared to assist him. He was very grateful, and eager to be off. I strapped on my pistol, and sent for the Committee Marshall, who on hearing the circumstances, cheerfully volunteered to accompany us.

On our arrival at the Camp, Ransome lingered behind, riding up to the door of every tent and peering in. Edwards and I dismounted at the tavern to get information and a drink. We were here only a few minutes when we saw Ransome galloping up like a madman; his face was flushed with excitement and as he approached he shouted:

"There she is! I have got her! Look! There she is at the door of that tent."

Pointing at the same time to a large tent on the opposite side of an *arroyo* or ravine, four or five hundred yards distant, in front of which was a woman occupied in preparing the morning meal.

We jumped on our horses, and off we started, but the husband distanced us. The rugged and dangerous bed of the *Cañada* was not hindrance to his headlong speed, urged by strong excitement and hope, and in a few seconds he was standing in front of the tent.

We saw in a moment he had been deceived by his own eagerness to believe in what he desired, and when we rode up, we found him the picture of mute despair, standing before a tall and handsome French woman, who was staring at him with an angry curiosity. I explained the circumstances to her and her manner changed at once. Her womanly instincts made her sympathize heartily with the bereaved husband, and she became all kindness and civility; and poor Ransome was so overcome with emotion caused by this sympathy, that he sat down on a log and wept like a child.

In this camp we left him, as he had no desire to return to Sonora with us. He has hopes that his wife may be in the vicinity, and he stays to prosecute his search. I hardly know whether we ought to wish him success, unless under the supposition that the proceedings of his wife are the result of force. The husband, however, most strenuously believes in his wife's affection, and is convinced that she has been coerced, and is anxious to return to his arms; and he, poor fellow, is ready to pardon every thing and take her again to her household affections and duties.

What strange romances are attached to the history of almost every female who has come to these shores. Mrs. Ransome's is the history of hundreds, modulated or aggravated according to circumstances. Perfect and flawless must be the virtue of the woman that may resist the licentiousness of California!

CHAPTER XXVI

SEPTEMBER FIRST. I have in my notes of passing events and life in this part of California refrained from touching on politics as much as possible. Personally I have had little to do with them; not because I am a foreigner, for a long residence in the United States and my early arrival in this country gave me certain rights that would have been cheerfully recognized by the authorities, had I been disposed to press them. In this county, I was proposed as a member to the first Legislature, an honor I declined; and although my position has obliged me to act in various official capacities in Sonora, yet the labors were more of a municipal character than political.[1]

Notwithstanding my silence on subjects that probably might not interest the reader, such as elections, candidates, gobernors, Members etc, it must not be supposed we are entirely strange to the excitement of political strife, or that we view with indifference the march of public events.

We have done our share for the organization of the Territory, and have worked hard to have it recognized as a state, taking its place in the

---

[1] Perkins had served as treasurer of Sonora, notwithstanding his status as a British subject. The *Sonora Herald*, February 22, 1851, contains a tax collector's notice signed by him.

Union as a worthy companion to the Atlantic States. Our house has been always the head quarters for the prominent personages in public life visiting Sonora, and our influence has, up to the present time, been paramount in this county; and in our house was commenced and perfected the opposition to the Tax Law I have already mentioned in another page; an opposition which had the effect of making the Law a dead letter, and thereby probably saved many lives, and prevented many thousands of people leaving the country.[2] It is with a pardonable pride that I feel myself authorized to state that the influence of myself, and my two excellent associates, Theall and Enyart, has always been inlisted in the course of Justice and Order.

Enyart and Colonel Weller came up this evening from San Francisco. We are supporting the latter as a candidate for Senator to the National Congress, and there is almost a certainty of his being chosen by the Legislature. He is winning golden opinions every where, and I believe will distinguish himself. He is a clever man; a better politician however than a lawyer. We left New Orleans together; I on my way to the Golden Gate, he, as Commissioner to determine the Mexican boundary, after the Treaty of *Guadalupe Hidalgo*. It was my intention, at first, to accompany him to San Diego, at the head of the Gulf of California, where he was to commence operations. We started in the "Sarah Sands" for Panamá, but circumstances described at the commencement of this work, altered our plans.[3] I made the trip through Mexico, and had a much more speedy and prosperous journey than the Commission, which met with great difficulties at Panamá.[4]

SATURDAY NIGHT. As I sit by the open window, holding my pen with listless fingers, and with thoughts ever straying from the scenes

---

[2] As seen in the Introduction, the Foreign Miners' Tax was repealed on March 14, 1851, but was reënacted on May 4, 1852, with the cost of a license reduced from $20 to $3 per month.

[3] Perkins got his facts a little mixed; as seen earlier, he sailed from New Orleans in the *Maria Burt*, not the *Sarah Sands*; John B. Weller sailed to the Isthmus in the *Alabama*, but possibly Perkins had originally taken passage in that vessel. Weller was then the U. S. Commissioner for the Mexican Boundary Survey, in 1852 was elected to the Senate from California, and in 1858 was elected governor.

[4] For independently written accounts of the Boundary Survey, see Carl I. Wheat, *Mapping the Transmississippi West* (San Francisco, 1959), Vol. III, pp. 204–246, and William H. Goetzmann, *Army Exploration in the American West, 1803–1863* (New Haven, 1959), pp. 153–208.

about me to scenes in other lands, my spirits are being awakened and lulled alternately by bursts of music from the many gambling saloons within a couple of hundred yards of the house. The music is generally of an admirable character, and forms one of the most expensive attractions of the brilliant rooms, where at tables piled with gold and silver sit the beautiful and fascinating Demons of Play, with a gracious and ready smile for every new-comer, be he arrayed in a black coat, or in a blue flannel shirt, be he a decent man or a blackguard.

Here, surrounded by ruffians, dirty Mexicans, or drunken Chilenos, you may see a lovely woman, richly dressed, brilliant with jewellery, that sparkles in vain to eclipse the eyes of the wearer. This is the veritable Demon of Gambling. The virtues of the Sex swallowed up in the love of Play. Vanity, the most constant companion of a French-woman is here secondary to the intense excitement proceeding from the passion for lucre; for I believe it is not so much a love of gaming as a desire of winning gold; entirely different in this respect from women of spanish race.

It is fearful to look upon these women at their Lansquenet Tables; to see the forms of angels in the employ of Hell; to witness the anxious and angry glare of disappointment when they loose; the feverish and eager glance of triumph when they win; the efforts to keep a calm exterior and clothe the tongue with honeyed words while the heart is beating with rage! Oh! it is terrible! and enough to make a gambler forswear his unholy trade. And to think that these lost women were once innocent children—once the joy and pride of happy mothers— pure virtuous girls—many of them once happy wives!

But I am talking flat treason against our only polka partners. It won't do. We must lay aside some straight-laced ideas and accommodate ourselves as we best may, to the extraordinary scene we find ourselves actors in. So I will try and picture Mad[me] Virginie, Madame Wharton, Madame Bremaire and half a dozen others of the *"elite* of beauty and fashion,"* as they were at our ball, graceful, chaste and *spirituelle,* instead of doing them the injustice of presenting them to the public in their uglier aspect as female blacklegs.

NINTH. This morning a fine fat Buck, seeking to escape the dogs in the mountains, ran into town, passing though the principal street. It was a novel sight, but the shouts of the crowd soon obliged the graceful animal to look about for some protecting shelter. Unfortunately, being a stranger in town, he sought refuge in the most fatal place he could have chosen—the eating house of Lecoq, where he was ruthlessly murdered and served up to the guests the same day at dinner. So much for confidence in the generosity of man! What if there be truth in the doctrine of metempsychosis, and this poor Stag should have been animated with the soul of some confiding and generous being, Wilberforce say, or Howard, and finding itself hard pressed by its natural canine enemies, it should have remembered its former noble instincts and have said to itself "I will throw myself on the generosity of man; perhaps he will pity and protect me." Poor fellow! he was mistaken.

The deer are fast disappearing from the *envyrons* of Sonora and, like the Indians, are seeking safety from the persecution of the white man in the higher ranges of the *Sierra Nevada.*

When I first arrived here, we had only to go a few hundred yards out of town to kill a buck. Now there are hunters who make a living by bringing game to the market, but they have to hunt far up in the mountains for it.

The finest game we have is the californian quail, or grouse, as the English call it. This is a delicious bird, of the size of a pigeon and distinguished from a similar bird in Canada and the United States, by a handsome compact plume of feathers, rising from the forehead and bending gracefully forward. They are very shy and difficult to kill.

Bear and Elk meat is common food in its season in the Mines, but both are coarse, the first greasy, the other dry. Of the bear, the only delicate part is the paw; still, dried bear meat is not unpalatable, and is certainly nutritious.

Ducks there are, though not plentiful; and pigeons are sometimes very abundant—other game (we beg pardon of the purist sportsman for ranking the two last as game) there is in the lower country, where animals, large and small, are more plentiful. The extensive plains are populated with many interesting members of the deer family; the american badger, the jackass hare, called so from its great size; [5] the rabbit, are all common. Animals valuable for their fur are also abundant; the ermine, mink, Martin, beaver and otter being amongst these latter.

---

[5] More commonly called the jack rabbit, but really a hare, as Perkins observes.

The most ferocious animal in the lower part of California, where the Grizzly Bear is not known, is what the natives call the *tigre colorado*, red tiger. It is the Cougar (*Fellis concolor*) of naturalists. Fortunately the Cougar is not very plentiful, otherwise it would be difficult to rear sheep and calves on the plains. The natives have been known to lasso a cougar on horseback, start off at full speed, and either choke the animal, or dash him to pieces. The lasso is the great arm of the Llanero, or man of the Plains. Two horsemen will never hesitate to attack a Grizzly; they each throw a lasso, and secure the bear by the legs or the neck, and then, separating in opposite directions, Master Bruin finds that one half of his body has a disagreeable tendency towards the north pole while the other is being attracted towards the south. When the bear is secured in this way, the horsemen dismount, and so exquisitely trained are their horses, that each stands like a statue, straining with all his force upon the lasso, with his body perhaps twenty degrees out of the line of the perpendicular. One hardly knows which to admire the most, the rider or his horse. The two men, as I have said, dismount and despatch the animal with their knives.

We have abundance of beef and good mutton. I have heard people say, the beef of the lower *pueblos* [6] is as fine as any in the world. But the long journey the animals make to arrive in the mines, and the want of good grass, often causes the beef to deteriorate greatly; but still it is very fair. The price is twenty five cents the pound. Mutton is worth half a dollar. As for vegetables, we have generally had to do without them. Lately the potato has been produced in the country, but as yet they are difficult to be had. We have used the large red Chile bean, as a substitute for roots and vegetables, and have almost forgotten to long for other food.

OCTOBER FOURTH. Since my last entry in this Journal I have been busily employed going to and fro between Sonora and San Francisco, preparing for the winter's business and the rainy season; with the determination if possible, of making a clean account next spring and returning home.

Theall has gone to New York on a visit. He has been already five years in the country, having come in 1847 with Stephenson's regiment,

---

[6] By "lower pueblos" Perkins refers to the ranches of southern California, a region he elsewhere calls Lower California. Strictly speaking, Pueblo de los Angeles was the lower, Pueblo de San Jose the upper, pueblo.

to take possession of the ceded territory. Mr. Fraser, our first Alcalde, has also gone home, to return in the spring.

When I saw them start off, and thought that in a few weeks they would be greeted by the "Old folks at home," I felt a something rising in my throat that was wondrously like homesickness; but I coughed away the feeling and bid them good bye like a man!

Shortly after, two more of our select private circle started for the Atlantic States, John Huntington, a lawyer from Boston, and a stirling good fellow, and Edward Marshall, a lawyer from Kentucky, who has been elected to the United States Congress; and for which election he may thank his Sonora friends, for we first "set the ball arolling." [7]

We have consequently lost the cream of our little clique, at least for a time, and Enyart and I are almost alone, for we have scarcely any other intimate friends besides those who have just left us.

The reader will pardon me these little personal paragraphs. Though possibly uninteresting to them the unknown names, it is a satisfaction to me to be enabled now and then to mention in affectionate terms, those with whom I have braved privation and dangers, and who have always proved staunch friends.

Letters from Home! a simple and common phrase, and yet what a world of varied feelings it contains! From the moment a man in a foreign land receives his letters from Home, until he has studied and restudied them over, he is no longer an exile; he is transported at once in spirit to the scenes he has left behind him, and finds himself snugly ensconced by the family fireside, shaking hands with, embracing and kissing, the companions of his childhood. There is a charm, a witchcraft in a letter from Home, that causes in one, a metamorfosis more complete than those of the naughty ladies in the Arabian Nights' Entertainments, who only changed their victim's physical form, and left him his original character. I have remarked in many instances and

---

[7] Edward Chauncey Marshall, who was born in Kentucky in 1821, was elected to the House of Representatives as a Democrat and served in the Thirty-second Congress (March 4, 1851—March 3, 1853). Although renominated in 1852, he withdrew before the election. He was an unsuccessful candidate for the Senate in 1856, afterward returned to Kentucky, where he practiced law for 21 years; resumed California legal practice in 1877, and was attorney general in 1883–1886. Marshall died in San Francisco on July 9, 1893. As Perkins remarks, he was practicing at Sonora when elected to Congress.

particularly in my own person, the softening influence of a letter from a
parent or a sister. The heart appears to undergo a complete revolution,
as if it were combatting and expelling the bad passions, of which all
hearts possess more or less, in order to prepare a worthy receptacle for
the pure feelings which the memories of home are sure to create.

My letters generally make me a little ashamed of finding myself in
this country, leading a kind of savage life merely for the accumulation
of gold. Lord! to "what base uses" do we put ourselves for the purpose
of gathering together a substance, the possession of which is certain to
take away half of our best virtues, and the greater portion of that
contentedness which is the principal ingredient of happiness in this
world.

The man who has little is generally happy, contented, generous,
charitable and kind hearted. The same man, when he has accumulated
a superfluity, becomes morose, discontented, selfish and insensible to
the sufferings of others; and still as we increase in years, the money
becomes more and more incapable of adding to our physical pleasures,
we hug it with a vain and absurd passion; we hoard it; we increase its
bulk by means more and more grasping and unscrupulous, and we die
to leave it to be squandered by those whose wishes perhaps would, were
it possible, hasten the catastrophe which puts them in possession of our
worshipped chests.

We each of us think, it may be, that we can withstand the
temptation of riches, and yet there is not more than one in twenty who
escapes the hardening of the heart, avariciousness and selfishness
incident to success in scraping together more than a sufficiency of this
world's goods.

While I was in San Francisco a short time ago, we had a very
narrow escape from Fire. The occupants of a house next to ours, had
put up a chimney that projected just under the overhanging eaves of
the roof, which one day was set on fire by it. Fortunately Huntington
discovered the flames in time, and they were extinguished before any
considerable damage was done. Theall and Enyart immediately afterwards armed themselves with a couple of axes, and in a few minutes
knocked the chimney down, much to the astonishment and disgust of
the French occupants, who protested with national volubility against
such a free and easy manner of removing the nuisance. But the
depredators were deaf to all french reasoning until the work of

destruction was completed; they then put a stop to the clamor by threatening to indict the people for endangering the safety of the town and have them fined, whipped, imprisoned, hanged and then banished the town!

The Black Tongue still rages in the vicinity. Some two hundred have fallen victims to this fatal disease in Sonora alone. A spanish doctor, who had made himself very useful in attending upon the sick, was seized this morning with the prevailing malady, and died in four hours. This event has created great alarm amongst the spanish population. When the medical men are carried off with so little ceremony, what is to become of the laity? Yesterday we were called upon to perform the last duties to another Brother Mason.

One of our worthy Judges [John G. Marvin?] was attacked, and came very near to death's door, more from fright I suspect than any thing else. It was something ludicrous to witness the alarm of the good gentleman, the same who arrested the combatants in a duel I have mentioned, and who after performing his duty, rode off the field at full speed, so as not to hear the report of the guns. For all that, the judge is an excellent gentlemanly fellow, and we could ill have spared him from our limited circle of intimates.

The disease of course has been more fatal among the lower classes, and particularly the Mexicans, whose intemperate habits and want of cleanliness make them specially susceptible of being attacked by contagious fevers. The absence of the commonest ideas concerning remedies is also peculiar to the Mexicans. I do not know a people so ignorant of the virtues of remedial plants, found in all countries. Their only idea of Hygiene is to shut the patient up in the darkest, and consequently the dirtiest, hole in the house, and give him no water. It is inconceivable, taking into consideration the half indian origin of the Mexican *peon,* the pertinacity with which he eschews water in ablutions or taken internally, in all cases of sickness. The practice of the Aborigenes of America and the Spaniards in this respect, is entirely at variance. While the Indian is the most complete hydropathist in the world, the Spaniard to this day fears to wash his hands or face if he be affected with a petty cold; and in the case of an infant being in delicate health, it is no uncommon thing to allow *years* to pass without bathing it! The large majority of people of Spanish race never wash their faces on rising from bed. They think it unhealthy.

CHAPTER XXVII

NOVEMBER FIRST. The leaves of deciduous trees have not yet begun to fall. The mountain sides are looking fresh and green, and we can scarcely expect rain until the foliage turns yellow—until autumn puts on its coat of many colors.

One of the prettiest and most respectable of our female friends, the little daughter of the Mexican prima Donna, was attacked with the Black Tongue, and was saved with difficulty. The Physician, I do not know who he is, has burned her face to the color and appearance of shrivelled parchment, the ignorant brute! As if a woman would not rather prefer loosing her life to having her beauty destroyed; and particularly in this country. What will poor Sophy do now? Who will be allured to hear her sing, and see her dance the graceful *Jaleo?* Where will be all the honey-sweet words that usually greeted the pretty Mexican on her coming off the boards? We are thinking seriously of lynching the inhuman practitioner who has thus destroyed the choicest flower in our parterre, and for no other reason than to save her life! Poor Sophy! her only alternative is to retire from the scene, and return home.

A handsome Mexican saddle has just arrived for me, ordered from Mazatlán. It costs me two hundred dollars, and its mountings, by my desire, are simple compared with the saddles of the better classes in Mexico, where it is not unusual for them to cost from five hundred to a thousand dollars.[1] The saddle becomes Kate very well, and she looks like an Indian princess under it.

A good light Mexican *montura* is, in my opinion, the best saddle in

---

[1] In a note Perkins remarks: "I remember when I arrived at Durango, Gen¹ [José] Urrea called on me, accompanied by his Aid-de-camp. He came in plain clothes, but *his horse was in uniform.* The saddle was heavy with solid gold, and the gold embroidery on the broad flappiers was exquisite. The high pummel was a mass of solid gold weighing probably ten pounds, and very finely chased or engraved. The broad elegant stirrups were also covered with curiously worked gold. Its value was ten thousand dollars."

the world. It ought not, however, to weigh more than twenty pounds. The common ones are very heavy, often weighing fifty; and the finer ones are generally unnecessarily burdened with ten or fifteen pounds extra in gold and silver. In the Mexican saddle you have an easy and comfortable seat, from which the wildest horse cannot shake you, and for a journey nothing can be more agreeable. The construction of the tree, pressing equally and firmly on the strongest part of the horse's back; the secure, simple though powerful girthing, straining from every part of the tree, and the consequent immoveability of the whole, constitute it the most perfect saddle that can be made; it is at all events the best I am acquainted with.

The stirrup is of wood; a broad thin band of hard wood is bent, so that the section forms a graceful triangle rounded at the angles. Were it not for the bands of gold or silver with which it is the custom to adorn the wood, this stirrup would not be heavier than the English hunting stirrup, perhaps some ounces lighter; and let any one who has plodded through the sandy hot plains of Mexico and parts of California, or through prickly cactii and thorny shrubs, with his feet in a pair of hot iron stirrups, and has exchanged them for the light, sheltering, cool and easy stirrup of a Mexican saddle, tell me which he prefers.

Englishmen are generally the most prejudiced of civilized people. They stick to old habits and old ways of thinking with a bigotted pertinacity. Thus when I was preparing for my journey through Mexico, I ridiculed the clumsy looking saddle and stirrup of the country, and bought, from an officer in the fort of Brownsville, an English saddle with light brass stirrups. It is well for pride to have a fall. After a few days journey through burning plains, densely covered with the *Nopal* or prickly pear, I was glad to adopt the *montura* of the country, and likewise profit by the lesson, although a little galling to British vanity.[2]

---

[2] "Mounted on the saddle I have described," Perkins says in a note, "I have seen a Mexican *Vaquero* gallop after a half wild bull, catch the animal's tail, pass it under his leg and twist it round the pummel of his saddle, give his horse half a turn round, and send the bull to the ground with fearful violence. He will also lasso a bull at full speed, check his horse at an angle, and the huge animal is thrown down with a shock like a 'small earthquake,' while notwithstanding the enormous strain, man, horse and saddle are as steadfast and firm as if the group were chiselled from a block of granite. These are common feats of the *Vaquero*, who may with justice be said to form part of the animal he mounts."

NOVEMBER FOURTH. It seems that Sonora possesses irrisistable attractions for the softer sex. They are pouring in from all quarters, white, brown and black, of all ages, and styles of beauty. They will soon be in goodly proportion to the men, and I should not wonder if we be soon so far advanced in civilization as to have female servants and cooks! The greater part of this immigration accommodate themselves as mistresses; others (not many though), ostentate a decent profession, such as sewing, washing, pastry making and selling knick-knacks; the handsome are always in demand to attract customers to the gambling tables and drinking saloons. These last are almost invariably French, for the American and English women are not graceful enough for this employment, and the spaniard is too proud. The latter are the best behaved of the female population; that is they pay more respect to outward forms of respectability, are more modest and do not tipple.

Yesterday I rode over to our gold quartz mines at Melones with my good friend [Charles] Lippencott, and brought back some interesting specimens for my collection, which I intend to be the finest in the country. I am more and more convinced that Quartz mining will prove a failure. The vein in our mine is rich; the gold is visible in all parts of it, and yet when it is crushed, with great trouble, the powder mixed with quicksilver, the amalgam does not contain a tenth part of the gold in the stone. The work does not pay, and will not for some years until labor be cheap, and machinery, worked by steam, be introduced. I brought away some choice *chispas,* in which the bulk of gold bears a proportion of thirty and forty per cent to the quartz.

Another arrival of a decided beauty in the person of a lovely Frenchwoman. I do not remember ever having seen a prettier woman. She is of course a *Parisienne,* and had induced a young Englishman, a scion of a well connected family in London, to accompany her from Paris to California. Foolish youngster! It appears that the act has separated him for ever from his family. They *say* they are married, and we take them at their word so as to keep up appearances and be enabled to add Mrs. . . . to our list of eligible visiting acquaintances; and she is an addition by no means to be despised, as she dances perfectly and is very correct in every thing that meets the public eye. Why should we desire to lift the curtain?

I wonder what the good farmers in Canada would say could they hear what I am this moment listening to:

"Seventy dollars for this fine fat pig! Only seventy dollars; five! seventy five dollars; going for a mere nothing. Five? thank you! Eighty dollars, going, going, gone!"

And this price is low, comparatively. Six months ago a hog was worth one hundred and fifty dollars.

Eventually there will undoubtedly be immense quantities of these valuable animals raised in California, for the climate is well adapted to the cultivation of maize, and there is abundance of mast from the pine and oak trees; and as the Indians will no longer come down from the mountain, as in former days, to gather it, the quadruped will have the whole harvest to himself.

I have just concluded a lunch from a huge bunch of delicious grapes. The bunch intact weighed two pounds and a half. This fruit grows to great perfection on the coast below San Francisco. It is too rich to make a good wine, although from it they distil an excellent brandy. There is an inferior grape from which a very good wine is made, I am told.

The fruit is sold here at seventy five cents the pound, which considering the amount of land carriage, is not extravagant. During the grape season there is a small steamer kept running between San Francisco and the southern ports for this trade alone, and immense piles of baskets of grapes are to be seen on the Long Wharf when the steamer discharges. They are sold there sometimes as low as ten cents the pound.[3]

NOVEMBER EIGHTH. The first rain of the season has fallen today in considerable abundance. Every body is wishing it to continue a month without intermission, for the long dry season has completely put a stop to gold digging about Sonora.

There was a little row last evening, and one innocent by stander got his face badly cut with a bottle. In the fight one of the combatants lost heart and retreated. He ran past the door of the store, where I was at the time weighing gold dust. His antagonist followed, pistol in hand, and as the flying man turned the corner of our house, the other fired, the ball entering the store a few feet from where I stood. How callous we become, and how indifferent to danger! The incident effected me

---

[3] So celebrated today are the grape-growing areas of northern California that it is salutary to have Perkins remind us that California viniculture had a different aspect in the 1850's.

so slightly that I did not desist a moment from my occupation, but this morning we had the imprudent gentleman tied up, and fifty respectable lashes applied as a corrective to his hot blood.

THIRTEENTH. Lippencott accompanied me again to the Quartz mine. The weather had cleared up and a few days of warmth had dried the roads. The atmosphere is pure and delightful. Mistress Kate is in excellent condition, and a gallop on her is a perfect luxury. To be on the road now on the mountains, with the cool bracing air kissing your face, and the sun, bright but not hot, looking down upon the tanned leaves and peering into the dark ravines of the *Cañadas,* raises such an abundance of animal spirits that you unavoidably feel inclined to whoop and yell like a Snake Indian.

The foliage has been blushing all sorts of colors within a few days past; the pines and evergreen oaks only retaining their summer dress.

> "The many colored woods
> Shade deepening over shade, the country round
> Imbrown; a varied umbrage, dusk and dun,
> Of every hue, from wan declining green,
> To sooty dark."

I think that in no climate in the world are the moonlight nights of California surpassed. I have heard this remark from several who have travelled through the old as well as the new World.

I think I have repeated already what a gentleman said to me one day in reference to the nights and climate generally of the great valley which lies between the *Sierra Nevada,* and the coast range. He remarked that only in one part of the world has he experienced the air so elastic and inspiriting, and the nights so gloriously lighted up, and that is in Greece, in the provinces of Achaia, Corinthia and Attica, all lying on the gulf of Corinth, and in latitude thirty eight, about the same we are in.

It would be overstepping the bounds of sober prose to attempt to describe the loveliness of our nights—to say that when the moon is half or three quarters full, hill, dale and plain are bathed in a light as soft, as intense, as *palpable,* as that of a hall lit with jets of gas in alabaster vases. The moon beams seem to have the power of softening the atmosphere and cleansing the air of the heated and impure exhalations of the day.

It seems a sacrilege on such nights to offend the tutelary genii of the balmy space by puffing the smoke of a cigar in their faces; but it must be confessed the luxury of an Havana or a pipe under the circumstances, is indubitable, although prosaic. I am not aware that pipes and cigars may even come under the category of poetical licenses.

Of course, little moonlight picnics are by no means uncommon. Just outside the town, which it overlooks on one side, while on the other is the Masonic Burying Ground, is a gentle eminence, on which a solitary block of granite stands sentinel, surrounded by a dozen evergreen oaks. For three months of the year this *Lomita* (spanish for a small hill or rising ground) is covered thickly with flowers, but at this season, by fallen leaves, and brown grass only. An evening or two ago,

> "When the sweet wind did gently kiss the trees,
> And they did make no noise"

half a dozen of us celebrated the beauty of the night, seated on the solitary granite rock, with a guitar and singing, sometimes a wild plaintive Argentine *Gaucho* song, sometimes a lively French *chansonette*. On this occasion a clever little woman, the handsome Mrs. —— already mentioned, made us all laugh heartily. Each of us had to contribute to the general fund of conversation with a love episode. Mrs.—— contributed with four.

She confessed to the soft impeachment of having had four offers of marriage before she contented herself with her present lord and master. The first wooer was a "very nice young man," and the match was in every way desirable, the old folks willing and all parties satisfied; when one day, the young girl discovered a pock mark on her lover's nose. She chose to consider the circumstance in a ludicrous light, and her mirth was excited to such an extent that she laughed all her love away, and at last refused to have the unfortunate man. There is nothing like ridicule to banish the little god, and when a girl finds any thing to laugh at in her lover, he had better at once raise the siege and decamp.

The second suitor was a young French painter, and an artist of some merit. On this occasion the course of true love appeared to be unobstructed. There was a tacit understanding that the parties pleased each other, and that Don Hymen was soon to bless the lovers. But, O Shakespear, thy "saw of might" was still to hold true! One unlucky day,

> "Upon a time (unhappy was the clock
> That struck the hour!)

the bridegroom got up a boating party on the Seine, and Annette's Mother and sisters were of the party with herself. During the excursion the boat got aground, and the Artist gallantly jumped overboard to shove it off. Alas! Upon what gossamer chains are hung our destinies! Before committing himself to the waters, the young man prudently took off his shoes and stockings.

"Well, what of that? Surely there was nothing in this simple and commendable action to offend a lady-love, and she a Frenchwoman."

No; but ye gods of female capriciousness; his toes were malformed! Could any one, could a barbarian expect a young and beautiful girl to unite herself in the strict bonds of matrimony with a man whose toes overlapped one another!

A third applicant, after getting swimmingly over the first preliminary difficulties of courtship, which of course kept him at a respectable distance from the object of his desires, was discarded for ever on his attempting to claim the first kiss of reciprocal love.

"Come, come!" I hear a lady reader say. "That is a little too much! Frenchwomen, *par excellence,* are not quite so squeamish as all that."

Not so fast, my fair and outraged Miss, or Madame. The kiss was all very well, *toute en règle;* but the gentleman was not blest with a sweet breath.

"Oh, that makes a vast difference; Annette was quite right!"

So I suppose.

The fourth suitor, Annette says, was just the very kind of a man for a husband. He was neither handsome nor ugly; clever nor stupid; good nor bad. What qualities he possessed were all negative. Listen ye handsome dandies and witty fops to the opinion of a Frenchwoman as to the *beau ideal* of a man for a husband!

Unfortunately the poor fellow had an awkward way of staring with one eye, and Annette took it into her little pate that the eye was of glass, and although the supposition was erroneous, imagination got the better of reality and the fourth lover was dismissed.

These episodes, related with all the vivacity of a *Parisienne,* afforded us much amusement, and the moonlight echoes became quite obstreperous in their mirth that night.

CHAPTER XXVIII

NOVEMBER TWENTIETH. The winter season has set in, and instead of the bright warm sun, and the gloriously soft moonlight nights, we have black lowering clouds, a continual rain, and ugly howling winds. But the universal sentiment is "pour on, I will indure." Even the gamblers and the Frenchwomen are resigned, for every puncheon of water from the clouds is good for an ounce of gold, and this estimable fraternity will get its share of the ounce. The weather is by no means disagreeable. It is not cold, and in the intervals, when it ceases to rain for an hour or two, the air is soft and pleasant. Colds and coughs are scarcely known here.

We are receiving the last of our winter purchases in the shape of five hundred sacks of Flour. Almost all the flour used in California is brought from Chile. It is packed in fifty, one hundred and two hundred pounds canvas bags. The larger sized is called a sack. Flour is worth now in San Francisco twelve dollars the hundred weight, and freight up to Sonora is four dollars more.

The Chile flour is better adapted for exportation to warm climates than the American, for the reason that it contains more gluten than the latter, in which a larger proportion of starch predominates, making it very liable to sour and ferment in its passage twice across the tropics to reach this country. The Chile wheat is equal to the grain of the Levant for making macaroni and vermicelli, thereby proving its superiority in gluten.

SUNDAY, TWENTY THIRD. We have lately had introduced in town a novel amusement for the million; something too, quite in keeping with the wild or half civilized state we are in, and the rough semi-savage propensities of our population. I allude to Bull and Bear baiting.

In Mexico I have seen Bull fighting in all its barbarous perfection. I have seen eight wild bulls slain in one afternoon, in the arena, and beautiful maidens greeting with a never-tired enthusiasm, the skill of the graceful *Matador,* as he gives the poor tired brute the *coup de grace.* It is difficult to say which of the two descriptions of combats is the most cruel. For my part, the contest between man and beast excites in me more sympathy from the fact that the latter fights at a disadvantage, and is always the victim; while between animals the combat is at all events, more or less on terms of equality, and when one of the combatants is conquered, at least he dies gloriously on the field of battle after a brave struggle, and is not killed traitorously and cowardly after having been baited and tortured by a host of tormentors for the gratification of a cruel and eager crowd. Yes, of the two I prefer witnessing a combat between beasts, unless more equal terms are given to the poor brutes in their contests with man, so as to give them a chance of coming off victoriously.

The great Bear of the Rocky mountains, better known as the "Grizzly," makes a very formidable antagonist for a good sized untamed bull. At liberty, they shun, but do not fear each other, like the Royal Tiger and the Lion in the East; each conscious of his own strength, yet each tacitly acknowledging a certain respect for that of his adversary, they agree to a system of non intervention.

The bears are taken in pitfalls, and, placed in iron cages, are sold to the owners of Bull rings, sometimes at as high a figure as two thousand dollars. There is quite a demand for them in San Francisco and the towns lower down on the coast.[1]

Each Sunday there is a combat between Bears and Bulls in the arena of Sonora, and, as the former are chained, they often get the worst of the fight, although the latter are generally so badly bitten that they are killed immediately afterwards.

I will now describe the scene in the Arena today which I witnessed, and the fatal circumstances which attended it will probably have the

---

[1] Here Perkins supplies a note: "Grizzly bear, *Ursus ferox.* This is undoubtedly the most formidable animal of the northern parts of the New World. When full grown it equals in size the great polar species, and is not only of more active habits, but of a fiercer and more vindictive disposition. Its strength is so enormous, that it will [carry off] the carcass of a buffalo weighing a thousand pounds. Encyc. Brit."

effect of obliging the Authorities to put an end to similar performances for the future.

The owners of the Bull Ring had secured a magnificent Bear at a cost of one thousand dollars. He was as large as a good-sized bullock, and weighed probably thirteen or fourteen hundred pounds. The inside of the huge tent was crowded; upwards of two thousand persons were present.

Bruin was secured with a free length of about ten feet of chain, and stalked to and fro with a savage dignity, stopping every now and then to look round upon and utter a low growl at the assembled multitude. Three bulls were turned into the ring, but were evidently scared and fought shy. The bear was turned over two or three times, but received no injury, and one of the bulls got pretty badly treated; all three were worsted and frightened. They were withdrawn amid the hisses of the spectators.

A splendid animal was now let in. This was a huge black bull, a magnificent fellow. His whole frame appeared to be quivering with rage; his tail was extended straight out in a line with the vertebrae, and his eyes, one could almost fancy, were flashing fire. He sprung with a single bound into the middle of the ring, and looked round proudly and fearlessly on the crowd; then commenced a low bellowing, and tossing the dirt up with his hoofs. In a few seconds he had caught sight of his antagonist, and immediately without the slightest hesitation, made a rush at him. Master Bruin curled himself up into a ball, and the furious bull rushed over him, missing his stroke. The bear, with wonderful quickness, sprung up at this moment, and caught the bull by the thigh with his teeth, and inflicted a ghastly wound. The noble animal gave a roar of mingled agony and rage, turned round, and, catching his adversary with his tremendous horns, raised him, notwithstanding his enormous weight, and made him perform a somerset that was only bounded by the length of the chain. the bear fell with a shock that seemed sufficient to break every bone in his body; but no; quick as a flash he had again given the bull a severe wound in the haunch, and the latter moved off to a little distance to breathe. In a few moments, he again made a gallant attack, again gave the bear a tremendous goring, and was again driven off by the frightful wounds he received from the teeth of the Grizzly, who appeared to keep his temper better than his antagonist, and consequently fought under greater advantage.

Four times did the brave brute make a desperate attack, and, although the bear was badly hurt, the bull always got the worst of it, until cowed and scared by a last fearful bite, when the bear caught him by the head, he turned, and collecting all his remaining strength, with one bound he topped the palisades and dropped like something more than a hot potato amongst a crowd of Mexicans. The terror was intense; such a scampering! such an outcry! Several people were badly hurt and one was gored to death by the infuriated animal, who however, more anxious to escape himself than to show more fight, quickly cleared the crowd and fled up the mountains, pursued by a score of horsemen with their *lassos*.

While this was going on outside, another interesting scene was being exhibited within the tent. The bear was lying panting and apparently exhausted, with his huge blood-red tongue hanging half a yard out of his mouth. A Mexican approached him with a bucket of water to pour on him, and thinking the animal was extended at the full length of his chain, walked close up to him. But Master Bruin was only "playing 'possum." With a sudden spring he caught the unfortunate fellow in his arms, threw him down, and with one effort of his tremendous jaws crushed the man's thigh as if it were a willow stick. We distinctly heard the snapping of the brute's teeth as they closed through the flesh and bone. In another minute, ay, in a quarter of a minute, all would have been over.

Then followed a scene that could only have taken place in California, and that, in truth, requires the testimony of an eye witness to be believed. The man was under the bear, and the beast was *crunching* his leg with his teeth. In an instant a score of revolvers were drawn and *fired*. The bear was riddled with balls, and the man was untouched! The most fatal shot was in the bear's head, and this proceeded from a man standing above the crowd on the topmost bench, and he fired over the heads of two or three hundred people. At least, this person claims the honor of having sent a ball within a few inches of the Mexican's body into the bear's head. The leg of the wounded man had to be amputated immediately, but it is doubtful if he live.

It is well that the Authorities intend putting a stop to these brutal exhibitions. They do no good, but keep the town in an uproar every Sunday, induce drinking and gambling, and, as was evidenced today, endanger life. It seems a miracle that so few people were hurt by the catastrophe of the bull jumping into a dense mass of people; but the poor animal, being as much frightened as were the bipeds, took advantage of the openings offered him by the flying crowd, and sought more eagerly to escape than to revenge his wrongs.

This will, I suppose, be the last exhibition of the kind we shall have here. In San Francisco, San José and Monterey, they are still allowed, but in these places they are not productive of so much scandal and vice as in the mines.

On the twenty seventh of November, two horse thieves were executed in Stockton. They were condemned under the new law just come into operation, and being the first criminals who have suffered capital punishment for this offence in California, their execution has created a good deal of excitement and feeling, and more so from the fact of the sufferers being white men.[2]

The incalculable injury done to the agricultural and grazing interests by horse thieves occasioned the enactment of this severe law.

The *Haciendas* or Estates are not fenced in like the farms at home. Over a vast extent of ground immense herds of horses, mules and horned cattle belonging probably to different owners, are allowed to roam; but every animal has the brand of his owner on the fore shoulder generally, but sometimes on the haunch, and when sold has a counter brand put on another part of the body.

Throughout all Spanish America, the law in reference to the branding of cattle is very strict. Each brand has to be registered in a book kept for the purpose in every District, and no alteration of it is permitted; and any one imitating or defacing this brand is punished as Forgers are with us.

In any part of Mexico a man may stop you on the high road, and if you be riding an animal with his brand, and not counter branded, he takes you before the first Alcalde, and, presenting his brand, swears

---

[2] The two horse thieves hanged at Stockton on November 28, as described in the *San Joaquin Republican* the following day, were James Wilson, alias Mountain Jim, and Frederick Salkmar. The law to which Perkins refers, passed April 22, 1851, amended the previous statute on crime and punishment by adding to the penalty for grand larceny (originally imprisonment for not less than one and not more than ten years), the more stringent alternative, "death, in the discretion of the jury" (*California Statutes*, 2d Session, 1850–1851, pp. 406–407).

that he never sold the animal; and it does not matter if in the meantime it shall have passed through the hands of a dozen purchases, he takes it without further ceremony. Of course many annoying incidents occur in this way, and which can only be avoided by taking especial care to secure a Bill of Sale or *Venta* as it is called, in which is noted every purchase and sale up to the original one. This Venta, a man travelling through Mexico should never be without, or he will probably run the risk of having his horse or mule taken from him at any moment; for if he be a foreigner, the natives will combine to swindle him, one giving another an animal to sell, and afterwards following the purchaser to claim it.[3]

The strict laws in reference to the marking of animals were salutary in the extreme in a country like Mexico, where the cattle of the different *Haciendas* had hundreds of miles of free pasturage to roam over, and consequently in constant danger of being stolen. When a *peon* was found with a horse or mule, he was demanded the bill of sale, and if he was not able to produce one, it was proof positive that he had stolen the animal, and he was punished accordingly, and the horse or mule was advertized by the mark, and soon found its way back to its legitimate owner.

Before the Americanizing of California the system was amply sufficient for the protection of this kind of property; but since that period the *Hacendados* have suffered greatly. Horse thieves would drive off hundreds of animals in one night; take them to the thickly populated mines, and find a ready sale for them; the purchasers little caring to whom they belonged, and never asking for a *Venta*; and if the veritable owner by any chance happened to find one of his stolen mules in the possession of a miner, and attempted to claim him, the threat of a pistol bullet was generally all the satisfaction he got.

But when the country, thanks to the Vigilance Committees, became more orderly, and the laws began to be respected, and justice to be administered, it was found that scarcely a horse or mule in the mines

---

[3] In a note Perkins says: "I remember on one occasion in travelling through Mexico, how enraged I was one day, finding myself stopped for a mule we had bought for the waggons, when on the Rio Grande, without having taken the precaution of demanding a Venta. It was taken from us by order of an Alcalde near one hundred miles from the place where we bought it, and no doubt by means of the very party from whom we purchased it."

was held by a legal right. No man was safe in making a journey of a dozen miles without having his horse claimed and taken from him. Almost every horse and mule had been stolen at some time or other.

This at last became such a serious evil both to the *Hacendado* and the Miner, and in fact to the whole community, that it was found necessary to make horse-stealing a capital offense. The law will probably only remain in force for a limited period; a few examples it is expected will have the effect of putting a stop to the system, and the next Legislature will repeal the law, or, what is more probable, they will let it remain as a dead letter.

We have now in Sonora two men, Mexicans, emprisoned for this offense, and if the Jury bring in a verdict of guilty, the Judge will have no alternative but to hang them. We want an example badly in this place. A large number of stolen animals are continually brought here and sold to the unsuspecting new-comers in the mines, who do not know any thing about the Cattle Laws of the country, and are ignorant of the consequences attending the illegal purchase of an animal.

The improvements in our building are completed. The front is thrown open with large doors, a balcony on each storey, an addition behind, and all handsomely painted and stuccoed. In fact the house has assumed such a fresh and handsome appearance that its old acquaintances scarcely know it. I wonder what friend Fraser would say were he to see the site of his brushwood hut he sold us for six hundred dollars, occupied by a large brick warehouse! When one looks back to that time, only two years ago, when the only description of dwellings were canvas tents and huts made of the branches of trees, and then walk through streets half a mile long, lined on either side with handsome structures in wood and brick, it is impossible not to be struck with admiration and wonder at a change that appears more like a tale of enchantment than sober reality.

Obtuse and stupid as the native Indians are, it must notwithstanding be a marvellous spectacle to them to see the beautiful valley, where a couple of years ago their women gathered and pounded the acorns of the forests of oak trees, filled up with big houses and a busy and strange crowd occupied in labors which must be a sad puzzle to the aboriginal understanding.

CHAPTER XXIX

DECEMBER FIRST. Rain, rain; and still the heavens are black with dense moisture-charged clouds. Although out door exercise is not possible in this weather, the rain has nothing depressing about it; on the contrary, it has quite an exhilarating effect on the system; probably from the mental satisfaction it creates in the thought of the immense benefits it brings to all classes of people.

In this country some two thousand miners have patiently or impatiently been waiting for rain in order to work their various claims in the plains and dry gulches. During the dry season the miner does little but prospect, and when he finds a spot which promises well, and by trials he is satisfied of the existence of gold, he marks off his claim, and waits for winter, sometimes taking a trip to the rivers, sometimes hunting, and too often drinking and gambling in the mean time.

Of our mining population, the most respectable, the most hard-working and economical men are the down Easters, or Yankees. It is true they are little liked for their stinginess and egotism, and their insolent contempt for the rights of others. On one occasion they invaded our yard and commenced sinking pits, and it was only the appearance of the barrels of half a dozen revolvers that induced them reluctantly to retire. The cool impudence of a Yankee, joined generally to skinflint habits, and a sharpness or "cuteness" of dealing, which verges at times rather palpably on to something very like roguery, have made him disliked by other people, and by none so much as his own countrymen from the Southern States and Texas. But although the latter are braver, more generous, kind hearted and make surer friends, the sterling solid qualities of the Yankee must not be overlooked.

As a friend, as a companion, the Southerner is preferable. He shows his descent from the Cavaliers; he is always more of a gentleman in his habits and language; more honorable too in his dealings; but he is more quarrelsome; too often intemperate; given to gambling, and ever too ready with his pistol or bowie knife. With these qualities of course it is not to be expected that the Southerner be a working man.

He is generally indolent, consequently, and as idleness is the parent of all kinds of evil, we find the Southerner, perhaps a gentleman of rank at home, a gambler by profession here.

The Yankee with all his disgusting vulgarity and self esteem and impudence, is an indomitable, energetic and industrious man; the real bone and sinew of a country. They are sober, do not gamble, and rarely fight except when driving off the poor Chinese, the Mexicans and the chilenos from their coveted claims; for it is only the Yankees who sustain and act up to the doctrine that none but Americans have a right to work the gold mines. They look upon foreigners with any thing but cordiality, and, as I have said, in instances where their interests have come into conflict with those of the Chinese or Mexicans, the Yankees have evinced a brutality which does them little honor. They act strictly up to the principle that they are the lords of the soil. And I think are very apt to go still further, and believe that the mines and the right of working them, belong exclusively to the immediate descendants of the Puritans.

The difference of idiosyncracy between the inhabitants of distinct parts of the United States is very great, and it seems something strange that so great an amount of political harmony should exist amongst people of such contrary habits and modes of thought. The American Nation may be said to be divided into four great sections of natives, in which manners and customs, dress, language are all as different as if they were distinct nations.

The Yankee I have already mentioned; and let it be understood I make use of the word "Yankee" in no disrespectful spirit, but because, even in the United States, it is generally used to designate the people of Massachusetts, Vermont, New Hampshire, Rhode Island, Maine and Connecticut.

The New Yorker is a type that stands alone as one of the sections; linked on one side to the puritans and old Dutch settlers, and on the other to the cavalier blood of the first immigrants to Virginia and Maryland. A New Yorker is certainly not a Southerner and yet he would be greatly offended were he to be designated a Yankee. He is shrewd and calculating, in which qualities he resembles his down East cousins; but here the likeness ends. The New Yorker is generous to ostentation; speaks a pure English; is well informed, and his manners are gentlemanly if they are a little free and easy. I am speaking of course, of the generality. Of the higher and privileged few, whose associations, education and family make them a distinct class, they are much the same in all the states, and in all parts of the world.

The third section contains the inhabitants of Virginia, Maryland, the Carolinas, Mississippi, Louisiana, and Texas; the latter perhaps ought to form another group, for they are entirely different from even the Mississippi "half horse, half aligator" planter. The Texan is a rowdy by nature; rough uncouth and sanguinary, but generous and faithful and brave.

The fourth section are the western people; Kentuckians, Ohio folks, Missourians etc; people who despise the refinements of civilization; with many of the vices of the down Easter and the southerner, and not without some of their virtues—a people in embryo, who partake of the wild nature of their forests and prairees, but a people who form the back bone of the body politic known by the name of the United States of America.

My lucubrations on American character are interrupted by the shouting and singing of a jolly party of lower Californians,[1] who are enjoying themselves in a building just behind ours. They are at this moment singing a favorite song of theirs, and, as I have the words, I will write them here in the original. The air is lively and the chorus quite jolly, being a laughing confession of a man to his lady mother that he comes home tipsy.

A California Drinking Song

Vámonos, Muchachos, a San Agustin } Bis
A tomar mescal de puro violin   }

Chorus

Como que me voy, como que me voy,
   Como que me vengo!
Ay! Señora Madre, que chispa tengo!

Como que me voy, como que me voy,
   Como que me caigo!
Ay! Señora Madre, que chispa traigo!

---

[1] By "Lower California" Perkins again means southern, rather than Baja, California.

Vámonos, Muchachos, para Santa Anita, } Bis
A tomar licor, del de mi chatita

Vámonos, Muchachos, vámos a Sonoma } Bis
A tomar licor de aquel de la Loma

I believe there are innumerable verses to this song, which is a great favorite with the people of the coast. Those of the interior are of a much harsher character; a compound of the barbarous music of the Indians, and the chants they have half learnt in the Catholic Missions, and which were imperfectly taught to them by the Jesuit [Franciscan] Padres. These singular strains they scream out with a piercing yet not inharmonious sound. This appears to be their only amusement. Athletic games they have none; they are the personification of laziness. Their most exalted idea of enjoyment is to sit on their haunches in a circle, wrapped in their *zarapes,* and passing a bottle of spirits from mouth to mouth, and singing their uncouth though not unmusical strains.

Their voices are what we would call broken; resembling the tone of an old woman, only with great compass and strength. They generally sing in two parts, in fifths.

The Lower Californians or Coast people are altogether a much superior race, as I have had occasion to observe in a former part of this Journal. They are very far in advance of the Mexicans. Their music is good; they display a taste for the violin, the guitar and the harp; they dance gracefully, and the men are inured to fatigue and labor, and have consequently much higher aspirations after liberty and good government than the inhabitants of any other part of Mexico. The Americans have already conceded them the privilege of the ballot box, and they are becoming familiar with the working of the American system of Government.

In the State Senate we have two distinguished Californians as members, General [Pablo] de la Guerra, and General [Mariano G.] Vallejo, and in the lower house there are two counties represented by them; General [J. M.] Covarrubias and another whose name I forget, being the members.[2]

---

[2] The other was Andrés Pico. Vallejo served as a Senator from Sonoma in the first session of the California legislature, 1849–1850; de la Guerra served in the first two sessions, but resigned at the close of the second, in May, 1851. Covarrubias, like de la Guerra, represented the Santa Barbara area, while Pico was an assemblyman from Los Angeles.

On the arrival of the first American force overland during the war with Mexico, the party was fiercely encountered by the Lower Californians, who fought with great bravery. It can hardly be said that they were conquered. Convinced that they would be benefited by changing masters and coming under the government of Uncle Sam, they gave in their allegiance, and have remained faithful ever since. When Stephenson's regiment arrived with the expressed purpose of subjugating the country, it was found that all the people were already living quietly and contently under the American flag.[3]

The advantages accruing to the Californians by the change are scarcely to be calculated. The value of their estates has increased twenty five to one. Before the Mexican War this coast was only visited by one or two ships in the year, with cotton cloths, Tea, Crockery, and a little finery etc. which were exchanged for hides and tallow, these being the only commodities the natives possessed worth exporting. Coin was scarcely known. A cowhide was current money and pieces of soap served for small change. A silver dollar or a gold doubloon were objects of curiosity.

Now, every thing a man grows or produces on his land he gets cash for, and good prices too. His herds of cattle, instead of being killed simply for their hides, are sold for food, and the hide is the least valuable part of the animal. His horses, before quite valueless, now command good prices. The product of the magnificent vineyards on the southern coast, was limited formerly to a few barrels of *aqua-ardiente* or brandy, and a little wine for home consumption. Now there is a never failing market for the fresh fruit, and the wines are gaining a popularity which, sooner or later, will bring them into universal use. One small vineyard has produced more for its owner this year than an *hacienda* with a thousand head of cattle did five years ago. And what is more important than all else, the *Hacendado* can live in perfect

---

[3] Concerning Stevenson's New York Regiment Perkins writes: "This was the regiment in which my partner Theall held a commission. A short time after its arrival it was disbanded and large numbers of the discharged soldiers have proved a sad nuisance to the country. Many of them have been already shot or hanged. 'Bill Ford' was of this regiment." No "Bill Ford" seems to be listed among those who served in the New York Regiment. Patrick Ford, a deserter, was killed by a desperado en route to Montana in 1868, as recorded in the Sacramento *Record*, September 11, 1868, so he cannot be identified with "Bill Ford."

security, making a rapid fortune without fear of being plundered by his own government.[4]

Among the many foreigners we have in Sonora, there are several from the Argentine Republic. All of them are educated men who have been driven from their native country by the tyranny of the Dictator Rosas. They first took refuge in Chile, whence they have come here to try their fortunes. These people are very reserved, mixing little with other spaniards. They are proud yet are very good fellows, when one becomes intimate with them. They hold in contempt the Peruvians, Chilians and Mexicans, to all of whom, at least those we have here, they are in truth vastly superior. Almost every Argentine I know plays the guitar and sings; and every night, the large room belonging to Elordí, a young man from Buenos Aires, and in which they congregate, and where no *Chileno* or *Peruano* is ever seen, resounds with the sweet mournful music of the Argentine Republic. Their national song, that is to say the hymn of the *Unitarios,* or enemies of Rosas, is very stirring and martial. It is a call to the Argentine people to assemble and destroy the tyrant; and when sung by a dozen manly voices the effect is almost as electric as that produced by the *Marseillaise,* or that exceedingly affecting patriotic song, *"Les Girondins";* and this puts me in mind that speaking of singing, I ought to do justice to our French population. In truth the French are the most musical of our community. Three or four of that gay and devil-may-care nation can never meet at night without singing all the old patriotic songs endeared to them by memories of past dangers, pleasures or hopes.

It has always appeared to me that the French as a nation cultivate "music for the million" to a greater extent than even the Germans. The latter are a musical people, no doubt; but only certain classes indulge in it to any extent, while almost every Frenchman can sing his national songs with taste and feeling. How often have I listened at night, with a sort of quiet enthusiasm, to the exquisitely mournful-heroic, half pathetic, half warlike chorus of the "Girondins"!

"Mourir pour la Patrie, mourir pour la Patrie,
C'est le sort le plus beau, le plus digne d'en vie!"

---

[4] Conditions were not so idyllic as Perkins intimates for all native Californians. Some of the land grants were overrun; and the Californios were as much discriminated against in the mines as the Mexicans and Chileans.

The chorus of the Argentine hymn I have mentioned, like most spanish war songs, only breathes defiance, and the verses are always self laudatory with the grossest epithets for the enemy.

Chorus of the Argentine National Song

"Ala lid! Argentinos corramos,
All combate, a la guerra marchad!
Guerra y muerte al cobarde tirano,
Guerra y muerte y despues habrá paz!" [5]

How strange it is that amongst the people who have less to congratulate themselves on the score of glories, we always find the most exaggerated pretentions. But the hyperbolism of the South Americans is no doubt a legacy of their ancestors, the Spaniards, the most preposterously hyperbolic of all nations if we except perhaps the Portuguese. A spaniard can't use ordinary language. His enemies are cowards, pigs, traitors, barbarians, bandits; his friends great, glorious, invincible, patriotic, virtuous. When he meets you in the morning, he is not only glad to see you; he is enchanted, transported with happiness. If you visit him he immediately puts every thing at your disposal, wife, daughters, house and lands. You admire a picture, "It is yours"—a horse "it is at your disposition"; but it is well understood to be all mere form; very few spaniards are capable of doing a generous action. All is pretention, nothing real. A spaniard will write a note, dating it *"La casa de Vd"* "Your house," placing every thing he has at your disposition, and if you ask him for the loan of a pound, he refuses you with a politeness and *sang froid* beyond all praise, and which does not prevent him from reiterating the next day his magnificient offers.

What I have seen in Mexico and what I have been enabled to judge of the character of South Americans in this country, convinces me that this peculiar idiosyncracy of the Spaniard is also very general amongst their descendants in those countries.

----

[5] "To the strife let us hasten, Argentinos! Let all march to the combat! War to the death to the cowardly Tyrant! War to the death, and then we shall have peace!" (Perkins' translation).

CHAPTER XXX

Christmas time, and with it letters from home, filled with all the quiet, holy, and affectionate feelings that congregate around the domestic hearth! How peaceful every tone! What a contrast to the restless passions encountered in the vortex of struggling duplicity in which we find ourselves in the great World! What trooping memories come up of home and childhood's reminiscences! Methinks I am again a youngster roaming about the old Farm and Homestead; my Father, my brothers, and sisters around me, and dim memories of a Mother! Again am I straying through the wild grounds of Argentieul, and every nook, and every tree are present—the poplars, silver birch and Balm of gilead trees in the "Little Wood," where our names were carved in the smooth bark—the strawberry field—the enclosure overrun with wild black and red raspberries, and where we were wont to play hide and seek—the quiet river at the foot of the flowery and sweet scented meadow, how often have we sat under the cool shade of the hazel-trees, and watched the sunfish sporting in its calm depths! See the effect of a letter from home at Christmas time, even in California; making a rose bloom in the Deserts of Sahara! It has done even more; it has actually inspired me, a three year resident in the gold mines, with poetic phrensy, and if my readers will be charitable enough to indulge me in this whim, I promise to sin no more. After all it is not too much, if amongst the many chapters of dry details one be found devoted to sentiment, let it be in prose or verse.

Half an hour has passed since I penned the last paragraph, and, on second thoughts, I will not inflict my poetry on the reader; but it is no less a fact that I have written, under inspiration, twelve verses, each verse consisting of four lines, each line consisting of no less than seven iambics, all strung together *segundum artem*. But I sacrifice the ambitious muse, not that I consider her unworthy, but that she would be out of place in a chronicle of Californian Life.

And what have we to do with the gentle memories of innocent days? what has sentiment to do with the terrible necessity of making money? Gold, gold, gilding a man's life but destroying his sympathies! O that it were possible to do without the yellow demon!

> "A curse on him who found the ore!
> A curse on him who digged the store!
> A curse on him who did refine it!
> A curse on him who first did coin it!"

But no; I will not endorse the sentiment in these lines, which undoubtedly were penned by some needy poet whose unacquaintance with the metal made him incapable of forming an impartial judgment.

Every physical thing is good to a certain extent, and gold may possess a double virtue: it incites to labor, to colonization, to civilization on one side, while on the other, its possession enables Benevolence and Charity to alleviate the sufferings of distressed humanity.

The Year Eighteen hundred and fifty one is growing old and feeble, and the sound of his steps will soon be lost in the mighty Past. Already we may fancy that we hear the panting of the Young Year, eager to commence his race. And yet how little noticed are these demarcations of time with us, solemn and suggesting as they are! Christmas and New Year's day bring no softening influence with them, except to a few whose thoughts are carried back to domestic hearths, and fancy they are listening to the affectionate conjectures of some loved and loving ones at home, and are forming, like myself, mental determinations that e'er another season shall pass away, they will be again united to those cherished beings.

Christmas day! The third I have seen in California! Will it be the last? This time last year we were wishing in vain for rain, a rain that did not come during the whole winter. Whether we are to be fortunate enough this season I cannot say, but the commencement promises well. This Christmas is as watery a one as can well be desired by even amphibious animals. Now is the time for any person hydromantically inclined to exercise the mysteries of his art. For five days, we have had a continued deluge falling upon us. Half a dozen of the Jew shops in the *arroyo* have been flooded off, and across the street in that quarter rushes an impassible river. It is quite a picturesque sight, and the roar of the waters is almost deafening. A handsome saloon has just been finished, built upon piles in the bed of the Arroyo; it belongs to the pretty Frenchwoman, Annette. We have just returned from assisting the fair owner to remove her household goods, four Lansquenet tables and the contents of a brilliant Bar, or liquor stand. The river soon broke into the house, and there is now a current two feet deep tumbling and rushing over the floor.

TWENTY SIXTH. The sun shone out warm and bright for a couple of hours this morning, but by twelve o'clock the heavens were again canopied with heavy clouds, which soon commenced discharging their contents again on the heads of the unprotected Jews in the *arroyo*.

Last night was, of course, celebrated by the correct number of drunken rows, sprees and fights. One man, a miner, got the upper part of his head shot off, but is doing well, *considering*. Enyart in trying to steal away from a party of noisy companions, fell into a miner's hole about ten feet deep, in which there was *some* water. He managed however, to scramble out and came home like a drowned rat. I retired to bed at nine o'clock; did not go out at all. The memories that Christmas is apt to bring up, should scarcely be mixed with the noisy drunken scenes by which I am surrounded. We, that is Enyart and I, drank a bottle of champagne to the health of the good folks at home, and were lulled to sleep by an agglomeration of sounds that baffles all attempt at description, and which are only to be heard in California.

A retrospective glance over the events of the past year, as far as I am personally concerned, offers abundant food for reflection. In worldly prosperity I have nothing to complain of; in health still less; and a few good friends have some what softened the inevitable asperities of Californian life. But here the bright side of the picture ceases. Notwithstanding the best efforts of a man, it is impossible not to be more or less infected by breathing continually a tainted moral atmosphere. The finer mental perceptions must suffer to a certain extent, and be more or less blunted by attrition with a society so completely vitiated as is that of California. It is true the past year has seen a vast improvement in all classes; and it is also true that, with the exception of blackguards from Sidney, and blacklegs from the United States, the immigration to this country has not been composed of naturally vicious people. On the contrary; there has always been a powerful element of Good to combat the surging bad passions that have found as it were a hotbed in California.

But the want of respectable female society, rational amusements, and books, has aided greatly to the demoralization of many whose natural character would have kept them aloof from temptation had there been other means but the gambling tables and drinking saloons, to have assisted them in whiling away the hours not devoted to labor.

The greatest deprivation I have suffered in this country has been the want of books, which probably were the only thing forgotten in the varied shipments to San Francisco in 49 and fifty. At the present time literature of all kind is abundant, and probably we owe the great improvement to be remarked in all classes, to this fact. Every town now has its daily, tri-weekly or weekly newspaper, and large book establishments are to be found in the Metropolis.

The acquisition of the Spanish language has interested me, and has enabled me to employ many an hour that might otherwise have been unprofitably dissipated. But it is no less a disagreeable fact that the want of books and a literary society causes a man to loose a valuable proportion of his acquired knowledge: History, composition, conversational powers, with the store of innumerable small but important items with which a man fills his brain in a civilized country, all must suffer neglect, and are consequently more or less forgotten, or at the best, leave such a confused medley of mixed-up recollections that nothing can be found ready burnished for immediate use. The melancholy result in my case and in that of many of my friends will be that we shall probably be likened to grizzly bears by our refined countrymen, should we ever have the good fortune to find ourselves again in their society.

Well, another year has passed away. A sixtieth part of a man's life is left behind us, in that course in which we are never permitted to turn back to amend an error or correct a false step in yesterday's journey! Has this portion of our life passed, and no monument been erected by the road side in which a shrine might have been raised for memory to worhip at? We should not say so. Providence assigns each man his station; gives every one his talent; and there is no position in life in which a man may not honorably aquit himself of the duties of the first, and give a just and righteous account of the use of the latter.

It is time to draw my Journal for this year to a close, and commence anew tomorrow on a clean sheet with the New Year. To the old one I bid a fair good night!

CHAPTER XXXI

New Year's Day 1852.—The progress of this country in the two last years is something marvelous, and will ever remain an historic curiosity in the lives of Nations. Two years ago the town of San Francisco numbered some three or four thousand inhabitants, tenanted in a few shanties, hovels and tents. An irregular monthly Steamer found its way into the magnificent harbor. Ships as soon as they arrived were deserted by their crews, from the Captain down to the cabin boy, and left to rot in the bay. The only means of getting up the rivers was by small ill-manned sailing boats, that were usually from ten days to a fortnight in reaching Stockton or Sacramento. These latter places being nothing more than a huddled up heap of tents. In the interior, no towns that deserved more than the name of encampments. The country without a Government, and without laws. The first necessaries of life, hard to be procured, while many articles such as tobacco, nails and bales of cotton, were to be seen paving the side walks of San Francisco.

What is the aspect of the country at this epoch, after passing through phases that appear to belong rather to romance than sober reality?

The insignificant little town known as *Yerba-Buena*[1] a few short months ago, is now a great city, with wharves lined by warehouses, extending half a mile into the sea. Magnificent marble, granite and brick edifices are in every street. A trade equal to that of a second rate city in the United States. A harbor full of ships, and arrivals and departures chronicled every hour. The rivers full of large and elegant steamers. Spacious storehouses full of the most valuable descriptions of merchandize. Fashionable ladies and well dressed men, walking or riding through the streets.

Up the country, the encampments like Sonora, changed into well

---

[1] In a note Perkins says: *"Yerba-buena,* which is the spanish name for peppermint, was the common denomination of San Francisco [until 1847]. This herb is very plentiful in the vecinity of the Golden Gate. Hence the vulgar name of the town."

built permanent towns; stage coaches on all the principal roads; good taverns by the road side, and large well furnished hotels in every town or village. All the departments of Government are now in as regular working order as in the State of Massachusetts, and the laws promptly administered. Large tracts of land have been reclaimed and cultivated and are now smiling with plentiful crops, the result of careful and laborious tillage of hundreds of hardworking farmers.

In every town there are newspapers conducted with more or less ability. In San Francisco there are four dailies, and in all the state there are fifty four papers published. Probably in no city in the world are the foreign news so varied as in the journals of the mercantile metropolis of California. Every day are to be seen notices in the Newspapers of arrivals from Europe, the United States, Chile, Perú, Mexico, Panamá, the Sandwich Islands, New South Wales, the Southern Ocean, China, the Eastern British possessions, Oregon etc. and we may read such notices as: "Late news from Owihee, Atovi, Shanghay, Sitka, Sooloo, Singapore or Kiwsin"; or something to this effect: "Important intelligence for our mercantile community from our correspondent in Eahei-Nomauwee, and Tavai-Poenammóo."

If two years have produced this extraordinary progress, what will San Francisco be at the end of the present century?

The new year is commencing gloriously. After an eight days rain the sun has made his appearance, accompanied only by some beautiful fleecy white clouds which serve to intensify the deep blue of the heavens. The poor devils of Mexicans are warming their chilled frames in the welcome beams. The women, and their name is legion, are again to be seen in the streets, picking their way daintily through the mud, with their white satin shoes, silk stockings, and rich *Rebozas*. The town is alive with people, walking about with cheerful countenances, inhaling the pure, invigorating atmosphere. The Miners are brightening up, and the merchants are calculating the extra profits on their pork and flour.

The day is mild and balmy as an Indian summer, and no snow is to be seen on the mountain tops about Sonora, although large quantities lie on the northern slopes. The young grass is shooting up on the plains and southern hill sides, soon to be covered we hope with a mantle of snow, for we have no desire for a long continuance of fine weather; only short breathing spells, to warm us up a little.

The town is remarkably quiet—most of the Mexicans have sallied out to the diggings to take advantage of the supply of water.

The new Jail is finished. It is not very secure, but thanks to the energy of the Vigilance Committee, there is not much need of a prison, except for the pickings-up of the Police. The "Committee" only exists now in name. Having accomplished its mission it has quietly delegated its powers to the legal Authorities, who, it is to be hoped, have now the power and the will to perform their duty and make the laws respected.

WEDNESDAY, SEVENTH. Corrales, the Mexican horse thief, one of the prisoners I mentioned some time back as being in custody and awaiting their trial, was hanged today by the legal Authorities. The scaffold was quite primitive; the cross beam was the horizontal branch of a large oak tree, and a low platform was erected below. The man did not fall more than eighteen inches, his neck was not broken, but he died immediately by suffocation.

Notwithstanding the positive proof of his guilt, he protested his innocence to the last. Perhaps he meant that he was innocent of any crime worthy of death, and probably it is a fact; but the peculiar circumstances I have already described as existing in this country, have made it necessary to use the most stringent measures to put a stop to the systematic stealing of cattle on a large scale. A few examples will be sufficient, when the enactment will be suffered to become a dead letter in the statute book.

When the criminal was about to be turned off, the sheriff, our old acquaintance George Work, had to cut a rope that sustained the hanging door of the platform. As this was the first execution Work had assisted at, he was very much agitated; so much so that he actually hanged the poor fellow some ten minutes before his time. In drawing his bowie knife to cut the rope, he drew it out, with the sheath, from his belt, and in his flurried state of mind not noticing the fact, struck, and with sufficient force to cut through the sheath and the rope at the same time. Dropping the knife, he then sank down and covered his face with both hands, greatly affected; and yet this man has been one of the biggest rowdies of the town, and offers a proof that not all the blackguards we have about us are naturally vicious, and that it is highly probable that when once good behaviour, honesty and sobriety shall be at a premium, hundreds, perhaps thousands of men who are now pests of society will be reclaimed and be made good citizens.

In the case of gamblers there is already a very salutary change. We seldom witness the arrogance and insolence which distinguished this class, even a twelve months ago. Their profession is no longer reputable and they feel it.

It is strange that even to this day there should be a superstitious belief in the existence of some potent virtue in the rope which has been used to hang a man. The one used today was eagerly sought after, and I have seen small pieces of it in the bosoms of young and old women of every class.[2]

I have drawn a sketch of a Californian Vaquero, and a Californian girl in her Sunday dress, which consists of a splendid skirt with a body; a silk *rebosa* to cover the head and bosom, and a pair of satin shoes with rose colored silk stockings. The latter are indispensable on Sunday, although amongst the poorer classes the satin shoes are often worn on week days without stockings. A great deal of pains is taken in the finishing of the skirt, which is generally of white muslin. A year is often expended in needle work, in white lace and colored silk embroidery round the flounces and the bottom of the dress.[3]

The rebosa is often laid aside on feast days to give place to a rich Chinese crape shawl, which is not satisfactory unless it be covered with the gaudiest description of embroidery, and is often worth a hundred dollars. In Mexico, the women use these articles of dress with a deal of coquetry in the house, giving a stranger whom they desire to fascinate, casual glimpses, by the apparently accidental disarrangement of the rebosa and shawl, of a swelling bust. This is done so gracefully and naturally that one would hardly suspect them of the intention, were not the movement accompanied by a furtive but expressive glance of a pair of black eyes that are watching the effect produced on you. However, I am running away from my subject which is the figures I have sketched and not the voluptuous Mexican women.

---

[2] Perkins appends a note: "Many people in Europe, even in civilized England, entertain the same belief. In Sweden I think it is that the people eagerly swallow the blood of executed criminals, believing it possesses a charm to drive off disease and death. The populace often have bloody fights with the military that is stationed round the scaffold to prevent them indulging in their disgusting propensity."

The execution of José Corrales on January 7, which inspired these remarks, is also described in the *Sonora Herald* of January 10, 1852.

[3] The sketches of the California vaquero and girl, in pen and pencil touched up with crayon, are included among our illustrations.

The *Vaquero* drawn is a very good representation of his class. He holds in his hand his *riata* or lasso, and in the *bota* of his right leg sticks his sheath knife. His pantaloons, open to the hips and adorned with rows of silver or gilt buttons, leave the white drawers visible, the latter being drawn in by the leather *bota* or high gaiters, usually ornamented with rich embroidery. It is seldom he wears a jacket; when he does, it is generally made of leather and scolloped with colored cloth, light blue being the most in favor. The *zarape* is his usual outside covering on horseback or on foot.

The *Vaquero* [4] is almost always on horseback, and to see him flying over the immense *llanos* on his half-tamed charger, amongst his herds of cattle, with his huge but not ungraceful hat perched on the top of his head, his brilliantly colored *zarape* flying in the wind, his enormous spurs, his graceful attitudes, altogether he forms by no means an uninteresting feature in a landscape.

TUESDAY, TWELFTH [thirteenth]. The weather still continues bright and warm notwithstanding our prayers for rain. We are not without interesting events to chronicle—1st the President's Message received; 2nd News of the arrival at New York of General [Lajos] Kossuth [hero of the Hungarian independence movement] 3rd letters from home; 4th a grand masquerade Ball, in which the women appeared gorgeously dressed; 5th the arrival from below of my friend Navarro, who has made his arrangements to return to Chile on the fifteenth of the coming month, and has come to bid me good bye; and 6th the intelligence of the probable removal of the capital to Sacramento.

The accommodations for the Houses of Assembly at "Vallejo" are of such a scanty nature, that the members have determined to change their quarters to the town of Sacramento. What effect this measure will have on the future of the General's great speculation, is as yet problematical.[5]

---

[4] Perkins' note says: "Vaquero in spanish means a cowherd; but the term is very generally applied to all the lower Californians below the class of *hacendados*. The name consequently is equivalent to the *guazo* of Chile and the *gaucho* of Buenos Ayres."

[5] Perkins explains in a note: "General [Mariano G.] Vallejo, the owner of large tracts of land in this state, made a proposition to this effect: He was to lay out the plan of a large town on his land near Benecia, to be called after him; he agreed to expend from his own funds a quarter of a million of dollars on the

It is shrewdly suspected that the honorable members found the new town rather dull and preferred the gaieties of Sacramento where there is a very good society, and they have found an excuse in the unfinished state of the public buildings. During the first session, and in such a short period after the acceptation of General Vallejo's proposition, it was hardly to be expected that the buildings should be in a complete condition, or the accommodations as comfortable as they might be, or that the society and means of amusements should be unexceptionable. The arrangement of the Government with Vallejo was an advantageous one for the State; the site is an excellent one for the capital, being within a few miles of Benecia, in a beautiful country, accessible by water from all parts, and at the same time retired from the commercial focus. I fear however, that the enemies of "Vallejo" will triumph in its overthrow. There is a powerful clique whose cry is *"Delenda est Cathargo"*!

The morning exercise of our little society in Sonora is pistol shooting. At the distance of a quarter of mile from the town is a secluded little valley in part of which is located the Masonic Burying Ground. The place has been respected on this account. No miners have as yet profaned it with their labors, and the original vegetation is intact and luxuriant. Here every fine morning as the sun begins to extricate itself from the maze of wooded mountains which form the Sierra Nevada, we cross the gentle hill that separates the valley from the town, and at one extremity where there stands a magnificent pine-tree a hundred and fifty feet high, we exercise our skill with Colt's

necessary public buildings, and the Government bound itself to make 'Vallejo' the capital of the State. The proposition was accepted, and the law passed in consequence was ratified by the people at the last Elections."

The bill making Vallejo the permanent seat of government was passed February 4, 1851. The third California legislature convened there on January 5, 1852, but, as Perkins says, on January 12 voted to reconvene at Sacramento on the 16th. At the time a committee was created to discuss the Vallejo question with the General, and proposals were made to move the seat of government to Benicia. The fourth legislature convened at Benicia, and later in the session made Benicia the "permanent" seat of government. The fifth legislature met at Benicia in January, 1854, but late in the following month changed the seat of government to Sacramento. Various legal proceedings kept the issue confused for another year, but from 1855 Sacramento has been California's capital. The technical reason given for removing the capital from Vallejo was that the General had failed to fulfill his bond.

Navy revolver. There are some half dozen of us, besides myself, whose names I immortalize by jotting them down here: William Hammond, our Banker; [Anson Akenside Hull] Tuttle our chief Judge; [S. H.] Dwinelle and [H. P.] Barber, Lawyers, Harry Ford and [F. E.] Dreyfous nothing in particular, all "good men and true." Practise makes perfect, and at twenty five paces it has become no great feat to cut the ace of hearts out of a card. The worst shot has to pay a fine of "Champagne Cocktails," a palatable tonic, a recipe of which I give for the benefit of the uninitiated.

Take one small tumbler of white Jamaica rum and burn it with three ounces of the best lump sugar until the latter is absorbed. Have two large glass or silver jugs ready; put into one a couple of pounds of dry ice broken into pieces of the size of a walnut, so that it shall not melt with too much facility; into the other pour the burnt rum, adding a small tumbler of the liquor known as sherry bitters, more or less according to taste. Now open a bottle of champagne and pour it over the broken ice; pour from one vessel to the other briskly eight or ten times, from the height of two or three feet, to liberate the fixed air, and serve out. Of the numerous "Drinks" invented by Young America, let me assure the reader this is not one of the worst.

Mr. Frank Marriatt, a son of the naval novelist whose works have so often charmed us, is established at "Mormon Gulch" a few miles from Sonora.[6] He is an active "go ahead" personage, and has already entered into various speculations. He brought out and put up some

---

[6] Frank Marryat, youngest son of Frederick Marryat, came to California by way of the Isthmus early in 1850. He left California in the spring of 1852, just ahead of Perkins (having taken passage in the *Northerner* to Panama), but after a stay in the West Indies returned to San Francisco early in 1853. He later went back to England, and in 1855 published an account of his California experiences, *Mountains and Molehills* (the English edition has illustrations much superior to the American edition, but both are "by the author"). It was not until September, 1851, that he found his way to Sonora, soon thereafter inaugurating his mining enterprise at Tuttletown in Mormon Gulch. He describes his associate as "a young Englishman of the name of Rowe," a surveying engineer of ability who had, before leaving England, "scarified that country to a considerable extent in the shape of tunnels and cuttings on railways." Rowe was engaged in constructing and surveying a plat of Vallejo when Marryat encountered him. Marryat died "of decline," in his twenty-ninth year, 1855. His California narrative, very different from that of Perkins, may profitably be compared with it.

good buildings in the new Capital, Vallejo, which will pay well if the state keep faith with the General; but, as I have already remarked, it is highly probable that all those who may have risked their capital in the new town, will meet with disappointment and loss.

Mr. Marriatt has put up a Quartz crushing machine at Mormon's Gulch, and it is proving a crushing business in every sense of the word, the proprietor's money being crushed even more rapidly than is the quartz. I often ride over to the Gulch for, besides Mr. Marriatt, we have many excellent friends established there. The place was originally settled by a company of gentlemen from Virginia and Maryland, and with whom we have always been on the best of terms. Regularly every Sunday, weather permitting, some of them come over, and remain with us until the following day. It was this same party who, on the occasion of the foreigners threatening the town in May 1850, rode over in full force, armed with their rifles, to protect the old house.[7]

Mormon Gulch is celebrated for the quantity of gold that has been there extracted. Three years constant working has not yet exhausted the supply, as is proved by the fact that many of its first explorers still continue to work there, never having left the place. The Mormon Gulch gold is also celebrated. It is very clean, in large grains and nuggets and of a brilliant and beautiful color.

Auriferous quartz is also abundant, and the surrounding mountains undoubtedly contain other valuable minerals. Several persons have entered into the business of quartz crushing, but as yet with little profit. The first operations meet with no difficulty; the quartz is blasted from the leads or veins, carted to the Machines, is primarily crushed and then ground; but here the continuance of the operations is stopped by the impossibility of extracting the pulverized gold from the equally pulverized stone. Amalgamation with quicksilver is found to be ineffective, and the disappointed operator after having with trouble and expense ground up a ton of stone rich in gold, is disgusted to find that his quicksilver is incapable of taking up the minute particles of the precious metal.

-----

[7] Compare Perkins' remarks at the end of chapter xvii.

CHAPTER XXXII

JANUARY TWENTY FOURTH. Sunday night. The weather is chilly and dry. A fire although comfortable is not indispensable. I am sitting alone in the *bodega* behind the store, the doors of which are closed for the night. A stove stands in the centre of the large room and a cheerful fire is to be seen between its grates. Around the walls are piled, nine or ten feet high, bags of flour, barley, biscuits, barrels of liquor and boxes of wine. The table (a pretty rickety one it is too) is covered with a handsome damask cloth. Four sperm candles illumine the pages of my Journal, but are not sufficient to dissipate the dense shadows caused by the piles of merchandise, in the angles of the room. The remains of a tumbler of arrack punch, and a plate of biscuit are beside me, and on the table lie also two very fine guitars, one of them Navarro's, the other mine. We have been practising tonight some of the plaintive Argentine music. By the side of the guitars is a *black hat*; my tile; and which speaks volumes in itself of the progress we have made towards civilized customs. The light sparkles upon the polished keys of a flute and a large and brilliant specimen of quartz and gold which was sent to me this evening to value.

The epoch of flannel shirts has disappeared for townsfolk. We now dress like christians, and I smile to think of the change as I witness myself equipped in a silken lined cloth frock, handsome vest and a black silk cravat, and over topped with a luxurious smoking cap of purple velvet and sable! There is however one of the ministers of civilization who has as yet been refused admittance into the minds. I mean the Barber. Razors are at a discount, and every man wears his face adorned as Nature intended the faces of the male of the genus *homo* to be.

To return. The rats are playing leap-frog on the floor and on the bags of flour, and two purring cats are complacently looking on enjoying their graceful gambollings. There is apparently a truce agreed to between the parties, a truce which is fatal to our bags of biscuit.

Frank, our Mexican boy, and one of the best boys I have known, is nodding drowsily from his low stool behind the stove. Frank, or rather Francisco, is our factotum; he sweeps the rooms, opens the stores, cooks our simple meals, and has even become expert in the concoction of a champagne cocktail.

Confused and uncouth sounds of the bands from the different saloons, Californians singing, and now and then the shouts and yells of the Mexicans intoxicating themselves in the low *chinganos* outside the principal street, mix themselves strangely and grotesquely with the domestic song proceeding from the teakettle on the stove; and this by the bye, puts me in mind that another tumbler of punch would not be amiss; or shall I wait until Navarro and Harry Askins come in? They are playing billiards with Mesdames Plannel and Martin, the latter a very beautiful woman with a very jealous husband, the former a very ugly woman but whose husband is even more jealous than the other. I shall not answer the question, and the reader will for ever remain in ignorance in reference to that other tumbler of punch.

The propositions urged upon me by Navarro to emigrate to South America have caused me to reflect seriously. It would be an agreeable change should we be able to realize the business plans formed, and enter Chile at the head of a great and beneficial undertaking, with all the advantages of position, consideration and society. Lord! how "flat, stale and unprofitable" will appear to us then the things that interest us here, often puerile, and too often vulgar. God grant we may not become divested of those feelings that may in another country be indispensable as a foundation on which to build a structure.

MONDAY, TWENTY FIFTH. I had written so far last night, when I fell asleep. So much for good thoughts and inspirations! In the mean time Navarro came in, took the pen from my hand, shut up my book and put all away. Sleeping and eating; all the spiritual part of humanity must succumb to their exigencies, as well as the physical. Milton doubtless was often obliged to leave off dictating some of the noblest passages of his grand epic, in order to satisfy the cravings of his stomach; and a man will pour forth all the impassioned eloquence of a fervid imagination to the being of his adoration, and immediately afterwards find a strong charm in a plate of oyster soup and a glass of brandy and water! Fie, fie upon the coarse wants of the human system!

Yesterday a Basque was brought in dead from "Los Cayotes" camp.[1]

---

[1] "Los Cayotes" otherwise known as Coyote Diggings, are described in the *Columbia Gazette* of January 22, 1853, as "on the hill between Columbia and Gold Springs." (See Lang, *A History of Tuolumne County*, p. 103.)

He was shot by the officers of Justice in an attempt to rescue a prisoner. He was buried last night by his countrymen by torchlight, and, according to one of their singular customs, several vollies of musquetry were fired over the grave.

These Basques are a strange people, and we have large numbers of them amongst us. Generally speaking they are peaceable, hard working men, but when their passions are roused they are very dangerous. They are probably the oldest people of Europe who have retained their customs and original language, if we except perhaps the Welsh. They are very powerful athletic men; their amusements after a hard days work being pitching quoits, and the iron bar, or heaving heavy stones.

These fellows would make the finest soldiers in the world but they are too proud to inlist in any service. Their language is a mixture of barbarous old french and older spanish, and not to be understood by the natives of either side of the Pyrenees.[2] The Mexicans view them with a species of stupid wonder. They can't understand the use of the vast physical exertions of the Basques exhibited for mere amusement. Their astonishment equals that of the Turkish Pasha, who was sadly puzzled at witnessing for the first a ball in England, and to see the continued and violent exertions of the ladies and gentlemen on the floor.

"Great Allah! why do not these people hire dancers to dance for them instead of killing themselves with fatigue!"

We have a policeman by the name of Soloman, a rather timid lymphatic individual.[3] Being on his beat last night, and passing behind Louis and Lecoq's large Hotel, in whose yard a number of horses were tied, he, being very shortsighted, imagined he saw a man trying to steal the cattle, and fired his pistol. He ran to the station, and pale with excitement, gave the alarm. Torches were at once put into requisition and a search instituted for the victim robber, for Soloman swore he shot him dead. A small pool of blood was in fact found, but the body had unaccountably disappeared. The thing was serious, and a deal of excitement there was amongst the police of course, until the following

---

[2] The Basques speak a tongue unrelated to any other, one of the most ancient of European languages.

[3] According to the U. S. census enumeration made in Sonora in May, 1851, T. L. Soloman, aged 29, was born in Kentucky; his occupation was "Miner."

morning, when old Louis was heard swearing vengeance against the scoundrel who had shot his fattest sow!

Soloman's story to the Marshall was: that in making his rounds he distinctly saw a man amongst the legs of the horses unloosening the *riatas* with which they were fastened.

"I called out" said he—"what are you doing there? There was no answer. I called out again—hallo! what are you about there with the horses? Again no answer. For the third time I called out to the robber, threatening to shoot him if he did not come forward and deliver himself up, and still he refused to answer."

"Well," said the Marshall, "and what did you do then?"

"Why Sir, then I shot him, by G——!"

The month of January has passed almost without a drop of rain, and there are serious fears that the winter being so far advanced we shall have a dry season. This will be very unfortunate for all kind of business. The faces that at christmas and New year time brightened with the copious falls of rain, are again lengthening in a very despondent manner, and the town is again full of miners out of work. *Paciencia y barrajar,* as the spanish gambler's proverb has it, and which we have translated literally in ours of, *patience and shuffle the cards.*

A respectable young man from Canada died suddenly day before yesterday, from eating the meat of a hog that had been poisoned.[4] The people of the town are poisoning the rats that have found their way up here and have become quite a pest. The hogs, eating the dead rats, sicken and are killed, and their meat sold by unprincipled vagabond dealers, who richly deserve lynching for their rascality.

FEBRUARY TENTH. I was amused last night, at the opening of Planel's new Theatre by a very characteristic incident. On this occasion a grand ball was given, and in honor of the important event the young men were all dressed up in their best, and Enyart was particularly fine; and a handsome fellow he is too when well dressed as he was last night, with black dress coat, black pantaloons, white vest and *white kids, toute*

---

[4] "It is said that pork intensifies the virulence of poison," Perkins comments in a note. "The horrible and celebrated poison which is now identified with the family of Pope Alexander VI (the Borgias) was made in the following manner: a large dose of arsenic was administered to a fat hog which was then hung up by the hind legs. The slaver was carefully collected from the mouth of the dying animal and chemically refined: making, it is said, a fearfully deadly poison."

en règle. There were of course plenty of handsome French women, and choosing one of the prettiest, Master Aleck stood up for a quadrille; when lo! for his *vis-a-vis* was another pretty frenchwoman, elegantly dressed and gallanted by a *"French gentleman,"* fresh from the mines, with huge muddy boots, canvas pantaloons, a dirty red flannel shirt, a part of which silently obtruded itself on public notice from a small rent behind. The contrast was so ludicrous between the two gentlemen that the whole room was in a roar of laughter. The Frenchman took it all in good part, observing that he had no other clothes, and he hoped his countrywomen and the townfolk would pardon him. He had no idea of meeting with parisian fashions so soon in Sonora.

These French women I have just spoken of, and whom I have mentioned in various parts of my Journal, are one of the peculiar features of California society. They are to be met with every where, and every where they are the same: money making, unscrupulous, and outwardly well-behaved; for rarely in any situation does a French-woman forget that grace and an affectation at least of dignity, are all-important attractions in her sex. Thousands have immigrated to this country as adventuresses. Some few are married and have come out with their husbands, but these generally have few personal attractions. Most are young girls who have found "protectors" in this country with whom they live in all respects as man and wife, and are for the most part excellent helpmates and valuable companions. They are always lady-like in their dress and comportment, and as virtuous as the generality of their class in France think it becoming or necessary in the sex.

Within a certain circle in France, the motto of married women appears to be faithlessness to the husband, and truth to the lover; and this fact has made more common the eschewing of the marriage ceremony, the more fascinating freedom of a contract of love taking its place, which has this advantage that when one of the parties gets tired of the other, or both desire a separation, they part amicably and at once. Under these circumstances—of course making use only of the arguments in favor of the system—the couple are careful how they offend each other; shunning subjects of dispute, and, not feeling a chain binding and fettering every action, they live on much happier terms than if they were married; and congugal fidelity is made certain, because there is no reason for concealing a new love for another person.

If the union be a satisfactory one to both parties, then each has an ever present interest in retaining by every means, the affection and good will of the other.

I suppose Madame George Sand has such arguments; but let it not be thought that I sanction them. I only repeat the arguments of the French people here.

A lecturer on Mesmerism has found his way to Sonora, and actually manages to humbug the hardfisted, matter-of-fact miner out of a few dollars. These itinerant vagabonds give quite an air of antiquity to our little three year old town. They bring back civilizing thoughts and feelings, and help to soften the acquired savageness of the people, although they be humbugs.

A spanish dramatic company is now performing nightly in M. Planel's new theatre; and Madame Abalos, ex-Prima Donna at the opera house in Mexico, sings, aided by her little daughter Sophy, the same I mentioned as having had her face burnt and her beauty destroyed during a dangerous attack of illness. Her voice however is uninjured and is pure and clear.

Madame Abalos must have been a superb-looking woman in her younger days, and undoubtedly triumphed as much by her beauty as by her singing. At the age of forty she is still an imposingly handsome woman. What a change for her; from singing to the gorgeous audiences of the opera house in Mexico, where the blaze of gold and jewels is even more dazzling than in the Theatres of Europe, to the boards of a wooden and canvas theatre filled with red and blue flannel shirts, bowie knives and Colt's revolvers!

The day is rainy, but we cannot hope at this season of the year, for much wet weather. The results of the continued drought will be disastrous to all classes. Another year must elapse e'er the gulches and plains can be worked. By next year however, the miners will not be so dependent on rain water as here to fore. Thousands of men are working on different canals which will bring the waters from the mountain streams. The Tuolumne Water Company have nearly completed their gigantic undertaking of bringing the head waters of Estanislao river over mountains and valleys to Shaw's Flats, and Columbia, near Sonora.[5]

---

[5] In this casual fashion Perkins first mentions Columbia, now a California state park and wonderfully evocative of the era Perkins described. The first

These works, taking into consideration that they are carried out by miners without the aid of engineers, or engineering skill, are stupendous, and are a wonderful commentary on what the search after gold enables men to perform. The work alluded to, when completed will make the fortune of all concerned in the undertaking, for the miners and owners of claims will pay any amount of money for a constant supply of water, without which their claims are valueless.

There are still in the vicinity of Sonora some five or six hundred acres of plain and valley almost untouched, and where, if the gold is not in great abundance, it is at least plentiful enough to pay the miner half an ounce a day.

Papers from the Atlantic side of the continent come to us full of excitement in reference to the presidential election. Out here in California however there is very little enthusiasm displayed, unless it may be amongst the government folks at Sacramento. We scarcely ever hear a surmise as to who will be the happy individual who will be called to king it over a nation of thirty millions for the next four years. Whigs and Democrats have in this country placed themselves quietly under the dominion of King Plutus, and the allegiance of the people must be changed considerably by "stump speakers" if half of them cast their vote at all next November.

On the twenty fourth, the French people got up a great banquet, in honor I believe of some republican triumph. I was of course the honored guest, as I always am in all the celebrations, balls and dinners given by the foreigners. This present banquet was a socialist meeting, and the walls of the room were hung around with a queer assemblage of names; amongst a host of others there were Fourier, Robespierre, Jesus Christ, Moses, Spartacus, Franklin—I thought they might as well have added Atila, Nero, and Caligula, and there then would have been an assortment.

The French are at this moment damning Luis Napoleon, and in

---

major discoveries in this locality were made as late as March, 1850, occasioning an immediate rush from the surrounding region. As set forth in Lang's *A History of Tuolumne County*, p. 100, the Tuolumne Water Company commenced work at Summit Pass on July 1, 1851, and turned the water of Five Mile Creek into Columbia on May 1, 1852; the following August, the ditch was completed to the South Fork of the Stanislaus. A map of the company's ditches, prepared in 1853 by Engineer John Wallace, is reproduced by Carlo M. De Ferrari in his edition of Stoddart's *Annals of Tuolumne County*.

the speech I had to make, I must have touched upon his tyranny
something in a shakesperian strain:

> "I have no words;
> My voice is in my sword! Thou bloodier villain
> Than terms can give thee out——"

for I had to undergo a separate hug from every Frenchman in the room.
Certainly the Nephew of the Great Man is not in the hearts of his
countrymen in California.

On this festive occasion, Madame Planel's house was tastefully
illuminated with colored transparencies, bearing the colors precious
and endeared to all republican Frenchmen, the bright *tricolor,* red,
white and blue.

After the dinner, we had a spanish drama, a french *vaudeville,* and
the "Casta Diva" from the Señora Abalos.

CHAPTER XXXIII

MARCH, SATURDAY SIXTH. Since last Sunday evening it has been
raining unremittingly, and there has fallen more water within these
days than during all the previous part of the winter. At this present
moment the rain is pouring down with no apparent intention of
ceasing. On Monday the election for City Officers was held. As I have
enjoyed the honor of being City Treasurer during the past year, I
allowed myself to be renominated, and had the satisfaction of being
beaten by thirty odd votes. The whole town was in a state of uproar and confusion and full of drunken loafers. I found by six o'clock
at night that electioneering implies any thing but soberness and
dignity. We pulled a poor vagabond out of a mud-hole in which he
probably would have been suffocated e'er morning, and putting him on
a blanket, allowed him to sleep on the store floor. At day light he got
up and walked off with my revolver and Enyart's fur cap.

> "O ingratitude,
> Thou are sharper than a serpent's tooth."

On tuesday we received letters from our absent partner Theall, and he may be expected back by next steamer. Enyart, who has been for some days at Sacramento arranging his treasury accounts, will be detained by the rain.

MONDAY, EIGHTH. Last night the rain cleared off, and today the sun is shining gloriously. The communication between Sonora and the lower towns is completely cut off for waggons. Adams and Co. sent down their Express this morning on horseback. It will probably be three days getting to Stockton. I do not know how Enyart will get up. An immense amount of water has fallen. Nearly all the Jew shops in the *Arroyo* have been carried off, and a turbulent and roaring river divides the two sections of the town. It is fortunate our house stands on a high and dry spot, or the adobe walls would have been washed away. Adobes being nothing more than dried clay, of course cannot offer any lengthened resistence to a current of water; as it is, the rain beating with fury on the southern side washed away the protecting lime stucco, and has eaten away part of the sun-dried brick wall. The town presents quite an active appearance, all the citizens battling against the water for there are few houses through which the swollen currents have not taken a short cut to the *arroyo*.

THURSDAY, ELEVENTH. On Tuesday the rain recommenced and has continued almost without intermission. The roads are completely broken up. The Estanislao river is three feet higher than it was known to be in the winter of forty nine. At Knight's Ferry, on the road from Stockton to Sonora, there are three or four hundred people weather-bound. Today an Express came up for Adams and Co. The man had to swim three rivers *on the plains*. His letters and papers are all wet and many destroyed. Snow fell this morning but melted as soon as it fell. No news from Enyart; I suppose he is weather bound at Stockton, and it is not improbable that he and Theall return together, for the latter with [John M.] Huntington is expected in the steamer now due.

FRIDAY. Enyart returned last night. He was obliged to walk most of the way from Stockton to the river, forty miles. From the ferry he rode up. Stockton is flooded as are also all the towns on the Sacramento river to above Marysville. In Stockton and Sacramento, boats navegate through the principal streets. We are fortunate here in Sonora that heavy rains can never have the same disastrous effects as in the towns of the plains. The reason is, Sonora is built on a rocky stratum and is some hundred feet above the plains. The water consequently runs off with great rapidity and only does damage in its headlong descent, to the houses in its path.

The Jews have built large numbers of small swindling shops in the broad bed of the *arroyo*, as the ground was unocupied, and being "miners property" belongs to every one. These shops as I have before said have been entirely washed away, and in their place "A river steep and wide" rushes down, completely breaking off all communication between the northern and southern portions of the town. The Jews receive very little sympathy from the community, for as their hand is against all men's pockets, their misfortunes only excite the mockery and risible faculties of the crowd.

There is a drove of a hundred and fifty head of cattle mired down near the river. This means they are all up to the belly in the mud and can not be extricated. They will all consequently perish; a loss for Sonora, as the beef was intended for this market.

WEDNESDAY, SEVENTEENTH. Yesterday the weather commenced clearing up, and today the sun is out and appears determined to submit no longer to the usurpation of the clouds. The Steamer "Tennessee" is in, and Theall has not arrived. The "North America" has been lost from San Juan del Sud [Nicaragua]. The rainy spell has caused a rise in many articles, amongst others barley, which we are selling at twenty dollars the hundred weight.

I rode over to "Campo Seco" day before yesterday and found the roads passable enough. The water does not soak into the ground here as on the plains, where it forms a general quagmire, in which a horse sinks to his belly.

The scenery is always worth a ride amongst the mountains. It is seldom so cold that grass may not be seen on the hill-sides and in the valleys, and the large number of ever-green oak-trees always enliven the scenery. The other day I picked sufficient flowers to form a handsome bouquet; amongst the flowers was the heliotrope and purple pansy.

The leaf of the evergreen oak is of dark green, stiff, pointed and armed with prickles. It forms the principal food of the deer during the winter season. There is another evergreen, belonging I think, also to the family of *Quercus,* bearing an acrid, astringent berry, and which grows in great abundance amongst the rocks and crags of the Upper

Sierras. I have seen whole mountains covered with it. The berries are red, and not unpalatable. I had to subsist on them for a couple of days on one occasion. The Indians are very fond of them, and during their season they scarcely eat any thing else. So highly are these berries esteemed by these people that when the season arrives in which they ripen, all the Indians at work on the plains, at once march off for the mountains. They say that the berry is absolutely necessary, once a year, to their health. Be this as it may, when Mr. Sutter employed whole tribes on his haciendas, before the discovery of gold, it was his custom to despatch them all to the hills for a couple of months, to enable them to rectify their system by the free use of the mountain berry.

The pine trees in California grow to a great height, and sometimes to an astonishing thickness. I remember on one occasion when out deer-hunting, I measured one a yard from the ground and found it thirty one feet in circumference; and I have heard of others of still more astounding dimensions. They are very peculiar on account of their trunk or rather the bark being generally perforated by the extraordinary labors of a certain woodpecker, called the *Carpintero*, by the natives. These perforations commence within a few feet of the ground and cover the whole trunk of the tree. The holes are about an inch and a half deep and half an inch in diameter, and are placed about an inch apart, so that many thousands, probably a hundred thousand might be counted in one tree. As soon as the acorns commence to fall, the birds begin their harvesting, and continue gathering the nuts and filling the holes until the tree is full, when it is studden with acorns very much as a flitch of bacon is with cloves. Each nut is put into a hole corresponding to its size, and with such nicety, with the apex outside, that with the fingers it is impossible to extract one. Here they remain fresh all the year around.

The oak bearing the fruit preserved by these birds in such a singular manner is the *Quercus longiglanda,* and the acorn is from an inch and a half to two inches long. The Indians use them to make the only bread they are acquainted with.[1] They pound the nut or gland in

---

[1] In a note Perkins explains: "The acorn is called in Spain *bellota* (pronounced *belyota*) the arabic *bollot; belot* being the scriptural term for the tree and the gland, which with water, formed the original diet of the aboriginal Iberian, as well as of his pig. When dry the acorns were ground, say the classical authors, into bread and when fresh they were served up as the second course. In

rude mortars scooped out of the surface of a rock. On visiting Indian encampments, even where they have been temporary, one will always see a number of these mortars in the large flat rocks about; sometimes a half a dozen in one stone. Round this stone we may imagine the ancient mothers of the tribe grouped, lightening their labors with reminiscences of their youthful days when the white man was unknown in the region.

The continual recurrence of these honey-combed rocks puzzled me considerably until I found out their history. They are made with the aid of flints and with obsidium, when this is to be got.

Speaking of Indians, there seems to be a great change come over the savage tribes within the last twelve months. Last year it was almost impossible to keep mules in safety any where outside the town. Almost every night the Indians were prowling about and driving off cattle. Now we scarcely ever hear of the robbery of a mule. The aborigines have received so many severe chastisements, that they are moving farther up into the fastnesses of the Sierra Nevada, and seldom venture down. Like the deer they are retiring before the tread of the white man. What will they do when the tide of population advancing from the shores of the Pacific meets the flood of immigration from the Atlantic side and hems them in on the snowy ridge of the Cordilleras? "The poor Indian!" His course is almost run on this vast continent once so exclusively his own. And yet there still exist some formidable remnants of some of the mighty tribes that defied for a lengthened period all the power of the European intruder. The Comanches and Apaches are yet strong enough to carry terror and devastation throughout the whole northern departments of Mexico. The Mexican Government is completely powerless against these warlike and fierce tribes of the Prairees.[2]

---

our times ladies of high rank at Madrid constantly ate them at the opera and elsewhere. They were the presents sent by Sancho Panza's wife to the Duchess, and formed the text on which Don Quixote preached so eloquently to the goatherds, on the joys and innocence of the golden age and pastoral happiness, in which they constituted the foundation of the kitchen. (Ford's Spain.)"

[2] "When I was travelling through Mexico, it happened to be the season of the year that the Indians usually choose for their predatory excursions. For many days and nights we were surrounded with bands of warriors, but as our party was pretty strong—twenty five men—we were unmolested. One evening on our arrival at a small town called *Quincami* [Cuencamé], we found the dense *chaporal* in front of the town occupied by hostile parties of Mexican soldiers and

On the *Rio Colorado* or Red River in the south of California, the Indians are giving the white settlers a deal of trouble, and in some places whole settlements have been butchered or driven off.³ But the savages are courting their own destruction in attacking the Americans. With the Mexicans it may be safe enough, and notwithstanding the clause in the treaty of *Guadalupe Hidalgo* obliging the Americans to protect the Mexican frontier from the Indians, as long as these respected "white property," they were not meddled with. But when they attack Americans, Yankee blood gets up, and Uncle Sam will soon find means to "annex" their savage territory and turn it into peaceful States. Half a century more and the Comanches, the Apaches, the Flatfeet [Blackfeet], powerful Tribes at the present time, will, in all probability, be totally exterminated, for there will be no "farther West"

Indians. They had been fighting for some hours and we came across several bodies of Mexicans already stripped by the Comanches. The latter were holding the *pueblo* in a state of siege, and had beaten back the parties sent out against them. On our appearance the Indians retired, although they were in sufficient numbers to have overpowered us without much difficulty, for they were all armed with lances and bows and arrows; with the latter they are exceedingly skillful, letting fly the arrow from under their horse's neck while the rider is slung on the further side of his animal. However, fortunately we were allowed to enter the gates, and just while we were doing so a huge gaunt wolf sprung across the roads. The shots we fired at the animal, the Indians undoubtedly thought were intended for them, and possessing as they do a most exaggerated idea as to the range and execution of an American rifle, the incident sent them scampering like mad to get out of sight, for they believe a rifle bullet will reach them at any distance that they can be seen at. Our presence in the town was hailed with the most frantic delight from the Alcalde down. Over and above the natural cowardice of the Mexicans, they have a mortal fear of the Indians, and the latter hold them in such contempt and abhorrence that a dozen Comanches will not hesitate to attack treble their number of Mexicans and will always end with scalping the greater part of them. In the *chaporal* we saved the life of a poor boy whose brother had just been killed. In the town I was kept up all night dressing the hurts of the wounded, which were usually in the *rear*. The Soldiers had managed to shoot and bring in *one* Indian, and the cowardly wretches had actually cut up the body and each soldier had a piece hanging to his saddle bow!" (Perkins).

³ The Indian difficulties to which Perkins refers involved the Yuma Indians of the lower Colorado River area and some of the coastal tribes living in San Diego County. All over California there was a great deal of excitement concerning these hostilities, characteristically reported in the *Alta California* of December 1, 3, and 4, 1851, and January 1, 2, 4, 6, 15, and 18, 1852. The militia was called out under Major General J. H. Bean, the Cahuilla Indians defeated, and their chief Antonio Garro shot by a firing squad on January 10.

to remove them to. They are on their last hunting grounds, and will undoubtedly defend them, although vainly, to the last.

There seems to be no doubt that in the range of Cordilleras in the Mexican province or Department of Sonora, there exists rich auriferous deposits as also silver mines in abundance, yet such is the terror inspired by the numerous tribes of warlike Indians in that district, that no one as yet has ventured on exploring the dangerous, but at the same time tempting, mountains. A short time ago however, a party was organized in California, composed principally of Frenchmen, many of them from this town of Sonora, with the object of penetrating into the Indian gold preserves and enrich themselves with the spoils. The party left San Francisco and has not been heard of since.[4]

There is no reason to doubt the distribution of the precious metals throughout the whole range of mountains in the new World, stretching almost from pole to pole, known in North America by the name of Cordilleras and Rocky Mountains, and in South America by the name of the Andes.[5]

If once the existence of gold in any considerable quantities in the mountains of Mexican Sonora shall be placed beyond doubt, American cupidity will soon do what Mexican valor and diplomacy have been unable to accomplish after many years of vain trial, and will probably lead to the Americanizing of the important and wealthy departments of Sonora and Durango, whose inhabitants are even now by no means unwilling to place themselves under the aegis of the Stars and Stripes.

----

[4] Perkins probably refers to a party of eighty-eight Frenchmen under Charles de Pindray which sailed from San Francisco for Guaymas on November 22, 1851, on the *Cumberland*. They were well received and commenced an agricultural colony at Cocóspera, but under Apache attack, the Sonoran government having become hostile, this venture was broken up in the summer of 1852. Pindray either killed himself or was murdered by Mexicans, probably the latter. See Rufus Kay Wyllys, *The French in Sonora (1850–1854)* (Berkeley, 1932), pp. 58–64.

[5] "In Mexico," Perkins explains, "these mountains as a complete range, are called *La Sierra Madre,* the mother of mountains; but every important eminence has its separate name, and *Cordilleras* is only a general name for any range. We have given a specific meaning to a general term. *Sierras* and *Cordilleras* are high ranges; *Cerro* is a small mountain. *Montañas* are high lands, although this and *Montes* are used to indicate as well, wooded lands; *Loma* is a hill of easy and gradual ascent."

CHAPTER XXXIV

MARCH, TWENTY THIRD. For some days we have had fine, warm and even sultry weather, and the roads are drying up rapidly. The trees are becoming green, and the flowers are springing up and flowering on every side. I walked out yesterday and plucked a half a dozen varieties, but it is still too early for the larger and finer descriptions. The youngsters have now an incentive to gather flowers to make bouquets for the purpose of throwing them at the feet of two very pretty and graceful dancers of the Chapman family, who are now performing in the Theatre.

Day before yesterday a bloodless duel came off between two chileno gentlemen. They used Colt's revolvers at twelve paces, and each fired four shots without effect. They must have been greatly frightened or else the pistols were loaded with powder only. But this however is not so strange as was the last duel between Judge Smith and Senator Broderick, both men of undoubted courage. They used the same weapon, and were to fire at the word the first time, and after that as they pleased. Six shots were fired on either side at ten paces. Only one was effective. Smith's third shot struck Broderick's watch, shattering it and inflicting a slight wound.[1] How two such men could fire six times at each other with such a deadly weapon as the revolver without greater damage being done, is unaccountable.

The penalties against duelling in California are very severe, but they have not been sufficient to check the practice. The principals and seconds forfeit their political rights, and if the duel ends fatally the survivors are incarcerated for life in the penitentiary.

I should be by this time in San Francisco on business, but an accident to Enyart who has sprained his ancle will detain me I fear. It

---

[1] David C. Broderick, who succeeded John B. Weller as U. S. Senator in 1857, at this time was serving in the California State Senate, its president in 1851. His duel with J. Caleb Smith of San Francisco is described in the Sacramento *State Journal*, March 10, 1852. Seven years later he was drawn into the celebrated duel with D. S. Terry in which he was mortally wounded.

is strange that any hurt to the limbs in this country seems to assume a much more serious aspect than in other places. It is difficult to account for this fact, for we are all very robust and enjoy excellent health, and the atmosphere is pure and bracing to an extraordinary degree. It may be perhaps accounted for in a peculiar state of the blood caused by abstinence from a vegetable and fruit diet, and indulgence in rich liquors of which there is such an abundance. Harry Ford has been laid up for nearly a twelve month from a little hurt in the knee, and another friend sprained his ancle very much as Enyart has just done, and he was confined for two months to his bed. All classes drink too much here. Half a dozen glasses of exquisite brandy and water, with a bottle of champagne or chambertin have no perceptable effects in this pure air, but I question if they improve the general system.

Sonora is very dull compared to what it used to be; and yet I suppose we must call it improved with its organized police, its halls of Justice, its lawyer's offices, library and printing office; theatres, hotels, balls, dinners and well dressed people; in fact civilization staring us in the face. We have now no rows, no fights, no murders, no rapes, no robberies to amuse us! Dr. Charneaux yesterday pitched a Frenchman from a window of the first floor of the hotel into the street, and we are so hard up for excitable incidents, that even this little affair afforded some gratification. The duel between Miranda and Carmaño was too ridiculous in all its phases to interest any one. I know not what we are coming to. What with peaceable citizens, picayunish yankees,[2] Jew clothing shops and down-East strong-minded women, Sonora will soon be unbearable, and all the old settlers will have to move off and seek more congenial shades!

On Friday twenty sixth I started in company with Harry Smith and Colonel Johnson on my trip to San Francisco and Sacramento, on horseback, and we reached the river after a pretty hard ride of three hours; distance thirty five miles. At Dent's ferry[3] we stopped all night.

---

[2] "For the information of my English readers, a picayune is the name given in New Orleans to the piece of silver of 5 cents. The most celebrated Journal in the South [the New Orleans *Picayune*] adopted the name, a Picayune being its daily price. The word as an adjective is applied to stingy people and particularly to the Yankees, whose habits are so opposed to the liberality of Southerners" (Perkins).

[3] The ferry on the Stanislaus commenced by William Knight in 1849 was completed and put in operation by John and Lewis Dent after Knight's death

While here the body of a poor fellow by the name of Telfair, a cattle drover, was brought in. He had been murdered it seems by his Mexican *vaquero*. The victim had a gash made with a knife in the face, and a silk banda or sash was tightly wound round the throat. He had evidently been choked to death. A party was out at the time in pursuit of the *vaquero*.

At Dents, Col. Johnson was so knocked up that we had to leave him, and the next morning, Smith and I taking the long river road as being the dryest, reached Heath and Emory's Ferry [4] by noon.

Let any stranger to Californian scenery ride through the plains at this season of the year and he will find no language to express his astonishment and admiration. None of the most carefully cultivated gardens of other lands can display the magnificent and gorgeous assemblage of colors with which the plains, the hills, the river banks as far as the eye can reach, are painted. Out of the road track, the eye cannot rest upon a spot which is not studded with floral gems. In some places is a patch of an acre completely yellow; another is all purple, another is blue; others are all white, while alongside is another all red and scarlet; again there are patches literally crowded with flowers of all hues and all descriptions.

The effect of the gorgeous and immense parterres of flowers on the senses is intoxicating, and on the river banks more particularly so, where the brilliantly clothed knolls bring to mind Shakespear's delicious lines:

"I know a bank whereon the wild thyme grows;
  Where oxlips and the nodding violet grows;

---

late that year or early the next. The firm name most often appears as Dent, Vantine & Co., James Vantine having become associated in the ferry at least as early as August, 1850.

4 Heath and Emory's Ferry was situated on the Stanislaus in the vicinity of present Oakdale. It had been known in 1849 as Taylor's Ferry, then operated by Nelson Taylor. The new proprietors were advertising in the *Stockton Times* as early as April 6, 1850. Several other Stanislaus ferries advertised their services, including T. B. Islip's, 6 miles below Taylor's Ferry, Cotton's New Ferry between these two, and "M'Lean, Jeffrey & Co." with a new boat on "the upper ferry (the oldest established ferry) on the main route from the Sonorian Camp, Woods' and Mormon diggings," etc. By August, 1850, Keeler's Ferry was advertising, and in November of the same year Sirey & Clarke were proclaiming their new lower ferry on the Stanislaus, 5 miles from its mouth. A history of these ferries would afford interesting reading.

Quite over canopied with lush woodbine,
With sweet musk-roses, and with eglantine.
There sleeps Titania sometime of the night,
Lulled in these flowers with dances and delight."

The imagination may hardly conceive any thing so superb as is the sober reality in this country. Once we dismounted to introduce a few drops of the sparkling water of the river to the contents of our "pocket pistols," and throwing ourselves down on a mattress of flowers, mingled the fragrant smoke of an *Havana* with their perfume. Without moving from where I lay, I plucked the flowers about me, and counted seventeen distinct hues; four of yellow, five of purple and blue, four of red, verging from brown to scarlet, one white, and the others perceptible shades without names. The Lubin, and the Marvel of Peru, the marigold, and amaranth, the Margarita, several varieties of Fuchia, the Larkspur of all colors, the golden Tulip, the violet, the cowslip, the golden rod, the wild flowering currant, and scores of others that I cannot name, all mingled in a most glorious and resplendent confusion, as if Nature meant to ridicule the comparative puny efforts of artificial cultivation.

And yet alas! how soon all this beauty vanishes like a short dream! In six weeks, pass over these same plains, these fairy banks, and where now you cannot find a spot to stand on without crushing a score of flowers, all will be desolate, bleak, sun-scorched and brown. One can with difficulty believe that the arid plains we see in summer are the gardens, *par excellence* of the Flower-World for one or two short months in the spring: "But the sun did beckon to the flowers, and they By noon most cunningly did steal away."

The road we travelled on this occasion is the old route from Stockton to the mines, and is much the longest. Stockton, Heath and Emery's Ferry and Knight's or Dent's Ferry form the three points of a triangle, the two former, being the base line. The new road across the plains in a straight line to Dent's ferry, naturally cuts off a distance equivalent to one side of the triangle. But the river road is much more picturesque, and in wet weather firmer and safer than the other. This is the route I took when I first went up to the mines, and as I was blind during nearly all the journey, it was entirely new to me, never having passed over it during my residence in Sonora. The scenery on the river bank is very lovely, even without the aid of the flowers. There is a perfect wilderness of trees and bushes, and farmers are beginning to settle on the borders.

Leaving the Ferry we crossed the plains to "French Camp," a little town rising up near the San Joaquin, and within five miles of Stockton.⁵ These five miles were completely overflowed, and it was with difficulty we managed to get into town, late at night.

The next morning at nine o'clock I went aboard the "Sophie" and in a few hours was put ashore at Benecia, where I was to wait for a Sacramento steamer from San Francisco. As bad luck would have it, however, no upper river boat left the city on Sunday [March 28], and I had to remain in Benecia until Monday night. I knew no one here, and the time passed slowly enough, enlivened a little by a visit to the palace of a steamer, the "Golden Gate" which is moored here repairing, and an introduction to a pretty American woman, Mrs. Davis, whose name in consequence will be immortalized in my volume. What a princely recompense for making herself agreeable for a couple of hours!

Benecia (or as it should be pronounced and written Venecia, the Americans having fallen into the error common with spaniards of confounding the pronunciation of the two letters) is the most beautifully situated town in this part of the state, and was for some time the ostensible rival of San Francisco. In former times its claims for preëminence were mainly supported by Mr. Semper, and Com. Jones ⁶, both largely interested in landed property here. The latter, in order to draw the commerce of the country to Benecia, made it the Naval Station for the squadron of the Pacific, making it also his head quarters. But somehow or other people could not be induced to believe that the position of San Francisco, situated on one of the grandest ports in the world, was inferior to that of Benecia, situated on a river, forty miles in

---

⁵ French Camp, or El Campo de los Franceses, was so named because during the 1830's it served as a rendezvous for the French-Canadian trappers comprising the California brigades of the Hudson's Bay Company. Later a town site called Castoria was laid out here, but the locality is known to this day as French Camp.

⁶ Robert Semple and Commodore Thomas ap Catesby Jones, who succeeded to the U. S. Naval command on the Pacific in 1848, are referred to here. Semple and Thomas O. Larkin purchased the town site from Mariano G. Vallejo early in 1847 for the nominal sum of $100, and Semple strove valiantly to promote the town (at first called Francisca) during the course of the next year. For details, see H. H. Bancroft, *A History of California*, V, 670–674.

the interior, and the more Messrs. Semper and Jones argued, the more obstinate the San Franciscanos became. But it was very evident from the beginning that all efforts to remove the commercial Metropolis from its present site would be futile.

Then came the establishing of the Capital at Vallejo, which is only a few miles from Benecia. This would undoubtedly have helped the latter place; but the Capital has been removed to Sacramento, temporally it is true, and it is quite impossible to say where it will be eventually located.[7]

Benecia is, without doubt, the best site for the capital. Situated in the centre of the State; at a respectable distance from the seashore; near the confluence of the two great rivers which form the highways to the northern and southern Mines; healthy; a magnificent agricultural country in its rear; a harbor capable of floating a whole navy; with banks to the river alongside of which ships of two thousand tons may moor; with favorable and elevated sites for public buildings, Benecia offers advantages which are possessed by no other town or locality in California; and it is really surprising, that, in properly rejecting it as the commercial metropolis, the people should not have been sensible of its great advantages as the Capital. The little *pueblo* on the opposite side of the river, called Martinez, looks like a birds nest in a laurel bush. It would form a lovely spot for a summer retreat from the cares of political strife, or from commercial perplexities. The country around is beautifully wooded, and the coast range of mountains is in its immediate vicinity.[8]

On monday evening I got on board the "Splendid Steamer, New World," where I had the good luck to find the Lieutenant Governor, Mr. Purdy, on his way up. Mr. Purdy is one of my oldest friends in California, and is one of the best fellows in the State. The people at large thought so too, when at the last election they voted him into his present position without an effort having been made by himself. I believe he did not spend an ounce in the whole canvass, that is, to secure his election.[9]

---

[7] See Chapter xxxi, note 5.

[8] Martinez was laid out in 1849 by W. M. Smith on lands granted to Ignacio Martinez. It became the seat of Contra Costa County.

[9] Samuel Purdy was born in New York in 1819, came to California in 1849, was elected the first mayor of Stockton in 1851, and later in the year was elected

On board the "New World" were also two hundred fresh arrivals from the Celestial Empire, on their way to the Northern gold-diggings. They were mostly dressed in the national costume, peticoat trowsers reaching to the knees, big jackets lined with sheep or dog-skin, and quilted, and huge basket hats, made of split bamboo. The lower part of their legs are encased in blue cotton stockings, made of cloth, and with soles fully an inch in depth. These people form a peaceable and hardworking class of our population, but are of very little service or benefit to commerce or to the state, as they consume little of the food or merchandise of the country. Rice, their great staple, they generally bring over with them in vast quantities, and when a Chinaman amasses a small amount of cash, he immediately returns home to the "flowery land." This determination seems to be in almost all cases premeditated, for none have brought their wives and children. Some time ago it was calculated that there were no less than fifteen thousand chinamen in California, and at the same time there were only three chinese women. Within the last six months however, Celestials of the softer sex have been speculating in the California mania. Some three or four scores of girls have come over. Their means of livelihood is uniform, and they help to add a darker shade to the profligacy of San Francisco.[10]

The first and almost only article which a chinaman buys when he lands, are boots; the thick, heavy, common yankee boot, which appears to take their fancy to such an extent, that one man will often purchase

---

lieutenant governor on the same ticket with John Bigler, inaugurated in January, 1852. He was again elected in 1853, having a far larger margin of victory than Bigler. Later he engaged in mine and land speculations, especially in Mexico, and died in San Francisco on February 17, 1882. Extended obituaries were published the following day in the San Francisco newspapers.

[10] According to H. H. Bancroft, *History of California*, VII, 336: "The first immigrants from China to modern California were two Chinese men and one woman, who arrived by the clipper bark *Eagle* in 1848. The men went to the mines, and the woman remained as a servant in the family of Charles V. Gillespie, who came hither from Hong Kong. In February, 1849, the number of Chinese men in California had increased to 54; and in January, 1850 to 787 men and 2 women. A year later there were 4,018 men and 7 women; and in January, 1852, 2,512 men and 8 women. By May they had increased to 11,-787, of whom only 7 were women. Like other immigrants some died and some returned, the whole number of both amounting to 476. By August, 1852, there were not less than 18,026 men and 14 women added to the Chinese population of California, brought chiefly from Hong Kong in British ships."

four or five pairs for his own particular use. The little conical, thick felt cap, shaped like a bee-hive, with the brim turned up, which we are accustomed to see on the heads of Celestials delineated on teacups etc, is rather a favorite "tile" for fancy gents among our lower orders. They were adopted as a sort of uniform by a famous set of blackguards called the "Tigers," the terror of decent people in 1849, but who are pretty well thinned out now by the gallows, revolvers and liquor.

We arrived at Sacramento on tuesday morning [March 30], and after a good look at the City, I may say I was disappointed. The town is very poor compared to San Francisco, and it seems to me that Marysville, which is situated at the head of the navegation, must eventually become much more important in a commercial point of view.

Sacramento is laid out on a magnificent scale, but it will be a very long while e'er a twentieth part will be built upon, for the simple reason that there is no need of a large town at this point. It is as easy to take up merchandise from San Francisco to Marysville as to Sacramento, and there are no diggings within eighty miles of the latter place.

The only Lion the town possesses, besides the Legislature, temporally lodged here, is Sutter's old Fort, which is situated about two miles from the river.[11] Coffroth, our representative, drove me out with Major Hammond's pair of Canadian ponies.[12] The Fort is a large enclosure, the walls of which are built of *adobes*, or sun-dried bricks. The fortifications are built in the modern style. The place was intended to withstand the attacks of the Indians, and was made large enough to contain all the cattle of the establishment in case of a foray from the tribes from the mountains. The walls were defended with one piece of ordinance, a small cannon, which, considering the arms of the probable assailants, was an ample and sufficient defence. The place is going to ruin, as, of course, since the advent of American immigration there is not much use for forts of protection against the Indians; but the curious old place gives rise to strange reflexions, particularly when we remem-

---

[11] Sutter's Fort, now a historical monument, restored and administered by the State, is still a principal attraction of Sacramento.

[12] James W. Coffroth was a representative from Tuolumne County. Richard P. Hammond, elected from San Joaquin County, was chosen speaker of the Assembly by a large majority on January 5, 1852.

ber that only four years ago it was the only abode of white men in a tract of thousands of square miles, and now a town of fifteen thousand inhabitants is alongside of it!

CHAPTER XXXV

The somewhat celebrated Captain Sutter, at one time the owner of thirty leagues of land on part of which Sacramento is built, and the lord of the entire Indian population, and proprietor of a military stronghold, is now comparatively a poor man! His lands have been taken possession of by unscrupulous squatters, and the law says that his titles under spanish or mexican grants are invalid. All he possesses now is a beautiful little estate up the river, called Hock Farm.

The history of John A. Sutter, and his settling in the wilds of California, where no white man had been his predecessor, would be interesting. What are the causes that could have induced such an expatriation? Sutter is a Swiss by birth, and has served in the French Army under Napoleon's generals, and has often seen the great man himself.[1] He afterwards emigrated to the United States, where he took out papers of naturalization. In 1839 he came to California, and obtained from the Mexican Government a grant of an immense territory along the river Sacramento, in the heart of the Indian possessions, and consequently surrounded by Savages. Here he built his Fort, and finally succeeded in reducing the Indian tribes and entered into peaceable terms with them. He induced them to labor, paying them in goods and cattle and food. His Fort and Estate he called New Helvetia.

At the epoch of the discovery of gold in 1848, Sutter had immense fields of corn and wheat, and possessed ten thousand head of cattle.

---

[1] Perkins was taken in by the prevailing Sutter legend. The expansive Swiss never served in the French army even of Charles X, to say nothing of Napoleon. See John Peter Zollinger, *Sutter, The Man and His Empire* (New York, 1939), the best biography.

The latter constituted the great, and we may say the only riches of the landed proprietors in those days, the hides, tallow and jerked beef being the only medium of exchange with the trading ships which visited the coast, bringing with them the necessaries and many of the luxuries of civilized life. Coin there was none. All business was conducted by barter and exchange.

Here Mr. Sutter lived the life of a Patriarch; his routine of life only broken by rare visits to his scanty neighbors, none of whom resided nearer than a couple of hundred miles and the yearly advent of the ship which brought him his supplies, and took off the produce of his estate.[2]

The principal amusement of Mr. Sutter was hunting the grizzly bear and the magnificent elk, both of which abounded in this region. He has been obliged more than once to withstand the united attack of numerous tribes of Indians, and on these occasions his cattle were all driven into the enclosure of the Fort, where a supply of fodder was always hoarded up for them; the walls were manned, and the solitary cannon thundered out its terrifying defiance, until the attacking party, beaten back, or despairing of success, came to terms, which were always dictated by the fearless Swiss.

At this epoch there is very little of a warlike appearance about the old fort. Before Sacramento was founded, Sutter rented the place to traders to store goods, and it soon presented a delapidated appearance; the outer walls are falling down, and the towers are covered with a green growth of rank vegetation, and many of the buildings inside are little else but heaps of rubbish. It is now interesting only as a curious memento of its founder's wild life, of days gone by, and of a people now completely subjugated and driven out of their old hunting grounds.

During my short stay in Sacramento, I became acquainted with a goodly number of the members of both houses of Legislature. They are a rum set for the most part. Othello would never have thought of addressing *them* as "potent, grave, and reverend signors." The President of the Senate Mr. Purdy lodged me in his room, and the Speaker of the house gave me his bed, so I have nothing to say against either branch of the Legislature on the score of hospitality, and there are more reasons than one for my qualifying both the Speaker and the President

---

[2] Perkins has an incorrect idea of Sutter's early situation at New Helvetia; in particular, no annual ship came to his establishment on the Sacramento, nor after the first few years, was he so isolated as Perkins thought.

as accomplished gentlemen and an honor to the country. I often attended the debates, in the Senate, sitting alongside of Van Buren and in the lower house by Coffroth, or Genl. Covarrubias, a Californian member from the lower country. Major Hammond is speaker of the lower House. On one occasion, sitting in the Senate chamber, a warm discussion got up, and pretty strong language began to be bandied from one side to the other of the benches. I noticed then several members, Van Buren was one of them, silently leave their seats, go out of the room and return immediately. It was to arm themselves with their revolvers! I could not help laughing when the namesake (and relation) of the little giant of Kinderhook, explained to me the cause of his leaving his seat.[3]

The late inundations have done considerable damage to Sacramento. Half of the town was at one time under water, and the Members of Legislature had to go to the place of their grave deliberations in boats. Through a break of the "levee" or embankment, the waters of the American river, which joins the Sacramento just above the town, rushed in with such overwhelming force, as to tear up by the roots several noble sycamore trees, of which there are large numbers adorning the city.

These trees must be very old. The circumference of some of them is at least thirty feet; Sacramento is the only place in which I have seen them, and I am ignorant of their existence elsewhere in the state.[4] How many centuries have passed since some little insignificant bird perhaps, deposited on this spot the seeds which were the parents of these magnificent patriarchs of the plains! Coming up the river, the only thing in the shape of trees we see, are the low bushes or *chaporal* of the banks, and the scanty stunted oaks on the plains, so that the effect produced by the appearance of the grand old sycamores in the landscape is very striking; almost what I suppose an oasis must be in an african desert, and very like the effect produced on the imagination

---

[3] All those mentioned here have previously been identified except Thomas B. Van Buren, who was the senator from San Joaquin County. Perkins visited Sacramento just after the "overflow" brought on by the March rains described in chapter xxxiii, a well-remembered flood, but less devastating than the inundation of January, 1850.

[4] The sycamore grows more widely in California than Perkins supposed, on all sides of the Central Valley, and down the coast from San Francisco to the Mexican boundary.

when, after traversing the three hundred miles of aridness between the Rio Grande in Mexico, and Monter[r]ey, we catch sight of the glorious clump of lofty trees, celebrated as the camp of General Taylor, and called "Walnut Grove," although there are fewer of these trees than of other species.[5]

After a stay of a few days [*i.e.*, one night] in Sacramento, I bid good bye to my friends and taking the "Antelope" Steamer at ten o clock in the morning found myself in San Francisco at the same hour at night, in time to hear Mad. Biscacciante sing, and see a Mad[lle] Celeste trip the light fantastic.[6] This Mad[lle] Celeste struck me as being won-

---

[5] "Nothing can exceed the beauty of this spot, which is some ten miles from Monter[r]ey. In the centre of the grove, rushes out of a pile of rocks and with the force of a mill race, a spring of delicious water, which in any but parched-up country like Mexico would become a respectable river within a dozen miles; but here the porous sandy plains and the scorching sun would drink up the waters of Lake Ontario in a score of days.

"It is only those persons who have travelled in tropical climates who know how to appreciate at their full value a spring of water and the shade of trees. It is impossible for those who have never left a northern climate, where they cannot ride or walk for half an hour without encountering a brook, a streamlet or a pond, to realize the want of water, that most terrible and unsupportable of all wants, which is so often experienced in countries where the sun is truly monarch of the land. In Ford's Spain, the author, with a full knowledge of his subject, says 'The flow of waters (in a tropical country) cannot be mistaken; the most dreary sterility edges the most luxuriant plenty; the most hopeless barrenness borders the richest vegetation; the line of demarkation is perceived from afar dividing the tawny desert from the verdurous garden.'

"Ask an Arab, a Mexican or a Peruvian, his idea of a paradise on earth, they will answer, a district with abundance of water; water, '*que no enferma, no adeuda, no enviuda*,' which nor makes men sick, nor in debt, nor women widows. I have learnt to love and almost worship water, and I can never see it running in sparkling globules under a canopy of leaves, which here and there allow the sunbeams to kiss the ripples, without experiencing a pious and thankful feeling to Providence. When I visited the Walnut Grove at Monter[r]ey I had to deplore the barbarity of the American Soldiers, who had wantonly cut down and destroyed to a shameful extent the magnificent old trees. How is it that these men had so soon forgotten the many filthy pools of slimy water they were obliged to slake their thirst at between the Gulf and Monter[r]ey, and the arid parched up soil where no green thing grows except the prickly pear, to offer a kindly shade? After passing through such a country, one might expect men to be thankful for shade and pure water, and to respect a blessing intended for many generations, and not for the sole use [of] a few" (Perkins).

[6] It is apparent that Perkins reached San Francisco on March 31 and therefore heard, not Mme. Biscacciante's fifth concert at the American Theatre that night, but her sixth concert on April 2; on April 1 he saw Miss Celeste dance as one of the featured performers at the Jenny Lind Theatre.

derfully like a certain Miss St. Clair, I once or twice saw dancing in Skerrett's company in the theatre at Toronto. What aristocratic people these actors and actresses are in their choice of *noms de guerre*. I have often wondered if it were possible for example, for a Mr. Jerry Grubbins to attain the eminence on the Histrionic boards so easily reached by Mr. Altamont Fitz Guelph.

There are two large theatres in San Francisco, one a brick building, the other a handsome cut stone edifice. The first was built in six weeks, the work going on night and day. It is pointed out as an astounding instance of what can be done in this extraordinary country.

Two steamers [the *Panama* and the *Col. Fremont*] came in from Panamá while I was in San Francisco [on April 1], bringing twelve hundred passengers, and amongst them Harry Gillingham, an old friend of mine, established with his brother in Stockton, and both excellent fellows. Harry went home to get him a wife, and sure enough he has succeeded, and has brought her out with him. This looks as if California were loosing its wild and adventurous habits, and putting on a civilized robe.

On Saturday evening [April 3] I again embarked in the Stockton boat, the "Sophie." The night was glorious, and I remained on the upper deck, walking to and fro all alone, until the night was far advanced. The moon and stars were in all their Californian splendor, and the rich perfumes of the flowers from the shores and the mountains on either side of us, seemed to be a natural adjunct to the glory of the heavens. The scenery of the river between San Francisco and Benecia, if it wants trees and forests, is yet not devoid of a wild and graceful beauty, and for a background it always has the imposing chain of the Sierra Nevada, with its golden tinted crowns of snow. The river, up to the junction of the Sacramento and San Joaquin, is broad, and often swells out into noble vistas. Up to Benecia it might be called a fresh water estuary of the sea, or a continuation of the noble bay of San Francisco, one of the grandest in the world.

We stopped at Martinez to take in some freight. It was the first time I had been there, and was struck with the quiet beauty of the little place, cooped up like a swiss cottage amongst mountains and forests. Long before the gold fever set in, Martinez was a *pueblo* or hamlet, the lands surrounding it forming a valuable Hacienda, through which roamed large herds of cattle. Lately Martinez has been mentioned as being a desirable locality for the Capital of the State.

On awakening on Sunday morning we found ourselves beside the busy wharf at Stockton, and I had to remain all that day to despatch my goods; and as Ramon Navarro had gone up to Sonora with my bonny mare Kate, that I left here when I embarked for Sacramento, I took a place in the Stage Coach the next morning [April 5], and on account of the heavy roads we were all day getting to the river, besides being upset once.

Here we found that another murder had been perpetrated in broad daylight on the public road the day before, and within hail almost of the populous ferry establishment. Two teamsters were on their way down, an old man and a young. About a mile from the ferry is a stretch of low land bordered on either side by hills. At the entrance near the river is a little roadside inn. Here the old man stopped for a few minutes to light his pipe, and the other went on with his team. Two or three hundred yards off, his companion found him lying in the middle of the road weltering in his blood. He had been shot and rifled within hail of his comrade, and within sight of the house, in the day time. The old man returned at once to the ferry. He says that they were followed by three Mexicans on horse back, whom he minutely described, and he had no doubt that these men committed the crime, as on entering the little valley he lost sight of them, and did not again see them.

This is the most open barefaced murder we have had for some time to chronicle, and is an evidence that there are some bold villains about, and people's lives are again becoming insecure. For some time back there have been stories rife of a certain "Joaquin," a valiant Mexican, who, for many injuries received from the Americans, has vowed a bloody revenge, and has formed a band of brigands who scour the country and assassinate white men whenever they can do so with impunity. This Joaquin is already a celebrated character, and many stories, that would do honor to Dick Turpin, are told of him by the spanish races, and some of them marvelous enough. Whether they be true or false, the fact is that many people have misteriously disappeared, and four murders committed on the Stockton road within a couple of weeks.[7]

---

[7] The bandit whom Perkins calls Joaquin will be immediately identified with Joaquin Murrieta, who ranks with Jesse James and Billy the Kid among famous American outlaws. There appear to have been a number of bandit leaders known as Joaquin during the period after the Foreign Miner's Tax brought

It was too late for the stage to proceed that night, so I borrowed a horse from friend Dent, crossed the ferry and pushed on for home. The sun was setting as I reached the opposite bank. The horse I rode was a large, powerful good brute, but so fat that it was with difficulty I got him into a gallop. I had barely travelled a couple of miles, and it was still light, when just in front of me I saw the very three men so accurately described by the old teamster, and said by him to have been the murderers of his companion. I am not ashamed to say that my heart jumped to my throat. The men were coming towards me and too close to give me time to escape if they intended attacking me; there was no help for it. I drew the pommel of my revolver to the front, grasped it with my right hand and cocked it in its pouch; with my other hand I pulled my horse out of the road and let him fall into a walk. All these actions proved to the men that I was prepared. They also pulled up their horses and we approached each other at a walk, they keeping the road. I put on as fierce and careless a look as possible, looking full at them as they passed me and turning well round in my saddle to keep them in view. They did not salute, as Mexicans almost invariably do on the road, if peaceably inclined.

The minuteness of the description given by the old man left no doubt as to the identity of these men with those who followed the teamsters, and who had assuredly murdered the young man, and I found myself in the presence, if not in the power of these men, the night closing in, and far from any habitation. I acknowledge to having felt very uncomfortable, and as I walked my horse past them, not venturing to increase his speed for fear of giving confidence to the Mexicans, and slowly increased the distance between us, I expected every moment to hear the report of a pistol and the whiz of a ball.

---

antiforeigner agitation to a climax, and folklore cherished by the writers of thrillers (commencing with John Rollin Ridge, "Yellow Bird," and his *Life and Adventures of Joaquin Murieta, the Celebrated California Bandit,* first published in San Francisco in 1854) has lumped them together in a composite biography. A Mexican was killed in 1853, declared to be the outlaw. His decapitated head was exhibited throughout California as that of Joaquin Murrieta, but questions remain. The pamphlet by Ridge was reprinted in 1955 with a critical introduction by Joseph Henry Jackson; and Francis P. Farquhar made a distinct contribution in editing for the Grabhorn Press in 1932 *Joaquin Murieta, The Brigand Chief of California.* Those interested in the subject might read Robert Greenwood, *The California Outlaw, Tiburcio Vasquez* (Los Gatos, 1960), pp. 11–14, and the researches by Frank Latta published at intervals in *The Pony Express,* 1961–1964.

As soon as I had got to a respectable distance, I dug the spurs into my fat horse's side, and got him into a gallop, with a thankful and lightened heart; but during my four hour's ride that night, my imagination was continually suggesting the sudden apparition of the three Mexicans from the bushes on either side of the road.

That these men were brigands there is no doubt. Two days before they were on the opposite side of the river; so that they could not be travelers; there are no Mexican encampments in this vicinity, and on meeting me they did not leave the road, nor did they salute me, something extraordinary, and enough of itself to prove the bad intentions and character of the men. I probably owed my safety to two causes. Mexicans are proverbially cowards (although there are of course exceptions), and do not like the idea of attacking a man evidently prepared for them, even should the odds be greatly in their favor. These fellows had not the slightest doubt that my hand was on a good revolver, and they know by experience the skill of the white man generally, in its use; and like the North American Indian they will seldom attempt a crime where there may be any risk attending it. They are the Thugs of America.

Another cause of my safety was the fact of my being on my way *up*, and consequently not supposed to be in the possession of much cash; not that it requires much inducement for a Mexican to murder; he is always ready for that; but it requires the incentive of plunder to induce him to run any risk. By eleven o'clock I was safely housed in Sonora, and very grateful for what I must always consider a Providencial escape.

CHAPTER XXXVI

APRIL TENTH. Crime is again on the increase. In the last chapter I mentioned the supposed existence of organized bands of brigands. Of this fact there is now no doubt. Whether the much talked-of "Joaquin" be a myth or a bona-fide personage, I can not say, but that murders and robberies on the plains, on the road and in the mountain fastnesses are becoming rife, is an indisputible certainty. There is no doubt at all that the ruffians of the country are systematizing their operations, forming bands, and acting under chiefs who form regular plans. We have already the names of some men who are said to be the heads of these bands. This state of things is a natural consequence of the laxity of the administration of the laws, and the unpardonable carelessness of the government, both of the State and at Washington, not to have foreseen the inevitable tendency to crime in a society constituted like that of California. We should have had small military piquets of cavalry stationed in all the principal places of the state, and a mounted police besides, under the orders of the district Magistrates. We have nothing of the kind, although more than a twelve-month ago, I urged, in the papers, the necessity of the measure, and we had a public meeting in Sonora, in order to petition the government to bestir itself in a matter of such paramount importance.[1] What course is there now to take? No other but the reorganization of the Vigilance Committees.

What a glorious field for organized bands of robbers and assassins is offered in the solitary plains, the mountain defiles, the unprotected roads over which gold laden pedestrians, and equestrians are continually travelling; many alone and unarmed. How many of these solitary travellers have already been quietly and secretly robbed and murdered, and the "Local column" of the Newspapers innocent of any knowledge of their fate! How many have perished in this manner will never be known, and yet what a picture would be presented for civilization to shudder at could we depict the secret hidden crimes that have been perpetrated in California! But the dead tell no tales, and the murderers, when they be Mexicans, are almost as taciturn.

The steamer "Northerner" arrived in San Francisco on the fifteenth [fourteenth], and it is with great satisfaction and pleasure we read among the passengers in the list, the names of Theall and Huntington.[2] So; the latter has again left home, wealth and a respectable position, to return to this wild country. It is strange. What fascinating attraction is there in California apart from its stores of gold? The only answer I can

---

[1] See Introduction and compare pages 168, 173.

[2] The *Alta California* of April 15, 1852, records the arrival early the previous day of the *Northerner* with upwards of six hundred passengers, among whom are listed H. W. Theall and "J. W." Huntington.

give is, that here there is freedom and independence that cannot exist in old societies. Here there is a wild liberty that grows upon a man's affections, in the same manner that the wild and solitary life of the Hunter of the Rocky Mountains soon acquires a charm so powerful that civilization offers no adequate inducement for a change.

SATURDAY, SEVENTEENTH. My birthday. With what joyous impatience, as youngsters, we used to hail this important epoch in a child's life, and count the days and hours in anticipation a month before-hand. Visions of presents, new clothes, and liberty from school, used to precede the auspicious season. How proud we used to be that each birthday brought us one year nearer to the bright, happy time when we were to be emancipated from lessons, and the control of pedagogues, to take our part in the bustle, the pleasures, the honors, and alas! What we could not understand then, the troubles, pains and cares of the great world. But when years are beginning to lay their heavy hand upon the tired heart, we are not apt to take much note of passing anniversaries; or if we do, it is to lament perhaps the passing away of that youth which memory never fails to gild with so much glory.

My birthday however was duly celebrated by the arrival of our two truants. Enyart, [F. E.] Dreyfous, and Judge [Green T.] Martin came up with Theall and John Huntington, and it is useless to say we had a regular "spree." All the old inhabitants flocked in to see Theall, and congratulate him on his safe return. He is a general favorite, and until two o'clock in the morning had to sustain a continual shaking of the hand, and answer pledges in the most expensive champagne the town afforded. No less a favorite is Huntington, but he dates from 1850, while Theall was making his fortune with a *barrel of rum*, when Sonora could not boast of a single tent.[3]

---

[3] In a note Perkins says: "The story is too good to be lost, and if ever this meets the eye of my old friend (a friendship of three years' standing in California is equivalent to one of twenty years in other countries) he must pardon my indiscretion. When the regiment in which Theall held a commission was disbanded in 1848, most of its members found their way to the mines, some to dig, some to gamble, and some to enter into business. It was difficult in those days to get heavy packages up to the mines, but Theall managed to reach Sullivan's Camp, two or three miles from Sonora, which was then only a small encampment, with a barrel of forty gallons of Jamaica Rum. This arrival created a tremendous excitement, for there was no liquor in the camp. Theall opened

I have decided on a trip home, now that Theall has returned. I shall leave California in its most beautiful season; and really it is difficult to imagine any scenery or climate more lovely and benign. I could never tire in the description of the flowers, the mountain scenery, and the moonlight nights of this country, but I might tire the reader, always disposed to believe that the author of a work like this is apt to exaggerate. But I candidly think that not even the famous George Robins[4] could endue these three characteristics of California with greater beauty on paper, than they possess in reality.

Out hunting the other day, I entered a little valley, or rather a hollow between two hills, and was charmed out of my sober senses. The surface of the ground was covered with a little flower exactly alike to our verbena. It grows close to the ground like moss, except where sheltered from the rays of the sun, when it shoots up to the height of several inches. Its color is a bright scarlet, and the people of the country call it *Sangre de Cristo*, blood of Christ. The hollow I have mentioned was carpeted with this brilliant little flower, so thickly that no spaces were vacant to step on. Here and there a Marvel of Peru lifted its golden head above its more humble companion, and gave variety to the picture, which was heightened by clumps of lylac-colored heliotropes. It is out of the question trying to describe this precious little scene; any language that would do it justice, might appear exaggeration.

---

his barrel and began to satisfy the demand at the rate of four rials, or half a dollar a glass. The measure was a broken tumbler, which held sideways, contained as much liquor as would fill a wine glass. The consumption the first day left no doubt that in two more the barrel would be empty. This would be a public calamity which it was a duty to try and avoid; so placing the barrel behind a canvas curtain with the front only visible and preparing some buckets of water, Theall awaited the attack on the following day. It commenced at daylight and continued without intermission all day, but thanks to the simple expedient of replacing with another liquid every glassful extracted, the barrel was in the same state in the evening as in the morning. The result was so satisfactory that notwithstanding the extraordinary consumption, the barrel of rum lasted fully a fortnight, and brought its owner the decent sum of a couple of thousand dollars. It was with this that Theall commenced business."

[4] Apparently Perkins refers to the auctioneer George Henry Robins (1778–1847), whose "ready wit and repartee in the rostrum," says the *Dictionary of National Biography*, "caused him to be one of the most successful and persuasive advocates in seducing his auditors to bid freely whatever appeared at the auction mart. He wrote his own advertisements, and, high-flown and fantastic as they were, in no instance was a purchase repudiated on the ground of misdirection."

SUNDAY, TWENTY FIFTH. In six or seven days more, I shall be probably on the Pacific, on my way home. Last night a party of my friends gave me a farewell supper and it is with pleasure I jot down their names in the event of memory playing me false in after years. There were Theall, Enyart, [John M.] Huntington, [A. A. H.] Tuttle, [Samuel H.] Dwinelle, [Charles F.] Dodge, [John H.] Richardson, [F. E.] Dreyfous, [Benjamin F.] Moore, [Green T.] Martin, [Hugh G.] Platt, [J. K. or H. K.] Swope, [Charles M.] Radcliff, [H. P.] Barber, and [Augustus C.] Imbrey.[5] The supper was really a magnificent affair, and in the centre of the table was a huge sugar-candy Steamer, at the mast-head of which was a miniature flag with the word, FAREWELL!

We were all a little low spirited. The anticipated separation of a member of such an isolated though jolly society as ours was enough to dampen our enjoyment. Here we were, a little party that had witnessed the rise of Sonora from a wilderness to a city. Members of the old Vigilance Committee, we had stood by each other, shoulder to shoulder, and a revolver in every hand, in the performance of a stern and fearful duty. We had participated in dangers of every kind and combatted together against them. Terrible scenes have we all gone through, and different as may be our respective characters, we have learnt to respect and like each other. One of our band was wanting, Edward Marshall, who is in Washington as Member of Congress, for this state.[6]

TUESDAY, TWENTIETH. Last night the weather suddenly changed. It became very cold, and rain, sleet, and hail fell in abundance. Stoves had to be put into immediate requisition. About two o'clock in the afternoon I witnessed one of the most brilliant natural phenomenons I ever remember having seen. The sun was reclining towards the west when a heavy cloud passed over the town, discharging for the space of a couple minutes, a perfect storm of large hail stones. During this time the sun was not obscured for an instant, and the effect of its rays shining obliquely on the chrystalized globules was magical. This was the farewell vouchsafed me by the beautiful heavens of Sonora; and it

---

[5] Most of those mentioned were lawyers and merchants. At the time of the census enumeration, May 18, 1851, Judge A. A. H. Tuttle was living in the same dwelling with Theall, Perkins, and Enyart (as was one E. Audrien, 39, a miner from France).

[6] See chapter xxvi, note 7.

cannot be said that they were not indebted to me, for the many panegyrics I have written and spoken of their loveliness.

On Monday, twenty eighth [twenty-sixth] of April, I started in the coach, with many cordial shakes of the hand, many kindly wishes, and, I believe, many regrets. For nearly three years has Sonora been my home, and I cannot help acknowledging, it has been a pleasant one. Many hardships, many perils and many pains, are indelibly attached to the memories of my residence here, yet I question if any other portion of my life has been so happy. From the commencement of our business up to the present time, we have been successful. As men of business we have enjoyed a respectability and consideration that no other commercial house in the southern mines has attained to such an extent. And we have never been without a select and pleasant little society of our own. In epochs of danger our house has always been the head quarters of the friends of order, and when the foreigners fancied it their duty to rise in defence of their rights—while swearing vengeance against the Americans, and threatening Sonora with destruction, our house and its inmates were to be strictly respected. In fact, in reference to the foreigners, as I have mentioned in a former page, I was known to them by the name of, *"El amigo de los Estrangeros."*

The many scenes, some of them strange, others wild and others dangerous, I have gone through during my residence in Sonora, if they have not endeared the place to me, have at least given it an interest that is akin to love. Here I lay at the point of death for a score of days, on the ground with the fierce sun burning through the shrivelled leaves of an *almada*. Here have I suffered hunger and thirst and fatigues and dangers in expeditions against the Indians. Here have I dodged behind trees and walls to avoid the angry pistol bullets of careless ruffians. Here have I been carried bodily out of my blankets by one of the fearful avalanches of water, so common in the Winter Season. Here have I assisted in the terrible duties assumed by the Vigilance Committees. Here have I seen three men shot or stabbed *by my side.* Here have I more than once stumbled over the dead body of a murdered man within a step of the threshold of my house. Here have I been shot at by lurking Indians and once narrowly escaped an attack from a grizzly bear. Here have I driven a team of mules, worked as a carpenter, mason, golddigger, guiltless for months and months of a clean white shirt; have slept in the field, on the mountains, in the snow, and in the rain, with no other covering but my Mexican *Zarape;* have carried carcasses of deer shot by myself, five or six miles on my shoulders; have seen Death in almost all its forms, until it had lost its horrors; have fought with my enemies, and alongside of my friends, and notwithstanding all this, now that I am about to leave Sonora, I cannot help feeling that my life here has been full of a wild charm, a kind of fascinating savageness, that is more akin to happiness perhaps than the enjoyments of civilized life; for as Armstrong says of happiness:

> "Few attain it, if 'twas e'er attained;
> But they the widest wander from the mark,
> Who through the flowery paths of sauntering joy
> Seek this coy goddess."

When I think over my life in California, so strange, so eventful, so full of perils, with the same heart that I humble in gratitude in the presence of a protecting Providence, I admire and wonder at the beneficent Wisdom that has given to man faculties and feelings which enable him to find contentment and enjoyment in every situation in which circumstances may place him. Custom will not only reconcile us to any mode of life, however opposed to our former associations and habits, but will eventually bring us pleasures and charms unknown to us formerly. Man carries about him his own world, his own little farm of contentment and enjoyment if he will but cultivate it.

On Monday evening the stage landed us safely at Stockton, nothing worth mentioning having occurred on the road, except that on one occasion the two leaders and one of the flankers broke loose from their tackling, and obliged us to walk half a stage. I remained in Stockton that night, and, accompanied by Ramon Navarro, paid some farewell visits, the last of which was to the family of the Ainsas, very respectible people from the Department of Sonora in Mexico, and the only decent Mexican family I have met in California. The girls stiched my new *Zarape* which had just arrived from Mazatlán.[7]

_____

[7] "The *zarape* is made by hand, of worsted and cotton, and those used by the lower orders are generally of a collection of brilliant colors. It forms the universal outer garment for all but the respectable classes of Mexicans. In shape it is nothing but an oblong square, about seven feet long by about four feet in breadth, and it is woven with such skill that the looms of England cannot imitate them, and they may be said to be almost water-proof. In the centre there is a slit to slip the head through, and on horseback in rainy weather, the long

On tuesday morning [April 27] I got on board the "Henry Clay" and on the following morning at ten, was alongside the "Long Wharf" in San Francisco, having been delayed as the Captain said, by a breakage in the machinery, but, as most of the passengers shrewdly suspected, in order to get the money for an extra breakfast. Every thing counts in California!

On my arrival I learn the disagreeable tidings that the "California" Steamer has broken down near San Diego, and that the "Tennessee" has not left Panamá; I shall consequently be detained some days here. Taking this fact into consideration, I may as well employ a few hours and fill a few pages with some last remarks about this extraordinary country and the wonderful City of San Francisco. Possibly I may never return.

---

ends are allowed to fall on either side, covering the legs and feet, while the breadth reaches before and behind to the saddle, thus completely covering the entire person. There is an interesting custom prevalent in Mexico in reference to the *zarape*. Young girls often work for years on one to be presented to their husbands as a wedding present; and this *zarape* is often worn for a lifetime by the husband, as it is counted dishonorable to part with it. The great mart for *zarapes* is Saltillo, where I bought a handsome one for fifty dollars. The finest ones however are made in Chihuahua, and are sometimes sold for two hundred dollars. Rich people in Chihuahua often carpet their parlors with these expensive articles" (Perkins).

CHAPTER XXXVII

It is now nearly three years since I landed here, and had to wade through a hundred yards of slime and mud to get ashore. Certainly the most sanguine down-Easter could have seen nothing prepossessing about the place. San Francisco then looked like an old broken-down caravansary, in which travellers were in vain looking for a corner to sleep in, or a supper to eat. There seemed to be no stability in the place. Great as was the rush to get into San Francisco, greater still was the rush to get out of it. A hundred dollars readily paid for a seat in a boat up to Stockton and Sacramento. And such water-craft! Old whaleboats, worm-eaten jolly boats, rotten launches, punts, any thing that looked as if it had been made to swim, all were put into requisition to convey the eager thousands towards the mines; and scarcely a day passed without some vessel entering the harbor, its decks packed with human beings, all eager to land and follow in the wake of the mighty living stream that flowed towards the *Sierra Nevada.*

In the returns made to the United States by its diplomatic agents in the Pacific in 1831, San Francisco contained three hundred and seventy one individuals; and there were certainly very few more in 1848 when gold was discovered at Sutter's sawmills on the Sacramento.[1] When I arrived here in June 1849, there could not have been more than a hundred houses, almost all of the most miserable description, mud hovels in fact. There was but one good house, and this was known for a long time as the "old adobe," and was used as the Post Office, even after the town had made considerable progress.[2]

From a little work called "Notes of Travellers" in a chapter on San Francisco, I quote the following, written evidently by a person who had seen what he describes, although ostensibly he draws his picture from two scetches of the City.[3]

"There now lie before us two prints; one of San Francisco taken in November 1848, soon after the discovery (of gold) was made, and another exactly a year afterwards. In the first we are able to count twenty six huts and other dwellings dotted about at uneven distances, and four small ships in the harbor. In the second the habitations are countless. The hollow upon which the City partly stands presents a birds-eye view of roofs, packed so closely together, that the houses they cover are innumerable; while the sides of the surrounding hills are thickly strewed with tents and temporary dwellings.

"On every side are buildings of all kinds, begun or half finished, but the greater part of them mere sheds, made of canvas, open in front,

---

[1] Sutter's mill was at Coloma, on the South Fork of the American River, a tributary of the Sacramento.

[2] The post office, as noted in Frank Soule, *Annals of San Francisco* (New York, 1854), pp. 259–260, was a small building at the corner of Pike and Clay streets. There were other well-constructed buildings (even a brick house) in San Francisco by 1849.

[3] We have not been able to identify the "little work" from which Perkins quotes the next two paragraphs.

and displaying all sorts of signs in all languages. Great quantities of goods are piled up in the open air, for want of a place to store them. The streets are full of people hurrying to and fro, and of as diverse and bizarre a character as the houses: Yankees of every possible variety, Native Californians, in *zarapes* and huge *sombreros,* Chilians, Sonorians, Kanakas from Hawaii, Chinese with long tails, Malays and others in whose embrowned and bearded visages it is impossible to recognize any especial nationality. In the midst of the *Plaza,* now dignified by the name of Portsmouth Square, is a lofty liberty pole. The *plaza* lies on the slope of the hill, and from a flagstaff in front of a one-storey adobe building, used as the Custom house, the American flag is flying.[4] On the lower side is the Parker House Hotel. The bay is black with the hulls of ships, and a thick forest of masts intercepts the landscapes of the opposite coast and the islet of Yerba Buena."

Were it possible to write a veridical history of California, it would be of astounding interest. Its sudden rise into preëminence; the extraordinary varieties of the human race we meet here, ranging from the Polynesian Savage to the most refined of individuals that Europe can produce; the reckless expenditure of wealth, and its sudden unbounded accumulation; the unheard-of vices ingendered by the love of gambling; the gambling mania itself; the unbounded confidence and the astounding roguery in business; the majical building up of cities; the recklessness of life; the thousands of miserable assassinations; the extraordinary facility with which "social order was shaped out of the human chaos"; the political anomalies, the country being at one time without any government; the organization of those terrible societies, the Vigilance Committees, and their wonderful effect and strange good conduct, not a single instance being on record of their having punished an innocent person; the herculean labors of the miners, mountains being bored, rivers turned out of their beds and channels, the Mother Earth perforated with gigantic chasms, and finally, agricultural labors turning the burnt up plains to smiling corn fields. A true history of all these things would be indeed interesting.

Now, the whole country is quiet; a good government organized and

---

[4] "It was from a rafter of this house," Perkins notes, "that the Vigilance Committee launched their first victim into eternity. The execution took place at night and more than five hundred men pulled at the rope."

the laws respected and well administered; order established out of chaos, and wild California turned into a peaceful, flourishing state. These Americans are a wonderful people, and deserve that we should apply to them the lines of Addison:

> "To civilize the rude unpolished world,
> And lay it under the restraint of laws,
> To make man mild and sociable to man,
> To cultivate the wild licentious savage
> With wisdom, discipline and liberal arts
> Th'embelishment of life! Virtues like these
> Make human nature shine."

But still we are tempted to exclaim with Macbeth:

> "Can such things be
> And overcome us like a summer's cloud
> Without our special wonder?"

The force of the golden mania of California has done what no other power had before accomplished—it has broken the chain of national prejudice of the Chinese, and they for the first time in their history have emigrated by thousands from their "flowery land" to the "El Dorado."

In San Francisco there is a quarter of the town entirely occupied by these singular people, who industriously pursue the professions of clothes washing, restaurant keeping and swindling.[5] Here a man may ask for and receive a fricasse of dog, cat, or rat, cooked in the best culinary style of Canton or Hong Kong.

Some few of the Chinese have sacrificed their pig tails and have adopted European customs; but the greater part stick with great pertinacity to all their national habits and dress. The pigtail is the glory of a John Chinaman, and he must have made up his mind never to return to his country who sacrifices it. In San Francisco there are not more than three or four tailless Celestials, and their countrymen undoubtedly look upon them with the same feeling of contempt which

---

[5] "Speaking of washing," Perkins observes in a note, "the fact is hardly credible but still no less a fact, that for many months after the building up of San Francisco, a large portion of the foul linen of the inhabitants was regularly sent to China by the clipper ships to be washed!"

was meted to the fox in the fable by his companions. A little while ago
a drunken American sailor quarrelled with a chinaman in the street,
and taking out his case knife cut off a yard of his carefully braided
pig-tail. The poor fellow was in despair. He had his barbarous assailant
taken before a Justice of the Peace, who very correctly fined him an
"Adobe." [6]

Bayard Taylor in his correspondence to the New York Tribune,
gives a good notion of the rapidity with which the City of San
Francisco sprung up, in the following terms:

"Of all the marvellous phases of the history of the Present, the
growth of San Francisco is the one which will most tax the belief of the
Future. Its parallel was never known, and shall never be beheld again.
I speak of only what I saw with my own eyes. When I landed there, a
little more than four months before, I found a scattering town of tents
and canvas houses, with a show of frame buildings on one or two
streets, and a population of about six thousand. Now on my last visit, I
saw around me an actual metropolis, displaying street after street of
well built edifices, filled with an active and enterprising people, and
exhibiting every mark of permanent commercial prosperity. Then, the
town was limited to the curve of the Bay fronting the anchorage and
bottoms of the hills, took hold of the Golden Gate, and was building its
warehouses on the open strait and almost fronting the blue horizon of
the Pacific. Then, the gold-seeking sojourner lodged in muslin (brown
cotton) rooms and canvas garrets, with a philosophic lack of furniture,
and ate his simple though substantial fare from pine boards. Now, lofty
Hotels, gaudy with verandahs and balconies, are met with in all
quarters, furnished with home luxury, and aristocratic restaurants
present their long bills of fare, rich with the choicest technicalities of
the Parisian *cuisine*. Then, vessels were coming in day after day to lie
deserted and useless at their anchorage. Now, scarcely a day passes but
some cluster of sails bound *outward* through the Golden Gate, take
their departure to all the corners of the Pacific. Like the magic seed of
the Indian Juggler, which grew, blossomed and bore fruit before the

---

[6] " 'Adobe,' " Perkins explains, "is the common and queer name given to a
California coin weighing about three ounces. It is octagon in shape and bears an
impression on one side only, and made from Californian gold without any
process of refinement. Its current value is fifty dollars." For a similar comment,
see chapter xix, note 1.

eyes of the spectators, San Francisco seems to have accomplished in a day the growth of half a century." [7]

The above extract from a very clever writer, and which my own experience enables me to corroborate, gives a good idea of the change, so fairy-like, that in the space of a few months made the City of San Francisco out of the shabby insignificant "Yerba Buena."

As I have already mentioned, the receding tide in old times used to leave two or three hundred yards of the beach a mass of slime, over which it was difficult to pass. The land on which the old town was built was full of inequalities, sand hills of some magnitude lining the coast. On my second visit to San Francisco, I found "steam paddies" at work; the sand hills had almost all disappeared, and with their contents, some twenty five acres reclaimed from the sea. Now the principal part of the town is built over what used to be the bay, and the outer line of houses is washed by several feet of tide water. The "Long Wharf" is in fact a street running out more than a thousand yards from the original shore; and built up on either side to its extremity, leaving slips for landing. [8]

On entering the Golden Gate, a handsome beach is perceived on the right. By water this landing is some four or five miles from the town, which is only seen on leaving the strait, and turning to the right on entering the bay. The landing I allude to is called North Beach, and was separated from San Francisco by almost impassable sand hills. These have all been removed, a gigantic labor, and now the North Beach forms part of the City, which on one side faces the straits and the Golden Gate, and on the other the bay and coast range of mountains.

Portsmouth Square which originally was almost on the sea shore, and is now five squares from the Bay is surrounded by superb edifices, one of which is the new marble Theatre, which occupies, if I mistake not, the site on which stood the first frame house erected in San Francisco, the Parker House, which was just being opened when I arrived in 1849.

The facilities offered to passengers and travellers may be briefly

---

[7] Perkins here quotes from Taylor's book (fashioned from his dispatches to the *Tribune*), *El Dorado, or Adventures in the Path of Empire* (New York, 1850), vol. II, pp. 55–56. Taylor first reached San Francisco August 18, 1849, several months after Perkins.

[8] The "Long Wharf" extended out into the Bay approximately from Montgomery Street; it became the extension of Clay Street as the Bay fill progressed.

summed up thus: seven steamers, most of them large, in the Sacramento line. Three to Stockton, and a number of small steam craft in the Bay. A steamer for the coast as far as Santa Barbara; another for the Columbia River; three large ocean steamers for the Nicaragua route and six, I believe, in the Panamá route. Stages and omnibuses leave every day for San José and Monterey. Besides the steamers there are several magnificent clipper ships that ply regularly between San Francisco and China, the Sandwich Islands, Australia, New York and Europe. In the interior there are stage coaches wherever they can run.

CHAPTER XXXVIII

Of all the vices with which California has been and still is cursed, gambling has been the most fatal. The legislature has been powerless to put a stop to it, and has consequently turned it to account by licensing it, and the ingress to the treasury through this means is quite respectable.

The immense, richly furnished and dazzling gambling saloons form the great attraction, the lions of San Francisco. From a score of such palaces of iniquity, nightly issue strains of the most ravishing music, and the street is inundated with the light of hundreds of lamps.

Let us pay a visit to the "Polka" Saloon, one of the largest and generally most crowded of the City. It is situated in Clay Street, a few steps from the Plaza. To the right on entering one of the numerous doors, is a bar of liquors, with marble counter; gold and silver and rich crystal of every form combining to make it attractive, and as if something more was necessary to induce people to drink, two beautiful girls, elegantly dressed, are behind the counter to serve out the liquor. They are French of course. How can a man resist their smiles? We can't; so we stop and after a compliment or two, ask for a glass of native wine, and with a bow which is answered by a fascinating smile (it could not have been more so, had it been an "adobe" instead of a two real piece I put on the counter) we move on.

The huge saloon is crowded with a motley congregation; well

dressed gentlemen, belonging to the City; sailors; miners in red and blue flannel shirts and long boots, ignorant of the existence of blacking; Mexicans in their long brilliantly colored *zarapes;* Chilenos in dark, and Peruvians in light colored *ponchos;* Californians in scolloped and silk worked leather jackets and wide brimmed *sombreros;* some like ourselves strolling about indulging merely their curiosity; but there are very few who do not stop now and then to put down a stake at one of the innumerable tables which crowd the saloon.

Here is a Monte table: let us approach; it is crowded with eager betters. In the centre is about a bushel of silver dollars, forming a bulwark around a peck of gold "Adobes," Eagles and half Eagles. Look at the Yankee dealer, and owner perhaps, of the pile of riches in front of him. See him as he slowly and deliberately draws card after card from the pack. He is the personification of Calm Villainy. You can no more detect a transient feeling in that man's face than you might from one chiselled out of marble. He may loose or win ten thousand dollars, staked at this moment on his table, but he will be the same, impassible, cold and silent. The practice of his trade has petrified his human nature. Look at these young men, these boys, staking fifty, a hundred dollars upon a card! Some of these will go home tonight, ruined, and from industrious sober men will, at one plunge, change to professional blacklegs and ruffians. There is a merchant, a rich merchant of the City, betting a thousand dollars. He is an old hand and remains calm under his losses; not so with that young sinner who has apparently lost his last coin; he is drinking madly of the liquor that is furnished at the table gratis, and savage imprecations are grinding through his hard set teeth. No one bestows a thought on him as he scowlingly watches the game, until impatient at not being able to join in it, he rushes out of the house perhaps to beg, borrow or steal another stake.

Cowper must have had a prophetic idea of California when he wrote the following lines:

> "The wings that waft our riches out of sight
> Grow on the gamester's elbows; and the alert
> And nimble motion of those restless joints
> That never tire, soon fans them all away"

The spacious saloon is thickly sprinked with *Monte,* Roulette and Lansquenet tables, round each of which is a crowd of votaries. The

Lansquenet tables are presided over by handsome, brilliantly dressed women, and their sparkling eyes are continually on the look-out to intice the young men to join the game. See, there is one pretty woman beckoning us to her side. I knew her in Sonora. What a bewitching smile she vouchsafes us as we shake hands with her! She does not ask us to play, and for a few minutes seems to forget her game. We will not detain her impatient customers.

"Je suis si content de vous avoir vu!"

"Good bye"

Don't look back; be satisfied with the beaming smile of adieu which gave an angel's expression to her handsome countenance. One minute later perhaps, and you may trace the passions of Hell in that face!

I have so often spoken of these fascinating votaresses of the Devil, that it would be repeating a thrice told tale, describing the dozens of beauties in the Saloons of the "Polka." Many of the gamblers have one by their side to serve the glasses of liquor to the players, and to chat and flirt with them, while the dealer fleeces their pockets.

At the further end of the Saloon are several well lighted rooms partitioned off from the body of the hall. You might imagine them to be refreshment rooms. Not so. It is here the Genius of the establishment resides. Here the *serious* business of gambling is carried on. Here nought is heard save the *clacking* of ivory counters. Here you have the princes of the profession assembled. These chambers receive the adventurous class who profess to "fight the Tiger." Here are the Pharo banks, and men will walk out of these dens fifty, a hundred, two hundred thousand dollars richer or poorer than they entered. Not a night passes that fortunes are not squandered in these places. This is the game that the master gamblers play amongst themselves; and many a blackleg has brought down a fortune from the mines, the proceeds of his iniquitous industry in the diggings, and lost it in a single night at a Pharo bank. The princes of the gambling profession seldom go out of San Francisco; they leave the inner towns to be gleaned by less ambitious rogues, and are content to fleece these same rogues on their arrival at the metropolis. Sometimes one of the "big-wigs" will also find himself ruined some fine night. In this case he quietly packs up his trunks, and makes the provincial tour himself.

It seems an extraordinary fact, and looks like a wise dispensation, that no gambler can hoard money. He can't give up playing and retire from business. An irrisistable impulse still pushes him on, and whatever may be his winnings, he invariably looses every thing at one time or other. Out of the thousands and thousands of blacklegs who have "exercised their profession" in California, there are not probably a hundred who have not been at one or various times, in the possession of a fortune. Some in San Francisco have been worth as much as half a million of dollars. But there is apparently a curse to their winnings. Like the gold of the Magician in the Arabian Nights Entertainments, after a few hours it turns to dried leaves and rubbish. Were it otherwise the United States would soon have been flooded with millionaire gamblers.

When I speak of gamblers in California, the word only applies to those who have adopted gaming as a profession; and it is a profession that lawyers, doctors and divines have embraced. The former and the latter are quite numerous in the brotherhood. Methodist parsons and temperance men seem to take very kindly to Monte, and one of the strangest phases of gambling in California is the great number of once respectable and educated men who are found professedly owning and conducting a gaming table. I have known dozens of young men, whose fathers stand among the proudest in the land in the United States, dealing Monte to a lot of dirty drunken Mexicans: one of them, I am sorry to say, being the son of a Canadian gentleman. It appears that as soon as a man looses all he possesses at a gambling table, a reckless impulse impels him to turn gambler himself, as the surest way to retrieve his fortunes; and once in the vortex, he is lost. He becomes vicious and quarrelsome; is continually in rows, and, after shooting, maiming or killing some half dozen, ends by being shot himself, or being strung up to the nearest tree by "Judge Lynch."

Such has been the fate of hundreds of this class. In Sonora at least fifty individuals have been killed in quarrels, by blacklegs, and a great many more wounded and maimed; and of the gamblers, three or four have been hanged and at least a score shot.

In San Francisco the rage for gambling is something fearful. Merchants, Lawyers, Politicians, Judges, Governors, all gamble to a frightful extent. How many failures of rich mercantile houses are due to the Pharo table, and the ill-luck of business to be accounted for by the ill-luck at a gaming table!

CHAPTER XXXIX

Very shortly, as the country becomes more densely populated, the game will disappear as it has done in the Eastern and many of the Western States; as the Americans appear to have an antipathy to restrictive laws in reference to seasons of killing game. The stately Elk and graceful deer will soon belong to the past, particularly as there are no forests out of the mountains for them to find shelter in. It is true that the "Tulare plains" will for some time offer a secure pasturage ground to the Elk; but these plains, subject to periodical inundations at present, and covered with a gigantic growth of rushes and other aquatic vegetation, are too valuable to be left for many years more in a state of nature. It will not be long before we shall see luxuriant fields of rice waving on these wild plains. Now they are the asylum of thousands, ay, hundreds of thousands of the magnificent Elk. This animal, the largest of the deer tribe known to exist at the present time, is of the height of an ox, and with a body about equal to that of a two year old colt, but considerably longer, and will weigh from four to five hundred pounds. The flesh is fully equal to the best beef in flavor, and is sold in large quantities in the markets of San Francisco. I never had the satisfaction of shooting one, although I have often seen their stately heads and antlers towering above the tall rushes of the "Tulare plains," that cover millions of acres between the San Joaquin river and the coast range of mountains.

The most dangerous animal in California, and perhaps in North America, is the Grizzly bear. I have mentioned him so often in this work that it is unnecessary to say any thing more about the gentleman. A description of panther or cougar exists in the lower part of the state, but I have not been able to learn much of his habits. He is not feared by the natives.

There are many species of deer, and although they are fast disappearing from the plains, are in immense numbers in the mountains. Up to fifty one, I have shot them within three miles of Sonora, but now one has to travel well up into the *Sierra* to get a shot. All attempts of the deer to get down into the plains are frustrated by the thousands of miners occupying all the passages; by the hunter's rifle, and by the continual noise of the blasting of rocks.

I have been told that a true species of wolf exists in the lower country, and, although perhaps rare, I do not doubt the fact. I think I have already mentioned having seen a large wolf in the Department of Durango, in Mexico, where the animal is very seldom seen. In the upper part of the state of California wolves are not known, at least in the part settled already. It is probable however that they will be found farther north. The prairee wolf or *cayoté* is very numerous. It is of dark color, and of the size of a large fox, which animal it resembles in many respects. Like the wolf it is often found in packs, differing in this respect from the fox. The *cayoté* is the noisiest devil one can imagine. His throat is a kind of orchestra of broken winded instruments. Out camping I have been scared out of a sound sleep by the impression of an attack of a score of Indians, when it would turn out to have been two or three of these noisy brutes. On one occasion, a pack of four or five cayotes ran over me as I lay rolled up in my blankets under a tree, and almost frightened me into fits, as a down-Easter would say. The row they made was equal to the yelling of fifty indians. I have often been amused witnessing the chase of a jack hare by cayotes. The hare is much the swifter animal, but the prairee wolf soon tires him out.

We have both the rabbit and hare in abundance. The latter is vulgarly called the Jackass Hare, on account of its great size.

The most beautiful animal in California is the Antelope, but it is so swift and so timid that it is very difficult to get within gun-shot of it. I have seen large herds browsing on the slopes of the coast range. Farther south they have the common american brown bear, the badger, and the mountain sheep, a species of antelope, with coarse short woolly hair, the *vicuña* of the northern hemisphere.[1] Of smaller animales, there are the marten, the chinchilla, and the prariee dog, foxes, and ferrets.

---

[1] The mountain sheep or bighorn, which in several species ranges from northern Mexico to Alaska, is unrelated to the antelope; its closest relative is the larger-horned argali of Asia. The vicuña to which Perkins alludes is a wild ruminant of the Andes, related to the domesticated llama and alpaca, and belonging to yet another species.

Birds in the interior are not numerous, particularly singing birds. Ducks and geese are seldom seen in the valley between the coast range and the *Sierras*. I was a twelve-month in Sonora without having seen one of the former, and I remember one day, when out deer shooting, I came upon a beautiful little pond of chrystaline water, in the centre of which was a magnificent drake, with all the brilliant metalic colors of the domestic fowl. The scene was so homelike, that I actually thought I was near some country house, and that the drake belonged to a civilized community; and it was only when the beggar rose up and flew away, that I discovered what a fool my imagination had made me; for notwithstanding I had nothing but a Mississippi rifle, still it would not have required great skill to put a ball into a duck at thirty paces. Woodcock there are none; at least I have no information of their existence here; but in recompense we have the Californian quail, a species of american grouse. O the dainty bird!

"Through the pathway of the sky
Quail with sharpen'd beak doth fly;
Christos praising with sharp beak.
What, O dun quail, doth thou seek?"

They are certainly the handsomest of the species. In shape and color they do not differ from their cousins on the other side of the Rocky Mountains; but they possess a head dress which distinguishes them from all others. This is a handsome jet-black plume of feathers, about an inch and a half long, projecting from their crest, and drooping down in front. They give equal pleasure to the hunter, and the gastronomer, and the tables of the restaurants in the mines have always been plenteously furnished with this delicate bird, of which there are large numbers. On the plains they are scarce; they prefer the brushwood of the first steppes [foothills] of the *Sierra*.

The woodpecker of California and its wonderful labors I have already mentioned. Humming birds, during the season of flowers, are very numerous, and of various plumage. Below San Francisco on the coast birds are less rare. There are to be found magpies, jays, crossbills, robins, swallows and many others, all familiar acquaintances.

On the coast is also to be found the great vulture [condor] (*sarcoramphus Californianus*) and other species; the golden, white headed, and bald headed eagle. The bays, inlets, and mouths of the rivers abound with waterfowl. Ducks, geese, swans, pelicans, gulls, flamingos, widgeon, teal, cranes, snipe and curlew.

There is no great variety of fish in the rivers in the interior. The noblest of the river denizens, the salmon, seems to have monopolized the upper waters; these fish are in great abundance, and very fine. In the bays, however, and the embouchures of the great streams, fish are in great variety and in incredible numbers, from the dogfish to white bait. Mackerel, halibut and turbot are common, as are also the pilchard, bonito, and sardine.

Of shell-fish, clams, mussels, shrimps, sea-urchins, limpets are plentiful, but there are few or no oysters. Some speculators have planted beds of this bivalve, but it appears that there exists some unknown enemy, that destroys them. It is probable however that somewhere on the coast oyster beds will be discovered.[2] The pearl oyster is plentiful in the Gulf of California.

The order Phocidae is well represented among the rocky inlets of the coast. Armies of seals are to be seen sporting in the water or clambering up the steep rocks. How they manage to climb up with their clumsy flappers has always puzzled and will continue to puzzle me. I have watched one for half an hour making its way laboriously up the side of a steep slippery rock, where a man with difficulty would be able to find a footing. It appears to me that the tail of the animal has the faculty of clinging to the face of a hard substance, probably for forming a vacuum with the soft portion of its nether extremities, and thus being enabled to support the weight of its body, while with its flappers it catches hold of the inequalities of the rock. At all events, it climbs up somehow, and to great heights, for thousands are to be seen on the coast basking in the sun on the top, and ledges of rocks fifty feet above the level of the sea. Outside the Golden Gate one can at any time get a glimpse of the formidable looking sea lion and the enormous walrus, which, next to the whale, is probably the largest animal known. I have seen them at least fifteen feet long and eighteen or twenty feet in circumference over the thickest part of the body. This animal with its tremendous tusks, and the sea lion with its savage look-

---

[2] So plentiful are Pacific oysters today that it comes as a surprise to learn of their scarcity during the Gold Rush period. The *Alta California* of May 17, 1850, expresses gratification for a gift of oysters brought down from Puget Sound, clearly the small and tasty Olympia variety.

ing mane, inspire terror to look at them; but the ferociousness of their appearance presents such a strange contrast to their exceeding timidity, that one is inclined to believe that dame Nature created these animals in one of her laughing moments. The features of the Walrus are small, the eyes have a tender expression, and were it not for those terrible tusks, the most pacific sheep could not have a more benign face.

There are few noxious animales. There are some kinds of snakes, though not numerous, of which the rattlesnake is the only venemous one. Centipedes and tarantulas there are, but rare, and not of the venemous nature of their congeners in Mexico. Scorpions, ticks, bugs, I have never seen here, although those pests of poor human nature, fleas, are unfortunately plentiful enough.

I must not forget the otter, which is found in the rivers, and sea coast in great numbers. The fur of the sea otter is of very valuable quality, superior to any thing I have seen on the Atlantic side of the continent.

CHAPTER XL

As gold was the great inducement which brought me as well as many thousands more to this far off region, let me devote one or two of the last pages of my Journal to the shining and coveted metal.

There are many theories as to the formation and existence of gold; but it is generally admitted now into the company of elements, a simple substance of which other things are formed and not being itself compounded out of others; and that it exists in this simple form in the primary formations.

Granite, the foundation of the crust of our earth, is composed of four substances: felspar, hornblend, mica and quartz. The existence of felspar, which is of an earthy nature, in granite, is the reason that the latter decomposes under the influence of air and water. Of the four substances, quartz is the most compact and heaviest, and consequently resists with greater force the action of the elements. Thus it is that quartz refuses to give up the gold which lies embedded in it, while the particles interspersed amongst the felspar, the horn blend and mica, soon separate themselves and are washed away by the first flood in the form of grains and flakes.

There appears to be no reason to doubt then, that gold is one of the primary elements existing in the molten masses of granite from the earlier periods of the globe; that it is in approximation with the different substances of which granite is composed, with perhaps more affinity and attraction for quartz than for the other parts. The question that naturally suggests itself is: Why then do we not find gold in granite in all parts of the world? Science answers us that no one of the metals is so widely diffused over the earth's surface.

Sir Roderick Murchison says that granites, greenstone, porphyry, serpentine, and I forget what others, are raised from "away down below," and form mountain ranges. When the oldest aqueous deposits happen to be superficial so as to be broken through by the internal forces, and the igneous rocks protrude, and particularly in the ranges running from north to south, there exists gold. And I will transcribe an account of where gold has actually been found, taken from a publicacion of last year. Until reading it I was not aware of the generality of this metal. But, however extensively diffused, it is only in some few favored spots where its extraction is largely profitable.

"In very ancient times the Scythian nations supplied gold from the Ural Mountains. Most of those sources were worked out or forgotten. Russia for centuries possessed the Ural, and forgot its gold. Many of us were boys when that was rediscovered. It is only within the last very few years that Russia discovered gold in another portion of her soil among the spurs of the Altai Mountains. The whole area of Country in Russia which fulfils the conditions of a gold-bearing district is immense. Eastward of the Ural chain, it includes a large part of Siberia; and also in Russian America there is nearly equal reason to believe that hereafter gold may be found.

"Before we quit Asia, we may observe, that the Chinese produce gold out of their soil; and although many of the mountain ranges in that country tend from east to west, yet the conditions of the surface and the meridional directions of the mountains too, would indicate in China some extensive district over which gold would probably be found in tolerable abundance. Gold exists also in Lydia and Hindostan.

"Now to pass over to America. In many places along the line of the Rocky Mountains, especially in that part of them included in the British Territory, gold may be looked for. The gold region of California, has been recently discovered. Gold in Mexico, where the conditions are again fulfilled, is not a new discovery. Gold in Central America lies neglected on account of the sad political condition of the little states there. There is gold to be found, perhaps, in the United States, some distance east of the Rocky Mountains. Certainly gold districts will be found about the Alleghanies. Gold has been found in Georgia, North and South Carolina and Virginia. It also exists in Canada, and may be found not very far north, on the British side of the St. Lawrence. In the frozen regions which shut in those straits and bays of the North Pole, to which early adventurers were sent from England on the search for gold, gold districts most probably exist. New Granada, Peru, Brazil, La Plata, Chile, and even Patagonia, contain districts which say 'look for gold.' There are one or two districts in Africa where gold exists; certainly in more districts than that which is called the Gold Coast, between the Niger and Cape Verde; also between Darfur and Abyssinia; and on the Mozambique coast opposite Madagasca. In Australia the full extent of our gold treasure is not yet discovered. In Europe, out of Russia, Hungary supplies every year one or two hundred thousand pounds worth; there is gold in Transylvania and Bohemia; the Rhine washes gold down with its sands from the crystalline rocks of the high Alps. The Danube, Rhone and Tagus, yield gold also in small quantities. There are neglected mines of gold in Spain." [1]

The article also makes mention of mines which have been worked in England, Scotland, Ireland and Wales. By this account it appears that there is not a country in the world in which gold has not been, or may not be found. But taking the history of mining from the beginning, it is pretty clear that, putting on one side California and

---

[1] "At the foot of the giant of the Andes, South America, the majestic Illimani, a large mass of gold was found by an Indian, in the seventeenth century. It weighed upwards of one hundred pounds with the quartz, and was purchased by the Viceroy for seven hundred ounces and remitted to the Cabinet of Natural History in Madrid. It was supposed to have been detached by lightning from the mountain" (Perkins).

Australia,[2] gold mining has never been so profitable as mines of tin, silver, iron, copper etc. And, taking even the teeming gold fields of California and Australia, a large proportion of gold seekers have not been able to do more than earn decent wages, although it must be said that the aggregate amount of the precious metal extracted has been wonderful.

The gold mines here have done in three years what all the other metals even were they congregated in this one spot, would have taken twenty years to accomplish; viz, turned a savage and sterile wilderness into a state studded with towns and teeming with a civilized population.

New discoveries are being daily made in this country to the North and to the South. The gold fields seem to be richer towards the North, and it is by no means improbable that British Columbia may be found to be incalculably rich in gold,[3] and tending farther towards the Arctic pole, verify what is said about in reference to Russian America. As yet little of the body of the *Sierras* has been explored; the outskirts only have been worked, and the Rocky Mountains are as yet untouched. Undoubtedly the *waste* gold has as yet only been carried off, and we shall find that this coast will produce gold in immense quantities for a vast number of years to come.

---

[2] Gold was discovered in Australia in February, 1851, by a California miner, E. Hargraves. The great Ballarat field was uncovered the ensuing summer, and by the time Perkins remarks, some two thousand gold hunters were pouring into Melbourne every week.

[3] By the time Perkins wrote his book, he must have known of the Fraser River discoveries of 1858 and the subsequent finds which made British Columbia viable as a crown colony, but he kept his narrative within its 1852 frame of reference.

CHAPTER XLI

On the thirtieth [twenty-eighth] of April, the "Winfield Scott," a large new Steamer arrived direct from New York, having made the passage in sixty four days by the way of Cape Horn. The Agents immediately set to work to prepare her for the Panamá line, and to take advantage of the large number of passengers waiting the steamers of the regular line. I secured a berth at once.[1]

On the fourth of May, Theall, having heard of my detention, arrived to see me off. John Huntington and Harry Ford also came down, and my last hours in California were cheered by the presence of many old friends.

The night of the fourth was quite an excitable one. On this night in 1850, and also in 1851, the City was destroyed by disastrous fires, and there seemed to be an impression that if San Francisco escaped this anniversary, it was safe for another year. The Firemen, with their Engines and hose carruages and ladders ready for action at a moments notice, were all on watch during the night. With the public feeling so strong and absorbed, it is not strange that an alarm, which was actually given, (it was caused by a stove pipe burning out) at about two o'clock in the morning, should have had the effect of filling the streets instantaneosly with a frightened population. The fact is, however, San Francisco can hardly ever be subjected again to the ruinous conflagrations that have so repeatedly laid the city in ashes.[2] The squares are now built up with stone and brick edifices, many of them thoroughly fireproof. A fire cannot now so easily gain an entrance into the centres of the squares as was formerly the case, when the flames, confined as it were in an oven, acquired such an intensity of heat, that I have witnessed a large iron warehouse, supposed to be fireproof, shrivel up and disappear as if it were made of lath slats. In former days there was no Fire Department either. The flames had their own way without any check whatever. Now San Francisco boasts a Fire department so complete in its organization, that probably there does not exist its equal in the world, in any City of four times the size of this.

I have by no means the elated feelings that I might be supposed to possess, on leaving California for a trip home; and I have no doubt that I shall be anxious to return in a few months. This feeling however may

---

[1] Perkins was not quite exact in saying that the *Winfield Scott* reached San Francisco direct from New York; the *Alta California* of April 29, 1852, records her arrival on the 28th, 14 days from Panama and 8 from Acapulco.

[2] H. H. Bancroft appropriately commented that its series of disastrous conflagrations "stamped San Francisco as one of the most combustible of cities, the houses being as inflammable as the temper of the inhabitants." Historic fires of great magnitude occurred on December 24, 1849; May 4, 1850; June 14, 1850; September 17, 1850; May 3–4, 1851; and June 22, 1851. After that, fires were kept in check to a large extent until the holocaust of 1906.

be temporary. One always feels somewhat loath to leave a place which custom and habit have reconciled us to. We forget the troubles, the cares and the dangers endured in it, and only feel that we are leaving well known scenes, and parting from associates and friends; and at first, the anticipation of meeting with older associates and dearer friends is not distinct enough to efface the feelings of the present moment.

As an instance of the mercurial temperament of Americans I will relate how two young friends become fellow passengers. On the evening of the day previous to that advertized for the departure of our steamer, I was spending part of the night with a number of friends in the stores of James McCrae. I casually remarked to the two young men referred to: "Take a trip with me to New York." They laughed; then looked serious; then commenced bantering each other, until the idea had taken consistency in their minds; and in two hours more were *packing up their trunks* for the voyage of six thousand miles.

On Thursday the sixth, the magnificent Steamer unloosed from the Long Wharf cheered by at least three thousand people, who had assembled to see us off. Radcliff, the Count Democomble and Forney accompanied me to the last moment of starting. Theall was obliged to return to Sonora two days before.[3]

Away we steam through the placid bay, past wharves, immense lines of warehouses, where three years ago there was nought but sandhills and filthy mud. We turn the point which shuts out the view of the City and enter into the majestic straits. Hugging the southern shore we soon come abreast of North Beach, and are startled by seeing a second San Francisco rising up, as if by enchantment; while in the openings of the hills we catch a last glimpse of the steeples of the Wonderful City.

On we rush in the face of a gale of wind which is forcing its way up the straits; now we are abreast of the Golden Gates, and in half an hour more out in the Great Pacific Ocean! The same ocean into which, upwards of three hundred years ago, Nunez de Bilbao plunged with the royal ensign of Spain in his mailed hand, and took possession of its unknown wilds in the name of his Royal Master![4]

---

[3] The departure of the *Winfield Scott* on May 6 was duly recorded in the *Alta California* next day, with "W. Perkins" included in the list of passengers.

[4] Vasco Nuñez de Balboa discovered the Pacific from the heights of Quarequá on the Isthmus in September, 1513. He took formal possession for his

Now, with the exception of some leagues of islands in the Indian [Pacific] Ocean, what is left to the once undisputed sway of Spain? Her colonies revolted and independent; the restless Saxon establishing his busy haunts in places where now the golden flag of Castile is scarcely ever to be seen. Her children degenerated into all but barbarism in countries to which flocked the flower of Spain under the glorious banners of Cortes and Pizzaro. Many grand tales might this Pacific Ocean relate, and many strange vicissitudes and wonderful scenes has it witnessed in its brief but stirring history!

The "Winfield Scott" is taking down eight hundred passengers, but we are not crowded by any means, as the separation of the Deck from the Cabin passengers is complete. Coming out of the harbor and through the Golden Gates, we had to encounter a gale that was stemmed with difficulty by the steamer; but once outside the wind was moderate, and the sea only rough enough to make four fifths of the passengers seasick, a great blessing to those who are not affected by the sea-demon, for the sick people keep their berths, and there is plenty of room to move about, and one can take his meals with some comfort.

Four days out, and we have only seen one whale blowing. On coming up this coast, in the same season of the year, in 1849, our ship used to be surrounded with whales, porpoises, dolphins, and blackfish, frisking about in fearless proximity; but then we were in a sailing vessel. The noise and splutter of steam vessels frighten away the denizens of the deep.

TUESDAY, ELEVENTH. Our trip down continues to be delightful. The weather cool, and a steady breeze accompanying the vessel. This morning the Cape of St. Lucas was plainly in sight on our larboard counter, about twenty five miles off. Cape St. Lucas is the extreme point of the long peninsula that locks up the narrow Gulf of California. We are now steering in a direct line for Acapulco, where we shall probably arrive late on Thursday. About nine o'clock this morning we passed through a school of Black-fish, and had a good view of the clumsy pig headed monsters. On these "grounds" the fishery of blackfish is productive; they produce a large quantity of oil. On my voyage up I remember having seen a line of these "fish," at least four miles long. Like the porpoise they are frolicsome creatures, one of their

sovereigns after reaching the shore, waiting for the tide to come in, then marching into the water with the banner of Spain held aloft.

favorite amusements being the game of leap-frog, in which they would put many "schools" on shore to shame. As I have before remarked, in these latitudes in a sailing vessel, one may see almost every description of the inhabitants of the sea, playing fearlessly about the silent ship. In the harbor at Mazatlán, a huge female whale lay with her calf for several hours under the stern of our vessel.

Last night I remained with Bours, to a late hour, on deck, smoking, and enjoying the beauties of the night. The white-caps were like clumps of dancing white feathers, dipped in phosphorous. These seas are surcharged with phosphoric animalculii, and at night every break of a wave is a flash of fire. The moon rose late, and the sea was black in the shadows of night, and consequently when the crests of the waves broke and tumbled over in a mass of brilliant sparkles, the sight was doubly attractive.

While enjoying ourselves, seated on the taff rail, the mate approached us, and we entered into conversation with him. He is an old Atlantic sailor, and is not yet accustomed to the extraordinary and sometimes startling phosphorescent phenomena so common in these latitudes, in the Pacific. As we were talking, we suddenly found ourselves in the midst of an immense sheet of what, in the surrounding obscurity, appeared to be foam and breakers. The mate made a jump for the bell to stop the engine, but before he could reach midships, we had passed through the white field into blue, or rather black water. The scene only lasted a few seconds, but it was fearfully beautiful. I never saw any thing like it, and may probably never witness such a sight again. I am certain that neither Bours nor myself drew our breath during the passage of the vessel through this little lake of fire. The appearance of the sea was that of a field of snow with myriads of fireflies on its surface. But it is absurd to try and describe it. Had there been in reality foam and breakers, I should not have felt my blood tingle more acutely. What appears to me most strange is, that we did not observe the mass of light before entering into it; and once passed through, it disappeared behind us. The mate said to us, a quarter of an hour later, when his fright had subsided, that he would not experience a similar sensation again, to be owner of the "Winfield Scott." His impression was that we had run out of our course and got into breakers.

At half past eleven o'clock the full moon rose in all her glory and eclipsed with her effulgent rays the ghostly lights of the ocean, and we, after making her a libation of brandy and water, descended to our berths.[5]

My usual occupation when the night sets in, and the decks are partly cleared, is to recline at full length on one of the deck sofas, and smoke cabano cigars. (They cost me twenty dollars the hundred in San Francisco.) Here I watch the top of the mainmast and calculate the number of stars it sweeps over as the ship sways and rolls; or mentally measure the expanse of horizon the heaving of the vessel allows me to discover each two or three seconds, under the life-boat that hangs on its davits over the port-quarter. Yes; and then I think of Home, and the number of strange little faces that will be popping up their lips to be

---

[5] Here Perkins provides an extended note: "The extraordinary phosphoric nature of the waters in the Gulf of California and particularly near Guaymas, makes it very difficult for the smugglers to land their goods, as each dip of the oar in the water is accompanied by a flash of vivid fire, which discovers the depradators to the Custom House officers. One of the most glorious sights it has been my fortune to witness is the tide coming in at a certain spot in the harbor of Mazatlán, at night. From two opposite points an unbroken wall of water rushes in, each wave about eight feet high, and when about a hundred yards from the sandy beach, slowly rolls over in an extended cascade of sparkling fire!

"Speaking of the singular phenomena of the lights in sea-water, Chambers says: 'The Medusa shares in another property possessed by most of the class, that of luminosity of phosphorescence. It is chiefly to the smaller tribes, accumulating in great numbers, and so transparent as to escape notice by day, that the occasional phosphorescence of the sea is due. In the midst of the diffused luminosity caused by the glow of innumerable multitudes of small acalephae, and even animalcules far smaller, the larger ones shine out like *stars in the milky way*. The cause of this beautiful appearance is ill understood. It has been ascertained to exist in a secretion from the surface, which can be washed off, and can thus communicate the phosphorescence to various fluids in which it seems to remain until decomposition has taken place. The light is rendered more brilliant when exhibited by the animal itself, by any thing that irritates it. And this fact is observed in the case of most luminous animals. '—Chambers' Zoology.

"Pfaff confirms the opinion that the appearance is due to the presence of microscopic animals, and principally *infusores*. In support of this opinion he quotes the careful observations of Dr. Michaelis, who has already determined several species, and noticed the most important circumstances of their phosphorescence. Pfaff observes that if an electric current be passed through a tube filled with sea-water, recently taken up, there is immediately seen in it an infinity of brilliant points, continually in motion, which remain visible only for a few moments."

kissed; the approaching happiness of again meeting with the dear associates of my childhood, and the many friendly hands that will soon be pressed in mine.

There is a youngster on board as Purser, whose brother was a frequent visitor to my bachelor quarters in C[incinnati]. His presence recalls many pleasant recollections of the quiet but jolly nights at the *"Den"* where George Woodward, John Groesbeck, George Febuger and Tom Gallagher used to stroll in to play cribbage at a cent a point. Why should I not give myself the pleasure of writing their names in full? I shall ever remain famous as having introduced cribbage into C——.[6] But many of my pupils and particularly Mr. Febuger, soon excelled their master, and the latter has often retired after a well fought field, the winner of fifteen to twenty cents!

The cry of, Land! on deck interrupts my reminiscences and relieves the reader from a subject of little interest except to the writer, and as the episode has been short and abruptly curtailed to boot, he will doubtlessly pardon me.

We entered the port of Acapulco on the fourteenth. The harbor is completely land-locked, and we cast anchor in front of the town, whence it is impossible to discover the entrance into the bay. It is more like a mountain lake than a harbor within hearing almost of the surf of the Pacific Ocean. The town is prettily situated on the high-lands on the inner side, and is shut out from the sea by a high range of mountains. The heat is intense, and I verily believe that plantains might be fried by the heat of the sun on the flag-stones of the Plaza.

The steamer was no sooner anchored than she was surrounded by copper-colored little imps from three years old and upwards, who seem to be amphibious. They will remain paddling about with arms and legs like huge bull-frogs for hours without any apparent inconvenience. These are the incipient pearl-divers, and they crowd round the steamers for the small pieces of silver coin that the passengers throw over board. You may see a little fellow not two feet long dive down entirely out of sight in pursuit of a silver picayune. Like the gipsies they disdain copper.

---

[6] Where Perkins' name should be thus held in grateful remembrance is shown by Cincinnati directories of the early 1850's which list several of the men he names.

The harbor of Acapulco swarms with sharks, but they are of a harmless species, for the native boys who almost live in the water, do not fear them. I have seen half a dozen sharks only a few feet under the legs of the little ruffians, and bipeds and fish appear to be on the most amiable terms. At night the presence of sharks is indicated by a phosphoric luminosity which surrounds them, probably owing to a multitude of minute parasitic animals attached to their skin.

Acapulco was established by the Spaniards some three hundred years ago, and the remains of an old Convent and the grand Cathedral, which were destroyed by an earthquake many, many years ago, are still visible. The church was almost entirely swallowed up. The tops of the walls only and about twenty feet of the towers are still above ground.

Amongst the ruins of the Convent on the top of a hill, an old white-headed blacksmith has put up two forges. I had a long conversation with the patriarch. He says the town was destroyed by a great earthquake before his time, and that since the Spaniards were driven out of the country there have no fine churches been built, and people were poorer, for now the silver mines were not worked as in former days. He did not say how in those fine former days, the Spaniards used to kidnap the poor Indians and bury them for life in these same silver mines; for seldom if ever were the poor wretches allowed to see the blessed light of day. Thinks I, old white-headed blacksmith, it is as well for humanity that the silver mines of Mexico are *not* worked as in former days.

The ancient Vulcan was working on an old fashioned anvil which *he* said came with the first bells and cannon. It was like a capital of a corinthian column inverted. The assistants were using American or English Anvils, but the old man would work on no other but the inverted capital.

From the ruins of the convent a fine view of the town and bay is to be had. Even from this point no opening from the harbor to the sea can be distinguished. It seems to be completely surrounded by mountains covered with trees.

The cocoa-nut tree forms the most beautiful feature in the scene spread out beneath the feet of one standing near the old Convent. The town is embowered and almost hidden by these graceful palms, the most aristocratic of the great family. Every house, rancho, or hovel has its group of cocoa trees, overshadowing the *patio,* or open space behind the edifice, and the weird-like noise the leaves continually make in the slightest breeze has a strange voluptuous effect on the senses.

From his group of cocoa nut trees the lazy Acapulqueño supplies his family with food, milk, oil and spirituous liquor; from its fibres he makes all kinds of mats, cordage, furniture and even clothing; and with its leaves he makes his dwelling. Thus, a family with twenty or thirty of these invaluable trees, is independent; and may even by the sale of nuts and oil, purchase the luxuries of life, which are for the Mexican a silver and gold embroidered manta, and, for the Mexican woman, an embroidered peticoat and silk stockings. Luxuries of other kinds they care not about. The most delicate food and liquor they would refuse, taking their *tortilla* with chile-pepper sauce in preference to all other food, and find more satisfaction in a "nip" of *mescal,* than in the best french brandy. Clothes, bedding, good and comfortable houses—what does a Mexican care for them in a climate where the greatest luxury one can imagine is to live night and day in the open air, under the cocoa-nut trees, and sleep in a hammock strung between two of them? We find our happiness in having so many wants; the Mexicans find theirs in having so few.

All kind of tropical fruit is abundant in Acapulco, and since the discovery of the gold region in California, the people are enriching themselves with its sale to the passengers of the steamers on their way up and down the coast. By a lucky chance I have an opportunity at this very time of giving an idea of the passenger trade between Panamá and Nicaragua, and San Francisco. On the same day with ourselves, arrived in the harbor of Acapulco the "Golden Gate" from Panamá, with eleven hundred and fifty passengers; the "Independence" from San Juan, Nicaragua, with seven hundred and thirty; the "New Orleans" from San Francisco, with four hundred and seventy five; and the "Columbus," from the same port, with four hundred and fifty. Our steamer has on board eight hundred. Nearly four thousand fruit ravenous men on shore at this little place the same day! We may safely calculate that one with another each of these four thousand spend half a dollar in fruit alone during the four and twenty hours which the vessels generally occupy in coaling. No wonder that the Acapulqueños are *muy aficionados á los yengis;* very fond of the Yankees.

Every house and hut has a fruit stall, and at night the streets are long continuous bazaars, where tables, lighted with tallow candles, are crowded and piled up with oranges, cocoa-nuts, shaddocks, mangos, pine apples, plantains, bananas, limes, melons; the *cherimoya* or custard apple and the *tuna*, fruit of the prickly pear, intermixed with savory hot dishes of *tortillas* fried in grasa and chile pepper.

The boatmen also make a deal of money taking the passengers ashore and bringing them off; so with one thing and another we may safely say that the California packet trade leaves a monthly sum of at least eight thousand dollars in this formerly insignificant little port.

The women are generally good looking, and keep themselves scrupulously clean. Like all Mexican women, they are lascivious, and sell themselves readily for love or money; but there is no grossness or vulgarity to be seen amongst them. All are graceful, goodnatured and well behaved, and not a word or gesture to offend the most delicate ear or eye. In our countries when a woman looses her virtue she looses her self respect. Not so with the Mexican woman. She not only does not part with her self respect, but she retains caste, and it would be only by descending into slovenness, vulgarity and drunkenness that she loses this.

In former days the mountains about Acapulco produced large amounts of silver. There are many rich mines still; but whether from the want of hands or fears of revolutions, scarcely any of them are worked. In the mountains on the opposite side of the bay, and fronting the Pacific, there is a mine which is being worked now, but I know not with what result.

CHAPTER XLII

Panamá in sight at four o'clock in the afternoon on Friday, twenty first of May. The rainy season was ushered in on the same day by the sudden fall of sundry small rivers from the upper regions of the atmosphere.

The entrance to the harbor, or rather roadstead of Panamá presents many striking beauties. Nothing can be more picturesque than the lovely groups of islands, with their two or three palm-leaf covered cottages or *ranchos,* half hidden by groups of banana and cocoanut trees. The stretches between the islands, as the steamer winds around them and opens and widens the views, are positively superb in their tropical beauty. There is nothing in my conception adds so much grace and life to a landscape as the palm-tree. Other trees may be handsome: and while some may be compared to beautiful woman attired for the opera, the palm-tree is like the same woman in deshabille, with wavy, undulating and floating drapery, that charms by its perfect freedom from restraint.

The island of Tobago is the principal one in the bay of Panamá, and is about ten miles distant from the city. A lofty hill rises from the centre of this island, and at its base is a little town, nestled close to the sea shore on a quiet harbor formed by an island in front, called Tobagocillo, or little Tobago. This is the rendezvous of the steamers after loading and discharging at Panamá, and is also the head quarters of the English Pacific Steam Navegation Company, which has a fine line of steamers between this point and Valparaiso. On account of the many improvements made in Tobago by this Company, the place has acquired a great maritime importance, and steamers and men of war are always to be found here taking in coals, provisions, water, or repairing. Here resides the manager of the English Company, a person of some consequence; in fact a small island king; for Tobago is very close upon being an English dependency.

There is a small steamer that plies between the island and Panamá, and makes four or five trips on steamer days. The harbor farther in is shallow and dangerous for any class of vessels, from the prevalence of sudden and violent squalls. The little ferry boat is often in great peril, and boating is a dangerous diversion, indulged in only in cases of necesity. Two officers of the English company lost their lives only a short time ago in one [of] these fatal squalls.

The passenger steamers run in as near as the shallow shore allows them, to land their passengers, or to take them on board, and then return to Tobago.

I had promised myself a couple of days of interesting research about the town of Panamá, and an examination of its many curious antiquities, but an incident entirely unlooked for, upset all my arrangements in a very summary manner.

Most of the passengers left the steamer on friday night, but the Purser requested Bours and me to remain on board that night, and he would take us ashore the next morning in the specie boat; an offer we were glad to accept as it would have been difficult to find lodgings in the town that night. We therefore remained on board, and the next morning at daylight started with the Purser, four sailors and the treasure.

The rain was pouring down in torrents and one of the men was occupied continually in baling the boat. Of course we were drenched completely. The distance from the anchorage to the beach in high tide, is about two miles. On our arrival we found the landing place deserted except by a party of twenty five or thirty black boatmen, who as usual rushed to the boat, through the water, long before we touched the beach.

These men are the scum of a bad race of people; treacherous, ferocious and thieving. This is the character I have always heard given to them. I have no doubt, however that their only intention at first was to secure the baggage, to carry up to the hotels, but when they surrounded the boat, up to their waists in the water, and caught a glimpse of the well-known packages in which the treasure is always put, and aware of the absence of a guard of soldiers who ought to have been on duty on the beach, their cupidity could not withstand the temptation, and they made a resolute attack to get at the gold dust. Fortunately they had no knives, and we were able to check them. Bours and I were both armed with pistols, but the effort to fire them proved unavailing, as the rain had saturated the powder and caps; but we did very respectable execution with the butt-ends in repelling the efforts of the scoundrels to upset the boat. One of the assailants wrenched an oar from the hands of one of the sailors, and used that as a weapon of attack, but Bours drew him towards him by the same oar, and laid his head open with a savage blow with his heavy revolver. The man disappeared under the water, but got ashore some way or other, for I saw him a few moments after, his face streaming with blood, on the beach, with a heavy stone in his hand, and the next moment I had to dodge the same stone which whizzed past my head like a bullet, and carried the Pursers hat half a dozen fathoms astern with it. At last the black devils retreated, and we were pushing off to await at a respectable distance the arrival of the Coast Guard, when we were saluted with volley after volley of large stones. One of these ended my glorious career for the time being, striking me on the side of the head, on the ear. My thick *Vicuña* hat broke the force of the blow somewhat; as it was, however, I was knocked head over heels in the boat, where I lay senseless during the rest of the fray. When I returned to consciousness, I found myself in a canvas hammock, in the house of the Agent, with a son of Apollo and Coronis busy with a pair of shears cutting away the "gory locks." The ear was pretty well mashed, and the scalp badly bruised, but the skull was all right.

The Doctor consoled me with the pleasant intimation that, "according to his lights, I had no business to be alive at that moment." He had doubtless never been at an Irish shindy, or he would known that it is not such an easy thing to kill a man by knocking him on the head. If he had examined the head then under his hands, he would have found a protuberance of the size of half an egg, the result of the any thing but gentle descent of a bludgeon upon my sconce, in a row in Sonora.

I learnt that very soon after my inglorious fall, the Coastguard appeared, and the black thieves beat a rapid retreat; but as for any hope of punishment being meted by the Authorities to the perpetrators of such outrages, it is not to be thought of.[1]

---

[1] The *Alta California* of June 16, 1852, in reporting the return of the *Winfield Scott* to San Francisco the previous day, picked up the following from the *Panama Star*:

"AN OUTRAGE.—On Sunday the 23d of May, as a boat-load of passengers were landing from the steamship Winfield Scott, a difficulty occurred between the natives and passengers which nearly resulted in the loss of life and a general row. The circumstances as told us, were about these: as the boat struck the shore, she was surrounded by natives, each eager to earn a few dimes by carrying baggage to the hotels; and in their efforts to obtain which, very little regard was paid to the owners wishes—in fact, it was a perfect scramble between the two parties; the one defending their baggage and the other endeavoring to obtain possession of it. A Mr. Perkins had a box of treasure which a persevering native seemed determined to get hold of.

"After pushing him away two or three times, Mr. P. drew off and hit him a blow with his fist, which sent him reeling, while at the same time a fellow passenger, who was equally annoyed, drew a revolver and attempted to shoot

Staying in Panamá was out of the question, with the rainy season setting in; and although my good Doctor intimated that it would be absolutely necessary to lay over until the next steamer, I could not make up my mind to such a sacrifice of time; so after quietly lying in my hammock for four and twenty hours, I mustered strength and resolution enough to mount a mule and start for Navy Bay.

O such a day! Small Mississippis were tumbling from the heavens, and larger ones flowing through the mountain gullies. Blinded with the pain in my head, wet, drenched to the skin, and I verily believe half an inch farther, so done up with fatigue that I had not strength to *fall off my mule*, we reached Gorgona, on the Chagres river, at six o'clock in the evening, performing the journey of twenty miles in twelve hours. Providentially the intelligence of my accident had reached this place somewhat earlier, and the ladies among the passengers had prepared a bed for me, the good souls. Women will under all circumstances show something of the angels' nature. The only spare room in the "hotel," (a ranch, divided into two departments,) had been given up to the women, and one of them, a beautiful and abandoned girl of San Francisco, gave me up her bed, and tended me with sisterly care although I had not spoken to her once during the whole voyage, and not one of the ladies showed me more quiet modest attention than this poor lost creature.

> "O woman in our hours of ease
> Inconstant, fickle, hard to please,
> And variable as the shade
> By the light quiv'ring aspen made;
> When pain and anguish wring the brow
> A ministering Angel thou!"

Hacknied as they are, I cannot refrain from quoting these beautiful lines of Scott. It is more than probable that I owe my life to the

one of his persecutors. Fortunately, or unfortunately, as the case may be judged by the reader, the pistol would not fire, although three caps were exploded. In the meantime the natives united, and hurled upon the beset passengers a perfect shower of stones, one of which hit Mr. Perkins on the side of the head, laid him senseless, and almost deprived him of life. Several persons were hit, but no other serious injury was sustained. Mr. P. was rescued from the crowd and carried to the private room of a friend, where his wounds were dressed, and on Sunday morning he was sufficiently recovered to proceed on his journey across the Isthmus."

thoughtfulness and care of these women; for had 1 not been able at once to undress and rub myself dry and get into a warm bed, I should certainly have been in a high fever before twelve o'clock at night; and fever in this country, and at this season is—death.

After being well scrubbed by Bours, whose friendly care I shall never forget, and my head dressed by one of the ladies, I fell into a deep sleep. Such a sleep; ye gods! Coleridge must have experienced such a one immediately before writing the famous verse in his *"Antient Mariner:"*

> "O sleep, it is a gentle thing
> Beloved from pole to pole;
> To Mary Queen the praise be given,
> She sent the gentle sleep from heav'n
> That slid into my soul."

It saved my life! The next day I felt so refreshed that I was able to enjoy the lovely scenery of Chagres river, down which we proceeded in open boats.

The vegetation between Panamá and Chagres is rank and luxuriant, with a great many false mahogany trees that grow to a great height. The road to Gorgona is nothing but a mule path, except where exist the remains of the old spanish stone causeway to Cruces, a pueblo a few miles above Gorgona. When I passed over it the air was oppressive with the dead weight of the smells from the rich and decaying vegetation, seething in the copious floods of warm rain. I saw no birds nor animales of any kind, and nothing in the shape of flowers; three months must elapse ere the Isthmus will be in all its glory, with fresh leaves and new vegetation; flowers not only covering the ground but the trunks and branches of the trees; birds of gay plumage, monkeys, lizards, iguanas, armadillos and insects of every description. At least so I am told. But I was in a poor plight to enjoy the beauties existing or lament the absence of others; and glad I was to ride into the narrow streets of Gorgona.

This little town consists of about two hundred thatched palm huts, and is situated on the Chagres river, half way between Panamá and Navy Bay, or Colon, or Aspinwall, as you will.[2] It is nine miles below Cruces on the same river. This latter place was important in the time of the Spaniards and, as I have mentioned, had a stone paved road to

---

[2] The name Colón prevails today.

Panamá, over which passed all the trafic of the "Indias," boats plying between the town of Chagres and Cruces. Gorgona is comparatively a new place, but as the route is somewhat shorter, and with less of river navegation, it is generally preferred to that of the old Spanish town.[3]

The extraordinary advent of passengers takes the people by surprise. They have not got into the way of providing for so many. The "Hotel" did what it could, and some two or three hundreds got a supper. The streets were full of prowling hungry men, foraging out grub, and when I arrived I do not think there was an egg, a chicken or a *tortola* in the whole pueblo. I expect the people must have taken to the woods in search of roots after our departure, for we left them nothing edible. I must add that the occasion was extraordinary, as the passengers from New York and San Francisco arrived simultaneously, and one night there were more than two thousand strangers in Gorgona.

On monday morning [May 24] we embarked on one of the numerous boats that ply the Chagres river, a kind of long flat-bottomed launch, with a canvas covering, propelled by negroes with long poles. These boatmen always used to go completely naked, but since the advent of numerous lady passengers, the Authorities have succeeded in persuading them to cover their loins with a napkin; but for many months females who passed up and down the river, had the agreeable satisfaction of being able to admire the "human and divine" in the persons of half a dozen stalwart nude black fellows.

The trip down the river was delightful. It had ceased raining and the country was lovely. The banks of the river are thickly populated, and men, women and children rushed out of their huts to see us pass, the former and latter being generally completely naked. I wished the voyage to continue to Chagres, but we were all obliged to pull up at a beastly little place called Frijole, to which *pueblo* the rails of the Rail Road have been laid.[4] The necessity of stopping, desembarking from the boats, and getting into the cars to be transported some few miles to

---

[3] During the dry season Gorgona was the favorite terminus for travel between Panama and the Chagres River; during the rainy season Cruces was preferred.

[4] The Panama Railroad Company, incorporated in New York in 1849, began surveys the same year and commenced construction in 1850. The road was completed to Panama in 1855. See F. N. Otis, *History of the Panama Railroad* (New York, 1867).

Aspinwall, is a bore; and what made the bore worse in our case, we were obliged to remain in this miserable little hole for a day and a night on account of an accident on the line, an embankment having given way.

The lady folks again made me up a bed in their own quarters, a brush-wood ranch divided off from the public room by a cotton curtain.

The night passed in continual alarms. Several rows occurred between the Americans and the natives, and two lives were lost. The place was surrounded with large numbers of negroes, who had congregated in the night in order to rob the passengers. They succeeded in securing a quantity of plunder. One poor old man had his trunk carried off, containing everything he possessed in the world, including several thousand dollars in gold-dust. We were suffered to depart the next morning, however, without molestation, thanks to a rather formidable show of rifles and revolvers.

The people of this country are most arrant thieves. Nothing is safe from them. They are not only rogues, but are a bad, vindictive, morose race. They are not of indian descent like the lower orders of most of the Spanish Americans, but are regular niggers; as black as the best polished boot, and all have a fierce hatred to the white race, and show it too, on all favorable occasions.

They do not cultivate the soil further than planting a few grains of Indian corn. They live upon the fruits growing wild in all parts of this beautiful land; bananas, plantains, melons, cocoa-nuts etc. What money the men get hold of is only used for the purpose of gambling, the great and universal vice of all spanish races. The men generally go naked, the women wear a long cotton shift, which is often nothing more than a peticoat, leaving the bust naked to the waist. The latter are pleasant bright-eyed creatures, and offer an agreeable contrast to the morose savage of the male sex.[5]

---

[5] "It is a notable fact," Perkins remarks, "That the female sex withstands the brutalizing effects of savage life to a greater degree than the male. I have had occasion to remark this in the various old spanish dependencies I have visited. From the universal laxity of the laws, from continual revolucions, wars with the Indians, cruel sports, such as Bull and Cock fighting, the Mexican, for instance, has become a sa[n]guinary beast, delighting in the most cowardly and savage acts of bloodshed; at the same time that the Mexican woman remains gentle, affectionate and charitable."

The holiday dress of the women of the Isthmus consists of a calico skirt fastened round the waist, while over the naked bust is thrown a richly worked gauze jacket, quite loose and transparent. This jacket does not quite meet the skirt, so that there remains a portion of the waist entirely uncovered. The glistening black skin and plump breasts shining through the thin gauze, has a comical effect. The common manner of wearing the hair is picturesque and attractive; two knots of braids fall on either side of the face, and in these are worked fresh flowers, replaced three or four times a day. These flowers, forming generally a vivid contrast to the ebony skin, give quite a pleasant aspect to the country girls. The men are strong and well formed, but have all the repulsive ugliness of the negro race, and wanting the good humored expression usually seen in the countenances of the North American Negro.

Loads are carried on the shoulders by a band passing over the forehead, as our Indian women carry their *papouses*. It is surprising what weights the men will carry strapped to their heads; but I may with confidence say that a weight an European would grumble at had he to bear it a hundred yards, one of these men will carry from Panamá over the mountains to Cruces, a distance of twenty eight miles. The great grandfathers of these same fellows used to carry the ingots of silver over the Isthmus, in the days when the old spanish government received yearly from her American colonies enough silver to pave the Grand Plaza of Madrid. Now the only silver that passes over belongs to the English, not wrung from the bloody sweat of millions of unhappy Indians, but the legitimate fruits of a flourishing commerce; while from a country then unknown, come millions of still more precious treasure, the product of a people also unknown in those days, all passing over the same rough paved road that the spaniards made in the sixteenth century. What a change in a couple of score of years!

On tuesday morning [May 25] we were taken into Aspinwall on the cars. This interoceanic Railway will be a great triumph of engineering skill. It is strange how English and French engineers allow themselves to be outdone by the practical American. The former, after most expensive surveys, made reports adverse to the practicability of building an iron road across the Isthmus of Panamá. After these gentry retired in disgust and dispair, over come a few Yankees, interested in the work, saying: "We want a road here, and if within human means, we will have it!" And lo! in less than a twelve-month, the route was surveyed, declared feasible, and five thousand men at work on it. The most difficult part of the road is already nearly finished. The first fifteen miles on the Darien side was certainly enough to startle an English engineer, being little more than a bog in the which the vegetation of centuries lay putrifying in ever stagnant waters. The labor of even surveying this stretch was very great, and the work of clearing the road so as to commence the making of a causeway, cost many lives amongst the laborers.

One of the principal difficulties instanced in the reports of the European Engineers was the climate. They were of the opinion that no workmen could live on the Isthmus. Well, the result has proved thus far, that the mortality has not been much more than that on any line constructed in the States; and now that the rails are laid to the river, and the works have reached higher and firmer and consequently healthier grounds, the men are almost entirely free from fever and sickness. I make this statement on the authority of the Superintendent; and he added that the greater part of the deaths occurred through habits of intemperance. The Navvies brought with them their habits of dram drinking and "spreeing," and these, comparatively harmless in a temperate or cold climate, where the violent action of heat is rare, are fatal in this country, where an excess of nitrogen and carbonic gases in the human system finds a fearful auxiliary in the intense heat acting upon the putrescent masses of vegetation, common in these countries.

At Navy Bay we found the Steamers "United States," "Crescent City" and the "Philadelphia." The "Northern Light," loaded with the first arrivals had already left. Mr. Bours, and two or three other friends went on board the "United States," bound for New York, while I made up my mind to go to New Orleans in the "Philadelphia"; so I put my luggage on board the latter steamer, and as Captain Berry had invited me to dine on board his boat, I rowed back to the "United States."

While at table a card was handed me on which I read the names of Mrs. H. y Mrs. M., two old and valued friends, who were on board the "Philadelphia," and had seen my name on my trunks. Wondering very much at this singular and unexpected occurrence, I immediately rowed back. I learnt that the two ladies had embarked at Havana in order to join the husband of Mrs. H. in Nicaragua, and the scoundrel of a Captain had refused under some pretext or other to land them there, telling them he would put them on board the English steamer at Chagres, by which means they would reach Nicaragua in twenty four hours. To understand the critical position in which they were placed, and the rascality of the captain, I must state that the English steamer was not expected for ten days: that when she does come, she does not put into Aspinwall at all, but lies off Chagres, a distance of ten miles from Navy Bay, and lastly the "Philadelphia" being obliged to return immediately, the ladies were obliged to land, to put up in some wretched hole ashore, in the midst of a ruffianly population, and wait for the English Steamer, then hire a boat and run ten miles to sea to board her. It was not surprising then, that we all looked on the extraordinary meeting as providential; and although my own trip would be considerably delayed, yet I could not but feel the most vivid satisfaction at having arrived so opportunely to relieve my lady friends from a most painful situation.

From the moment of my appearance all doubt and perplexity vanished. I immediately went ashore, got the best quarters the town afforded and made as comfortable arrangements as I could under the circumstances, and brought the ladies ashore with bag and baggage, and of course a due proportion of bandboxes; all of us with a full determination to make the best of our position and be good humored and jolly. And I believe I should have enjoyed myself, had the wound in my head permitted me. An abscess had formed inside the ear, and I suffered tortures. Had it not been for the care and continual attention of Mrs. H. I think I should have died. For two or three days I was delirious with the pain.

CHAPTER XLIII

An act of summary justice took place on the mountains, the day I passed over. A party of three Americans had hired a Native to take over their small stock of baggage, which contained amongst other things, a carpet bag rather heavy with gold-dust. On the way the negro absconded, and sought to secrete himself, with his mule in the dense vegetation that covers the country in every direction. The Americans followed his track and caught him. The fellow, however, had managed to hide the carpet bag, and no threats would induce him to reveal where. He maintained a dogged silence, undoubtedly expecting to receive a good whaling, and triumphantly carry off the plunder afterwards. But, unluckily, he did not quite understand the Yankee character. When the owners of the gold found that menaces were futile to induce the rogue to give up the treasure, they took the *latigo,* or raw-hide rope from the mule, and hung the black rascal to the nearest tree.

I knew one of the party, and when I saw him on board the "United States" without his beard, I asked him what was his reason for shaving before reaching New York. He then related me the above circumstances, and added that he and his comrades had cut off their beards to avoid being recognised should the Authorities get wind of the affair before the steamers left the harbor. A few such examples as this would be of service on the Isthmus.

Great expectations are entertained by the projectors and founders of the town of Aspinwall in Navy Bay. As yet there is only a small slip redeemed from the surrounding swamps, and on which are built the railroad offices. The few houses occupy a small space between the swamp and the sea, on what has been formerly a coral reef, now joined to the mainland.

An enormous wooden Hotel is still unfinished. Here during the arrivals of Passengers from New York and San Francisco, it is possible to get something to eat, but in the *interregnum,* the house is all but closed, and nothing is to be had but liquors. We were obliged to forage for ourselves and pick up eggs, fowls and fruit from the natives, and with the help of preserved meats, of which there are immense stores in Aspinwall, we managed very well.

Every thing must have a beginning, and I should not wonder if some fine day, Aspinwall shall see her "coral shores" covered with granite warehouses, and her surrounding swamps smiling with orange trees, corn, and, shades of Uncle Sam, perhaps pumpkins! At all events its position is advantageous to an extraordinary degree.

The substratum of all this coast is coral. The beach is a ragged plain, smelling villainously of decayed shell-fish and cast-up seaweed; and yet the beach offers the only amusement in the place. When the heat of the day subsided, we always found ourselves scrambling among the jagged coral, racing after its numerous occupants, crabs, star fish, sea-devils, lizards, and searching after rare shells. This of course when the wound in my head permitted me to move. Fortunately my health continued good, so that in the intervals when the pain left me, I was well enough.

Why have we no ship canal across the Isthmus? When we think of the Britannia tubular bridge, the Thames Tunnel, the Croton aqueduct, the canals which unite Lake Erie with the Hudson river and with Lake Ontario, we may safely assert that it is not on account of engineering difficulties that the work has not already been commenced.

Forty years ago Humboldt declared the project feasible, and English and American Engineers have confirmed this declaration by actual survey.[1] The Princes of the Plutus family, say or did say that the work would not pay. Here we have the secret. Had a Canal across the Isthmus offered the certainty of profitable dividends, we should not now be sending our ships to the Pacific and Indian Oceans, some nine thousand miles out of their way, round the stormy and ill-named Tierra del Fuego, or the distant Cape of Good Hope. Was it not Stephenson who said, in refusing to admit of Engineering imposibilities, that a railroad to the moon was only a question of expense? An extravagant but brilliant phrase, indicating the unbounded confidence of a man of genius in the capacity of science to meet any exigency, and over come any difficulty; a vaunt, cousin german to the celebrated one of Archimedes.

Forty years ago a canal was not so necessary as at present. When Humboldt wrote, the decadence of Spain had reached a point verging upon dissolution. Her golden blood-stained flag was about to be driven from the Pacific, where it had for three hundred years sanctioned so many atrocities, and the infant Republics, like newly hatched chickens, were helpless, and timorous. With the exception of Valparaiso and Lima, there was not a point of commercial importance from the

---

[1] " 'The Isthmus of Panama is suited to the formation of an oceanic canal, one with fewer sluices than the Caledonian canal, capable of affording an unimpeded passage at all seasons of the year to vessels of that class which sail between Liverpool and New York, and between Chile and California.' 1st ed. of Humboldt 'Views of Nature.' " (Perkins).

Straights of Magellan to the Russian settlements, north of Oregon. A yearly ship carried cottons, crockery, tea and some few articles of luxury to California, to exchange for hides and dried beef. A yearly ship more than sufficed for the trade between Acapulco and the Philipines. The subjects of the Czar had a small trade in furs with Kamschatka. The whole group of the Polynesia, a small world of itself, had not yet been introduced into respectable society. Tahiti, Honolulu and New Zealand were still serving up missionaries and their wives "hot with plenty of gravy," and the European trade to the Indian Ocean went by the way of the Cape of Good Hope.

Capitalists were, in the main, not far out in their prudent calculations. They were wrong only in being short-sighted. They ought to have been able to have foreseen the future importance of the Pacific. But what shall we say of the apathy of speculation in this epoch? The events of the last eight or ten years surely showed plainly enough the growing magnitude of this region and its important trade, and we might have expected some steps towards carrying out the dream of the great German. The Pacific is dotted with white sails. Chile has risen up to be a respectable commercial nation, freighting yearly a couple of hundred vessels with her agricultural products, and her valuable ores. Peru, miserable degraded Peru, saved from bankruptcy by the ignoble excrements of birds, freights whole fleets of ships at the Chincha Islands, the proceeds not inriching the wretched country, and improving the condition of the people, but lining the pockets of the rapacious rogues who constitute her public men.

The Sandwich Island trade is being fostered into importance by enterprizing Americans. New Zealand is becoming a flourishing English Colony; Australia is already a powerful nation, and, lastly, Golden California with her wondrous city, raised as if by magic on her magnificent bay, Columbia and Oregon, swell the list. All these points cry out for a short cut to and from the old world.

Twenty five years ago it was calculated that twenty five ships would not annually pay toll for passing through the canal. Now, with perhaps greater accuracy of calculation, it is said that in eighteen hundred and sixty, about which time the canal might be finished if commenced now, one hundred and fifty thousand tons of shipping would take advantage of the route, and this figure is very moderate.

How is it that in this age of mechanical wonders, the project of uniting the two oceans has been so entirely neglected? Had not the great and brilliant project of Paterson failed, who knows but that at this moment we should have had, not only a canal, but a powerful Saxon Empire on the Gulf of Darien! [2]

[2] Perkins explains: "Paterson was an obscure Scotch clergyman, yet this person formed one of the most brilliant colonizing schemes ever devised. Sir John Dalrymple, in his memoirs of Great Britain and Ireland, says—'Paterson having examined the places, satisfied himself that on the Isthmus of Darien there was a tract of country running across from the Atlantic to the Pacific, which the Spaniards had never possessed, and inhabited by a people continually at war with them; that along the coast, on the Atlantic side, there lay a string of islands called the Sámbolos, uninhabited, and full of natural strength, and of forests, from which last circumstance one of them was called the island of Pines; that the seas there were filled with turtle and the Manati, or Sea-cow; that midway between Porto-Bello and Carthagena, but nearly fifty leagues distant from either, at a place called *Acta,* in the mouth of the Darien, there was a natural harbor, capable of receiving the greatest fleets, and defended from storms by other islands which covered the mouth of it; and from enemies by a promontory which commanded the passage and by hidden rocks in the passage itself; that on the other side of the Isthmus, and in the same tract of country there were natural harbors, equally capacious and well defended; that the two oceans were connected by a ridge of hills, which by their height created a temperate climate in the midst of the most sultry latitudes, and were sheltered by forests, but not rendered damp, because the trees grew at some distance from each other, and had very little underwood; that, contrary to the usual barren nature of hilly countries, the soil was of a black mould two or three feet deep, and producing spontaneously the finest tropical fruits and plants, roots and herbs; that roads might be formed with ease along the ridge, by which mules, and even carriages, might pass from one sea to the other in the space of one day, and consequently that this passage seemed to be pointed out by Nature as a common centre to connect together the trade and intercourse of the universe.'

"Many others were the advantages pointed out by Paterson, and, after some disheartening failures when at last he procured a statute from Parliament, such was the extraordinary enthusiasm created by his project that nearly a million sterling was contributed at once. Young and old, male and female, threw their little fortunes into the stock, and widows sold their jointures for the same purpose. In the mean time the jealousy of trade was undermining the infant Scotch company. The East India Company had sufficient influence with the English Government which the [*i.e.,* with] pitiable want of common sense, discountenanced the scheme, to the great rage of the whole Scotch nation. The people however, were not discouraged, but built six vessels, carrying from thirty six to sixty guns, and on the twenty sixth of July, 1698, the whole city of Edinburgh poured down to Leith to see the colony of twelve hundred persons, besides the crews of the vessels off. The colony established itself at Acta, calling it New St Andrew. But in the mean time their enemies were not idle. Orders were sent to the Governors of the West Indies and other American Colonies, to issue proclamations against giving assistance or even holding correspondence

Thanks to the go-ahead genius of the American branch of the Saxon family, we are in a fair way of having an excellent iron road joining the two oceans, and naked boatmen, and extortionate muleteers, and muddy mountain passes, and the old Cruces road, paved with great round stones, and strings of mules heavily laden with ingots of silver, so large and heavy that therein lies their safety from being robbed—will all be of the past. They will cut down the luxuriant forests for woods to feed the engines. The noise of the steam whistle will frighten away the jolly little monkeys and the brilliantly painted birds. The Native will remove his picturesque palm-leaf hut from the "line of road," and, very soon, passing the gorgeous Isthmus of Panamá will be like going over fifty miles of railroad in Vermont, barring the heat.

Felicitation then for what we shall gain in the Useful, but regrets for what we shall loose in the Beautiful, which, unfortunately, is too often knocked on the head by the iron hammer of Utility. I have probably looked for the last time on the wild date and feathery cocoa-nut trees, and magnificent mahogany trees and limes that line the old road; on the comely black damsel, naked to the waist who, for two rials, sold me enough of delicious bananas to stock a fruit store in Broadway; on the noisy little monkeys, talking in bad spanish from the trees that overhang the banks of the river: on the white woolly-headed patriarch, who came out of his road-side hut, naked as the day he was born, to request me to *lend* him some tobacco *por el amor de Dios;* to the wild, picturesque, luxuriant, tropical scenery of the old route across the Isthmus of Panama, *en fin.*

The day after our little party had established itself in its humble quarters in Aspinwall, to wait for the English Steamer, I was informed that a poor fellow, calling himself a Canadian, lay sick with a fever, in a garret in the new Hotel. I at once went to see him, and Mrs. H. insisted on accompanying me. We found the man very far gone, and

---

with the Colony. Thus the Scotch who had not anticipated such disgraceful persecution, in want of food, and other aid, suffered great misery, looking in vain for the aid promised from the mother country. In eight months all had either died or quitted the settlement. Two more attempts were made by Paterson, but the Government allowed the Spaniards to conquer the Colony. This was not done however without their being gallantly opposed by Capt Campbell, who stormed Tubucante and dissipated a force of sixteen hundred men with a party of two hundred. In the mean time the Spanish fleet of eleven ship captured St Andrew, and so ended this promising scheme."

entirely out of his head. The people of the Hotel had left him alone to die! Mrs. H., woman-like, immediately set to work, in a manner that only women are capable of, to alleviate the situation of our poor countryman, although her kindness was little appreciated by its unconscious recipient, for the man in his delirium made efforts to strike and bite her.

I searched out the American physician and with much difficulty persuaded him to accompany me to see the sick man. When we entered the bare garret room, we found Mrs. H. at the bedside, much to the astonishment of the Doctor, who could not understand how a lady could find the courage, which he lacked, to risk the danger of a contagious fever, when the object of such abnegation was an utter stranger to her. The patient was apparently free from fever but speechless. The man of Drugs, without touching him, shook his head.

"He is a gone case" said he, vulgarly; but recollecting the presence of a lady in the room, he turned to her, and added:

"He can't live over the day."

"Is there no way of saving him?" asked Mrs. H. anxiously.

"I know of none" replied the Doctor.

"But supposing he was some dear friend of yours, Doctor, you would not give him up without at least making an effort to save him. In such a case, tell me, what would be your course?"

The physician thought for a little while, or pretended to think, and answered:

"I would put him into a warm bath."

"Well, we will try the remedy in this case," said the brave lady.

"But" said the doctor, "You do not know the difficulties, the impossibilities that will oppose you, in what you propose to do. There is not a kettle in the place large enough to boil the water in, nor is there such a thing as a bathing tub to be found in Aspinwall."

Notwithstanding the discouraging intelligence of the doctor, Mrs. H. nothing daunted bade me search for a tub and she would have the water ready.

I had my doubts as to the *medical legality* of the remedy. The fever had only left the patient to give place to the chills and debility of the last moments of life. A warm bath in my opinion was only to hasten the catastrophy. I suggested this to the doctor, but he insisted that he would advise no other remedy, at the same time stated his opinion that nothing could save the man.

I set out on my search for a tub. The doctor was right; not such a thing was to [be] found in the place, but I procured a tin lined box, in which had been packed french goods, and carrying my prize to the house, I found the good Samaritan in the yard, beside a large fire (the thermometer must have stood at a hundred and ten in the shade) on which were placed about a score of teakettles, earthen pots, and tin cups of all sizes. Our efforts merited success! We got the box and the numerous vessels of hot water into the room. A white man volunteered his assistance. We undressed the patient and with some difficulty, and with the greatest care, got him into the bath. In about one minute we took him out—dead!

CHAPTER XLIV

I have mentioned the name of General Covarrubias once I believe in these pages. He was one of the first persons of distinction who gave in his adhesion to the Americans, when the latter invaded California, and he did so under the firm conviction that his country would be happier and more prosperous under their rule, than under the anarchical domination of Mexico. Since that period he has been regularly elected to the state Legislature by his county, Santa Bárbara, and recently was elected member of the Democratic Convention that is to meet in a short time at Washington, for the nomination of a future President.

Accident prevented us from being fellow passengers, and the "Columbus" in which he embarked arrived at Panamá on the day I was wounded. Although I had not seen him on the Isthmus, I supposed of course that he had embarked on board one of the steamers at Aspinwall, and that he was then half way to New York. Much to my astonishment, he made his appearance one morning at the Hotel, black with exposure to the sun, his clothes muddy and torn, and a beard of ten days growth. He was as much surprised to see me still here as I was to see him. After a mutual explanation, he washed and dressed himself and I presented him to the ladies. He had lost his baggage on the Isthmus, and was delayed hunting it up, and only succeeded in finding a part of it. His is a worse plight than mine. My delay is caused by a duty which is in itself a pleasure, while he will be too late to join the Convention and will thus have made his journey in vain. However, with the greatest good humour he made up his mind to his fate and joined our little party, determined on accompanying us to Nicaragua, where we hoped to find a Steamer for New York; and we, setting aside our sorrow for the misfortune that deprives him of taking his seat in the Convention, were very well satisfied in securing a gentlemanly and jovial companion.

The English steamer at last hove in sight, passing outside of Navy Bay, at the distance of three or four miles, without touching. The English are too stupidly dignified to change a custom without an immense amount of red-tapeism and diplomacy. Ever since the Royal West India Steam line was established, the treasure and passengers from the Pacific are embarked at Chagres, where vessels are obliged to lie out some two or three miles from shore, on account of the shallows formed by the deposits brought down by the river. Now when the Railway is in working order for a portion of the way, all the passengers of course take advantage of it, and one would naturally suppose the English would be glad to leave such a wretched deadly hole as Chagres, where the Steamer has to anchor out at sea, and receive their passengers and treasure at the commodious bay and wharves of Aspinwall. No such thing! Their lordly pride stupidly ignores the existence of a Railroad, safe harbor and fine piers at the ancient Porto-Bello, and passengers have to get to Chagres the best way they can, in small open boats. In this manner we reached the Steamer; and the passage of ten miles was a very disagreeable, not to say a dangerous one. But we were embued with the spirit of Mark Tapley and were determined to be jolly under all circumstances. When we did get on board, all of us drenched with salt water and the ladies suffering from sea sickness, we found a gentlemanly set of officers, who received us with a cordiality and attention that made us forget our past troubles. The name of the Steamer is the "Great Western," the same old boat that attained such a celebrity as one of the first Steamers on the line between Liverpool and

New York. She is commanded by Leut." Woolley, of the Royal Navy, and I set down the name of her surgeon, Dr. Finlay, in order not to forget a man who tended me with the greatest care during a night of anguish. The drenching I got in the open boat irritated my wound, and I suffered great tortures during a whole night.

The town of Chagres was, once upon a time, a place of some note. Its open roadstead has borne many a gallant vessel decked with the proud flags of Spain. On the right bank of the river, opposite the town, and commanding the entrance, was a strong fort, well garnished with the magnificent brass cannon of the time of Philip the Morose, the bigotted son of the great Emperor. This fort is now a heap of ruins, but being built on a prominent and lofty point, might with little trouble be put into a decent state of defence.[1]

The cannon have never been removed, and are valuable for the quantity of silver they contain. In the sixteenth century it was common for the gentry to attend the founding of cannon, and they vied with each other in throwing into the molten mass trinkets of gold and silver and money, sometimes to an amount hardly credible.

Chagres is now only a collection of palm huts, and is said to be the most unhealthy place in the world. The Agency of the English Steam Navegation Company, as I have before intimated, is still retained here, and large quantities of silver from the Pacific are here shipped for Europe.

On Saturday, the twenty ninth [of May], we landed at Greytown, or San Juan del Norte, where we found Mr. H. anxiously expecting his wife and sister-in-law. He had suffered great anxiety of course, but all was forgotten in the joy of an unexpected meeting, for he never dreamed of finding his folks on board the English steamer from Carthegena. The party is on its way to California, and had chosen this route, very unadvisedly. Mr. H. left his wife in New Orleans, to come down in the next steamer, and preceded her to Greytown to have all ready to ascend the San Juan. He made a pretty mess of it, and had it not been for the providential meeting with me, on the Isthmus, his imprudence might have had seriously disagreeable results. He had his

---

[1] Those who crossed the Isthmus during the Gold Rush landed at Chagres, at the mouth of the river of the same name, some 8 miles west of present Colón. Fort San Lorenzo was an object of the liveliest curiosity, and the artistically inclined sketched it in its ruined condition.

launch, or flatboat, nearly completed, and in the mean time we took up our quarters in the "Franklin House," where one room was given for the use of whole party. Fortunately the room opened to a balcony, and the General and I removed our cots outside and defied the mosquitos.

As we had some days to pass in this place, we made ourselves as comfortable as possible. The hotel was three storeys high, and about twenty feet square, and we being at the top of the house, enjoyed one storey to ourselves in an airy and commanding position. It was a great house, the "Franklin!"

The harbor of San Juan del Norte, now called Greytown, receives the waters of the river San Juan, which flows from the great lake of Nicaragua, and after a course of about eighty miles, joins the Caribbian Sea at this point. The river is of considerable depth, but there exist shallows at either end, and numerous rapids obstruct the navegation.

There is much talk of an interoceanic canal here, but it is my opinion that the scheme is all but impossible. All the proposed routes centre at Nicaragua lake, and the river San Juan, on the Atlantic side, is the only line to the ocean; but from the Lake to the Pacific coast, there are five or six different routes proposed.

One is taken through the lake Managua to the Bay of Fonseca; but this line would be very long, the distance from ocean to ocean being more than three hundred miles. Two other routes from the same lake to Realejo and Tamarinda, would be much shorter; but there are no harbors at these two points. Another route runs directly from Nicaragua lake to San Juan del Sur, a distance of ten or twelve miles; but here it would be necessary to make a *ship tunnel* between one and two miles long.[2]

Two English men of war were in the port when we arrived, one of which had just brought down his Royal Highness and copper colored Majesty, the King of the Mosquitos, to Greytown, from his capital Blewfields. His Kingship is a goodlooking, tolerably educated Indian. There is a dispute between him and the Nicaraguan Government in

---

[2] In a note from which several words are now missing, Perkins writes: "Capt. (now Admiral) Fitzroy says: 'Enough is known to discourage any attempt to construct either canal or railroad.' He considers the climate pestilential particularly in the low grounds on both sides of the river, which holds its course amidst forests, swamps and mud banks. The American Minister however in his pleasant book on Nicaragua, gives quite a different idea of the climate which [. . .]"

reference to the possession of San Juan del Norte. In the mean time the Americans are quietly colonizing the town and go in for the claims of Nicaragua against the red-skinned *protegé* of her Britannic Majesty. The Americans have the Municipal Authority entirely in their own hands.[3]

We arrived in times of great excitement. Some Californians had been attacked by a party of Natives, and robbed of a large amount of gold dust. Three of the culprits had been caught the day before and lodged in the Blockhouse, guarded by about two hundred Californians, who are here waiting the arrival of the steamer from New York.

A fourth and, as it is believed, the most guilty of the robbers, had escaped up the river with the greater portion of the booty, and a large party was out after him. The three prisoners were tried by the Municipal Authorities and sentenced to be hanged. Some hours after our arrival they were led just outside the town to a scaffold, and one of them hanged at once. The other two, in consideration of further confessions made, were pardoned after receiving fifty lashes, and being branded on the right hand.

To all intents and purposes this was Lynch law, for the town authorities possess no powers of Life or death, legally; but being Americans they became puppets in the hands of the exasperated Californians. *Sin embargo,* the effect will be beneficial in this land of degradation and crime.

Some officers of the Men of War came ashore to witness the fun, but they did not interfere in any way. In fact it struck me that neither his Majesty of Blewfields, nor the Government at Granada, exercised or enjoyed much right of sovereignty at Greytown.

Greytown, as a locality for colonists, is much superior in beauty and salubrity of climate, to Aspinwall. The harbor is spacious and picturesque, but shallow on account of the deposits that are continually thrown into it by the two mouths of the San Juan. On the long peninsular, running out in a semi-circular form, enclosing the harbor, are the buildings of the Nicaragua Transit Company.

The town is surrounded by dense forests, where the undergrowth of mimosa lianas and parasitical plants, has interlaced itself with the

---

[3] The Mosquito Territory on the Caribbean shore of Nicaragua at this time had a semi-independent character, its Indian sovereign backed by the British. In 1860 the British government ceded the protectorate to Nicaragua, which soon established effective sovereignty over the area.

huge trunks of the *ceiba* and mohogany, into an impenetrable wall of vegetation, which only the axe or fire can conquer. The tract of clear land on which the town is built is covered with a bright, clean sward, interspersed with fruit trees, mangoes, mimosa and wild roses. There is not much fruit grown in the vicinity of San Juan, but about eighty miles from here there are many islands, one of which, "Corn Island," the property of an old man by the name of Sheppard, by all accounts, must be a perfect paradise.[4] The English Government offered Mr. Sheppard seventy five thousand pounds for his property, which he refused. All kind of the most exquisite fruit is brought down from these islands. The finest pineapples I ever tasted came from Corn Island. If one can imagine a rich juicy "Hoovey" strawberry of the size of a melon, he will be able to form an idea of these delicious pines.

Corn, yams, eggs, poultry etc, are brought down the river from Granada in large quantities, for the supply of the shipping. Granada is the capital of the Nicaraguan Republic, and, not lying in the route across the Isthmus, is little known; besides, the people are jealous of foreigners and oppose all attempts at intercourse and reciprocity of trade.

Those who have seen the place describe it a fine town of about forty thousand inhabitants (a figure which I consider exaggerated), and situated in the midst of a fertile and beautiful country.

The temptation of gain hardly induces the poorer classes to come into contact with the heretic Yankees; and yet my impression is that these same heretics are fated one day to be the possessors of the soil, the lords of the land, and the deliverers (perhaps extinguishers) of the enslaved and slavish population. They have already "staked out their claim" in Greytown.

The *Nicaraguenses* are a superior race to the *Novo Granadinos*. The first is Indian, the second is strongly mixed with the Negro; and notwithstanding the opinion of some writers on Ethnology that the latter is superior to the former, I hold the contrary. The admixture of white with negro blood soon destroys or swallows up the characteristics

---

[4] "I heard it stated that this old gentleman had been a notorious pirate in former times, and had his rendezvous in the San Juan where he accumulated hoards of treasure. When I went to see him, I found him lying in his hammock, from which he seldom moves. He is nearly blind with age, but with mental faculties still in full vigour. He is fond of conversing with strangers. He told me he left Scotland more than" [the rest of Perkins' note, several words perhaps, is missing from the manuscript].

of the latter; while the whole of Spanish America shows that the mixture of the White with the Indian has proved fatal to the Caucasion race. This seems to be an evidence of physical superiority which the Negro does not possess.

In Canada and the United States, the *cuartaroon* is not distinguishable from the White; but let one take a person of indian blood in the same degree and he will find most decided evidences of the aboriginal origen.

The intractability of the Indian and his enmity to all species of European civilization only show that he possesses more obstinacy or doggedness than the Negro; and possibly indicate a higher order of reasoning faculty.

There is a large lagoon just behind the town, which communicates in some mysterious manner with the sea, as its waters are influenced regularly by the tides. This lagoon is full of alligators of very large size, and it is somewhat of a fearful sight to see the repulsive looking monsters disporting on the surface of the water, or in the slimy mud on the wooded side of the lagoon. They are not to be held in contempt, for over and above unwary dogs, young pigs, sheep and even donkeys, they do not dislike a "cold man." It was only a few weeks before my arrival that an emigrant Irishman and his wife lay down under a mango tree, some two hundred yards from the lagoon and fell asleep. The woman was awakened by the screams of her husband, who was carried off in the jaws of an immense alligator, and in a few minutes the water was red with the blood of the poor fellow, who was torn to shreds by dozens of these ferocious brutes. I never heard of a more horrible thing related of the crocodiles of the Nile; but I believe these are nothing to compare, in point of size and ferocity, to the Cayman of tropical America.

Perkins' original manuscript is preserved only to this point, its concluding pages now lost. The missing portion is restored by retranslating the corresponding pages of the Buenos Aires edition of 1937.

The bay is also full of sharks, and it is very dangerous to bathe in deep water: the people of this country never go farther than a yard from shore.

The city is very well built up, with excellent, wide streets, and since as yet there are neither carts nor horses, all streets are like beautiful lawns covered with luxuriant green grass. This is the most attractive part of Greytown. The houses are far superior to any I have seen in Central America: all are surrounded by thick hedges of tall bamboo and are so well built that it would seem that the Americans must have had a hand in their construction. The houses are roofed with the broad, durable leaves of the wild date; but the government now requires that all newly constructed houses have tile roofs; the reason for this measure is that some time ago a fire destroyed the entire city.

Since Central America is the perfect land for monkeys, it is an almost universal custom to have a large one hitched on a chain in the patio of the house. Here there are many, and they are frequently used in place of dogs, which are less common. Some have a very attractive appearance but others are repulsive.

What a wonderful land this would be if it were cared for and cultivated! If, in place of the fanatic, ignorant, and lazy people who live here today, there came vigorous, civilized people to occupy the fertile, rich fields; what a difference that would make! One needs the pen of Camoëns to describe the exquisite landscape and natural beauties of Central America. The vegetation, the impenetrable forests which are veritable gardens; "the wild luxuriance which clothed the humid shores; the rose-coloured Flamingoes fishing at the mouth of the rivers in the early morning and giving animation to the landscape." This is what Humboldt tells us (*Cosmos*, Vol. II), and how frequently I have had the opportunity to recall these phrases. How true they are! And the flamingos balancing themselves on their long legs in the dark waters or unfolding their brilliant plumage in the rays of the sun! Never to be forgotten scenes!

Among the most curious plants that one sees here are the mimosa or *sensitiva* and the mango. Of the first there are a great variety and they reach a height of five or six feet.

Who doesn't recall that delightful poem by Shelley, which begins:

"A Sensitive Plant in a garden grew,
And the young winds fed it with silver dew,
And it opened its fan-like leaves to the light
And closed them beneath the kisses of Night."

One of my most pleasant pastimes was to walk along the shore of the lake and see how the leaves, upon being touched, immediately curled up as if frightened; so much so, that at last I began to believe that the plant knew when I was approaching or heard my footsteps, since it closed its leaves before I could reach out and touch them with my cane or hand. It is almost enough to make one believe that these plants possess understanding and feeling, and when one sees them for the first time one is amazed to see how the fan-shaped leaves fold up and close like the hand of a child at the lightest touch.

The people of this country are likeable. They are attentive, quite clean, and, as I have said before, their houses and patios are neat. The women have pretty eyes, are dark-skinned, very industrious, and appear very healthy.

As I mentioned above, the owner of the "Franklin" placed a whole room with four beds at our disposition. A great kindness; but since we were two ladies, a husband, and two other men, unfortunately bachelors, we found ourselves in the same situation as the man with the fox, the goose, and the corn. Nevertheless, just as that man solved his problem, so we, by means of our intelligence, succeeded in resolving ours. We gave one bed in the room to the married couple, another to Mrs. M., and the General and I took ours out on the balcony. We were a happy group and found our comical situation most amusing; I, at least when the pain in my head permitted, enjoyed it enormously; and Mrs. H. cared for and bandaged my wound so expertly that my pain was half of what it would have been under other circumstances. The following morning we faced one serious difficulty: I had caught a cold sleeping in the open air; in my state, this was dangerous, and after a council of war, it was decided that I should be admitted to the "citadel." How we laughed at this phase of *Life in California*. I remember that while crossing the Isthmus we stopped one night in the little town of Frijoles, and the women, numbering six or seven, occupied the only available room where not even husbands were allowed; and they insisted I sleep in that room and prepared a very comfortable bed for me in one corner where I rested undisturbed all night.

Mr. H.'s launch was completed on Wednesday, and he and his wife and Mrs. M. made their departure, leaving the General and myself very much alone and sad since we had another four or five days to wait for a ship. Lacking excellent care, my wound began to trouble me greatly; until a Californian told me I should apply steam to my ear. This I did, and the pain vanished. I felt a new man and the wound immediately began to heal; I suppose the steam opened the abscess in my ear and, since this was the cause of the extreme pain, I was left with only some slight inconvenience until scar tissue formed.

Two days after the departure of our friends, the General and I, lonely and depressed, were strolling along the wharf waiting in vain for the arrival of a steamer from New York, when our attention was attracted by a launch slowly entering the bay, with a very curious flag hoisted from an oar. To our surprise, we saw that it was H. and the ladies who were returning.

H. thought he would be able, without any assistance, to get the launch to the lake; but under the burning rays of the sun the task proved impossible. Sickness overtook them, and they had to return and do what they should have from the first: hire a crew from among the local inhabitants. We passed a very enjoyable evening together, and the next day they left. Let us hope they will have better luck this time!

Sunday, the sixth [of June], despairing that a steamer would ever arrive, we took the "Great Western" to Aspinwall where we had the luck to find the "El Dorado" for New Orleans, and the General and I immediately embarked; at last, I was headed home.

Few passengers. Bad seas; worse boat; one passenger died on board, and we threw him over the side. A death on shipboard produces a terrible effect on all passengers: first the illness, then death, afterwards the body wrapped in a flag is brought on deck, the corpse is placed on an inclined board passed through one of the stanchions; iron weights are tied to the body; then a rapid religious ceremony, the momentary halt of the engines, the body falls, the Captain gives the signal to proceed, and the ship continues on its way while the eyes of all the passengers remain fixed on the spot where the body disappeared, even though it has plunged to a depth of many fathoms. All this is truly more terrible than on land.

At dawn of the fifth day we sighted the lighthouse of San Antonio, situated at the western tip of Cuba. Here the two extremes of Cuba and Yucatán draw together to form the narrow canal generally known as the Gulf of Mexico of the Caribbean Sea. We arrived that same night at Habana; ships cannot enter the port at night, and since they are in open waters they are continually exposed to accidents. Sailing vessels prefer to remain far off shore for fear of sudden storms in the Gulf and only enter the following day. The entrance to the port of Habana is very narrow. On the left is the famous *Castillo del Morro*, surrounded by cannon. On both sides and wherever there is room to install a battery, we can see the black mouth of a 32. As I note the long lines of cannon facing each other across the several intervening yards, I recall the words of the Bastard of Falcombridge, when Austria and France, united with England to attack a city, placed themselves on opposite sides:

> "Oh prudent discipline! From north to south,
> Austria and France aim at each other."

It seems strange that the entrance to the small port of Habana should be so strongly fortified, for the city can be bombarded from outside, and troops can disembark two miles away where there are no defences.

I paid a peso to land and attempted to make use of the short time we had at our disposal. I had the luck to find a Cuban gentleman, Señor Perera, to accompany me as guide and show me the prettiest sights of the city: *Jesús del Monte, Cres,*[5] *Puentes Grandes.* We visited the palace of the Count of Villanueva: what beautiful gardens! what paintings! In the dining room there was a small chapel hidden by a curtain which when drawn back disclosed a magnificent altar, glittering with gold, silver, and precious stones, and crowned with a painting of the Virgin and Child, worth, I was told, a fortune. The coconut trees in the garden were so well cared for that each trunk was like a marble column, and the foliage appeared to be a crest of feathers. From the observatory in one wing of the palace, there is an excellent view of the city. The drives are a delight; never have I seen their equal.

I visited the spot where Crittenden and his followers were executed. Only a fortnight ago the steamer "Saranac" was here to request that the government permit the repatriation of the remains of those unfortunate

---

[5] It is not clear in the Spanish translation what location is referred to by *Cres.*

men. The Spanish authorities immediately acceded to the request; I understand that the bodies were buried along the seacoast.[6]

Wherever there is any high ground which dominates the city there is a fort; Habana is surrounded by them. Within the city there are thirty thousand troops; each street has its barracks and picket of soldiers, and the police, with sword and revolver, patrol the streets continuously. All offices, from the highest to the lowest, are staffed with Spaniards, and the Creoles groan under a terrible tyranny which they are powerless to resist. Spain well knows that they will seize upon any opportunity to revolt and has taken as her motto, "oderint dum metuant." But this cannot last: there will be a war, and then, poor Spaniards! There will be a repetition of the Jacquerie in France. The hatred between the two races is terrible. While in a café, I saw two well-dressed young men arrested and dragged off to jail for the sole reason that they were discontented with certain acts by the government.

The prison is the largest building in Habana; it covers more than a thousand square feet, with patios on the inside. It is the first thing one sees upon entering the port. At the moment there are more than eight hundred political prisoners held there. The upper part is occupied by soldiers; now they number about two thousand.

The streets are narrow, and many without sidewalks; large coaches cannot turn around in the street, and often a carriage will have to continue for several blocks before a place wide enough to turn around in will be found. The *volanta*, or Spanish carriage, is one of the

---

[6] Perkins says in a note: "Mr. Crittenden of New Orleans disembarked in Cuba with one hundred Americans in order to help López liberate the country. After winning one brilliant victory over the troops sent against them, they were defeated, taken prisoners, and all of them were shot. López was captured shortly thereafter and garroted."

By way of further explanation, Colonel William S. Crittenden was one of the principal officers under General Narciso López, a Venezuelan-born Cuban who mounted an unsuccessful effort to oust the Spanish rulers in the summer of 1851. A force mainly consisting of Americans landed at Cabañas Bay but was quickly defeated. Having fallen into the hands of the Spaniards, López was garroted at Havana on September 1. Crittenden, who had become separated from López soon after reaching Cuba, was shot with some fifty fellow captives on August 16 at Atares, the fortress at the head of Havana Harbor. Others were eventually released. The first issue of the *New York Times*, October 18, 1851, recounts this melancholy history, and it may be followed serially in the *Alta California*, September 8, 18, 19, October 3, 8, 1851.

curiosities of Habana: it is a type of four-wheeled coach with very long shafts; the larger wheels are located just behind the single seat. The shaft poles are more or less twenty feet long; the coachman rides postillion and is a very picturesque sight; he is generally dressed in a coat with long tails and covered with gold lace. He uses leather spatter dashes; his naked feet have huge spurs attached to the heels. The spatter dashes are richly embroidered in gold and silver. The coaches are driven with great speed, which is a nuisance to anyone wanting to take notes; but the movement is smooth and agreeable; the coachmen are always Negroes. The tails of the horses are braided and tied with pretty ribbons to the left side, so that the poor animal is left to the mercy of the flies, which lose no time in taking advantage of such a favorable circumstance.

The palace of the Viceroy is situated in the center of the city and occupies a whole block. It is an imposing edifice; on one side is the palace of the Intendancy. In front there is an attractive plaza with trees and flowers, and on one of the sides of this plaza is the Cathedral, of very ugly architectural appearance, but quite imposing on the inside, with its richly decorated altars and costly paintings.

There are three principal cafés, all sumptuously decorated. One is for the Creoles; another is solely for Spaniards, where one never sees a Cuban; the third is for foreigners from all parts; the main room has no roof and is filled with flowers, trees, and fountains. The floors are of mosaic, the tables of marble, and these places are always delightfully cool. Here the people gather to pass the warm hours at midday; they drink all types of cool beverages and eat sweets. These are the only cafés there are.

One thing that attracts attention from a commercial point of view is the number of cigar factories. In every street there are two or three such houses whose trademarks are known perhaps throughout the civilized world. I bought a thousand cigars of different classes in one factory in the street of the *Obispo*. The favorite trademark was *El Combate*. Here smokers wait for a dozen cigars to be made up in their presence, for Cubans prefer their cigars fresh; while we think that a cigar is not ready to be smoked until the tobacco's essence has mellowed with time.

There is an attractive characteristic of the roads in Habana: entire streets are gardens, and here every evening one can see elegant ladies in their private coaches dressed in brilliant gowns: here one sees the Negro women in their striking dress and also the elegant and pallid Spanish damsels. The scene is one of extreme merriment: the avenues are graced with statues and fountains and on the principal one is the theater *Facon*, the most beautiful theater in America.

The people are proud of their avenues and never walk on the grass or cut the flowers. The Avenue of Marble starts at the port and from here dominates the *Casa Blanca*, the forts, barracks, *Campo de Marte*, etc., on the other side of the water. It is a thousand feet long. The streets are adorned with statues of the Spanish sovereigns. A pretty statue of the little "sugar eater" Isabel is situated in the center of the principal avenue.

The glow worms of Cuba are worthy of their name: they are large and shed a continuous light. Negroes gather them by the dozens in cages and sell them. I have been able to read easily by the light of a glow-worm cage. The Negro women often put them under their muslin gowns when out strolling at night; they appear as diamonds in the darkness.

> "I mark the glow-worm as I pass,
> Move with green radiance through the grass,
> An emerald of light."

I concluded my wanderings with a visit to the cemetery of Habana. This consists of a large plot of ground closed off by a high wall. In this wall are four rows of niches, one above the other, and here the coffins are deposited. One hundred pesos secure the privilege to leave the coffin in the niche for ten years. If, at the end of this period, the niche is not once more rented by the family (which is what usually happens), the bones are taken out and burned, the niche is cleaned, whitewashed, and ready to receive another tenant. This procedure appeared to me to be excellent, all except burning the bones. The doors to the niches are generally closed by attractive tombstones, some gilded and very well worked, and the first impression that one receives is that the wall is covered with paintings, accentuated even more by the fact that these tombstones are usually decorated with bouquets of natural or artificial flowers. The interior plot of land is occupied by the graves of the former aristocracy of the island. Perera cautiously pointed out to me with a gesture the location of the remains of López, the patriot. After his execution, his body was buried near the seashore in unconsecrated ground; but two or three faithful friends with extreme care dug up the body, and, leaping the wall of the cemetery at night, succeeded in burying it without leaving a trace of its location. Through its spies, the government heard about the act but has not been able to find the place where López was buried. The brave men who carried out this deed have had to flee the country. Alongside the cemetery is the Asylum for the Feeble-Minded. Above the entrance to the cemetery are these words: "To Religion, to the public health," and this message from the Pope: "Let forty days of indulgence be given to all those who humbly enter this sacred spot to pray for the souls of those who rest here. May no one profane this spot by smoking, eating, or hurting another, under the penalty of excommunication."

With the very sincere impression that Habana is the most enchanting place that I have ever known, I embarked once more on Tuesday, the sixteenth [of June], and after three days of stormy weather, I arrived at New Orleans, after an absence of three and one-quarter years.

Appendix

THREE LETTERS BY "LEO"

THREE LETTERS BY "LEO"

William Perkins' journal has made it possible to identify him as the author of three letters contributed to Stockton newspapers in 1850–1851 over the nom de plume "Leo." Published while he was living in California, with no possibility of later revision, they provide an arresting counterpoint to his journal. The first letter was printed in the *Stockton Times*, March 30, 1850; the *Alta California* of April 3, 1850, reprinted all but the first paragraph of this letter, identified only as by a correspondent of the *Times*.

The second letter, of May 19–22, 1850, provoked by the attempt to collect the Foreign Miner's Tax in Tuolumne County, was printed in the *Stockton Times* of May 25, 1850, and reprinted in the *Alta California* two days later. This letter, word for word the same as some passages in Perkins' journal—the essential clue to the identification of "Leo"—was prefaced by the *Stockton Times* as follows: "We have received the following extremely interesting communication relative to the disturbances in the mines from a gentleman who is universally respected, who is largely interested in the prosperity of this district, and whose opinions ought to have great weight with the community. In most of the opinions expressed we cordially agree."

The third letter was printed in the Stockton *San Joaquin Republican,* successor to the *Times,* on October 25, 1851. It returns to some of the themes of the first letter, but has a wider range and more facts, a valuable contribution to the literature of the Gold Rush and the history of the Southern Mines.

TOWN OF SONORA, March 25, 1850.

To the Editor of the Stockton Times:

SIR—With the presumption that communications from any part of the district that owns your paper as its public organ, will prove acceptable not only to yourselves, but to your readers also, I shall commence a series of letters that may, I hope, convey acceptable information to the people of the plains, as well as to the many thousand strangers who are continually arriving in the country. Not boasting of, as yet, a press in our own growing town, we must *per force*, use your columns as a means of disseminating that information, which, coming from creditable and respectable sources, may form valuable statistics for the "fresh hands."

The cry that has gone abroad against the Southern mines is hushed at last. Experience has brought its overwhelming evidence of the richness, the extent, and the working facilities of the placers to the south of the Mocalome—(I believe there is no *legal* rule of orthography for the word. I offer my mode of spelling the word to the public gratis.) The rivers are now being worked with great success—the bars containing large quantities of fine gold, and the banks large deposits of coarse gold. It was near the river Stanislado (pardon my egotism again) that the mass of quartz and gold was found, weighing upwards of ninety pounds! The proportion of the precious metal, I understand, was about one-twelfth.

One great advantage that the Southern mines possess over the Northern, is that the gold is found *everywhere*. It is not confined to wet arroyos or deep gullies, but lies in the sides of mountains, on hill tops at times, in plains and beautiful vallies. The famous Sonora lump of twenty-two pounds was found in a shallow gully, about three hundred yards from, and about twenty-five feet above, the town of Sonora. This gully had been superficially worked before, and it was at the second digging that this piece was taken out.[1] A day or two ago another piece of pure solid gold weighing *fifty-one ounces* was taken out by a party of Americans, (W. G. Sterling & Co.,) from the same locality; and the diggings of last year are now being worked over, and with eminent success. Heretofore the surface only of the earth has been mined, but experiments fully bear out the truth of a theory I have always entertained, that gold is of much more ancient origin than quartz or even boulders, and that it must lie in large quantities *underneath the formation of rock*. If this theory is correct, the result will be very important to California. Be this as it may, however, one thing is certain, that the ground has been very superficially worked, and the second digging, in many places, has turned out very profitably; and this remark applies with strong force to the placers of Sonora, which are, without exception, the richest in the Southern mines—not in individual holes and corners, but spread over millions of acres of ground.

The town of Sonora itself has sprung up as if by magic, amongst the first spurs of the lofty Sierra Nevada. It now forms the depot for all the mining region of the Tuolumne and Stanislado, and already commands a

[1] See chapter vi, note 7.

very great influence from its position and the wealth and enterprize of its inhabitants. The value of property is increasing daily, as handsome and durable buildings are in progress of being erected.

LEO.

SONORA, Sunday, May 19, 1850.

To the Editor of the Stockton Times:

SIR—As I anticipated, the advent of the Tax Collector [L. A. Besançon] was the signal for trouble and alarm.[2] Little, if any, excitement was displayed in town until this morning, when reports reached us that large bodies of Mexicans, Chilians and Frenchmen were assembled outside the town, holding meetings and consulting on means to evade the payment of the imposition of $20 per month. No notice was taken of these demonstrations, for the citizens of this place have so uniformly treated foreigners well, that we could hardly entertain any fears for the peace of the town.

About noon, two deputations came in from the assemblies to see the authorities, and ascertain if any action of the Governor could arrest the consummation of the contemplated taxation; or at least, to have it explained to them, and the justice of it shown to them.—They asserted that it was impossible that such an amount could be paid; that they would willingly pay four or five dollars per month, but that it would be out of the power of more than half of the miners to pay the sum contemplated. A great many diggers hardly getting more gold than sufficed for a mere livelihood.

During the discussion, an American who wished to get out of the crowd, began elbowing his way from the place where he stood, when a Mexican or Chilian in front of him drew a pistol. In a moment a dozen revolvers were out, and a precipitate retreat was made by the foreigners. No shot was fired, but the Mexicans were alarmed and the town was cleared in five minutes. Our peace now seemed threatened by about 5,000 men outside, and no inconsiderable alarm created in town. The citizens armed themselves, and expresses were sent to Mormon Creek and Sullivan's Diggings, from which places about five hundred well armed Americans arrived, and marched through the streets with guns and rifles on their shoulders. The demonstration was sufficient; the crowds in the vicinity soon dispersed, and quiet was restored. The only thing to be feared is the misguided zeal of our own citizens, who although generally sympathising with the discontent occasioned by the unjust tax, are incensed that the for-

---

[2] See Perkins' parallel account in Chapter x.

eigners should presume to take the law into their own hands, and may not be willing to allow the affair to rest where it is.

A very serious affray took place this afternoon, in which a Mexican was seriously wounded. A man was noticed parading the street with two or three pistols and a knife in his belt; the man was intoxicated, and the sheriff arrested him, or rather took his arms from him. While in the act, a Mexican came up behind and made a stab at the officer with a large knife. The murderous intent was frustrated by a bystander, who with a bowie knife struck the man, wounding him severely. Mr. [George] Work, the sheriff, was happily untouched.

This state of affairs, if allowed to last, will ruin the prosperity of the whole southern mines, and your own town of Stockton will be the first to suffer thereby.

Monday, May 20.—A guard was kept up all last night, but everything was quiet, and as I said yesterday, I believe the danger, if any was to be apprehended, has passed away. But the excitable feelings of the hundreds of Americans now under arms had to be indulged and hearing that a camp, mostly composed of foreigners, situated about seven miles from Sonora, had mounted Mexican, Chilian, and French Flags (what truth there is in the report I know not) they have started out this morning to avenge the insult, and chastise the temerity of the "greasers" and outsiders. I sincerely trust there will be good sense enough in the party to refrain from wanton aggression. The foreigners are acting under a strong excitement, prevailing from this sudden and *unexpected* call for a heavy tax. Few if any of them, have heard the collector's name, and are not aware who are authorised to collect the tax. They complain, and most justly to my thinking, that they never received the slightest intimation to prepare them for this action on the part of the government, before men unknown to them, with no apparent authority, demanded a payment of twenty dollars for the privilege of working one month in the mines. The consequence is an indecision and a repugnance, mingled with strongly incensed feelings towards the "powers that be." What will be the result is perhaps difficult to say; but the commercial interests of the country in the meantime must suffer severely.

A very respectable portion of the foreign population of Sonora, held a meeting on Saturday, in order to memorialize the Governor on the subject of the tax. I have translated a portion of this memorial, to show the moderation of these people. After stating their conviction that it (the tax) will destroy all their interests, along with the commercial interests of the southern mines, causing so many thousands to leave them, they go on:—"Without doubting for a moment the power of the present government to make a difference between American citizens and those of other countries, we humbly draw your excellency's attention to the fact, that it is altogether contrary to the institutions of the free Republic of the United States, to make such a difference as amounts in reality to a prohibition of labor. Without assuming any tone other than that of the deepest respect for the government under which we live and are protected, we beg humbly to suggest to your excellency that a larger state income could be raised, and that too, without causing the slightest dissatisfaction, by the imposition of four or five dollars per month, instead of the large sum of twenty."

Est modus no rebus! The Legislature would have done wisely to have studied this phrase. The latter part of the above memorial speaks truly, not only the opinion of the foreign commercial population, but the great bulk of Americans are convinced likewise of its truth.

I am sorry to be obliged to say that the Mexican hurt yesterday has since died. He has paid the penalty of his attempt at crime.

The passage and action of this taxation law is a subject that has become one of earnest discussion. That it is illegal for men who are cognizant of law, no one will question. No territory or incipient state has any right to interfere with the proceeds of public lands. No state has a right to set aside the treaties of the Federal Government. These are two acknowledged facts, consequently no set of men at San Jose or any where else in California had a right to impose such a tax. Have we not treaties of reciprocity with France? Have we not given large immunities to Mexicans by our treaty of peace with them? Has not our government offered every assistance to the efforts of emigrants to reach the haven of our free Republic? Has she not promised and accorded to them, in every part of her territory the same immunities that she favors her own sons with—the right of franchise alone excepted —with its concomitant privileges? An answer in the affirmative must be given to these questions. I therefore look upon the act passed by the last legislature, as illegal, unjust, abortive and extremely prejudicial to the best interests of the state. Illegal for it wars against existing treaties of the United States; unjust to those who have adopted California for their home, accelerating her prosperity and growth by their labor and capital; abortive for three fifths of the tax will be evaded; and prejudicial to our interests, for business has been prostrated since the collectors have been among us.

Notwithstanding my opinion of the illegality of a tax on foreign miners, I was in favor of a moderate sum being raised from them, in exchange for a legal (as far as the State could make it a legal) warrant to dig. The miners themselves desired this, for the license would have protected them from many an outrage and indignity. For this license a sum of from three to four dollars per month would have been quite sufficient for legislative purposes, and a larger amount seemed to display a desire either to drive the foreign population entirely out of the country, or to amass an amount of money that could hardly be expended in the legitimate business of the government.

Let us be a little statistical. Our foreign working population in this county is estimated at ten thousand, and the estimate is, I assure you, from what experience I have, not exaggerated. Supposing twenty dollars per month to be collected from each one of these, we have an income from public lands placed at the private disposal of a state or territory of $200,000 per month, or nearly two millions and a half per annum, from one county alone. It is not to be wondered if Uncle Sam should deem this a little too large a bite for our State to indulge in. Again, the collector, I understand, has a commission of $3 on each license. This is a monthly income of $30,000, or an annual income of $360,000. Uncle Sam might object to the public money being disposed of so very summarily. This simple statement of facts is conclusive proof of the recklessness of our legislators, and is another of the many reasons why we should press an immediate union with the parent country.

The party of Americans who went out this morning, has returned. They met no opposition; everything was quiet, and I hope will remain so. Upwards of five hundred Sonorians have left, it is supposed for home. A Frenchman, it is said, has been apprehended for inciting the foreigners to rebel; he is now in custody.

I am happy to be able to close my letter with an assurance of perfect quietness.

May 22d, 1850.—All is quiet. A large body of Frenchmen under arms encamped near the town yesterday, and met [*i.e.*, sent?] in a deputation. They had received word from men badly disposed that the French inhabitants were in danger of their lives, and they armed themselves to assist their countrymen. Upon discovering the falsity of the report, they peaceably dispersed. Do not believe any of the numerous reports flying about the country. I will keep you posted up in regard to *facts*, if any occur of importance.

LEO

SONORA, [October] 24th, 1851.

MESSRS. EDITORS.—It has always been a matter of surprise to me, an old resident in the Southern mines, to see the small amount of information that reaches the eastern half of the dominion of the "stars and stripes," having reference to this particular portion of the Golden State.

When we consider the class of population that has settled the southern mines, principally emigrants from the educated middle-classes of the southern and south-western States, men endowed with all the energy of the "Universal Yankee Nation," coupled with the superior intelligence of their class, we may naturally feel some astonishment when we witness the development of the wonderful resources of these regions, the country filled with a dense population, agriculture advancing with rapid strides, large towns built up, and enormous sums of treasure forwarded to the sea port, all in such a quiet and unostentatious manner, that scarcely a paragraph is in papers—otherwise teeming with accounts of the discovery of petty northern placers, appearing to indicate other sources of wealth than the Yuba, Feather river, Scott's river, and the Gold Bluffs.

It is true that the unexampled rise of an inland city like Sacramento might be apt to draw the admiring and fascinated gaze of our Atlantic brethren towards that quarter of California, and the large interests that the city of San Francisco possesses in the northern mines, *may* be reason sufficiently strong to account for the extraordinary neglect with which the interests of the southern portion of this State have been treated by the Metropolitan press.

But, after all, perhaps it might be easier to trace this ignorance and neglect to our own supineness and carelessness. We are certainly a more indolent and ease-loving people than out brethren in the north. I mean we are more apt to let every thing take its own course, without any extra aid from ourselves, than our go-ahead, inquisitive and restless countrymen from the eastern states, who have generally found their way to the northern latitudes of California, under the impression probably, that the Coloma valley was nearer than the Tuolumne river to Connecticut. The Lord knows! possibly the same *primum mobile* may have induced the southerner to prefer the Tule lands of the San Joaquin, from a fancied resemblance to the cane brakes of the Mississippi!

Whatever may be the reason, I feel that we have been much aggrieved by the scanty and meagre meed of admiration we have received, and I call upon the people of Stockton, instead of puzzling their own brains and astonishing those of the public, by their magnificent schemes of municipal financial aggrandizement, viz: taxing merchandize, teams, mules and stray *Greasers*—to enter nobly into the game of emulation with their northern neighbors, and make their town rival that of Sacramento; no hard matter where there is a will, and the intelligence to make the most of great natural advantages.

Desiring strongly that our Atlantic brethren should be made aware of the fact that there is a southern as well as a northern California—desiring to counteract the effect of the San Francisco press, which, up to a few months ago, used to confound SONORA with Sonoma, I propose to give some detailed account of a portion of the southern mines, and, as far as I shall be able, give an idea of the extraordinary amount of treasure taken from this region. To avoid losing myself amongst the vast placers lying between the Moquelumne and King's rivers, I shall confine myself, on this occasion, to the county of Tuolumne.

The geographical portion [*i.e.*, position?] of Tuolumne county makes the name appropriate, the river bearing that name draining about seven-eighths of the county. The head waters of the Tuolumne are within two or three miles of the south fork of the Stanislaus, the dividing ridge being much closer to the latter than to the former river. The consequent immense extent of auriferous land sweeping down to the Tuolumne, gave rise to the conjecture of General Vallejo (since proved to be a fact) that this part of the country was the richest in the State.

The first diggings, on arriving into the mining region by the Stockton road, are Jamestown, Georgetown and Wood's Creek, at first known collectively by the latter appellative. This is one of the oldest placers of California, having been worked as early as the Fall of 1848.[3] Wood's Creek takes its rise in the mountains a short distance from Sonora, and flowing through that town, continues in a south-west direction, watering Jamestown, Georgetown, and many a populous camp on its way, until it empties itself into the Tuolumne river at the important and flourishing town of Jacksonville.

In the early part of the summer of 1849, when the writer of this found his dusty way through the scorched plains to the mountains of the Stanislaus and Tuolumne, Wood's Creek, was, at that time alive with busy miners. Two thousand men had been working on that creek for five months, making an average of from one ounce to twenty-four dollars per day. From that time to the present, there has been continually at work, an average of twenty-five hundred laborers, the proceeds of whose work is calculated to have been six dollars per day. You must understand me as speaking of the average yield,—for while many were fortunate enough to acquire a rapid fortune, others were content to make a good living. From the most rigid enquiries, and nicest calculations, we find that upwards of fifteen millions of gold has been taken from the bed of this stream, of twenty miles in length; and in which, at this moment at least, three thousand men are gaining good wages. Northern placers are somewhat thrown in the shade by this!

Another very productive stream is that commonly known as "Sullivan's

---

[3] Thus Perkins agrees with the history developed in the Introduction.

Creek," and running for some distance parallel with Wood's creek. On this creek five and a half millions of gold have been taken out. From Sullivan's camp to the junction of the stream with Wood's creek, the whole distance has been worked for nearly three years, and is still worked with very satisfactory results.

The immediate vicinity of the town of Sonora has, perhaps, produced more gold than an equal space in any other part of California. From the time when the camp was first formed by a party of Sonorians, in April, 1849,[4] up to the spring of 1850, when the camp became Americanized, upwards of twelve tons of gold had been taken out; without including a vast amount dug by the lower orders of Mexicans.

The extensive placer of Columbia, four miles from Sonora, was opened last year, and on account of the dryness of the season is still almost in its virgin state. The small amount of labor already expended there has resulted in a benefit of two millions of dollars. In anticipation of the rainy season, already have upwards of two hundred and fifty good and substantial houses sprung up as if by magic. But no magic is required—no necessity here for "Alladdin's Lamp"—the genie of gold is more powerful than the famed genie of the ring.

The Chinese Camp, Campo Seco, Yorktown, Shaw's Flat, all within two or three miles of Sonora, have been, and are yet as productive as the richest placers of the north. At Campo Seco a canal four miles long was made to supply the place with water. In dry seasons like the present, want of water is the great drawback to the enterprise of the miner in the southern counties. The "Tuolumne Water Company," got up for the purpose of supplying Columbia, Yankee Hill, Shaw's Flats, Sonorita, and the environs of Sonora with water from the south fork of the Stanislaus, has been busily at work since the commencement of July. The canal will be twenty-two miles in length, and calculated to supply ten cubic feet of water. It is already graded and ditched; and taking into consideration the surface of country through which it passes, it may be looked upon as a work of wonderful magnitude. The cost will be about four hundred thousand dollars. One hundred and sixty men have been at work on the canal for about three months. The completion of this work will throw open four thousand acres of land to the miner's shovel and pick.[5] Virgin soil, teeming with the precious metal, as yet untouched by the votaries of the blind son of Ceres!

Taking the results, as published by the journals of the day, of the

---

[4] Here is the earliest direct statement about the time of Sonora's origin.

[5] In this letter Perkins remarks more largely upon the Tuolumne Water Company and Columbia than he does in chapter xxxii.

canal or sluice at Nevada city, which is, I believe, eleven miles long, and gives a daily income of eight thousand dollars, what are we warranted in anticipating from the existence of a canal in Tuolumne county, with a sufficiency of water in its first flow for the working of five hundred "long toms!" And what would be the result if a sufficient quantity of water could be produced to supply upwards of fifteen thousand acres of auriferous ground now lying untouched for the want of that indispensable element?

I have been disappointed in securing such reliable information in regard to the operations on the Tuolumne river, as would warrant me in incorporating it in this article. I shall only state, that works of great magnitude have been contracted, and a vast amount of capital expended. I learn that very large returns are now being received for the outlay of that capital. The fact of so many flourishing little towns studding the bands [banks] of the Tuolumne, sufficiently attests the general success of mining operations in that quarter; Jacksonville, the principal town containing no less than two thousand inhabitants.

The most successful point on the Stanislaus river has been the "Pine Crossing," a beautiful deep dell, surrounded by the most majestic mountains. Here the sun is visible for only a small portion of the day, and then his fervid rays are neutralized by the cooling influence of the bright waters fresh from their snowy sources in the Sierra Nevada. In this delightful spot, the river has been turned from its bed; and a rich and golden harvest has rewarded the miner's toil.

Besides the placers whose names I have already mentioned, there are scores of small camps, from which it is impossible to acquire information to be relied on: but taking the amount of the precious metal known to have been extracted from the richest placers, and making a moderate allowance for the proceeds of the smaller diggings, we have respectable sum, in round numbers, of seventy millions of dollars from the county of Tuolumne, of which sum I suppose fifteen millions has found its way to Mexico. And yet this is a portion of California, which, through the ignorance of the San Francisco press, is scarcely known to the community of the Atlantic States.

The city of Sonora, situated in the centre of this Plutonian paradise, is usually spoken of as a little mountain camp, when, in reality, it is the largest inland town in California; having a population of upwards of five thousand. It contains one hundred and fifteen mercantile establishments, thirty-five hotels and restaurants, eight butcher shops, four drug stores, three bath houses, nine bakeries, two express offices, and two banking houses, with all the other establishments of trade that a town of its size would naturally support. Its real estate is valued at six hundred thousand dollars; and the amount of merchandize and capital at a million and a half.

The house of Reynolds, Todd & Co., have sent down through their office, since the commencement of their express business within a fraction of three millions of dollars, and about the same amount has been shipped through other houses. With two daily lines of stages, we are within thirty-four hours travel of the Commercial Emporium [Stockton], whence all our supplies are drawn.

The quartz mining interest, that may be said to centre itself in Tuolumne county, forms a subject of so much importance, and involving such stupendous results, that I am afraid to touch upon it. I have, however, requested a gentleman of great mining experience, and a good practical chemist and mineralogist, to prepare a paper which will accompany or precede this communication.[6]

LEO

---

[6] The technical paper Perkins mentions was not published. A regular correspondent of the *San Joaquin Republican* living at Big Oak Flat, who signed himself "Mountaineer," remarked in the *Republican* of November 25: "I notice a very interesting communication from Sonora, in one of your papers, signed 'Leo,' in which he gives an account of the Northern part of Tuolumne county, seeming to forget that the Tuolumne river was not the Southern boundary of this county; and all the large tract of country lying between this river and the height of land between it and the Merced is passed over in silence. Now there have been spots found in this region as rich as any about that favored place, Sonora. At some future time I will give a full description of the creeks upon this side of the Tuolumne." The promised account of the more southerly mines in Tuolumne County was written from Big Oak Flat on December 16, printed in the *Republican* of December 20, 1851.

Index

INDEX

Abalos, Señora: daughter Sophy, 251, 266; sings in Sonora, 304, 306

Abduction, 256–258

Abernathy, Dr., defines somnambulism, 136

Acapulco, 355; Perkins in, 358–361; trade with Philippines, 374

Acorns, Perkins re, 309–310

Adams & Co. Express, 307

Adobe: brick, 108, 112, 149, 205; coin, 215, 339, 342

Agustin, mute Indian, 23

Ainsas, family, 334

Alabama, 5, 259

Alabamans, 7

Alcalde: authority of, 98, 115; Ham, 95; Fraser, 98, 115; Theall, 98, 115; Dodge, 115, 127, 153; elective office, 115

Alexandria, Va., 5, 9

Alice Tarlton, 15

Allen, Capt., 39

Allen, David, 160–161

Alric, Father Henry, 210

Alta California, 13, 19, 26, 29–30, 36–37, 99, 395

American Camp: Jamestown, 19; Columbia, 39–40

American River: gold discovery on, 13, 184; rush to, 14; foreigners driven from, 30; breaks levee, 323

Anderson, William, death of, 200–202

Angel, George, 15

Angels Creek, 15, 221

Animals, wild: antelope, 346; big horn sheep, 346; cougars, 262, 267, 345; coyote and wolf, 109, 346; deer, 101, 260–261, 334; elk, 92, 345; jack rabbits, 261, 346; seals, 348; fur-bearing, 261; 346; deer meat, 261; *see also* Grizzly bear

Annette, 268, 271–273; builds saloon, 288–289

Antelope, 324

Antiquities, 177–178, 346

Argentieul, Christmas at, 2, 287

Argentina, Perkins in, 48–56

Argentinos: money belts of, 103; dances, 163; attitude of Yankees toward, 202; character, 222–223, 245, 285; hymn of Unitarios, 285–286

Arnault, Father, 210

Askins, Harry, 203, 300

Aspinwall (Colon): Perkins to, 366, 368–369; expectations for, 372; Mrs. H. helps man at, 376–378

Audubon, John Woodhouse: in Webb's party, 76; reaches California, 76, 79

Australia, 71–72, 351–352, 374

Bachman, J. H., 76, 79

Baker, L., 3, 5, 88

Balboa, Nuñez de, 354–355

Bald Mountain; *see* Bear Mountain

Balls; *see* Fandangos

Barber, H. P.: at banquet, 291; at target-shooting, 297; at farewell party for Perkins, 332

Barley: from Chile, 165; price, 165, 308

Barry, Richard C., 160, 171; duel, 205–208; docket of, 229

Basques, 300–301

Baton Rouge, 4

Bean, J. H., 311

Bear (Bald) Mountain, 91, 100–101; gold strike on, 230

Belden, Josiah, 17

Belt, George G., 186–187

Bengal, 251

Benicia: harbor, 91; headquarters for Pacific fleet, 91; name, 91, 317; site, 295–296; seat of government,